CENTRAL STATISTICAL OFFICE

Social *WITHDRAWN* Trends 19

1989 Edition

Editor: TOM GRIFFIN

Associate Editor: JENNY CHURCH

A publication of the Government Statistical Servic

London: Her Majesty's Stationery Office

Contents

Introduction

This new edition of *Social Trends* updates its broad description of British society. The material in it is arranged in 12 chapters, corresponding closely to the administrative functions of Government. The focus in each chapter is on current policy concerns, as the primary user of *Social Trends* remains Government.

Article

This year *Social Trends* includes an article on trends in social attitudes by Roger Jowell, Lindsay Brook and Sharon Witherspoon of Social and Community Planning Research. *Social Trends 15* included an article presenting some results from the first British Social Attitudes survey which was conducted in 1983. Since then the survey has been repeated annually, and because some topics have been covered every year it is now possible to study trends over a five-year period.

New material and sources

To preserve topicality, almost a third of the 189 tables and half of the 103 charts in *Social Trends 19* are new compared with the previous edition. Latest available data are included wherever possible, in particular from the General Household Survey, the Family Expenditure Survey and the Labour Force Survey. The source of the data is given below each table and chart, and published sources are named where appropriate. The fifth edition of the CSO's *Guide to Official Statistics* also gives a list of sources of various items that appear in *Social Trends*. Further details on each subject are given in specialist departmental publications such as *Population Trends* produced by the OPCS, the *Employment Gazette* by the Department of Employment, *Economic Trends* by the CSO, and the White Paper on *The Government's Expenditure Plans 1988-89 to 1990-91*. In particular, regional and local authority analyses of much of the information in *Social Trends* may be found in the CSO's publication *Regional Trends*.

Contributors

The Editor and Associate Editor wish to thank all their colleagues in the Government Statistical Service and their contributors in other organisations, without whose help this publication would not be possible. Within the Central Statistical Office the *Social Trends* production team was: David Blunt, Mark Camley, Ian Goode, Charles Lound, Kathy Marsh, Sally Perry and Brenda Sturge. Thanks are also due to Neil Bradbury, David Frazer and Peter Stokes who were involved during the early stages of preparation of this edition, and to our colleagues in the Graphic Design Unit and Word Processing Unit.

Appendix

This edition of *Social Trends* again includes an Appendix, giving definitions and general background information, particularly on administrative structures and legal frameworks. Anyone seeking to understand the tables and charts in detail will find it helpful to read the corresponding entries in the Appendix. Statistical notes are also included as footnotes to the tables and charts. A full index to this edition is included at the end.

Social Statistics Branch
Central Statistical Office
Great George Street
London SW1P 3AQ

Symbols and conventions

Reference years. Because of space constraints, it is generally not possible to show data for each year of a long historical series. When a choice of years has to be made, the most recent year or a run of recent years is shown together with past population census years (1981, 1971, 1961 etc) and sometimes the mid-points between census years (1976 etc). Other years may be added if they represent a peak or trough in the series shown in the table.

Rounding of figures. In tables where figures have been rounded to the nearest final digit, there may be an apparent discrepancy between the sum of the constituent items and the total as shown.

Billion. This term is used to represent a thousand million.

Provisional and estimated data. Occasionally data for the latest years shown in the tables are provisional or estimated. To keep footnotes to a minimum, these have not been indicated; source departments will be able to advise if revised data are available.

Non-calendar years. Unless otherwise stated, the symbol - represents financial years (eg 1 April 1986 - 31 March 1987). In Chapter 3 the symbol / represents academic years (eg September 1985 / July 1986).

Italics. Figures are shown in italics when they represent percentages.

Symbols. The following symbols have been used throughout *Social Trends:*

..	*not available*	.	*not applicable*
—	*negligible (less than half the final digit shown)*	0	*nil*

REGIONAL TRENDS 23

1988 Edition

HMSO £18.50 net

ISBN 011 620344 7

What the newspapers say about Regional Trends

'...provides a fascinating insight into the differing lifestyles of particular regions...'
- *Financial Times*

'...all-embracing data...covers every aspect of life in Britain...' -*Daily Telegraph*

'...provides a snapshot of the British at work, at leisure, at school, and in birth, marriage and death. It looks at the nation's eating habits, spending habits, its sickness and its health.' - *The Independent*

'...Details of life drawn from thousands of pieces of information...' - *The Times*

'...throws a statistical spotlight on the state of the nation...' - *The Guardian*

'...brings together comparative information about variations in lifestyles from all over Britain.' - *Morning Star*

List of Tables and Charts

Numbers in brackets refer to similar items appearing in *Social Trends 18*

Social Trends 19, © Crown copyright 1989

1988 Edition
FROM THE CENTRAL STATISTICAL OFFICE

KEY DATA

Comprehensive,
compact and cheap,
Key Data is the ideal
research aid for students.
It provides key statistics in each
social and economic domain,
taken from such well-established
and acclaimed CSO sources
as *Social Trends*, *UK National
Accounts* and *Monthly Digest
of Statistics*

£3.50

ISBN 0 11 620345 5

**HMSO
BOOKS**

Recent Trends in Social Attitudes

Lindsay Brook, Roger Jowell and Sharon Witherspoon

Social and Community Planning Research

Lindsay Brook and Sharon Witherspoon are Senior Researchers at Social and Community Planning Research (SCPR), and Roger Jowell is the Director of SCPR. They co-direct SCPR's British Social Attitudes Series. The views expressed in this article are those of the authors.

Introduction

SCPR's British Social Attitudes Series (BSAS) started in 1983. Its aim is to monitor public attitudes to a range of social, political, economic and moral issues during the 1980s and into the 1990s. Its primary source of data is an hour-long annual interview survey, with a self-completion supplement, among a probability sample of around 3,000 people throughout Great Britain. Brief technical details of the series are given in the Appendix at the end of the article. Each questionnaire differs somewhat from its predecessors in that some topics are included every year, and others less often; at least one fresh module is introduced at each round. Summaries of the findings, and commentaries on them, appear in an annual book produced by SCPR. [1]

The series is core-funded by the Sainsbury Family Charitable Trusts, with supplementary funds from a number of government departments, quasi-government bodies, other foundations and companies. There is an international component too, each year some of the BSAS questions are replicated in up to ten other countries (see the Appendix for further details).

The content of each survey, and control over the publication of findings, remain entirely within SCPR's hands, ensuring the independence of the series from any of its various funders.

The focus of the BSAS is on people's underlying attitudes, not on their opinions about topical issues or personalities. The mass media already commission and publish regular polls that aim to chart transitory fluctuations in public opinion. This series tries instead to reveal long-term changes in the nation's values. The cumulated datasets form a sort of moving picture, portraying how British people see their world and themselves and, through their eyes, how society itself is changing. The movements we chart are bound on the whole to be gradual, because a nation's values are essentially part of its culture and are hardly likely to shift dramatically between one year and the next in any but exceptional circumstances. Indeed, if we were to uncover mercurial annual movements, we should certainly look for a more plausible explanation than that people's underlying attitudes were themselves so volatile. Other explanations, such as measurement errors, would be much more plausible, and they would need systematically to be discounted before we could safely construe a 'difference' between two readings, however large, as a 'change'.

In any time-series, whether it measures behaviour or attitudes, it is important to keep the questions constant over time to ensure that they record rather than create movement. But this is not always possible. Some questions, despite careful piloting, do not work very well and need to be amended if they are to survive. Other questions may work well at first, but subsequently become inappropriate as circumstances alter. Suppose, for instance, that a module of questions had been designed for the 1983 survey to tap attitudes to nationalisation. At that time neither the concept of 'privatisation' nor even the word had entered the public's consciousness. It would have taken a peculiar kind of obstinacy merely to repeat these questions year in and year out, without taking account of the radically changing circumstances in which the questions were being asked. At a minimum, some new questions would need to have been added to the existing ones. But it is likely too that some of the original questions would not have worked in the new context, and they would have had to be adjusted or discarded.

It is not only political changes that create these sorts of problems. Questions designed in 1983 about sexual permissiveness would fast have become out of date with the growing awareness of AIDS. When this series started, AIDS had barely been heard of in Britain. Yet,

---

[1] The latest book is *British Social Attitudes: the 5th Report*, edited by R Jowell *et al*, Gower, Aldershot, 1988 (referred to in this article as *The 5th Report*).

by 1987, we felt the need not only to add some questions and to amend others, in recognition of the new issue, but also to include a special module devoted entirely to the subject.

So, simply by keeping our questions the same between readings, we cannot assume that the differences we uncover are 'real' changes in attitudes. Nor can we employ tests of statistical significance as strong supporting evidence, since they relate only to random sources of error, not to systematic sources of bias. We recognise instead that identical questions may well mean different things to respondents at different times or in different contexts. Even apparently unrelated changes in the questionnaire, such as the introduction of new topics or the alteration of earlier items, may somehow modify the message that a particular question conveys, affecting the answers accordingly.

The safest way of counteracting these difficulties is, where possible, never to rely on only a single question on any subject to do any serious work, but to approach each topic from a variety of angles. When several supporting measurements all move in the same direction, they help to reinforce the conclusion that a change, rather than a fortuitous fluctuation, is actually taking place.

The problems we have referred to are not, of course, unique to attitudinal measures. They arise, in varying degrees, on all surveys. The notion that all attitudinal data are 'soft' and 'subjective', and behavioural data 'hard' and 'objective', is wrong in both respects. Survey measurements by their nature are prone to errors, inaccuracies and biases of one sort or another. Yet if we want to know something about the nation's collective character and characteristics, and whether and how society is changing, there is no real substitute for asking people directly, and for treating their answers as an approximation of the truth - in the absence of 'contrary indications'. But the search for 'contrary indications' is vital, and it makes the analysis and interpretation of attitudinal data both intriguing and frustrating. The intriguing part is trying to discover whether apparent changes are, after all, illusory. The frustrating part is having to invent fresh ways of saying that things *are* what they used to be.

Economic expectations

In *Social Trends 15*, we commented on the widespread pessimism revealed in 1983 about prospects for both inflation and unemployment. Since then, although there have been fluctuations in attitudes, the public mood has become markedly more bullish. True, few people believe that prices will actually stand still or go down; nearly four people in five expect them to rise. But the proportion believing that they will go up *a lot* has fallen from a peak of 40 per cent in 1985 to 26 per cent in 1987. On unemployment too, forecasts have become decidedly more optimistic, indeed in 1987, for the first time in the BSAS, a majority of the sample (57 per cent) predicted that unemployment would not rise, and a further quarter thought it would fall.

We also reported in *Social Trends 15* a close association between a person's expectations and his or her circumstances - income, economic status and so on. And this still holds true. Even in a generally more optimistic climate, the less well-off remain much gloomier about prospects for the economy than are their more prosperous counterparts (Table A.1).

Closer comparison of these data with those from 1983 show that, on prospects for inflation, the differences between the better-off and worse-off have narrowed somewhat, while on prospects for unemployment they have widened. Moreover, the unemployed themselves, in comparison with their counterparts in work, now seem to be less convinced than ever that unemployment is on the wane.

A.1 **Expectations of prices and unemployment: by household income, occupational status, and economic status, 1987**

Great Britain — Percentages and numbers

	Percentage in each economic group who believe that		
	Prices will rise a lot in year ahead	Unemployment will rise a lot in year ahead	Weighted sample sizes (= 100%) (numbers)
Household income			
High (£15,000 or more pa)	16	11	663
Middle (£7,000 to under £15,000 pa)	23	16	856
Low (less than £7,000 pa)	35	21	889
Occupational status			
Non-manual	20	12	1,359
Manual	32	21	1,219
Economic status			
Self-employed	18	10	188
Employee	23	15	1,342
Unemployed	33	31	189
All respondents	26	17	2,766[1]

1 The base includes some respondents who gave no information or were not classifiable into the above groups.

When we asked employees about the economic prospects for their workplace in the year ahead, the mood was once again more optimistic than it had been five years earlier. For instance, the proportion of employees believing that their own wage or salary would keep abreast or ahead of the cost of living has risen from 61 per cent in 1983 to 70 per cent in 1987. There has been a similar fairly steady increase - from 16 per cent to 23 per cent - in the proportion of employees forecasting that staffing levels at their place of work will rise.

These findings are reflected, perhaps, in people's forecasts about their personal financial circumstances. As Table A.2 shows, although pessimism about personal living standards seemed to increase between 1984 and 1985, it has receded somewhat since then. The latest figures reveal a generally more optimistic mood than at any time since we began asking this question in 1984.

A.2 Financial circumstances: comparisons with past and predictions for future

Great Britain   Percentages and numbers

	1984	1985	1986	1987
Percentage considering that over the past year or so, household income has:				
fallen behind prices	46	55	47	45
kept up with prices	44	37	41	44
gone up by more than prices	8	7	9	9
Percentage considering that in the year ahead, household income will:				
fall behind prices	43	49	43	39
keep up with prices	45	39	43	46
go up by more than prices	8	8	9	10
Weighted sample sizes (= 100%) (numbers)	1,645	1,769	3,066	2,766

Once again, however, there are exceptions to this sense of increasing prosperity. For instance, over two thirds (68 per cent) of the unemployed and 60 per cent of pensioners feel that their household income had fallen behind prices in the preceding year, and nearly 60 per cent of both groups are just as despondent about the year ahead. People living in Scotland, in the north of England and in Wales are also noticeably more pessimistic than are their counterparts in the Midlands and (especially) in London and the South (see also Curtice, pp. 131-33, in *The 5th Report*). The most striking differences were, however, between those on different levels of household income. Not surprisingly perhaps, as Table A.3 shows, the more prosperous one is the more confident one is that the prosperity will continue.

A.3 Financial circumstances: comparisons with past and predictions for future, by household income, 1987

Great Britain   Percentages and numbers

	Annual household income		
	Under £7,000	£7,000 – £14,999	£15,000 or more
Percentage considering that over the past year or so, household income has:			
fallen behind prices	67	38	24
kept up with prices	28	53	52
gone up by more than prices	3	8	23
Percentage considering that in the year ahead, household income will:			
fall behind prices	61	33	19
keep up with prices	28	56	58
go up by more than prices	5	7	21
Weighted sample sizes (= 100%) (numbers)	889	856	663

So despite a clear overall increase in public optimism about the economy, the picture is still somewhat patchy. Inflation and unemployment are seen as ever-present threats, and a sizeable minority of the population, largely concentrated in the lowest income groups, seem to be sceptical that any general improvements in the economy will actually benefit them. Concern about unemployment in particular, despite the lessening gloom about its likely growth, remains very high. By a margin of over three to one (73 per cent to 23 per cent), respondents feel that the government should give higher priority to bringing down unemployment than to reducing inflation. Indeed, this view has slightly hardened in the last five years, possibly because inflation during the period has been consistently rather low. Something approaching a consensus among the various population subgroups exists on this issue, although pensioners and (more noticeably) the self-employed are more likely than average to give priority to tackling inflation.

This general concern about unemployment is reinforced by responses to other questions. A majority (57 per cent) believes it is the government's responsibility to ensure that everyone who wants a job can have one, only 22 per cent disagree. Moreover, from a wide range of possible policies presented to respondents as a way of helping Britain's economic problems, the Keynesian solution of the 'government setting up construction projects to create more jobs' attracts the consistent support of around 90 per cent of respondents over the years. Other interventionist measures, even those directed at controlling inflation, are far less popular, and getting less so. For instance, in 1983, 'control of wages by legislation' had the support of almost half of respondents; by 1987, only around a third (34 per cent) were in favour. 'Control of prices by legislation' is more popular, but support has fallen steadily from 70 per cent to 58 per cent over the years.

Anxiety about unemployment emerges in answers to a number of questions. For many people, however, it seems to be at one remove, expressing itself more as a general policy concern than as a personal worry. For instance, when we ask people which is of greater concern to *themselves and their families* - unemployment or inflation - we find a solid majority (55 per cent to 41 per cent) nominating inflation. If, however, inflation were to rise substantially, then concern about unemployment, or the sense that it should have priority, might well diminish.

The moral climate and the spread of AIDS

A time-series would have been especially valuable over the last twenty-five years or so during which, for instance, homosexuality, abortion, censorship and divorce have all been subject to radical legislative reform, some more than once. Nonetheless, the BSAS does provide data back to 1983, and episodic opinion poll data are available before then, on some issues.

If pressed to speculate in 1983 on the likely direction of public attitudes to issues such as these, we would probably have predicted - on the basis of US data, notably their *General Social Survey* - a gradual movement towards a more 'liberal' (or less censorious) stance on the majority of 'personal-sexual' matters. And we would have been quite simply wrong. Our results show that on attitudes to extra-marital sex, homosexuality, the availability of pornography, contraception for the under 16s and some methods of assisted reproduction, such movement as there is has been towards greater censoriousness. Some changes are small, others greater, but their direction is constant. Attitudes to abortion are the only exception. We give some examples here (see also Harding, pp.36-42 in *The 5th Report*).

Regularly, we have asked respondents to judge various kinds of sexual relationships, giving them a choice ranging from 'always wrong' to 'not wrong at all'. We show just three years' data in Table A.4.

A.4 Attitudes towards sexual relationships

Great Britain	Percentages and numbers		
	1983	1985	1987
Percentage thinking that pre-marital sexual relationships are:			
Always/mostly wrong	28	23	25
Sometimes wrong	17	19	21
Rarely wrong/not wrong at all	50	52	50
Percentage thinking that extra-marital sexual relationships are [1]:			
Always/mostly wrong	83	82	88
Sometimes wrong	11	11	9
Rarely wrong/not wrong at all	3	3	1
Percentage thinking that homosexual relationships are:			
Almost/mostly wrong	62	69	74
Sometimes wrong	8	7	8
Rarely wrong/not wrong at all	21	16	13
Weighted sample sizes (= 100%)			
(numbers)	1,719	1,769	1,391

1 The item wording in 1983 referred to husband and wife separately. The answers were almost identical, so averaged responses are given here.

Attitudes towards pre-marital sex have been fairly stable, but there has been a steady climb in the proportion strongly critical of homosexuality and a sharp rise in the last two years in the proportion censuring extra-marital sex. At first sight, it looks as though AIDS has had something to do with these trends. In the early to mid 1980s, AIDS was widely believed to be a specifically gay disease. Only more recently has it been suggested that the heterosexual population is also at risk. But the advent of AIDS is unlikely to have affected attitudes to the availability of pornographic material, or to contraception *per se,* or to artificial fertility measures. Yet on these subjects too the pendulum appears to be swinging against the more liberal attitudes that were said to be characteristic of the 1960s and the 1970s.

For instance, in 1983 the proportion of respondents in favour of an outright ban on pornographic magazines and films was 33 per cent, as opposed to 52 per cent who were prepared to allow them in 'special adult shops'. By 1987 the gap had narrowed to 38:42 per cent respectively. Similarly, on the question of whether 'doctors should be allowed to give contraceptive advice and supplies to young people under 16 without having to inform parents,' the proportion disagreeing rose from 50 per cent in 1985 [2] to 60 per cent in 1987. Trends in attitudes towards methods of assisted reproduction [2] are less easy to discern, but the suggestion is of a continuing widespread acceptance of techniques which involve the husband (AIH and *in vitro* fertilisation using AIH), and far less - and diminishing - sympathy for those techniques which involve an 'outside' person. Indeed, only one half of our respondents thought that even such a long-established practice as artificial insemination by donor (AID) should be allowed by law. Around a third of the sample (it was nearer one half in 1985) would permit unpaid surrogacy arrangements, but fewer than a quarter would allow paid surrogacy.

All these subjects have, of course, been the focus of recent parliamentary debate and of well-publicised legal cases with the aim of challenging or reversing earlier 'liberalising' measures. To some extent at least, then, public attitudes seem to be in tune with such moves and - on the evidence of our most recent data - are becoming more so.

As we have noted, an exception to this apparent movement towards greater censoriousness on personal-sexual matters is the issue of abortion. Here the results are unequivocally in the opposite direction. Public support for allowing legal abortion in a range of circumstances has increased substantially over the last five years, and, as Table A.5 shows, the increase has been fairly steady.

Moreover, support for abortion has risen among all main demographic subgroups within the population, including both men and women. Indeed, the attitudes of the two sexes differ in one respect only, men are rather more likely to approve of abortion on social grounds when both the man and the woman are involved in the decision. They are no less likely than women, however, to support the woman's right to decide.

---

2   Questions on these two topics were first asked about in the BSAS in 1985.

A.5 Attitudes towards legalised abortion

Great Britain   Percentages and numbers

	1983	1985	1987
Percentage agreeing that abortion should be allowed by law when:			
The woman decides on her own she does not wish to have the child	37	49	54
The woman is not married and does not wish to marry the man	44	54	56
The couple agree they do not wish to have the child	46	55	59
The couple cannot afford any more children	47	58	58
There is a strong chance of a defect in the baby	82	86	89
The woman became pregnant as a result of rape	85	89	93
The woman's health is seriously endangered by the pregnancy	87	91	94
Weighted sample sizes (= 100%) (numbers)	1,610	1,502	1,243

We urge caution in interpreting the rank ordering of support for abortion in Table A.5, since we have found that support varies somewhat according to the order in which we present the items to respondents. But, the general trend is real enough.

Against this background of change in respect of a wide range of 'personal-sexual' mores, we devised a module of questions for the 1987 survey to establish benchmark data on public attitudes towards AIDS and those suffering from the disease. These questions had five particular themes. First, we asked which groups in society were thought to be most at risk from AIDS - specifically to discover whether or not it was still widely thought of as a gay disease. Second, we asked about its likely spread and the prospect of a 'cure'. Third, we included a series of questions to help us gauge levels of prejudice against AIDS sufferers - in particular, support for or disapproval of various possible discriminatory measures. Fourth, we asked about the resources that should be devoted to treating sufferers and to finding a 'cure'. Lastly, we tried to tap the wider moral questions which the appearance of AIDS raises.

Fieldwork took place in the wake of the large government advertising campaign which warned the public not to 'die of ignorance', reassuringly, we found that most people are now aware of many aspects of the disease and how it is spread. For instance, almost everyone regards homosexual men and abusers of intravenous drugs as being at high risk from HIV infection. Only a tiny minority exempt from risk sexually active heterosexuals with more than one partner: indeed nearly three in four people regard them as 'greatly' at risk too. Rather worryingly, younger men (especially the 18-24 year olds) take a more sanguine view about the vulnerability of sexually active heterosexual people to the virus. This suggests a need for further health education efforts among this group at least.

The near-unanimous recognition that homosexual men are at high risk from HIV infection may, as we have suggested, have led to the increased censoriousness

we found towards homosexuality. But it has not led to increased support for discrimination against homosexual people; tolerance of them as teachers in schools, colleges and universities, or as occupants of responsible positions in public life has, if anything, increased slightly between 1983 and 1987. True, tolerance was never high: around half the population would bar homosexual people from teaching posts, and around 40 per cent from other positions of authority. But there are signs of a decrease in prejudice and, in any event, there has been no increase to correspond with the rise in censoriousness of homosexual activities we reported earlier. In this respect anyway, the advent of AIDS has not produced the 'gay backlash' which some had predicted and feared.

We also asked a number of questions to gauge feelings towards AIDS sufferers. In particular, we asked whether or not there should be a legal right for employers to dismiss people known to have the disease, or for doctors and nurses to have a right to refuse them medical treatment, or for schools to have a right to expel pupils with AIDS. Table A.6 shows the results.

A.6 Attitudes to discrimination against AIDS sufferers, 1987

Great Britain   Percentages and numbers

	Should there be a legal right for		
	Employers to dismiss employees?	Doctors and nurses to refuse treatment?	Schools to expel children?
Percentage answering:			
Definitely	13	11	8
Probably	25	20	16
Probably not	29	26	30
Definitely not	28	41	40
Don't know/not stated	5	2	6
Weighted sample sizes (= 100%) (numbers)	1,391	1,391	1,391

Although only a small minority of the population is firmly in favour of discrimination in any of the three situations, a rather larger number is inclined towards some curtailment of sufferers' legal rights. But the balance of opinion is against any of these draconian measures. As on many matters to do with sexual morality and civil liberties, education influences attitudes. People with degrees, for instance, almost regardless of their other political or social values, tend to be more 'liberal' on these sorts of issues; and that is true in their attitudes to AIDS sufferers too. But it is equally true that the gap between graduates and others in their attitudes to moral issues has been diminishing since 1983, with graduates tending to become less permissive, rather than non-graduates more so (see Brook, p.73, in *The 5th Report*). We shall keep track of this apparent movement in future rounds.

To acknowledge that AIDS, in common with other sexually transmittable diseases, has a moral dimension is self-evident; but the disease's variable and often long period of latency, and the lack as yet of any vaccine - let alone a cure - seem to give AIDS an almost uniquely menacing character.

Three in five of our respondents are deeply pessimistic about the continued spread of AIDS [3], believing that within five years it would cause more deaths in Britain than any other single disease. Only a third are hopeful that a cure would be found during that period. This may explain why the public's response to the disease is so ambivalent. On the one hand, 60 per cent of people feel that AIDS sufferers 'get much less sympathy from society than they ought to get'. On the other hand, almost the same proportion (57 per cent) believe that 'most people with AIDS have only themselves to blame'. Broad sympathy for sufferers does not seem to preclude a degree of censure of the behaviour that has brought about their plight. A similar pattern emerges when we ask how resources should be deployed in combatting the effects of the disease. By a clear margin (58 per cent to 38 per cent) people feel that 'more money should be spent trying to find a cure for AIDS, even if it means that research into other serious diseases is delayed'; nonetheless around half of the population (52 per cent) is against the NHS spending 'more of its resources on giving better care to people dying from AIDS'.

The strong link between morality and the disease is demonstrated most starkly in the finding that two-thirds of the population endorse the proposition that 'official warnings about AIDS should say that some sexual practices are morally wrong'. The under 45s are much less enthusiastic about this approach than their elders, but even so a (bare) majority of even the 18-24 year olds support it. Such a morally interventionist approach in government advertising would be more or less unprecedented, and the level of public support for it is therefore surprising. It remains to be seen whether such support would be sustained if a campaign of this kind were actually to be mounted.

Public spending and the National Health Service

As part of the background to our questions about attitudes to social provision of one kind or another, we have asked respondents each year to weigh the claims of public expenditure on health, education and welfare against the claims of tax cuts. Although attitudes are slightly ambivalent, the proportion of respondents favouring rises in taxes to pay for increased social provision has grown each year - from just under a third in 1983 to one half in 1987. People may, of course, be plumping for what they think is the most 'socially acceptable' option of the three offered. It should also be remembered that rates of personal taxation have come down over the same period. Even so, around 90 per cent of the population, in each of the five readings, say they are against reductions in social spending, even in return for tax cuts.

On the other hand, almost nobody felt, when we asked them in 1986, that their own incomes were currently undertaxed. Only 24 per cent feel that their present tax levels are acceptable, while 61 per cent feel they are too high or much too high. (The remaining 15 per cent did not pay tax or did not express a view one way or the other.)

Moreover, as we reported in Social Trends 15, a very large majority (in 1987 over three-quarters of people in all income brackets) feels that the less well-off in particular pay too much in taxes. Since 1987, the basic and higher rates of income tax have, of course, been further reduced, but it seems unlikely - given the large and stable majorities - that this last round of tax cuts would have changed attitudes radically.

Another background question we ask is about people's priorities, if any, for extra government spending. Ten items of public expenditure are shown to respondents on a card; they include defence, police and prisons, housing, education, social security, health, and so on. The proportion naming health as first priority has always been higher than that for any other item; even so, it has risen from 37 per cent in 1983 to 52 per cent in 1987. Indeed, almost four in every five respondents (79 per cent) now give health first or second priority from among the ten items offered. Education, the second choice, comes way behind (55 per cent), while 'help for industry' has plummeted from 29 per cent in 1983 to 11 per cent in 1987. More important, perhaps, these views are shared by and large by all the main population subgroups, revealing a degree of consensus that is uncommon among respondents to this series.

It was always anticipated that health and education would be popular candidates for increased provision. But why does there seem to have been such a large increase in the proportion feeling that more should be spent on the NHS - in spite of overall real increases in expenditure in the last few years? Our data reveal answers that seem at first glance to be contradictory. On the one hand, satisfaction with particular services within the NHS is - almost without exception - high, and has scarcely decreased since 1983. On the other hand, as Table A.7 shows, more and more respondents over the years are expressing a sense of general dissatisfaction with the 'way the NHS runs nowadays'. In 1983, the ratio of 'satisfied' to 'dissatisfied' respondents was greater than 2:1. In 1987, respondents are more or less equally divided.

Those subgroups within the population - notably younger women, and people between 35 and 54 years of age - who were the most discontented with the NHS in 1983 are even more likely to voice complaints now. People over the age of 55, many of whom probably still

---

3   This general view is shared by research scientists too: see, for example, Anderson, R.M., Medley, G.F., Blythe, S.P. and Johnson, A.M. 'Is it possible to predict the minimum size of the AIDS epidemic in the UK?' *The Lancet*, (1987), pp. 1073 – 75 .

A.7 Overall satisfaction with the National Health Service

Great Britain		Percentages and numbers	
	1983		1987
Very satisfied	11 }		7 }
		55	41
Quite satisfied	44 }		34 }
Neither satisfied nor dissatisfied	20		20
Quite dissatisfied	18 }		24 }
		25	39
Very dissatisfied	7 }		15 }
Weighted sample sizes (= 100%) (numbers)	1,719		2,766

remember pre-Beveridge days, tend to be less critical both of the NHS and of other aspects of state provision.

But this is only a part of the picture. General questions like these are useful for monitoring changes in 'mood' over the years, but they do not tell us about attitudes to specific parts of the NHS, or how people feel about their own experiences of the NHS. One regular question in the series asks people to say, from their own experience or from what they have heard, how satisfied or dissatisfied they are with specific aspects of the NHS. Now we see that dissatisfaction with particular services is low, as Table A.8 shows, and has not risen much since 1983 - except in the case of hospital services.

A.8 Attitudes towards particular aspects of the National Health Service

Great Britain	Percentages and numbers	
	1983	1987
Percentage of respondents either very dissatisfied or quite dissatisfied with:		
Local doctors or GPs	13	13
NHS dentists	10	9
Health visitors	6	8
District nurses	2	3
Being in hospital as an in-patient	7	13
Attending hospital as an out-patient	21	29
Weighted sample sizes (= 100%) (numbers)	1,719	2,766

So, while primary health care services are generally highly regarded, aspects of the hospital service are thought by increasing proportions to be in need of improvement. But what sorts of improvements, if any, did people have in mind? In 1987, we included a question for the first time, nominating twelve aspects of the NHS 'in your area', and inviting respondents to say for each whether (and if so how much) it was in need of improvement. The distribution of responses, and a commentary on it, is given by Bosanquet on pages 101 and 102 of The 5th Report. Here we refer only briefly to the broad conclusions. For further evidence on this subject in another context, see also Focus on Health Care, P. Prescott-Clarke, T. Brooks and C. Machray, SCPR and RIPA, 1988.

In general, people appear to be more than satisfied with the quality of medical care available to them under the NHS, whether by GPs or by hospitals. Nursing care too is judged satisfactory or very good by over three-quarters of the population. To the extent then that dissatisfaction is expressed, and improvement is called for, it is largely confined to problems of resources available to hospitals and especially the perennial problem of waiting times both for appointments with consultants and for non-emergency operations. In contrast with the widespread approval of the quality of medical and nursing care, only around one in ten people express satisfaction with waiting times for hospital treatment. Concern about other aspects of NHS hospitals, such as the condition of buildings, staffing levels of doctors and nurses and the standard of casualty departments is at a rather lower level, but even so between a half and three-quarters of the sample saw at least some room for improvement.

What then of attitudes to private medicine? There is certainly considerable public support for the availability of private medicine, with only one in ten respondents against private medicine, per se. But a further 51 per cent believe it should be confined to private clinics and hospitals. Support for the principle of private provision thus seems to be tempered by worries about its impact on the quality and availability of state-provided health care. Respondents therefore continue to support (by 54 per cent to 41 per cent, in 1987) the right of NHS doctors to take on private patients, but the preference is for this to happen outside NHS hospitals. By a margin of 44 per cent to 23 per cent, people feel that private treatment in NHS hospitals harms rather than benefits the NHS. On the other hand, by a similar margin (39 per cent to 20 per cent), people feel that the availability of private medical treatment outside the NHS is actually a good thing for the NHS.

In sum, our various pieces of evidence suggest strongly that the NHS continues to matter a great deal to the British public. Among all the possible targets for increased public expenditure (including other 'popular' ones such as education and housing), it commands by far the greatest and most consistent support. That this support should be rising may stem in part at least from a growing sense of public concern about the strains that NHS hospitals in particular are seen to be under, leading to too-long queues for treatment of one sort or another. Even so, most people express continuing contentment with standards of medical and nursing care in hospitals, as with primary health-care services such as GPs and dentists.

The domestic division of labour

Who does what in the home, and is the demarcation of tasks held to be appropriate? The answers to these questions are among the most widely quoted from the BSAS. In *Social Trends 15*, we reported that the majority of time-consuming household tasks were done by women. Our most recent data, presented in Table A.9, show that this is still so. Among respondents who were married or living as married, it is still overwhelmingly the case that the woman is responsible for looking after the home. Only in repairing household equipment, organising bills and doing the evening dishes do men begin to play a leading role.

A.9 Household division of labour, 1987

Great Britain Percentages [1]

Household tasks:	Mainly men	Mainly women	Shared equally
(percentage allocation)			
Washing and ironing	2	88	9
Looking after sick children [2]	2	67	30
Household cleaning	4	72	23
Preparing evening meal	6	77	17
Household shopping	7	50	43
Teaching children discipline [2]	13	19	67
Doing evening dishes	22	39	36
Organising household bills	32	38	30
Repairing household equipment	82	6	8

1 Sample size (weighted): 983 respondents, married or living as married.

2 Asked of 422 respondents, married or living as married and with children aged under 16 living in household.

Even in households where the woman works full-time outside the home, tasks are not shared equally, though more so than in households where the wife works part-time or not at all. Indeed, our figures suggest that women who have part-time paid jobs may have the worst of both worlds, extra responsibilities outside the home and only limited sharing of activities within it. Thus for most items we ask about - household shopping, preparing the evening meal, household cleaning, washing and ironing - households in which the woman has a part-time job are more or less indistinguishable from those in which the woman is not in paid work at all. And, as Table A.10 shows, when we ask respondents a summary question, *'Who is mainly responsible for general domestic duties?'*, we find that this pattern holds.

Some women may, perhaps, take a part-time job because domestic chores prevent them from working full-time outside the home; others may choose to work part-time specifically in order to have more time for household responsibilities. We cannot attribute causes or motives from our data. What we can say, however, is that it seems to be part of some arrangement, explicit or otherwise, that working men do not participate much in most household duties, including childcare, especially - but by no means exclusively - when the woman in the household does not herself work full-time outside the home.

But so far we have dealt only with how domestic tasks *are* shared. How do respondents - married, cohabiting or single - think these tasks *ought* to be shared? As might be expected, there is a noticeable gap between what people say does happen and what they say ought to happen. Table A.11 shows that by far the most egalitarian answers come from people, male or female, who have never themselves been married. Their views are, perhaps, not (yet) tempered by experience. Even

A.10 Main responsibility for domestic duties, 1987

Great Britain Percentages and numbers

	Respondents in households where		
	Man works, woman works full-time	Man works, women works part-time[1]	Man works woman does not work
Mainly women	72	88	91
Shared equally	22	7	5
Weighted sample size (= 100%) (numbers)	406	369	557

1 'Part-time' is defined as 10-29 hours a week.

A.11 Actual and prescriptive household division of labour, 1987

Great Britain Percentages and numbers

		Married people [1]	
	Never married people considering tasks should be shared equally	Considering tasks should be shared equally	Tasks actually shared equally
Household tasks			
Washing and ironing	41	27	9
Looking after sick children	58	51	30 [2]
Household cleaning	62	52	23
Preparing evening meal	55	42	17
Household shopping	77	65	43
Teaching children discipline	80	83	67 [2]
Doing evening dishes	74	69	36
Organising household bills	59	62	30
Repairing household equipment	34	23	8
Weighted sample size (= 100%) (numbers)	234	983	983

1 Including co-habitees.

2 Percentages based on 422 respondents who are married or living as married and with children under 16 living in household.

so, although they are *more* egalitarian than the rest, they do not by any means prescribe an equal allocation of tasks. There have been only slight increases (between around 2 per cent and 8 per cent) since 1984 in the proportions saying that the tasks *should* be shared equally.

We looked at these responses too according to whether the woman in the household had a full-time job, a part-time job, or no job outside the home. Not unexpectedly, we find that full-time working women are much more egalitarian than their male partners. The gap between part-time working women and their male partners is less marked, and in households in which the woman does not work, women are sometimes *less* egalitarian than their partners. Of course, women with full-time jobs tend to be younger than average, which may explain why they are more likely to be egalitarian. But it seems equally likely that full-time women workers just feel that the burden they carry is unfairly heavy.

In the 1987 survey, we widened the scope of the module to cover the question of whether, or in what circumstances, it was appropriate for women to go out to work. We touched on a number of issues, but we concentrate here on the answers to one question for which we have comparative data back to 1965. We included a question first asked in Hunt's 1965 study of working-age women, [4] and then again in Martin and Roberts' 1980 *Women and Employment Survey,* [5] both conducted by the Office of Population Censuses and Surveys. So,for three specified family circumstances, respondents were asked in surveys spanning more than two decades to choose one of these options for the woman:

> *She ought to go out to work if she's fit*
> *It's up to her whether to go out to work or not*
> *She should only go out to work if she really needs the money*
> *She ought to stay at home*

We confine our BSAS data to the answers of women aged 18-59 to make them comparable to those of the other two surveys.

Even in 1965, women overwhelmingly felt that being married was not in itself a disqualification from working. But there has been an enormous change since then in beliefs about married women going out to work. For instance, in 1965, nearly four in five women felt that mothers of under-fives should stay at home; by 1980 that proportion had fallen to around three in five; and by 1987 it had dropped further to well under a half (Table A.12).

A.12 Trends in attitudes to women going out to work

Great Britain — Percentages and numbers

	1965[1]	1980[2]	1987
Percentage of working age women who considered that:			
Married woman with no children			
Ought to work	13	33	27
Up to her [3]	75	62	69
Only if she needs money	9	4	3
Ought to stay at home	1	1	—
Married woman with children under school age			
Ought to work	—	—	—
Up to her [3]	5	15	26
Only if she needs the money	15	25	29
Ought to stay at home	78	62	45
Married woman with children at school			
Ought to work	3	3	3
Up to her [3]	35	50	61
Only if she needs money	39	36	29
Ought to stay at home	20	11	7
Weighted sample size (= 100%) (numbers)	7,391	5,888	503

1 Source: A Hunt, *A Survey of Women's Employment,* Government Social Survey, London, 1968.
2 Source: J Martin and C Roberts, *Women and Employment: A Lifetime Perspective,* HMSO, London, 1984.
3 There was a wording change to the second option in 1980, which we have followed: "She has a right to work if she wants to" (1965); "It's *up to her* whether to go out to work or not" (1980 and 1987).

So in one of those rare instances in Britain where we have a solid attitudinal time-series stretching back until 1965, we find evidence of a radical change in attitudes. The 'working woman' is now not only a reality but accepted as one (by other women at any rate and, as our data reveal, by men too) in almost all circumstances, even - increasingly - when she has children under school age. Yet this greater acceptance of a woman's right to work outside the home does not (yet) appear to have translated itself into a sense of egalitarianism in the allocation of tasks, either actual or prescribed, within the home. We shall continue to monitor trends.

4   *A Survey of Women's Employment,* A. Hunt, Government Social Survey, London, 1968.

5   *Women and Employment: A Lifetime Perspective,* J. Martin and C. Roberts, HMSO, London, 1984.

Appendix

Each annual survey, (there have been five to date, from 1983-1987), is designed to yield a representative sample of adults (aged 18 or over) living in Great Britain. For practical reasons the sample is confined to those living in private households whose addresses were included in the (then-current) electoral registers. People living in institutions are excluded, as are (necessarily) those living in private households whose addresses are not on the electoral registers.

The probability sampling method employed is based on a multi-stage stratified design, the final stage involving the selection of addresses from sampling points throughout England, Scotland and Wales. Before analysis, the data are weighted to correct for unequal probabilities of selection (arising from differences between the number of people listed on the registers and the number found at the address).

Fieldwork takes place each spring. The achieved sample varies somewhat from year to year depending on response rates (usually around 70 per cent overall). In the first three rounds, we interviewed around 1800 respondents, annually, increased to 3000 in the last two rounds. This larger sample size has enabled us to ask some questions of a random half of the sample, others of the remaining half, thus giving greater scope for the introduction of fresh modules in most years.

Core-funding for the series (secure until 1992) comes from the Sainsbury Family Charitable Trusts. It is supplemented by fixed-term commitments of funds (usually for three-year periods) by other bodies, mainly government or quasi-government. The Department of Employment, the Department of the Environment and the Department of Trade and Industry all give financial support to modules of questions on attitudes to the labour market, housing, and business and industry respectively. The Countryside Commission supports a module of questions about attitudes to 'green' issues; the Nuffield Foundation has helped to fund questions on public and private morality; and the Economic and Social Research Council has supported questions on political culture. Other government departments, quasi-government organisations, grant-giving bodies, universities and private industry have also provided funding.

Each year, SCPR produces a book on the findings - an edited volume of commentaries on some of the survey's principal results, together with selected tabulations. The series is published by Gower and to date comprises *British Social Attitudes: the 1984 Report; the 1985 Report; the 1986 Report; the 1987 Report;* and the volume on which most of the findings presented in this article are based, *the 5th Report,* which appeared in autumn 1988. From 1989, SCPR will also produce an annual cumulative sourcebook of findings, once again to be published by Gower, and to be sponsored initially by Shell UK Ltd. The datatapes of all the BSAS surveys are lodged in the ESRC Data Archive at the University of Essex.

Through its links with the *International Social Survey Programme* (ISSP), which SCPR co-founded in 1985, the BSAS regularly includes a module of questions on a rotating set of topics, designed by and mutually agreed with its ten other partners. Countries now collaborating in this venture are (besides Britain) Australia, Austria, Holland, Hungary, the Republic of Ireland, Israel, Italy, Norway, the USA and West Germany. Each nation includes a module of identical (or at least equivalent) questions in a self-completion supplement as part of its own annual survey series. These data are placed each year in the Data Archive at the University of Cologne, and are also available publicly.

Chapter 1: Population

Population structure and changes

- In 1987 the population of the United Kingdom was just under 57 million and is expected to reach 60 million by the year 2025. *(Table 1.2)*

- The population aged 85 or over is projected to rise from 0.8 million in 1987 to 1.4 million by 2025. *(Chart 1.1 and Table 1.2)*

Births and deaths

- In the United Kingdom there were 776 thousand live births and 644 thousand deaths in 1987. Between 1971 and 1987 the annual number of deaths has remained about the same, but live births have fallen by 14 per cent. *(Table 1.9 and Table 1.13)*

Migration

- In recent years more people have been entering the United Kingdom than leaving it. Averages for 1983-87 show there were 220 thousand new residents (including British citizens) per year and 190 thousand who have left the country to reside elsewhere. *(Table 1.14)*

- In 1987, 46 thousand people subject to immigration controls were accepted for settlement in the United Kingdom. *(Chart 1.15)*

- Provisional figures suggest that there were just over 4.5 thousand applications for refugee status in 1987, slightly down on 1986 but nearly twice as many as were made in 1981. *(Table 1.16)*

International comparisons

- In 1986 the United Kingdom with 233 inhabitants per square kilometre was more densely populated than most EC countries, and was well above the EC average of 143 inhabitants per sq km. *(Chart 1.17)*

- In 1985 the ratio of the number of persons aged 65 or over to the number of working age (15–64 years) was greater for the United Kingdom than for any other EC country. *(Chart 1.18)*

1.1 Population: by selected age bands

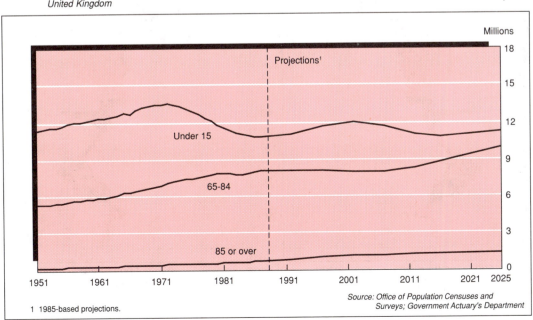

United Kingdom

Millions

Projections[1]

Under 15

65-84

85 or over

1 1985-based projections.

Source: Office of Population Censuses and Surveys; Government Actuary's Department

1.2 Age and sex structure of the population[1]

United Kingdom

Millions

	0— 4	5—14	15—29	30— 44	45— 59	60— 64	65—74	75— 84	85+	All ages
Mid-year estimates										
1951	4.3	7.0	10.3	11.1	9.6	2.4	3.7	1.6	0.2	50.3
1961	4.3	8.1	10.3	10.5	10.6	2.8	4.0	1.9	0.3	52.8
1971	4.5	8.9	11.8	9.8	10.2	3.2	4.8	2.2	0.5	55.9
1981	3.5	8.1	12.8	11.0	9.5	2.9	5.2	2.7	0.6	56.4
1986	3.6	7.2	13.5	11.5	9.2	3.1	5.0	3.0	0.7	56.8
1987										
Males	1.9	3.6	6.9	5.8	4.6	1.4	2.2	1.1	0.2	27.7
Females	1.8	3.4	6.6	5.8	4.6	1.6	2.8	1.9	0.6	29.2
Total	3.7	7.1	13.5	11.6	9.2	3.0	5.0	3.0	0.8	56.9
Projections [2]										
1991	3.9	7.1	12.9	12.1	9.5	2.9	5.0	3.1	0.9	57.5
1996	4.1	7.6	11.6	12.6	10.5	2.7	5.0	3.1	1.1	58.3
2001	3.9	8.1	10.8	13.2	11.0	2.8	4.8	3.2	1.2	59.0
2006	3.6	8.1	11.0	12.6	11.6	3.2	4.8	3.2	1.2	59.3
2011	3.5	7.5	11.7	11.3	12.1	3.7	5.2	3.1	1.3	59.4
2025	3.8	7.4	11.2	11.3	11.1	4.1	6.0	3.9	1.4	60.0

1 See Appendix, Part 1: Population and population projections.
2 1985—based projections.

Source: Office of Population Censuses and Surveys;
Government Actuary's Department

Table 1.2 illustrates that the population of the United Kingdom grew steadily between 1951 and 1971 but since then the overall total has grown more slowly. Only slow growth is projected for the years up to 2025. The age structure of the population has changed more perceptibly in recent years, with a lower proportion of children aged under 15 in 1987 than in 1971, and a higher proportion aged 65 or over (see also Chart 1.1). More detailed information on population projections can be found in Table 1.8 and in the Appendix (Part 1: Population and population projections).

The number of people aged 65 or over (8.8 million in 1987) is now over 50 per cent greater than in 1951 (5.5

1.3 Population: by sex and age, 1987 and 2021

United Kingdom

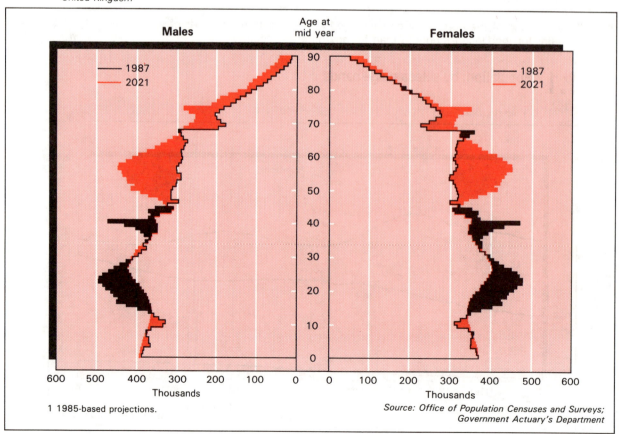

1 1985-based projections.

Source: Office of Population Censuses and Surveys;
Government Actuary's Department

million). The number in 1987 represented just over 15 per cent of the population compared with nearly 11 per cent in 1951. The size of this age group is expected to increase to 11.3 million by the year 2025. The slow-down in projected growth is due to the effects of low birth rates in the late 1920s and the 1930s. However, within the broad 65 or over age band, the balance of different age groups is expected to shift towards the older ages. In particular, the population aged 85 or over is projected to grow most rapidly, from some 0.8 million in 1987 to over 1.4 million by 2025. At the lower end of the age range, those aged under 15 formed 19 per cent of the total population in 1987 and by 2025 this proportion is expected to be broadly unchanged.

The age and sex distribution of the UK population in 1987 is compared with the projected distribution in 2021 in Chart 1.3. This shows how different peaks and troughs in births in past years have determined the current age structure and will continue to do so in the future: for example the peak in births in 1964 gives rise to a peak in the numbers in their early twenties at mid-1987, which becomes a peak in those in their mid fifties in 2021. Another factor affecting the age structure is increased life expectancy, which is partly responsible for the expected growth in numbers of the elderly, especially those aged 75 or over, which can be seen from the red-shaded area at the top of the two sides of the chart.

Chart 1.4 shows the marital composition of the population of England and Wales. In 1986 30 per cent of males aged 16 and over had never married compared to 22 per cent of females. About 5 per cent of males aged 16 and over and 6 per cent of females were divorced and had not remarried. Among both men and women the 40-44 age group had the highest proportion

of divorcees who had not remarried (trends in marriage and divorce are discussed in greater detail in Chapter 2). In 1986 there were over four times as many widows as widowers aged 65 and over, reflecting the greater number of women than men surviving into old age.

1.4 Population: by sex, age and marital status, 1986

England & Wales

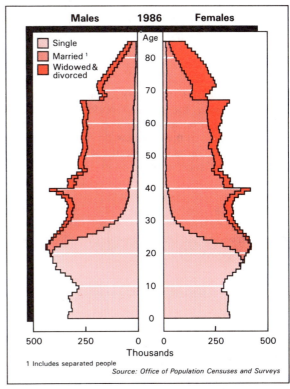

1 Includes separated people

Source: Office of Population Censuses and Surveys

Table 1.5 and Chart 1.6 use combined data from the 1984, 1985 and 1986 Labour Force Surveys. About 4.5 per cent of the population in Great Britain were from

1.5 Population[1]: by ethnic origin and age, 1984-86

Great Britain   Percentages and thousands

	Percentage in each age-group					Total[1] all ages (= 100%) (thousands)	Percentage UK-born	Percentage resident in English metropolitan areas[2]
	0—15	16—29	30—44	45—59	60 or over			
Ethnic group								
White	20	22	20	17	21	51,107	96	31
All ethnic minority groups	34	28	20	13	4	2,432	43	69
of which								
West Indian or Guyanese	26	33	16	19	6	534	53	81
Indian	32	27	23	13	5	760	36	66
Pakistani	44	24	17	12	2	397	42	66
Bangladeshi	50	20	14	15	1	103	31	79
Chinese	28	28	28	11	5	115	24	52
African	26	31	27	12	4	103	35	75
Arab	17	40	28	10	5	66	11	62
Mixed	53	27	11	7	3	235	74	58
Other	28	25	30	12	4	119	28	63
Not stated	29	24	18	13	17	691	68	37
All ethnic groups	21	22	20	17	20	54,230	93	33

1 Population in private households.
2 Including Greater London.

Source: Labour Force Survey, combined data for 1984 to 1986 inclusive, Office of Population Censuses and Surveys

the ethnic minority groups (Table 1.5). Of the ethnic minority population, over two thirds were either from the West Indian/Guyanese, Indian or Pakistani ethnic groups. All the ethnic minority groups have markedly different age structures from that of the White population; for example, 21 per cent of the White population was aged 60 or over compared to the West Indian/Guyanese ethnic group with 6 per cent. Correspondingly children form a.smaller proportion of the White population than they do of the different ethnic minority populations. As the ethnic minority population ages however, these differences are expected to lessen.

Chart 1.6 illustrates the marked difference in age structure between the United Kingdom-born and the overseas-born members of the ethnic minority population. Most of the overseas-born entered the UK as young adults, or as dependents, while the UK-born are the first or second generation children of these earlier immigrants. Consequently, about half of the UK-born ethnic minority population were aged under 10 and less than 7 per cent were aged over 25. In contrast, less than 5 per cent of the overseas-born ethnic minority population were aged under 10 while over three quarters were aged above 25.

Chart 1.7 compares annual population growth rates in different parts of the United Kingdom between 1981 and 1987 with those projected for the period between 1985 and 2001. Between 1981 and 1987 there was population growth in most non-metropolitan areas. Growth in East Anglia was nearly 1 per cent per annum, but that in Wales and the non-metropolitan parts of the north of England was slight and in Scotland there was a population fall. The populations of all metropolitan areas fell, reflecting the movement of people from urban to more rural areas. The greatest rates of fall were in Merseyside and the West Midlands.

Projected population changes between 1985 and 2001 are expected to continue the trends observed between 1981 and 1987, with continued growth projected in several areas, particularly East Anglia and the South East and South West of England. Greater London is expected to reverse its trend of population loss, and slight growth is projected between 1985 and 2001. More detailed information on the regional variations within the United Kingdom can be found in the CSO publication *Regional Trends*.

1.6 Ethnic minority population: by age and whether UK-born or overseas-born, 1984-86 average

Great Britain

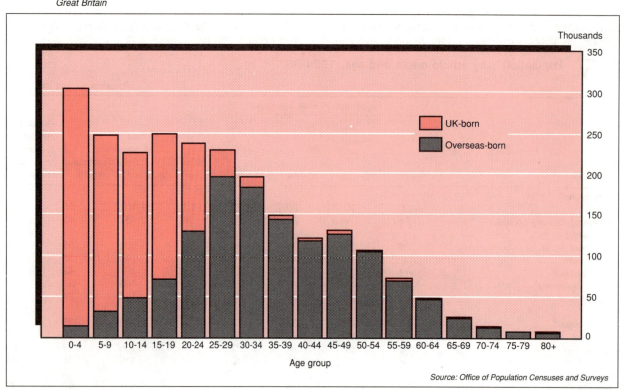

Source: Office of Population Censuses and Surveys

Social Trends 19, © Crown copyright 1989

1.7 Recent and projected future rates of change in total population: by region and country

United Kingdom

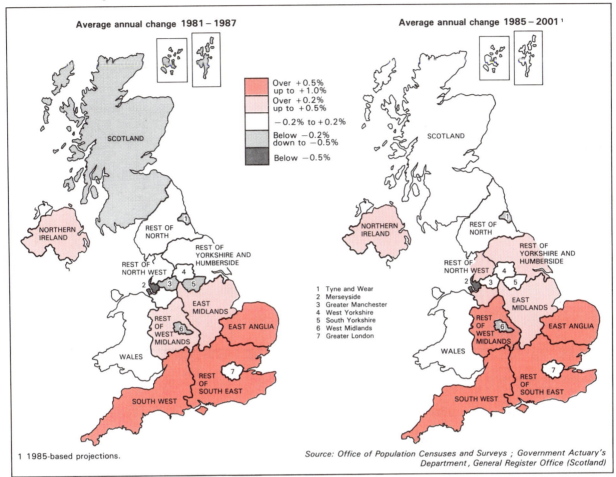

Average annual change 1981 – 1987

Average annual change 1985 – 2001 [1]

Over +0.5% up to +1.0%
Over +0.2% up to +0.5%
−0.2% to +0.2%
Below −0.2% down to −0.5%
Below −0.5%

1 Tyne and Wear
2 Merseyside
3 Greater Manchester
4 West Yorkshire
5 South Yorkshire
6 West Midlands
7 Greater London

1 1985-based projections.

Source: Office of Population Censuses and Surveys ; Government Actuary's Department , General Register Office (Scotland)

Population Trends

Population Trends, now in its 12th year, is the journal of the Office of Population Censuses and Surveys (OPCS). It is published four times a year in March, June, September and December.

Each issue brings together articles on a variety of population and medical topics giving in-depth analysis to particular subjects.

Population Trends also contains regular series of up-to-date statistical tabulations on population, births, marriages, divorces, deaths, migration and abortion.

The Winter 1988 edition will be the 54th issue of **Population Trends.** Published by HMSO, it can be obtained from Government bookshops and through good booksellers.

1.8 Population changes and projections[1]

United Kingdom   Thousands

| | Population at start of period | Average annual change | | | | | |
		Live births	Deaths	Net natural change	Net civilian migration	Other adjustments [2]	Overall annual change
Census enumerated							
1901-11	38,237	1,091	624	467	− 82	.	385
1911-21	42,082	975	689	286	− 92	.	194
1921-31	44,027	824	555	268	− 67	.	201
1931-51	46,038	785	598	188	+ 25	.	213
Mid-year estimates							
1951-61	50,290	839	593	246	− 9	+ 15	252
1961-71	52,807	963	639	324	− 32	+ 20	312
1971-81	55,928	736	666	70	− 44	+ 17	42
1981-86	56,352	732	662	70	+ 9	+ 3	82
1986-87	56,763	764	634	129	+ 31	+ 4	167
Projections [3]							
1987-91	56,891	804	647	157	− 17	0	140
1991-96	57,452	834	645	190	− 17	0	172
1996-2001	58,312	795	648	146	− 17	0	129
2001-06	58,957	732	654	78	− 17	0	61
2006-11	59,259	713	663	50	− 17	0	33
2011-16	59,422	736	677	59	− 17	0	41
2016-25	60,015	765	715	50	− 17	0	33

1 See Appendix, Part 1: Population and population projections.
2 Changes in numbers of armed forces plus adjustments to reconcile differences between estimated population change and the figures for natural change and net civilian migration.
3 1985-based projections.

Source: Office of Population Censuses and Surveys; Government Actuary's Department

Table 1.8 shows how the different factors which determine the total size of the United Kingdom population — births, deaths and migration — have changed since 1901 and how they are expected to change up to the year 2025. Between 1986 and 1987 the population increased by 167 thousand; this increase was similar to those in the two previous years, but greater than the average increase experienced in the period 1981-84. While the future population loss due to deaths and to net emigration is assumed to remain fairly stable until the year 2006, with deaths rising slowly after that date, births are projected to rise until the mid-1990s, then to fall until around 2011 and to rise again thereafter. Moderate overall growth is expected to produce a population of almost 59 million by 2001 and slightly over 60 million by 2016.

Births and Deaths

There were 776 thousand live births in the United Kingdom in 1987 (Table 1.9), 18 per cent more than the trough in 1977 but nearly 24 per cent fewer than the post-1950 peak year for births — 1964. These changes are reflected in the crude birth rate (that is not adjusted for women's ages) and the other measures of fertility shown in the table; the crude birth rate in 1987, at just over 13½ births per thousand population, was 28 per cent lower than the 1964 peak of nearly 19 births per thousand population, but about 16 per cent higher than the trough of less than 12 in 1977.

1.9 Live births: totals and rates

United Kingdom

	Total live births (thousands)	Crude birth rate[1]	General fertility rate[2]	Mean age of mothers at birth (years)	Total period fertility rate[3]
1951	797	15.9	73.0	28.4	2.15
1956	825	16.1	78.8	28.0	2.36
1961	944	17.9	90.6	27.6	2.80
1964	1,015	18.8	94.1	27.2	2.95
1966	980	17.9	91.5	26.9	2.79
1971	902	16.1	84.3	26.4	2.41
1976	676	12.0	61.3	26.7	1.74
1977	657	11.7	58.9	26.8	1.69
1981	731	13.0	62.1	27.2	1.81
1985	751	13.3	61.4	27.7	1.80
1986	755	13.3	61.1	27.7	1.78
1987	776	13.6	62.3	27.1	1.82
Projections[4]					
1991	827	14.4	67.0.	27.5	1.90
2001	759	12.9	64.3	28.4	1.99
2011	721	12.1	66.4	27.7	2.00
2025	760	12.7	67.4	28.1	2.00

1 Total births per 1,000 population of all ages.
2 Total births per 1,000 women aged 15-44. Includes also births to mothers aged under 15, and 45 or over.
3 The average number of children which would be born per woman if women experienced the age-specific fertility rates of the period in question throughout their child-bearing life span.
4 1985-based projections.

Source: Office of Population Censuses and Surveys

1.10 Live birth rates: by age of mother[1]

England & Wales

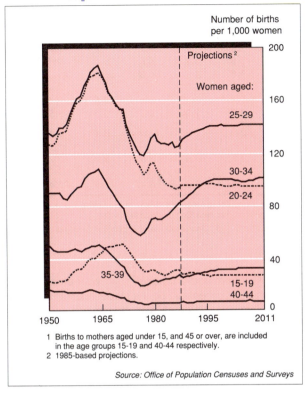

1 Births to mothers aged under 15, and 45 or over, are included
  in the age groups 15-19 and 40-44 respectively.
2 1985-based projections.

Source: Office of Population Censuses and Surveys

Chart 1.10 shows that in England and Wales the number of births per thousand women at all ages over 20 peaked in the early 1960's while for those aged 15-19 the peak was in 1971. Since then birth rates have fallen, and in 1987 for all women except those aged 15-19, birth rates were lower than they were in 1950, particularly amongst women aged 35-39 (down 45 per cent) and 40-44 (down 66 per cent). Since the trough in the mid 1970's birth rates for women over 25 have generally risen, and are projected to continue their rise into the next century, but those for women aged 20-24 are projected to remain stable and those for the under 20's to decrease slightly.

Births to mothers born outside the United Kingdom fell from 12.2 per cent of all live births in Great Britain in 1981 to 11.2 per cent in 1987; this was however, still higher than the corresponding figure of 10.6 per cent in 1971 (Table 1.11). Similarly the proportion of births to mothers born in the New Commonwealth and Pakistan (NCWP), which had risen from 5.3 per cent in 1971 to 7.8 per cent in 1981, fell to 7.1 per cent in 1987. Over this period the percentage of births to mothers born in the Irish Republic fell from 2.6 per cent of all live births in 1971 to 0.8 per cent in 1987. These trends partly reflect changes in the number of women of child-bearing age born in different parts of the world. It is important to note, however, that birthplace does not necessarily equate with ethnic group. In particular, there are an increasing number of women from the ethnic minority population in the younger child-bearing ages who were themselves born in this country (see also Chart 1.6). Conversely, some women, although born in countries of the NCWP, are not of ethnic minority descent.

1.11 Live births: by country of birth of mother

Great Britain

Thousands and percentages

Area/country of birth of mother	Live births (thousands)				Percentage of all live births			
	1971	1981	1986	1987	1971	1981	1986	1987
United Kingdom[1]	773.3	617.3	641.9	663.8	88.9	87.7	88.3	88.8
Outside United Kingdom								
Irish Republic	22.5	8.6	6.4	6.2	2.6	1.2	0.9	0.8
Old Commonwealth	2.7	2.6	2.7	2.8	0.3	0.4	0.4	0.4
New Commonwealth and Pakistan								
India	13.7	12.6	10.8	10.2	1.6	1.8	1.5	1.4
Pakistan and Bangladesh	8.5	17.0	18.9	18.3	1.0	2.4	2.6	2.5
Caribbean	12.6	6.3	4.7	4.6	1.4	0.9	0.6	0.6
East Africa	2.2	6.7	7.3	7.3	0.3	1.0	1.0	1.0
Rest of Africa	3.0	3.6	3.8	4.0	0.3	0.5	0.5	0.5
Other New Commonwealth[2]	6.2	8.4	8.7	8.6	0.7	1.2	1.2	1.1
Total New Commonwealth and Pakistan	46.2	54.6	54.3	53.0	5.3	7.8	7.5	7.1
Other European Community	} 20.4	{ 6.1	7.2	7.4 }	} 2.3	{ 0.9	1.0	1.0
Rest of the world		{ 14.1	14.2	14.4 }		{ 2.0	2.0	1.9
Total with mother born outside UK	91.8	86.0	84.8	83.9	10.6	12.2	11.7	11.2
Not stated	4.8	0.2	0.1	0.1	0.6	—	—	—
Total live births	869.9	703.5	726.8	747.8	100.0	100.0	100.0	100.0

1 Includes Isle of Man and Channel Islands.
2 Includes Hong Kong, Singapore, Malaysia, Sri Lanka, Malta, Gibraltar
  Cyprus and other New Commonwealth Islands.

Source: Office of Population Censuses and Surveys

1.12 Fertility rates and births outside marriage: by country of birth of mother

England & Wales Rates and percentages

	Total period fertility rates [1]				Percentage of births outside marriage			
	1971	1981	1986	1987	1971	1981	1986	1987
Area/country of birth of mother								
United Kingdom [2]	2.3	1.7	1.7	1.8	*8.1*	*13.4*	*22.9*	*24.8*
New Commonwealth and Pakistan								
India	4.1	3.1	2.9	2.7	*1.7*	*1.2*	*1.7*	*1.8*
Pakistan and Bangladesh	8.8	6.5	5.6	5.2	*0.8*	*0.5*	*0.6*	*0.8*
Caribbean	3.3	2.0	1.8	1.9	*36.3*	*50.0*	*48.3*	*48.7*
East Africa	2.4	2.1	2.0	2.0	*3.7*	*2.4*	*3.4*	*3.8*
Rest of Africa	3.8	3.4	2.8	3.2	*4.6*	*13.0*	*22.1*	*25.0*
Other New Commonwealth [3]	2.6	2.0	2.0	1.9	*5.2*	*6.3*	*9.9*	*10.5*
Total New Commonwealth and Pakistan	3.8	2.9	2.9	2.8	*11.9*	*8.4*	*8.4*	*9.0*
Rest of the world	2.7	2.0	1.9	1.9	*8.9*	*9.4*	*13.7*	*15.4*
All countries	2.4	1.8	1.8	1.8	*8.4*	*12.8*	*21.4*	*23.2*

1 See Table 1.9 footnote 3.
2 Includes Isle of Man and Channel Islands.

3 Includes Hong Kong, Singapore, Malaysia, Sri Lanka, Malta, Gibraltar, Cyprus and other New Commonwealth islands.

Source: Office of Population Censuses and Surveys

Fertility rates dropped between 1971 and 1987 for all women in England and Wales, no matter where they were born (Table 1.12). The total period fertility rate (TPFR) for women born in Pakistan and Bangladesh, although still much higher than for other countries, fell by over 40 per cent between 1971 and 1987. In the same period the TPFR for Caribbean-born women fell by approximately the same proportion and is now only just above the rate for UK-born women. Between 1971 and 1987 the percentage of births outside marriage to United Kingdom and Caribbean-born women increased by 17 and 12 percentage points respectively though the trends have been different, with the percentage of births outside marriage to UK mothers continuing to rise while that for Caribbean mothers appears to be stabilising. In contrast the very low proportions of births outside marriage to women from India, Pakistan and Bangladesh have remained almost constant over the same period. (Chapter 2 contains further details on births outside marriage.)

1.13 Death rates: by age and sex

United Kingdom Rates per thousand population and thousands

	Age											All ages	Total deaths (000's)
	Under 1[1]	1—4	5—14	15—34	35—44	45—54	55—64	65—74	75—84	85+			
1961													
Males	24.8	1.1	0.4	1.1	2.5	7.5	22.3	55.1	125.0	258.6		12.6	322.0
Females	19.3	0.8	0.3	0.6	1.8	4.5	11.1	31.5	89.1	215.9		11.4	309.8
1971													
Males	20.2	0.8	0.4	1.0	2.4	7.2	20.5	51.4	114.7	235.6		12.2	328.5
Females	15.5	0.6	0.3	0.5	1.6	4.4	10.3	26.8	75.2	189.5		11.1	316.5
1976													
Males	16.4	0.7	0.3	1.0	2.2	7.2	20.1	51.4	118.5	250.8		12.6	341.9
Females	12.4	0.5	0.2	0.5	1.5	4.4	10.5	26.6	75.9	203.0		11.8	338.9
1981													
Males	12.7	0.6	0.3	0.9	1.9	6.3	18.1	46.3	106.3	226.6		12.0	329.1
Females	9.5	0.5	0.2	0.4	1.3	3.9	9.8	24.7	66.9	178.4		11.4	328.8
1986													
Males	10.9	0.4	0.2	0.8	1.7	5.5	17.0	43.6	102.0	217.1		11.8	327.2
Females	8.1	0.4	0.2	0.4	1.1	3.3	9.5	24.0	63.2	172.4		11.5	333.6
1987													
Males	10.3	0.4	0.2	0.9	1.7	5.2	16.4	42.0	97.3	194.3		11.5	318.3
Females	7.9	0.4	0.2	0.4	1.1	3.3	9.4	23.3	60.8	159.9		11.2	326.0

1 Rate per 1,000 live births.

Source: Office of Population Censuses and Surveys

There were just over 644 thousand deaths in the United Kingdom in 1987, a fall of 16½ thousand over the 1986 total (Table 1.13). The crude death rate was 11.5 deaths per thousand population for males in 1987 and 11.2 for females, although this takes no account of the changing age structure of the population. There were declines in the death rate for all age groups and both sexes between 1961 and 1987, though men retained higher mortality rates than women at almost all ages. Chapter 7 gives information on life expectancy at different ages, causes of death and infant mortality.

Migration

Estimates of the effect of overseas migration on the size of the population are made annually by the Registrars General. For demographic purposes they use the agreed international definition of migrants, such that a 'new resident' is someone who, having lived abroad for at least twelve months, declares an intention to reside in the United Kingdom for at least twelve months. The definition of a 'departing resident' is the converse. The main source of data on such movements is the International Passenger Survey (IPS).

Table 1.14 shows five-year averages for migration into and out from the United Kingdom. In 1983-87 more people came into the country than left it, while in 1973-77 and 1978-82 the opposite was the case. The number of migrants from the European Community has more than doubled between 1973-77 and 1983-87, and there has been a 50 per cent increase in the number of residents from the USA moving to the United Kingdom over the same period. Migration to South Africa has decreased by 71 per cent over the period covered in the table, and all Commonwealth countries (excluding the 'other' category) have experienced declining popularity. In 1983-87 47 per cent of all migrants into the United Kingdom were UK citizens compared to 44 per cent in 1973-77 and 41 per cent in 1978-82.

1.14 International migration into and out of the United Kingdom: by country of last or next residence

Thousands

	1973-1977			1978-1982			1983-1987		
	Inflow	Outflow	Balance	Inflow	Outflow	Balance	Inflow	Outflow	Balance
Country of last or next residence									
Commonwealth countries									
Australia	25.0	42.6	− 17.5	13.3	35.2	− 21.9	15.3	27.4	− 12.0
Canada	8.0	28.9	− 20.9	5.8	18.9	− 13.1	6.1	7.5	− 1.4
New Zealand	8.5	17.0	− 8.5	6.6	9.6	− 3.0	8.8	7.4	1.3
African Commonwealth	19.2	13.1	6.2	13.6	10.5	3.1	13.8	7.0	6.8
Bangladesh, India, Sri Lanka	12.4	3.9	8.5	17.5	3.9	13.6	14.2	3.7	10.5
Caribbean	4.4	4.9	− 0.5	4.1	3.2	0.9	3.6	2.8	0.8
Other	16.0	8.3	7.6	15.6	12.9	2.7	16.6	14.9	1.7
Total Commonwealth	93.6	118.8	− 25.2	76.5	94.3	− 17.8	78.5	70.8	7.7
Non Commonwealth countries [1]									
European Community [2]	23.8	30.0	− 6.2	29.2	32.0	− 2.8	51.9	44.6	7.3
Rest of Europe	12.6	15.9	− 3.3	11.0	12.2	− 1.2	8.4	8.0	0.4
United States of America	16.9	20.6	− 3.7	16.2	26.8	− 10.6	25.3	30.3	− 5.0
Rest of America	4.2	3.6	0.6	3.6	4.8	− 1.2	2.6	2.3	0.3
Republic of South Africa	9.0	18.5	− 9.4	7.6	14.4	− 6.8	11.6	5.4	6.1
Pakistan	8.3	2.6	5.7	12.9	1.5	11.4	10.3	1.8	8.5
Middle East [3]	—	—	—	12.6	24.8	− 12.2	15.6	17.4	− 1.7
Other [3]	17.6	24.5	− 6.9	12.5	9.6	2.9	15.4	8.6	6.8
Total Non Commonwealth	92.5	115.6	− 23.1	105.6	126.1	− 20.5	141.1	118.4	22.7
All countries	186.1	234.4	− 48.4	182.1	220.4	− 38.3	219.6	189.2	30.4
Of which:									
UK citizens	81.3	165.0	− 83.7	75.3	150.8	− 75.6	103.8	119.0	− 15.3
Non-UK citizens	104.8	69.5	35.4	106.8	69.6	37.3	115.8	70.2	45.7

1 Excluding the Irish Republic.
2 Spain and Portugal are included with rest of Europe for 1973 – 1982 and with European Community for 1983 – 1987.
3 Middle East included in Other for 1973 – 1977.

Source: Office of Population Censuses and Surveys

1.15 Acceptances for settlement: by category of acceptance

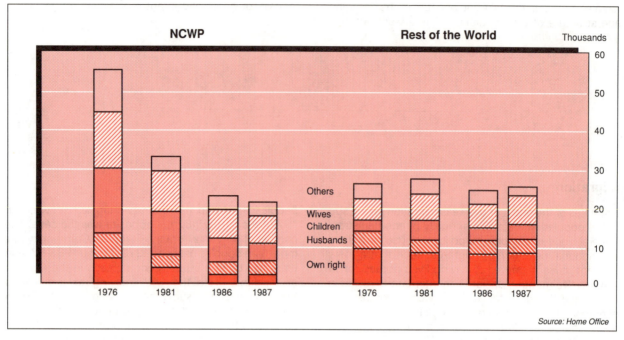

United Kingdom

Source: Home Office

An alternative measure of immigration — the main measure for persons subject to immigration control — is the number of people accepted for settlement in the United Kingdom under the Immigration Act 1971 (Chart 1.15). These statistics are on a different basis from those from the IPS and relate only to people who are subject to immigration control and not to people who have the right of abode in the United Kingdom. In 1987, 46.0 thousand people were accepted for settlement, 34.8 thousand less than in 1976. Citizens from the NCWP accounted for 20.8 thousand — just over 45 per cent of the total. About 56 per cent of the NCWP citizens granted settlement in 1987 were wives and children.

Table 1.16 shows the total number of applications for refugee status or asylum in the United Kingdom between 1979 and 1987 and the decisions taken in those years. Provisionally, there were just over 4½

thousand applications in 1987, slightly down on 1986 but nearly 3 times as many as were made in 1979. The table excludes 20 thousand Vietnamese refugees who have settled in the United Kingdom between 1979 and 1987 and who are dealt with under separate arrangements.

Just over 3 thousand decisions on refugee status or asylum were reached in 1987. Of the decisions taken, 13 per cent were granted asylum or refugee status and 63 per cent were granted leave to remain on exceptional grounds. Exceptional grounds include circumstances under which the applicants are given leave to remain in the United Kingdom on an annual basis because they could not be expected to return to their country of origin in the prevailing circumstances (see Appendix Part 1: Population - Refugees). The remaining 25 per cent of decisions were refusals of refugee status or exceptional leave to remain.

1.16 Applications for refugee status [1] or asylum, and decisions taken [2]

United Kingdom   Numbers

	1979	1980	1981	1982	1983	1984	1985	1986	1987
Number of applications	1,563	2,352	2,425	4,223	4,296	3,869	5,444	4,811	4,508
Decisions taken									
Granted asylum or refugee status	525	1,147	1,473	1,727	1,185	649	866	536	378
Granted exceptional leave to remain	215	238	278	311	939	779	2,121	2,713	1,891
Refused asylum or exceptional leave to remain	209	412	607	904	826	556	751	729	749
Total decisions	949	1,797	2,358	2,942	2,950	1,984	3,738	3,978	3,018

1 See Appendix, Part 1: Refugees.
2 Decisions in a particular year do not necessarily relate to applications made in that year.

Source: Home Office

International Comparisons

The United Nations (UN) estimated that in 1974 the world's population was 4 billion; 13 years later the UN designated 11 July 1987, 'Day of 5 billion', as the symbolic focus of a worldwide celebration of the day the world's population reached 5 billion. By comparison it took about 35 years to grow from 2 billion in the middle of the 1920s to 3 billion in 1960 and more than a century to grow from 1 billion to 2 billion. It is projected that the world's population will reach 6 billion by 1999, 7 billion by 2010 and 8 billion by 2022.

Chart 1.17 shows population densities for each of the European Community member countries in 1986. The United Kingdom, with 233 inhabitants per square kilometre was well above the Community average of 143, while Ireland, with only 50 inhabitants per square kilometre had the lowest population density in the Community.

The total population of the European Community is expected to show a slight decline between 1985 and 2025, having risen to a peak of about 330 million in the year 2000. However, significant changes in the age structure are expected over the period. In the EC the number of people aged under 15 as a percentage of those aged 15 to 64 is expected to fall in most countries

1.17 **Population density: EC comparison, 1986**

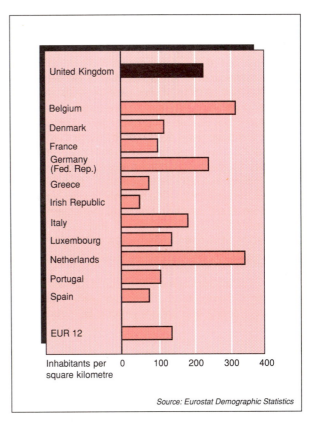

Source: Eurostat Demographic Statistics

1.18 **Dependancy ratios: EC comparison, 1985 and 2025[1]**

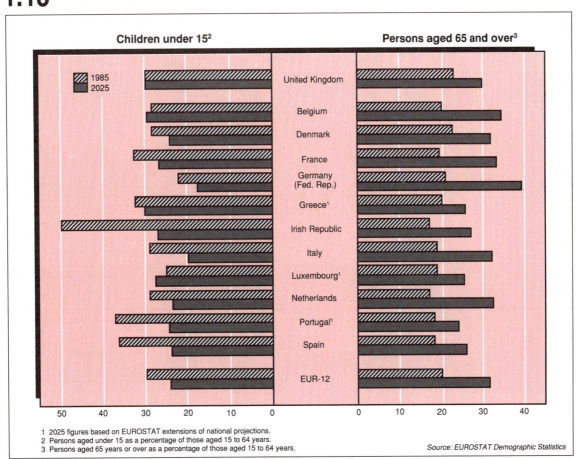

1 2025 figures based on EUROSTAT extensions of national projections.
2 Persons aged under 15 as a percentage of those aged 15 to 64 years.
3 Persons aged 65 years or over as a percentage of those aged 15 to 64 years.

Source: EUROSTAT Demographic Statistics

between 1985 and 2025, nearly halving in Ireland from 50 per cent to 27 per cent but remaining stable in the United Kingdom (Chart 1.18). The number of people aged 65 or over as a percentage of those aged 15 to 64 is projected to show an increase in all EC countries, nearly doubling in the Federal Republic of Germany from 21 per cent in 1985 to 40 per cent in 2025. In 1985 the UK had the highest percentage of elderly dependents, but population projections indicate that by 2025 it will have been overtaken by more than half of the other EC countries. The number of children in the EC under 15 years, which fell from 72 million in 1965 to 64 million in 1985, is expected to decline to 49 million in the year 2025. The number of elderly persons (aged 65 or over), on the other hand, which amounted to 32 million in 1965 and to 43 million in 1985 is projected to have risen to 64 million by the year 2025.

Table 1.19 compares demographic data for each of the European Community countries alongside figures for the USA, Canada and Japan. Among EC countries in mid-1986 the Federal Republic of Germany (FRG) had the largest population (61.1 million) followed by Italy (57.2 million) and the United Kingdom (56.8 million). By the year 2025 it is projected that the United Kingdom will have moved into first place with a population of 60.0 million. Of the countries shown in the table Belgium, Denmark, Luxembourg, the FRG, the Irish Republic and Italy are all expected to have slightly smaller populations in the year 2025 than they had in 1986. In the FRG and in Denmark the birth rate was below the death rate in 1986 while in a number of other countries the birth rate scarcely exceeded the death rate. The highest birth rate of the countries shown in Table 1.19 was in the Republic of Ireland (17.4 live births per 1000 population) followed by the USA (15.5) and Canada (14.8). Japan had the lowest death rate (6.3 deaths per thousand population). Expectations of life at birth were greatest for both men and women in Japan being 74.5 and 80.1 years respectively compared with 71.7 and 77.5 years in the United Kingdom. They were lowest in Belgium and Luxembourg for men, and in the Irish Republic for women.

1.19 Population structure of selected countries, 1986

	Population (millions)	Birth rate [1]	Death rate [2]	Expectation of life at birth [3] (years)		Projections [4] (millions)	
				Males	Females	2000	2025
United Kingdom	56,763	13.3	11.7	71.7	77.5	58,859	60,015
Belgium	9,862	11.9	11.3	70.0	76.8	9,679	8,910
Denmark	5,121	10.8	11.3	71.6	77.5	5,154	4,740
France	55,394	14.1	9.9	71.5	79.7	57,879	58,152
Germany (Fed. Rep.)	61,066	10.2	11.5	71.2	77.8	60,484	51,140
Greece	9,966	11.3	9.2	72.2	76.4	10,334	10,633[5]
Irish Republic	3,541	17.4	9.5	70.1	75.6	3,479	3,283
Italy	57,246	10.1	9.5	71.4	78.1	57,226	50,900
Luxembourg	369	11.7	10.7	70.0	76.7	378	365[5]
Netherlands	14,572	12.7	8.6	72.9	79.7	15,588	15,325
Portugal	10,208	12.4	9.4	70.3	77.1	11,077	10,834[5]
Spain	38,616	12.1	7.7	72.5	78.6	40,691	40,381
USA	241,596	15.5	8.7	71.3	78.8	266,194	300,796
Canada	25,612	14.8	7.3	72.8	80.1		
Japan	121,492	11.5	6.3	74.5	80.1	129,104	128,596

1 Live births per thousand population.
2 Deaths per thousand population.
3 Latest available year.

4 Latest national projection, except where otherwise stated.
5 SOEC extension of national projections.

Source: Statistical Office of the European Communities;
Office of Population Censuses and Surveys

Chapter 2: Households and families

Households

- A quarter of all households in Great Britain were one-person households in 1987, compared to only about one-eighth in 1961. *(Chart 2.1 below)*

- One-person households in Great Britain are projected to increase further from 5.3 million in 1987 to 7.1 million in 2001. *(Table 2.5)*

Families

- In 1986, 14 per cent of dependent children in Great Britain lived in lone-parent families; almost twice the proportion as in 1972, the earliest year for which data are available from the General Household Survey. *(Table 2.10)*

- The proportion of women aged 18-49 years who were cohabiting nearly doubled between 1981 and 1987 in Great Britain, from 3.3 per cent to 6.4 per cent. *(Table 2.11)*

Marriage and divorce

- Since 1971, bachelors and spinsters have formed an increasing proportion of the population. Between 1901 and 1971 the trend had been the reverse. *(Chart 2.14)*

- In 1986, the United Kingdom had both the highest marriage rate and divorce rate of the EC countries. *(Table 2.20)*

Family building

- The average interval from marriage to the birth of a first child in England and Wales was 27 months in 1987, having fallen from a peak of 31 months in 1978. *(Chart 2.22)*

- Births outside marriage have risen very quickly in recent years. They accounted for 23 per cent of all births in the United Kingdom in 1987 compared to only 12 per cent in 1981 and 6 per cent in 1961. *(Table 2.26)*

2.1 **One person households as a percentage of all households: by age**

Great Britain

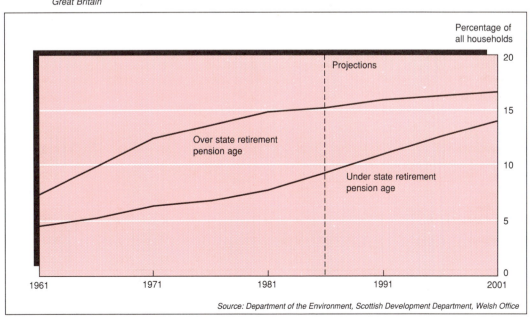

Source: Department of the Environment, Scottish Development Department, Welsh Office

Households

Whereas Chapter 1 looked at statistics about people as individuals, this chapter examines the structure and characteristics of the households and families in which they live. The tables and charts in this chapter generally exclude the population of institutions, ie those living in boarding schools, hospitals,. halls of residence, old people's homes, prisons, and other communal establishments.

2.2 Households [1]: by size

Great Britain					Percentages
	1961	1971	1976	1981	1987
Household size					
1 person	12	18	21	22	25
2 people	30	32	32	32	32
3 people	23	19	17	17	17
4 people	19	17	17	18	17
5 people	9	8	8	7	6
6 or more people	7	6	5	4	2
All households	100	100	100	100	100
Average household size (number of people)	3.09	2.89	2.76	2.71	2.55

1 See Appendix, Part 2: Households. The data for 1961, 1971, and 1981 are taken from the Population Censuses of those years; the 1976 and 1987 data are from the General Household Survey.

Source: Office of Population Censuses and Surveys

One of the most notable features of the period since the second world war has been the increase in people living alone: in 1987 a quarter of households in Great Britain contained only one person, compared with about one eighth in 1961 (Chart 2.1 and Table 2.2). At the same time the proportion of households containing five or more people has halved, and is now less than one tenth.

These changes have inevitably led to a reduction in average household size, from 3.09 people in 1961 to 2.55 people in 1987 (Table 2.2). The increase in the proportion of one-person households is not caused simply by an increase in the proportion of elderly people living alone; Chart 2.1 shows that the proportions of people living alone aged both under and over state retirement pension age (65 years for men, 60 years for women) have increased. However, the proportion of two-person households has increased slightly over the last 25 years, while households with 3 or more people have decreased as a proportion of all households.

Table 2.3 confirms the growth in the proportion of one person households shown in Chart 2.1. Whilst the proportion of one person households both above and below state retirement pension age has been increasing, the proportion containing a married couple with dependent children has been decreasing and the proportion of other households has remained fairly constant. The fall in the proportion of households with dependent children reflects the falling birth rate during the late 1960s and 1970s although this rate started to rise again in the 1980s (see Table 1.9). With smaller households and an increasing population, the total number of households has been increasing which in turn means there is an increase in demand for dwellings (see Chapter 8: Housing).

In 1987 the average size of households containing children under the age of 16 was 4.0 persons. Between 1971 and 1985 there was a gradual reduction in the average size of such households, from 4.3 to 4.0 persons, but there was no further perceptible change between 1985 and 1987.

2.3 Households [1]: by type

Great Britain								Percentages and thousands
	Percentages					Thousands		
	1961	1971	1976	1981	1987	1961	1971	1981
One person								
Under pensionable age	4	6	6	8	9	726	1,122	1,469
Over pensionable age	7	12	15	14	16	1,193	2,198	2,771
Two or more unrelated adults	5	4	3	5	3	804	748	922
Married couple [2] with								
No children	26	27	27	26	27	4,147	4,890	4,989
1 – 2 dependent children [3]	30	26	26	25	23	4,835	4,723	4,850
3 or more dependent children [3]	8	9	8	6	5	1,282	1,582	1,100
Non-dependent children only	10	8	7	8	9	1,673	1,565	1,586
Lone parent [2] with								
Dependent children [3]	2	3	4	5	4	367	515	916
Non-dependent children only	4	4	4	4	4	721	712	720
Two or more families	3	1	1	1	1	439	263	170
All households	100	100	100	100	100	16,189	18,317	19,493

1 See Appendix, Part 2: Households. Data for 1961, 1971 and 1981 are taken from the population censuses for those years; the 1976 and 1987 data are from the General Household Survey.

2 Other individuals who were not family members may also have been present.

3 These family types may also include non-dependent children.

Source: Office of Population Censuses and Surveys

2.4 Households [1]: by type, Northern Ireland

Percentages and numbers

	1983	1986	1987
One person			
Under pensionable age	6	7	9
Over pensionable age	14	13	15
Two or more unrelated adults	4	4	4
Married couple [2] with			
No children	19	18	18
1 – 2 dependent children [3]	25	24	23
3 or more dependent children [3]	13	13	12
Non-dependent children only	8	9	8
Lone parent [2] with			
Dependent children [3]	4	6	6
Non-dependent children only	5	6	5
Two or more families	1	1	1
Sample size (= 100% numbers)	2,940	2,759	3,167

1 See Appendix, Part 2: Households.
2 Other individuals who were not family members may also have been present.
3 These family types may also include non-dependent children.

Source: Continuous Household Survey

2.5 Household projections [1]: by household type and age of head

Great Britain   Millions and numbers

	1987	1991	1996	2001
Households (millions)				
One person households				
Head aged 16-29	0.6	0.7	0.7	0.0
30-44	0.6	0.8	1.0	1.3
45-59/64 [2]	0.9	0.9	1.1	1.3
60/65 [3] or over	3.3	3.5	3.7	3.9
Total	5.3	5.9	6.6	7.1
All other households				
Head aged 15-29	2.2	2.1	1.9	1.6
30-44	5.2	5.4	5.4	5.6
45-59/64 [2]	5.5	5.5	5.9	6.1
60/65 [3] or over	3.0	3.0	3.0	2.9
Total	15.9	16.1	16.2	16.2
All households	21.2	22.0	22.8	23.3
Average household size				
(numbers)	2.57	2.50	2.45	2.42

1 1985-based for England and Wales, 1983-based for Scotland.
2 45 – 59 for females, 45 – 64 for males.
3 60 or over for females, 65 or over for males.

Source: Department of the Environment;
Scottish Development Department;
Welsh Office

In recent years Northern Ireland has conducted a similar survey to the General Household Survey (GHS) in Great Britain, the Continuous Household Survey (CHS), and estimates on an equivalent basis to those in Table 2.3 are presented for the Province in Table 2.4. This shows that the pattern of household composition differs from that in Great Britain in several respects. There is a lower percentage of married couples without children in Northern Ireland than in Great Britain and a higher percentage of married couples with 3 or more dependent children in Northern Ireland than in Great Britain. The proportion of households in Northern Ireland consisting of a one parent family was slightly higher than that for the rest of the United Kingdom.

The number of households in Great Britain is projected to rise by 2.1 million to 23.3 million between 1987 and 2001 (Table 2.5). This projected increase is largely the result of the projected growth in the number of one-person households from 5.3 million in 1987 to 7.1 million in 2001, an increase of a third. However people over state retirement pension age are projected to form a declining proportion of one-person households, 55 per cent in 2001 compared with 62 per cent in 1987. The falling trend in average household size is expected to continue, with the average dropping below 2.50 well before the turn of the century.

General Household Survey 1986

General Household Survey

The sixteenth edition of this annual publication from the Office of Population Censuses and Surveys contains statistics on population, family information, contraception, housing, burglary, employment, education, health, smoking, leisure and the elderly. Published by HMSO, it can be obtained from Government bookshops and through good booksellers.

2.6 Marital status of men and women living alone: by age, 1985

Great Britain

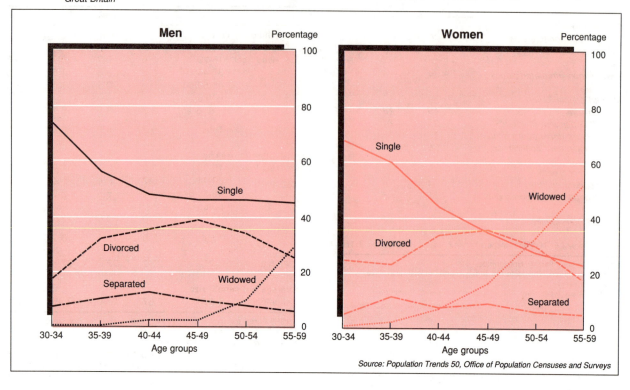

Source: Population Trends 50, Office of Population Censuses and Surveys

Profiles of the marital status of those living alone in the middle years of life derived from the Labour Force Survey, appear in Chart 2.6. The age patterns of the proportions of men and women who are divorced are fairly similar, as is the case with those who are separated. However, the proportion of women living alone who are single declines far more rapidly with each successive age-group than does that for men, whilst the proportion who are widowed increases more rapidly. Widows account for over one half of women in their

2.7 Household type· by ethnic group of head of household, 1984-1986

Great Britain

Percentages

		Ethnic group of head of household					
	White	All ethnic minority groups	West Indian or Guyanese	Indian	Pakistani or Bangladeshi	Other ethnic minority groups	All groups (including bit stated)
Household type							
One person households	24	14	18	6	5	21	24
One family households (with or without other persons)							
Couple with no children	26	11	11	10	6	14	26
Couple with children							
with dependent children [1]	29	47	28	59	68	41	29
with non-dependent children only	8	4	5	5	2	4	8
Lone parent							
with dependent children [1]	4	11	23	4	4	8	4
with non-dependent children only	3	3	6	2	2	2	3
Two or more family households with children	1	6	2	11	10	2	1
Other households [2]	4	5	5	4	3	8	4
All households	100	100	100	100	100	100	100

1 Aged under 16 years of age, or under 19 years of age and never married and either in full-time education or else on a government scheme.

2 Households which contain either two or more families with no children or two or more persons not in a family.

Source: Labour Force Surveys, 1984–1986 average, Office of Population Censuses and Surveys

late fifties who are living alone. The total number of men and women living alone varies from age-group to age-group declining to a minimum for those aged from 40 to 44, and there after increasing for each successive age-group. Thus the pattern of numbers of those living alone by their age and marital status is somewhat different to Chart 2.6.

The proportion of households containing just one person is much higher in the White population than in the ethnic minority population (Table 2.7); 24 per cent of households where the head is from the White population consisted of a person living alone, compared with 18 per cent of West Indian/Guyanese households, 6 per cent of Indian households and 5 per cent of Pakistani/Bangladeshi households. The reason lies mainly in the White population being more elderly (see Table 1.5); which results in higher proportions living alone. Indian and Pakistani or Bangladeshi households are the most likely to contain two or more families with children; they are also the most likely to consist of a couple with dependent children. There is a higher proportion of one parent families among the West Indian and Guyanese ethnic group.

Within the European Community in 1981, the United Kingdom had marginally the largest proportion of two person households (Table 2.8), although several of the countries had a similar proportion. Portugal, Spain and

2.8 Household size: EC comparison, 1981 [1]

Percentages and thousands

	Number of persons in household				All house-holds (= 100%) (thousands)
	1	2	3 to 5	6 or more	
United Kingdom	22	32	42	3	19,949
Belgium	23	30	43	4	3,569
Denmark	29	31	38	2	2,069
France	25	29	42	4	19,590
Germany (Fed. Rep.)	31	29	39	1	25,099
Greece	15	25	54	6	2,974
Irish Republic	17	20	43	19	911
Italy	18	24	54	5	18,632
Luxembourg	21	28	46	5	128
Netherlands	23	30	43	4	5,011
Portugal	13	25	52	10	2,924
Spain	10	21	56	13	10,586

1 Data are derived from population censuses carried out in 1981 or 1982, the exceptions being the Netherlands and the Federal Republic of Germany who drew on population registers and large-scale sample surveys.

Source: Statistical Office of the European Communities

the Irish Republic were the most likely countries to have 3 or more persons in a household and indeed to have over 6 persons to a larger extent, whilst Denmark and the German Federal Republic were the most likely countries to have 2 or less persons per household.

Families

Whereas a household is usually defined simply as a person or group of people living together, the term family as used here comprises a married couple either living alone or with their never married children, or a lone parent with his or her children (see Appendix, Part 2: Families). This section examines some of the characteristics of families as opposed to households.

Just over 77 per cent of people living in private households in Great Britain in 1987 lived in families headed by a married couple, a proportion which has fallen only slightly since 1961 (Table 2.9). About 57 per cent of these people, that is almost 44 per cent of all people living in private households, lived in 'traditional' family group households consisting of a married couple with dependent children; the remainder had either non-dependent children or none living with them. The proportion of people living in households consisting of a married couple and no children has risen, whilst the proportion of married couples with children has fallen. The proportion of people living in one-parent families with dependent children doubled from 2½ per cent in

1961 to almost 5 per cent in 1987, largely reflecting the rise in divorce and the increasing incidence of births outside marriage (see Table 2.16 and Chart 2.27).

2.9 People in households [1]: by type of household and family in which they live

Great Britain   Percentages

	1961	1971	1981	1987
Type of household				
Living alone	3.9	6.3	8.0	9.9
Married couple, no children	17.8	19.3	19.5	21.5
Married couple with dependent children [2]	52.2	51.7	47.4	44.1
Married couple with non-dependent children only	11.6	10.0	10.3	11.8
Lone parent with dependent children [2]	2.5	3.5	5.8	4.7
Other households	12.0	9.2	9.0	8.0
All households	100	100	100	100

1 See Appendix, Part 2: Families. The data for 1961, 1971 and 1981 are taken from the population censuses for those years; the 1987 data are from the General Household Survey.
2 These family types may also include non-dependent children.

Source: Office of Population Censuses and Surveys

The majority of dependent children in Great Britain in 1986 lived with one or more siblings and a married couple, in other words in a 'traditional' family (Table 2.10). However, the General Household Survey (GHS) indicates that the proportion living in such families has fallen from 76 per cent to 68 per cent between 1972 and 1986, whilst the proportion of 'only children' has risen slightly. The proportion of children living in lone-parent families rose from 8 per cent in 1972 to 14 per cent in 1986; however, the proportion living with a lone father is still very small, compared with those living with a lone mother.

In 1986, the Continuous Household Survey (CHS) in Northern Ireland showed that 77 per cent of dependent children were living in 'traditional' families, whilst 11 per cent were the only child of a married couple. About 12 per cent of dependent children lived in one-parent families which is a slightly lower proportion than that for the rest of the United Kingdom.

The average number of children in families in Great Britain containing dependent children has remained the same since 1981, after falling from 2.0 to 1.8 children between 1971 and 1981. The number of children in families headed by a lone parent tend to be smaller than those headed by a married couple: in 1987 families headed by a lone parent contained 1.6 children on average. The average family size is not equivalent to the number of children that women may have born to them in total (see Chart 2.21) since they are based on the number of dependent children, including adopted and step-children actually living with one or both parents, and therefore excludes, for example, children who have grown up and left home.

'Cohabitation' is defined as living together as husband and wife without having married legally. The prevalence of cohabitation has increased in Great Britain in recent years; GHS estimates suggest that the proportion of women aged 18 to 49 who were cohabiting more than doubled between 1979 and 1987 (Table 2.11). In 1987 over 11 per cent of women aged 18 to 24 were cohabiting compared with 5 per cent of those aged 25-49 years.

2.10 Dependent[1] children: by family type

Great Britain			Percentages and numbers
	1972	1981	1986
Percentage of dependent children			
1 dependent child living with			
Married couple	16	18	18
Lone mother	2	3	4
Lone father	—	1	1
2 or more dependent children living with			
Married couple	76	70	68
Lone mother	5	7	8
Lone father	1	1	1
Sample size (= 100%) (numbers)	9,474	8,216	6,031

1 See Appendix, Part 2: Families.   Source: General Household Survey

Cohabitation is more prevalent at ages 25-29 years for men and 20-24 years for women; men tend to be a few years older than their partners. In both cases the proportion cohabiting was 11 per cent. Women and men who were divorced were more likely than those of other marital status to be cohabiting in 1986. The proportion of divorced women aged 16-59 years cohabiting in 1986 was 24 per cent whilst 28 per cent of divorced men aged 16-59 years were cohabiting. The proportion of divorced women cohabiting was 22 per cent for those with dependent children and 25 per cent for those without. For single women, 32 per cent of those with dependent children were cohabiting compared with 9 per cent of those without dependent children.

2.11 Percentage of women aged 18-49 cohabiting: by age

Great Britain			Percentages and numbers		
	1979	1981	1985	1986	1987
Age group (percentages)					
18—24	4.5	5.6	9.1	9.0	11.5
25—49	2.2	2.6	3.9	4.6	4.9
18—49	2.7	3.3	5.0	5.5	6.4
Women in sample (= 100%)(numbers)					
18—24	1,353	1,517	1,182	1,194	1,277
25—49	4,651	5,007	4,182	4,320	4,379
18—49	6,004	6,524	5,364	5,514	5,656

Source: General Household Survey

Marriage and divorce

2.12 Marriages

United Kingdom   Thousands and percentages

	1961	1971	1976	1981	1984	1985	1986	1987
Marriages (thousands)								
First marriage for both partners	340	369	282	263	259	257	254	260
First marriage for one partner only								
Bachelor/divorced woman	11	21	30	32	32	32	34	34
Bachelor/widow	5	4	4	3	2	2	2	2
Spinster/divorced man	12	24	32	36	38	38	38	39
Spinster/widower	8	5	4	3	2	2	2	2
Second (or later) marriage for both partners								
Both divorced	5	17	34	44	46	47	48	47
Both widowed	10	10	10	7	6	6	6	5
Divorced man/widow	3	4	5	5	5	4	4	4
Divorced woman/widower	3	5	5	5	5	5	5	5
Total marriages	397	459	406	398	396	393	394	398
Remarriages[1] as a percentage of all marriages	*14*	*20*	*31*	*34*	*35*	*35*	*35*	*35*
Remarriages[1] of the divorced as a percentage of all marriages	*9*	*15*	*26*	*31*	*32*	*32*	*33*	*32*

1 Remarriage for one or both partners.

Source: Office of Population Censuses and Surveys

The number of marriages in the United Kingdom rose slightly from 394 thousand in 1986 to 398 thousand in 1987 (Table 2.12). The number of marriages between bachelors and spinsters increased slightly between 1986 and 1987 after previously declining, though such marriages constituted only 65 per cent of the total in 1987 compared with 86 per cent in 1961. There was a large increase between 1971 and 1976 in the proportion of marriages where one or both partners were remarrying, coinciding with the period during which the number of divorces doubled after the *Divorce Reform Act 1969* came into force (see below). Since 1976 the proportion of remarriages has risen comparatively slowly to reach 35 per cent.

Whilst the number of marriages involving at least one divorced partner increased from 34 thousand to 129 thousand between 1961 and 1987, the number involving a widow or widower has fallen from 29 thousand to only 18 thousand over the same period.

Chart 2.13 gives some indication of the extent of intermarriage between the various ethnic groups resident in Great Britain. These estimates are based on combined results from the 1984, 1985 and 1986 Labour Force Surveys, and are restricted to marriages between the partners from White and ethnic minority populations. Persons of mixed origin were more likely than persons from any of the other ethnic minority groups to be married to a partner from the White population. About half of Arab men were married to White women, but relatively few Arab women were in mixed marriages.

Persons of West Indian or African ethnic origin were roughly twice as likely to be in mixed marriages as their South Asian counter-parts. Unlike other groups, Chinese women were more likely to be in mixed marriages than Chinese men.

During the second half of last century, about 40 per cent of all men and women aged 15 and over had never married (Chart 2.14). From 1901, bachelors and spinsters formed a diminishing proportion of all men and women aged 15 or over until 1971 when 25 per cent

2.13 Percentage of husbands and wives from the ethnic minority population married to White partners: by ethnic group, 1984-1986

Great Britain

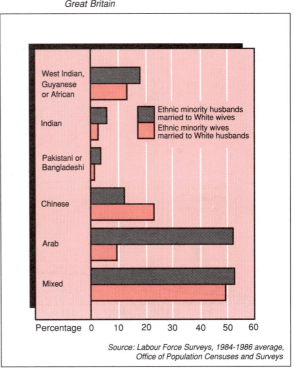

Source: Labour Force Surveys, 1984-1986 average, Office of Population Censuses and Surveys

2.14 Percentage of population who were single[1]: by age and sex

England & Wales

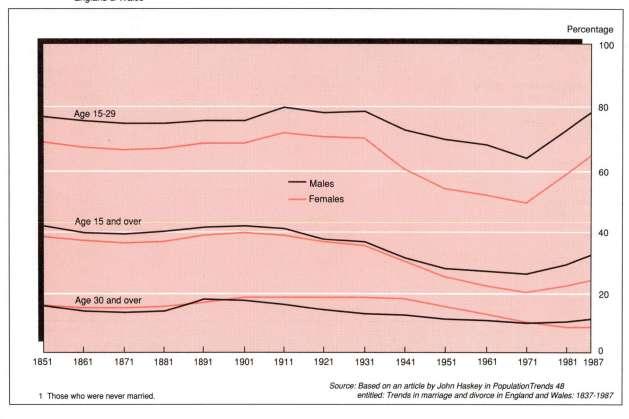

1 Those who were never married.

Source: Based on an article by John Haskey in PopulationTrends 48
entitled: Trends in marriage and divorce in England and Wales: 1837-1987

2.15 Marriage, remarriage and divorce: rates

Great Britain

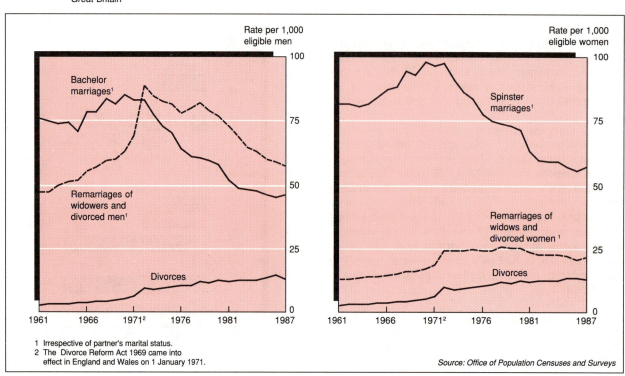

1 Irrespective of partner's marital status.
2 The Divorce Reform Act 1969 came into
effect in England and Wales on 1 January 1971.

Source: Office of Population Censuses and Surveys

2: HOUSEHOLDS AND FAMILIES

2.16 Divorce[1]

	1961	1971	1976	1981	1983	1984	1985	1986	1987
Petitions filed [2] (thousands)									
England & Wales									
By husband	14	44	43	47	45	49	52	50	50
By wife	18	67	101	123	124	131	139	131	133
Total	32	111	145	170	169	180	191	180	183
Decrees nisi granted (thousands)									
England & Wales	27	89	132	148	150	148	162	153	150
Decrees absolute granted (thousands)									
England & Wales	25	74	127	146	147	145	160	154	151
Scotland	2	5	9	10	13	12	13	13	12
Northern Ireland	0.1	0.3	0.6	1.2	1.5	1.6	1.6	1.5	1.5
United Kingdom	27	80	136	157	162	158	175	168	165
Persons divorcing per thousand married people									
England & Wales	2.1	6.0	10.1	11.9	12.2	12.0	13.4	12.9	12.6
Percentage of divorces where one or both partners had been divorced previously									
England & Wales	*9.3*	*8.8*	*11.6*	*17.1*	*20.0*	*21.0*	*23.0*	*23.2*	*23.5*
Estimated numbers of divorced people who had not remarried (thousands)									
Great Britain									
Men	101	200	405	653	784	846	916	988	. .
Women	184	317	564	890	1,036	1,104	1,177	1,257	. .
Total	285	517	969	1,543	1,820	1,950	2,094	2,245	. .

1 This table includes annulment throughout. See Appendix, Part 2: Divorce.
2 Estimates based on 100 per cent of petitions at the Principal Registry together with a 2 month sample of county court petitions (March and September).

Source: Office of Population Censuses and Surveys;
Lord Chancellor's Department

of men and 20 per cent of women were single. The proportions began to rise about 1971. The increase from 1971 coincides with the increase in one person households (Chart 2.1 and Tables 2.2 and 2.3) and the increase in the proportion of births outside marriage (Chart 2.25).

The number of marriages each year depends partly on the age and marital status structure of the population and on the ratio of males to females. Changes in the number of marriages could in theory therefore reflect the changing size and characteristics of the population eligible to marry. Marriage, remarriage and divorce rates for men and women are shown in Chart 2.15 in terms of numbers per thousand eligible. The remarriage rate for men increased substantially during the 1960s and early 1970s reaching a peak in 1972, the year after the *Divorce Reform Act 1969* came into force in England and Wales. Since 1972 the rate of remarriages for men has fallen in most years, and in 1987 the rate was two-thirds that of the 1972 peak, at a level comparable with that recorded in the mid-sixties. For women, the changes in the remarriage rate over time have been much more gradual: as for men, the rate rose sharply in 1972, and since then has remained fairly stable. In 1987 the remarriage rate per eligible man was two and

a half times the corresponding rate for women, though the actual number of remarriages is similar. The rates of first marriages, which have fallen since 1972, increased in 1987.

Section 1 of the *Matrimonial and Family Proceedings Act 1984* which became law on 12 October 1984 had an immediate and marked effect on divorce proceedings. This legislation allowed couples to petition for divorce after the first anniversary of their marriage, whereas under former legislation they could not usually petition for divorce unless their marriage had lasted at least three years. The new legislation led to a record 191 thousand divorce petitions filed in England and Wales in 1985, a 6 per cent increase over 1984 (Table 2.16). In 1986 the number of petitions fell back to the 1984 level, suggesting a backlog effect caused by a larger than usual number of couples who were first able to divorce in 1985, ie those who in 1985 had been married for only one or two years. However the number increased again slightly in 1987. A total of 165 thousand decrees were made absolute in the United Kingdom in 1987, a fall of 6 per cent since 1985, but still over double the number in 1971 when the *Divorce Reform Act 1969* came into force in England and Wales. Despite the fall in the number of petitions filed and decrees

Social Trends 19, © Crown copyright 1989

43

2.17 Divorce: by duration of marriage

Great Britain

Percentages and thousands

Duration of marriage				Year of divorce					
	1961	1971	1976	1981	1983	1984	1985	1986	1987
Duration of marriage *(completed years)*									
0–2	1.2	1.2	1.5	1.5	1.3	1.2	8.9	9.2	9.3
3–4	10.1	12.2	16.5	19.0	19.5	19.6	18.8	15.3	13.7
5–9	30.6	30.5	30.2	29.1	28.7	28.3	26.2	27.5	28.6
10–14	22.9	19.4	18.7	19.6	19.2	18.9	17.1	17.5	17.5
15–19	13.9	12.6	12.8	12.8	12.9	13.2	12.2	12.8	13.0
20–24	} 21.2	9.5	8.8	8.6	8.6	8.7	7.9	8.4	8.7
25–29		5.8	5.6	4.9	5.2	5.3	4.7	4.8	4.9
30 or over		8.9	5.9	4.5	4.7	4.6	4.2	4.3	4.3
All durations (= 100%) (thousands)	27.0	79.2	135.4	155.6	160.7	156.4	173.7	166.7	163.1

Source: Office of Population Censuses and Surveys

absolute granted between 1985 and 1987, the proportion of partners divorcing for the second or subsequent time rose slightly; nearly a quarter of divorces in England and Wales in 1987 involved at least one partner who was divorcing for a subsequent time.

The impact of the 1984 Act can also be seen in Table 2.17. Whereas in 1984 only 1.2 per cent of divorces in Great Britain occurred within 2 years of marriage this proportion has been around 9 per cent since 1985 (the 1984 Act did not apply in Scotland). There had already been a steady increase in the proportion of divorces occuring before the fifth wedding anniversary, from just over a tenth in 1961 to around a fifth in 1984 and over a quarter in 1985, although the proportion has

2.18 Children of divorcing couples: by age

England & Wales

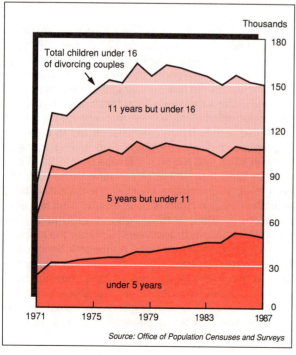

Source: Office of Population Censuses and Surveys

subsequently declined. The proportion of divorces occurring after 20 years of marriage fell from 24 per cent in 1971 to 17 per cent in 1985, before increasing slightly to 18 per cent in 1987.

In England and Wales in 1987, 73 per cent of all decrees were granted to wives, the highest proportion ever recorded. The *Divorce Reform Act 1969* introduced a solitary ground for divorce: the 'irretrievable breakdown of marriage' which can be established by proving one or more of five 'facts'. Ever since 1973, the most frequently used 'fact' on which wives have been granted decrees has been the unreasonable behaviour of their husbands, and in 1987 over one half of the decrees granted to wives was on this fact. On the other hand, the fact most frequently used by husbands has been adultery: 45 per cent of divorcing husbands were granted decrees on their wives adultery in 1987. The effect of the 1969 legislation was to allow divorce for the first time to certain groups, the most important being those who wished to divorce because they had lived apart from their partner for more than five years, and the effect was to produce the high proportions of decrees granted on five years' separation for both men and women in 1971. This proportion has since declined, indicating that the 1971 figures probably represented a backlog effect.

The substantial increases in the numbers of divorces in England and Wales over the last fifteen years has meant that the number of children under 16 directly affected rose to peaks of 163 thousand in 1978 and 1980 (Chart 2.18). Since 1980 the number has fallen, and was 149 thousand in 1987. The proportion of children of divorcing couples aged under 5 has increased from 23 per cent in 1972 to 32 per cent in 1987, whilst the corresponding proportion of those aged between 5 and 11 has decreased from 49 per cent to 39 per cent.

According to results from the 1986 General Household Survey (GHS) three-fifths of divorced husbands and half of divorced wives in Great Britain whose first marriage ended between 1975 and 1982 before they were 35 years old had remarried within 3 years of their divorce.

2.19 Attitudes to marriage and divorce: by marital status, 1986

Percentages and numbers

	Married now	Living as married	Separated/ divorced/ widowed	Not married	All adults
Percentage of those questioned who thought that:					
Divorce in Britain should be made more difficult to obtain than it is now					
Agree	40	19	44	36	39
Neither agree nor disagree	34	31	22	38	33
Disagree	26	50	32	24	27
As a society, we ought to do more to safeguard the institution of marriage					
Agree	74	39	77	59	71
Neither agree nor disagree	20	37	13	31	21
Disagree	5	22	7	9	6
Most people nowadays take marriage too lightly					
Agree	77	64	76	62	74
Neither agree nor disagree	13	24	11	29	15
Disagree	9	11	10	8	9
Bases (weighted) (numbers)	956	36	184	204	1,387

*Source: British Social Attitudes Survey, 1986,
Social and Community Planning Research*

The British Social Attitudes Survey, 1986, conducted by Social and Community Planning Research, asked respondents about their attitudes to marriage and divorce and some of these results are shown in Table 2.19. More than two-thirds of respondents felt that 'as a society we ought to do more to safe-guard the institution of marriage', and only 6 per cent disagreed. A little over a third of people thought divorce should be made more difficult to obtain whilst a little under a third disagreed and a third neither agreed nor disagreed. Three-quarters of those surveyed thought that people take marriage too lightly whilst one in ten disagreed.

Those who were married or either separated, widowed or divorced tended to have a higher regard for the institution of marriage than those who were living as married or not married though the majority of all these groups thought that marriage is taken too lightly nowadays. However, such inferences need to be made with caution since the sample sizes, particularly for those living together are quite small.

Men and women in all EC countries for which data are available were getting married for the first time at an older age in 1986 than their counterparts in 1981 (Table

2.20 Marriage and divorce rates and age at first marriage: by sex, EC comparison

Years and rates

	Age at first marriage (years)				Marriage per 1,000 eligible population		Divorce per 1,000 existing marriages	
	Men		Women					
	1981	1986	1981	1986	1981	1986	1981	1986
United Kingdom	25.4	26.2	23.1	24.1	7.1	6.9	11.9	12.9
Belgium	24.8	25.5[1]	22.4	23.3[1]	6.5	5.8	6.1	7.3
Denmark	27.9	29.2	25.1	26.5	5.0	6.0	12.1	12.8
France	25.3	26.6	23.2	24.6	5.8	4.8	6.8	8.5
Germany (Fed. Rep.)	26.3	27.5	23.6	24.9	5.8	6.1	7.2	8.3
Greece	27.2	27.3[1]	22.3	22.8[1]	7.3	5.8	2.5	3.0[1]
Irish Republic	26.5	27.1[1]	24.4	25.0[1]	6.0	5.2	0.0	0.0
Italy	27.2	. .	24.0	. .	5.6	5.2	0.9	1.1
Luxembourg	25.9	26.9	22.9	24.0	5.5	5.1	5.9	7.5[1]
Netherlands	25.6	27.1	23.3	25.0	6.0	6.0	8.3	8.7
Portugal	25.2	25.4	22.6	22.9	7.7	6.8	2.8	. .
Spain	25.9	. .	23.5	. .	5.4	. .	1.1	. .

1 1985.

Source: Statistical Office of the European Communities

2.20). In the United Kingdom in 1986, the average age at first marriage was 26 years for men and 24 years for women. The marriage rate increased between 1981 and 1986 in Denmark and the Federal Republic of Germany, remained the same in the Netherlands and decreased in the remaining countries, including the United Kingdom which nevertheless still had the highest rate of all the countries shown in 1986. The rate of divorce in the same period increased in all countries for which the data are available except Ireland where divorce is not legal. The United Kingdom had the highest divorce rate in 1986, followed very closely by Denmark.

Family building

Estimates and projections of the number of children per woman and of the future numbers of births in terms of their birth order are important elements underlying the population projections discussed in Chapter 1, and the assumptions used for England and Wales are illustrated in Chart 2.21. Women born in the earlier years shown will have already completed their families, but for the younger women evidence from the General Household Survey is taken into account, where women are asked about their future child-bearing expectations.

2.21 Estimated and projected total number of children per woman: by woman's year of birth

England & Wales

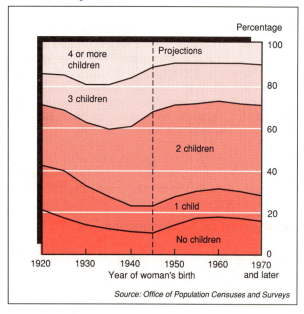

Source: Office of Population Censuses and Surveys

per cent of women born in 1955 and later years are assumed to have at least one child.

For all the women covered by the Chart, the most likely number of children is two, though this proportion has risen quite steeply from those born in 1920 to a peak for those women born in 1945. The proportion of women having four children fell from 20 per cent of those born in 1930 and 1935 to 12 per cent of those born in 1945 and a further fall is projected.

Details of successive registrations of births to women in the Office of Population Censuses and Surveys Longitudinal Study have been linked and therefore provide information about the lengths of intervals between marriage and births to women in the sample. The trends in the interval from marriage to first birth by father's social class (see Appendix: Part 2, Social class of father) during the period 1972 to 1987 are shown in Chart 2.22. For each social class the median

2.22 Median intervals from marriage to first birth[1]: by father's social class[2] at birth registration.

England & Wales

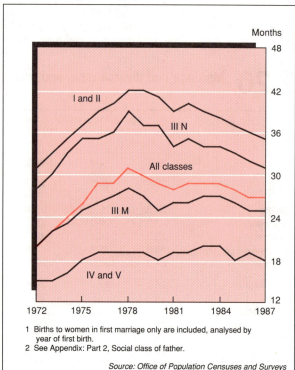

1 Births to women in first marriage only are included, analysed by year of first birth.
2 See Appendix: Part 2, Social class of father.

Source: Office of Population Censuses and Surveys

Most women have children, though families are on average becoming smaller. Chart 2.21 shows that the percentage of women who had a child at all increased steadily from about 80 per cent of those born in 1920 up to a peak of 90 per cent of women born in 1945. For women born more recently the likelihood of remaining childless has increased and it is estimated that 17 per cent of women born in 1955 will not have any children. Corresponding to the upward trend in the proportion of women remaining childless, the proportion of women having two children is now estimated to have fallen. It is assumed that the proportion of women remaining childless will level off, so that just over 80

2.23 Maternities with multiple births: by age of mother

Great Britain   Rates and numbers

| | Rate per 1,000 maternities | | | | | Numbers | | |
| | | | 1987 | | | | | |
Age of mother	1966	1976	All	Twins	Other	1966	1976	1987
Under 20 years	6.4	6.2	6.0	5.9	0.1	622	405	381
20 – 24 years	9.1	7.6	8.4	8.3	0.1	2,880	1,557	1,772
25 – 29 years	11.8	10.5	11.2	11.0	0.2	3,338	2,548	2,927
30 – 34 years	14.4	12.4	13.8	13.4	0.4	2,211	1,234	2,041
35 years and over	15.3	13.2	5.8	15.5	0.3	1,521	480	930
All ages	11.1	9.6	10.8	10.6	0.2	10,572	6,224	8,051

Source: Office of Population, Censuses and Surveys

interval lengthened up to about 1978. Since then, however, the trends in each social class have differed.

In the non-manual groups I and II, and IIIN, the general trend in the median interval has been downwards, but in the manual groups IIIM, and IV and V, the trend was more stable.

In 1987, the mean age of mothers at the birth of their first child inside marriage was 26.5 years, compared to 25.0 years in 1977. The mean age of the mother at the first birth by social class of father in 1987 increased by social class so that it was 28.4 years for Classes I and II, 27.0 years for IIIN, 25.8 years for IIIM and 24.5 years for classes IV and V.

The total number of maternities in 1987 was 743,306, of which 7,907 were twins, 135 triplets and 9 quadruplets. As the age of the woman giving birth increases, so does the likelihood of her having a multiple

birth (Table 2.23). Although the likelihood of multiple births increases with age, the actual number of maternities by women over the age of 30 years decreases. The number of multiple births decreased from 11 thousand in 1966 to 6 thousand in 1976 but has since risen to 8 thousand in 1987.

The 1938 *Population (Statistics) Act* provided for the previous numbers of births to a married woman, first by her present husband and second by any former husbands, to be collected as part of the birth registration process. In 1960 the schedule of questions to the Act was amended and the number of previous births either by the current husband or previous husbands was required as an aggregate. A new question was introduced, however, asking whether the mother had been married more than once. From this question and indirectly from the information provided by the 1938 Act, it is possible to obtain the information shown in Chart 2.24 about the trends in the proportion of women giving birth who were in their second or later marriages.

2.24 Births to women in second or later marriages as a percentage of all births inside marriage: by age of mother

England & Wales

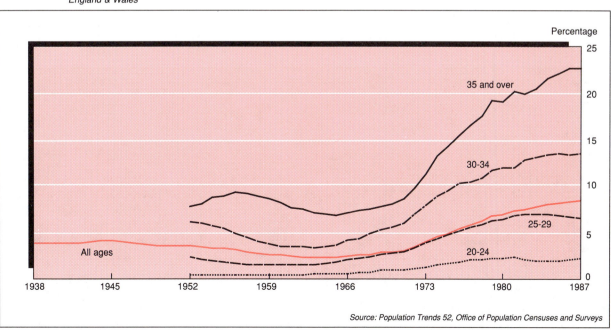

Source: Population Trends 52, Office of Population Censuses and Surveys

2.25 Live births outside marriage as a percentage of all births

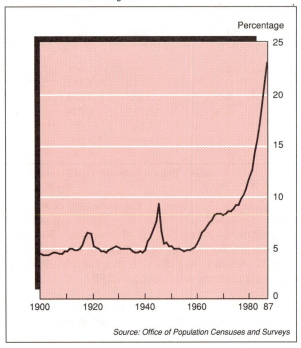

United Kingdom

Source: Office of Population Censuses and Surveys

From the start of birth registration in 1837, children who were neither conceived nor born within marriage were classified as 'illegitimate' or children born outside of marriage as they are now termed. The percentage of births in England and Wales which were outside marriage fell steadily from a level of 6 to 7 per cent of all births during the 1840s to around 4 per cent at the turn of the century. There were substantial increases in the number of children born outside of marriage during both World Wars, but the ratio fell again after each period so that in the early 1950s the percentage of births outside marriage in the United Kingdom was still only slightly higher than it had been 50 years earlier (Chart 2.25). During the past 30 years the percentage of births outside marriage has risen steeply, stabilising only for a brief period in the 1960s, and by 1987 it had reached 23 per cent of all births (Table 2.26). At the same time there has been an increase in the proportion of births outside of marriage registered by both parents, from 38 per cent of births outside marriage in England and Wales in 1961 to 68 per cent in 1987. Further, it is known that in 70 per cent of these joint registrations in 1987, the mother and father gave the same address as their usual place of residence. These figures suggest that at least half the children born outside marriage in 1987 had parents who were living together and were likely to be bringing up the child within a non-marital union.

Between 1938 and 1951 the proportion of births which were to women who were in their second or later marriage fell slightly. This downward trend continued at a faster pace between 1951 and 1964. The trend reversed after 1964 and by 1977 the overall proportion of births to women who were in their second or later marriage had more than doubled. This change stemmed from the sharp rise in the divorce rate and the consequent increase in the numbers of divorced women of all ages who remarried and went on to have children. From 1977 to 1987 the upward trend continued but at a reduced pace. In 1987, 23 per cent of all births to women aged 35 or over were to women in second or later marriages whilst this proportion was 13 per cent for those aged 30-34, 6 per cent for those aged 25-29 and 2 per cent for those aged 20-24 years.

2.26 Live births outside marriage

Thousands and percentages

	United Kingdom		England & Wales
	Live births outside marriage (thousands)	As percentage of total live births	Percentage registered in joint names
1961	54	6	38
1971	74	8	45
1976	61	9	51
1981	91	12	58
1986	158	21	66
1987	178	23	68

Source: Office of Population Censuses and Surveys

Population Trends

Population Trends, now in its 12th year, is the journal of the Office of Population Censuses and Surveys (OPCS). It is published four times a year in March, June, September and December.

The Winter 1988 edition will be the 54th issue of **Population Trends**. Published by HMSO, it can be obtained from Government bookshops and through good booksellers.

2.27 Conceptions: by outcome, 1976 and 1986

England & Wales

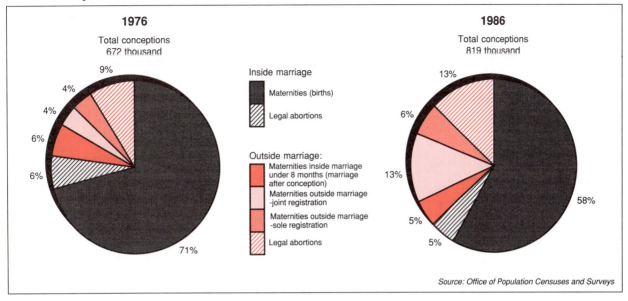

1976

Total conceptions
672 thousand

9%
4%
4%
6%
6%
71%

1986

Total conceptions
819 thousand

13%
6%
13%
5%
5%
58%

Inside marriage

■ Maternities (births)

▨ Legal abortions

Outside marriage:

■ Maternities inside marriage
under 8 months (marriage
after conception)

■ Maternities outside marriage
-joint registration

■ Maternities outside marriage
-sole registration

▨ Legal abortions

Source: Office of Population Censuses and Surveys

There were an estimated 819 thousand conceptions to women of all ages in England and Wales in 1986, an increase of almost 3 per cent over the previous year. The pattern of outcome of conceptions has changed considerably between 1976 and 1986 (Chart 2.27). Whereas in 1976 83 per cent of conceptions either were inside marriage or marriage took place between conception and birth, this proportion had fallen to 68 per cent in 1986. The proportion of conceptions which were terminated by legal abortion rose from 15 per cent in 1976 to 18 per cent in 1986 (Table 2.28 gives more details on abortions). For the same period, the number of conceptions to women aged under 20 years has increased from 106 thousand in 1976 to 119 thousand in 1986. In 1986, 14 per cent of these conceptions to women aged under 20 were inside marriage, 10 per cent resulted in births inside marriage though conception took place outside marriage, and 34 per cent were terminated by legal abortion.

The *Abortion Act 1967* does not affect the provisions of the *Infant Life Preservations Act 1929*. This latter Act says that it is an offence to destroy the life of a child capable of being born alive. Evidence that the pregnancy has lasted for 28 weeks is *prima facie* evidence that the child is capable of being born alive. Thus, under the 1967 *Abortion Act,* abortions can be performed up to 28 weeks gestation. However, there is currently a voluntary agreement that 24 weeks is normally the upper limit.

The number of abortions to women resident in Great Britain in 1987 rose to 166 thousand, an increase of almost 6 per cent on the previous year which continued the steady upward trend since 1983 (Table 2.28). These

recent increases have sometimes been attributed to the lower proportions of women using oral contraceptives after publicity in late 1983 concerning claimed health risks for women who use oral contraceptives with a high hormonal content, though these claims have since been disputed. In 1987 over two-fifths of abortions were carried out on women aged under 20 compared with just over a fifth in 1971. There has been some change in the gestation period at which the abortion takes place: the proportion of terminations under 13 weeks has increased from 74 per cent in 1971 to 87 per cent in 1987.

2.28 Legal abortions [1]

Great Britain		Thousands and percentages	
	Women resident in Great Britain		
	1971	1981	1987
Age of woman (thousands)			
Under 16 years	2	4	4
16-19 years	19	34	38
20-34 years	60	81	106
35 years or over	18	19	19
Age unknown	2	1	—
Total	101	139	166
Gestation period (percentages)			
Under 13 weeks	*74*	*84*	*87*
13-17 weeks	*20*	*11*	*10*
18-19 weeks	*2*	*2*	*2*
20-23 weeks	*1*	*1*	*1*
24 weeks and over	*—*	*—*	*—*
Unknown	*3*	*1*	*—*
Total	*100*	*100*	*100*

1 Legal abortions carried out under the Abortion Act 1967.

Source: Office of Population Censuses and Surveys;
Scottish Health Service, Common Services Agency

Education Statistics for the United Kingdom

This annual publication provides basic statistics for the whole of the United Kingdom. It illustrates the size and nature of education in the United Kingdom and international comparisons can be made. The responsible departments, Department of Education and Science, Welsh Office Education Department, Scottish Education Department and Department of Education Northern Ireland, make available a selection of statistics concerning the education services for which they are responsible. Two-thirds of the tables in the volume provide time-series, usually spanning twenty years.

DES Education Statistics Publications

Volumes
These contain detailed education statistics and include time series and regional data.

Schools (England)
School Leavers, CSE and GCE (England)
Further Education (England)
Further Education Student: Staff Ratios (England)
Teachers in Service (England and Wales)
Finance and Awards (England and Wales)

These annual publications are available at £12 each from:

Department of Education and Science
Room 337
Mowden Hall
Staindrop Road
Darlington DL3 9BG

Chapter 3: Education

Schools and their pupils
- The total number of school pupils in the United Kingdom rose by 2.4 million between 1961 and 1976, but then fell by 1.9 million between 1976 and 1987. *(Table 3.2)*

Qualifications and activities beyond age 16
- In 1986/87, 60 per cent of girls leaving school in the United Kingdom held at least 1 higher grade result at GCE 'O' level or CSE grade 1 compared to 53 per cent of boys. *(Table 3.9)*

- In 1986/87, girls in Great Britain were more likely than boys to have gained higher grade results at GCE 'O' level or CSE grade 1 in English whilst boys were more likely than girls to have higher grade results in Mathematics. *(Chart 3.11)*

Further and higher education
- The number of full-time higher education students in the United Kingdom rose by 19 per cent between 1975/76 and 1986/87 to stand at 613 thousand whilst the number of part-time students rose by 64 per cent in the same period to stand at 359 thousand. *(Table 3.16 and 3.17)*

- In 1986, 44 per cent of all first degrees were awarded to women compared to 39 per cent in 1981. *(Table 3.18)*

Educational standards of adults
- In 1987, 11 per cent of those aged 25-29 in Great Britain held a degree or equivalent qualification compared to 6 per cent of those aged 50-59. *(Table 3.21)*

Resources
- The number of full-time teachers employed in the United Kingdom fell by 7 per cent between 1980/81 and 1986/87 to stand at 526 thousand. *(Table 3.23)*

- In 1987, the average number of pupils per teacher in public sector schools in the United Kingdom was 18.3 compared to 23.2 in 1971. *(Table 3.24)*

3.1 Public sector school pupils: by type of school

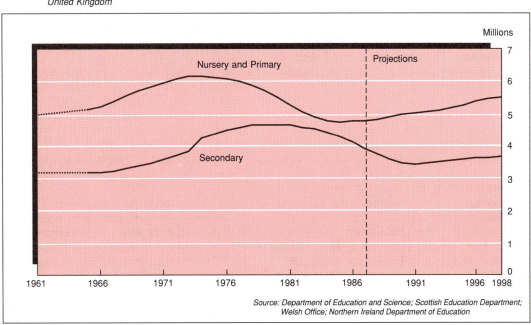

United Kingdom

Source: Department of Education and Science; Scottish Education Department; Welsh Office; Northern Ireland Department of Education

Schools and their pupils

3.2 School pupils [1] — summary: by type of school [2]

United Kingdom   Thousands

	Actuals at January of each year						Projections [3]			
	1961	1971	1976[4]	1981[4]	1986[5]	1987	1988	1991	1994	1998
Public sector schools (full and part-time)										
Nursery schools	31	50	75	89	96	97	98	101	105	105
Primary schools										
Under fives	} 4,906	{ 301	466	459	547	731	549	582	620	642
Other primary [6]		{ 5,601	5,532	4,712	4,088	3,936[7]	4,162	4,321	4,444	4,753
Secondary schools										
Under school leaving age	..	..	..	4,202	3,681	3,519[7]	3,352	3,074	3,230	3,306
Over school leaving age	..	..	..	404	399	384	392	330	299	336
Total	3,165	3,555	4,448	4,606	4,080	3,902	3,745	3,405	3,529	3,642
Total public sector	8,102	9,507	10,522	9,866	8,810	8,666	8,553	8,409	8,698	9,141
Independent schools	680	621	629	619	607	619[8]	575[9]	582[9]	599[9]	624[9]
Special schools (full-time only)	77	103	149	147	128	123	121	113	113	117
All schools — total pupils	8,859	10,230	11,300	10,632	9,545	9,407	9,249	9,104	9,409	9,882

1 Part-time pupils are counted as one.
2 See Appendix, Part 3: Main categories of educational establishments and Stages of education.
3 Projections are 1987-based for England, 1986-based for Northern Ireland and 1985-based for Wales and Scotland.
4 Figures for Scottish components are at previous September.
5 Data for Scotland are estimated.

6 In Scotland 11 year olds are customarily in primary schools.
7 218 pupils in hospital schools in Northern Ireland have been included in the enrolment figures for their normal schools.
8 Including pupils in voluntary grammar schools in Northern Ireland.
9 Great Britain only.

Source: Department of Education and Science; Scottish Education Department; Welsh Office; Northern Ireland Department of Education

The tables and charts in this section cover all pupils in public sector schools, assisted and independent schools and special schools for the handicapped.

An increase in the birth rate in the United Kingdom in the late 1940s and most particularly in the mid-1960s led to an increase in the number of pupils in public sector primary schools and secondary schools between 1961 and the late 1970s (Chart 3.1 and Table 3.2). The raising of the school-leaving age from 15 to 16 years of age in 1972/73 also helped to increase the number of secondary school pupils. The number of pupils in public sector primary schools then fell by 23 per cent between 1976 and 1986, reflecting falling birth rates in the late 1960s and 1970s, but increased slightly in 1987 and is projected to continue to increase until 1998. The number of pupils in public sector secondary schools fell between 1981 and 1987 and is projected to continue to fall until 1991, but then to increase for at least the next seven years.

The large increase between 1971 and 1981 in the number of pupils at special schools was due mainly to the *Education (Handicapped Children) Act 1970*, under which local education authorities in England and Wales assumed responsibility from April 1971 for all establishments catering for mentally handicapped children. Previously, the most severely mentally handicapped children had been the responsibility of the health authorities. The *Education (Mentally Handicapped Children) (Scotland) Act 1974* made similar provisions in Scotland. The *Education Act 1981* abolished the ten statutory handicap groups into which pupils had previously fallen. Instead local education authorities assess a child's particular educational needs, providing a statement of these needs where necessary.

Statistics from 1984 onwards refer to children with statements of special educational need.

In 1987, as in 1971, 23 per cent of pupils in public sector schools in England were attending voluntary schools which are mainly denominational, ie Church of England, Roman Catholic, Methodist, etc. There were just over 1 million full-time pupils in voluntary primary schools in 1987, of whom 63 per cent were in Church of England schools, 35 per cent in Roman Catholic schools and 2 per cent in schools of other denominations and religions. There were also 575 thousand pupils in voluntary secondary schools, of whom 51 per cent were in Roman Catholic schools, 25 per cent in Church of England schools and 23 per cent in other denominational schools. In recent years these proportions have remained almost unchanged.

The National Curriculum will be introduced in September 1989 and it will require all pupils aged 5 to 16 to study 3 core subjects - English, Mathematics and Science and 7 other foundation subjects. Pupils' performance will be assessed and reported on at the end of 4 'Key Stages' - at ages 7, 11, 14 and 16. The first assessments and tests will be on a trial basis for 7 year olds in 1991.

Table 3.3 shows the change in the structure of maintained secondary education in Great Britain, with a movement from selective to comprehensive school education (see Appendix, Part 3: Stages of education). In 1971, 36 per cent of pupils in maintained secondary schools in England attended comprehensive or middle deemed secondary schools (for definition, see Appendix, Part 3: Stages of Education) compared to 59 per cent in both Wales and Scotland. However, by 1987

3.3 Pupils in public sector secondary education [1, 2]

England, Wales, Scotland and Northern Ireland   Percentages and thousands

	1971	1981	1987		1971	1981	1987
England *(percentages)*				**Scotland** *(percentages)*			
Maintained secondary schools				Public sector secondary schools			
Middle deemed secondary	1.9	7.0	6.5	Selective	28.3	0.1	..
Modern	38.0	6.0	4.1	Comprehensive	58.7	96.0	..
Grammar	18.4	3.4	3.1	Part comprehensive/part selective	13.0	3.8	..
Technical	1.3	0.3	0.1				
Comprehensive	34.4	82.5	85.8	Total pupils (= 100%)			
Other	6.0	0.9	0.4	(thousands)	314	408	..
Total pupils (= 100%)							
(thousands)	2,953	3,840	3,240				
Wales *(percentages)*				**Northern Ireland** *(percentages)*			
Maintained secondary schools				Public sector secondary schools			
Middle deemed secondary	0.1	0.1	0.1	Secondary intermediate	87.7	88.6	88.5
Modern	22.3	1.8	0.6	Grammar	11.8	11.4	11.5
Grammar	15.4	1.3	0.5	Technical intermediate	0.5	—	—
Comprehensive	58.5	96.6	98.5				
Other	3.7	0.3	0.3	Total pupils (= 100%)			
				(thousands)	96	119	109
Total pupils (= 100%)							
(thousands)	191	240	210				

1 See Appendix, Part 3: Main categories of educational establishments and Stages of education.

2 Counts at January except 1981 data for Scotland which are at the preceding September.

Source: Department of Education and Science

this proportion had increased to 92 per cent in England, 99 per cent in Wales and, by 1985, 96 per cent in Scotland.

The *Education Reform Act 1988* empowers the Secretary of State for Education and Science to enter into funding agreements with sponsors for the establishment of city technology colleges (CTC) and city colleges for the technology of the arts. Plans for 7 CTCs have been announced to date and further sponsors have been pledged.

Almost half of nursery schools have 50 pupils or less (Table 3.4), although between 1979/80 and 1986/87, there was a small increase in the proportion of larger schools. The size of primary schools remained fairly constant between 1979/80 and 1986/87 with over a third having 100 to 200 pupils, and a further two-fifths having over 200 pupils.

There was a tendency in comprehensive and other secondary schools for the number of pupils on the register to fall between 1979/80 and 1986/87 (Table 3.5). In 1979/80, 32 per cent of secondary schools had over 1,000 pupils but this had fallen to 24 per cent by 1986/87. This reflects the continual fall in the number of secondary school pupils between 1979 and 1987, although a rise is expected in the early 1990s (see Chart 3.1).

Between 1977 and 1987 approval for the closure of 1,417 primary schools and 463 secondary schools in

3.4 Public sector nursery and primary schools: by size, 1979/80 and 1986/87

United Kingdom   Percentages and numbers

	Nursery		Primary	
	1979/80	1986/87	1979/80	1986/87
Number of pupils on school register *(percentages)*				
50 or under	52.4	46.3	11.0	10.8
51–100	39.0	43.1	13.6	14.0
101–200	8.6	10.5	31.5	36.1
200 or over	—	0.2	43.9	39.1
Total schools (= 100%) (numbers)	1,236	1,299	26,764	24,610

Source: Department of Education and Science; Scottish Education Department; Welsh Office; Northern Ireland Department of Education

3.5 Public sector secondary schools: by size, 1979/80 and 1986/87

United Kingdom   Percentages and numbers

	Comprehensive	Other [1]	All
Number of pupils on school register *(percentages)*			
1979/80			
400 or under	5.5	31.7	13.0
401–800	30.0	55.3	37.2
801–1,000	21.6	7.9	17.7
1,001 or over	42.9	5.2	32.1
Total schools (= 100%) (numbers)	3,982	1,589	5,571
1986/87 [2]			
400 or under	6.5	47.5	16.3
401–800	38.8	43.3	39.9
801–1,000	23.8	5.4	19.4
1,001 or over	30.1	3.8	24.4
Total schools (= 100%) (numbers)	3,872	1,217	5,089

1 Includes Middle Schools deemed secondary, secondary modern, grammar schools, technical and other schools.
2 1987/88 for Scotland

Source: Department of Education and Science; Scottish Education Department; Welsh Office; Northern Ireland Department of Education

3.6 Class sizes as taught [1]

England	Percentages and numbers		
	1977	1981	1987
Primary schools			
Percentage of classes taught by:			
One teacher in classes with			
1—20 pupils	16.1	20.0	16.4
21—30 pupils	46.3	54.9	59.7
31 or more pupils	33.7	21.8	18.1
Two or more teachers	4.0	3.3	5.8
Average size of class (numbers)	27.5	25.5	25.8
Number of classes (thousands)	170.6	160.6	142.8
Secondary schools			
Percentage of classes taught by:			
One teacher in classes with			
1—20 pupils	42.3	44.4	46.2
21—30 pupils	41.7	45.1	45.4
31 or more pupils	12.5	8.2	5.0
Two or more teachers	3.5	2.4	3.4
Average size of class (numbers)	22.4	21.5	21.0
Number of classes (thousands)	165.4	174.4	150.1

1 Class size related to one selected period in each public sector school on the day of the count in January. Middle schools are either primary or secondary for this table - see Appendix, Part 3: Stages of education.

Source: Department of Education and Science

England had been given by the Secretary of State for Education and Science or determined by local authorities. School closures are recorded on the date upon which closure proposals were decided rather than the date on which the schools were actually closed.

The average class size in public sector schools in England fell between 1977 and 1981, from 27.5 to 25.5 in primary schools and from 22.4 to 21.5 in secondary schools (Table 3.6). In 1987 the class size was slightly higher than in 1981 for primary schools but slightly lower for secondary schools. The proportion of classes with 31 or more pupils taught by one teacher has also continued to decline since 1977, in both primary and secondary schools.

Many initiatives were undertaken in 1986, designated as Industry Year, to stimulate links between school and industry. Whilst some schools had been engaged in this field for years, and some of those had developed co-operation to a high degree, many others reported to the Industry Year organisers that the initiatives in 1986 provided their first real contacts with industry. A survey of 500 maintained primary schools and 500 maintained secondary schools in England was carried out in February 1987 on schools' links with industry during Industry Year 1986, with response rates of 73 per cent and 65 per cent respectively.

The survey showed that over 90 per cent of secondary schools had links with industry in 1986 spanning a wide range of activities, compared with half of primary schools. Around 10 per cent of the teaching staff in primary schools and 12 per cent in secondary schools had previously worked in industry, and 1 per cent of primary schools and 25 per cent of secondary schools had seconded staff to industry in 1986. The percentage of schools linked with manufacturing or service industries was greater than with leisure or other industries, and was more so for secondary schools. Nearly 90 per cent of secondary schools reported that some of their pupils had been involved in work experience during 1986. Among pupils in their last year of compulsory schooling an average 66 per cent were involved, the average length of placement per pupil being 12 days. Other activities included visits to industry, curriculum development activities involving industry, special Industry Year activities, mini enterprises and twinning of schools with local companies.

Table 3.7 shows that 6.4 per cent of all pupils in Great Britain attended independent schools in 1987 compared to 5.4 per cent in 1981. Pupils aged 16 or over form the highest percentage of children of all age groups attending independent schools. The gap between the proportions of boys and proportions of girls attending independent schools widens with age.

The number of children under five who went to private or public sector schools in the United Kingdom rose from 280 thousand in 1966 to 676 thousand in 1985, but fell to 671 thousand in 1986 before increasing again to 681 thousand in 1987 (Table 3.8). However, provision for the under fives can be better measured by expressing the number attending school as a percentage of the population aged 3 to 4, the age group most relevant to pre-school education. This proportion rose from 15 per cent in 1966 to 48 per cent in 1987. Much of this increase occurred between 1966 and 1981 and was accounted for largely by an increase in the number attending for part of the day. Estimated public sector current expenditure on pre-school education in the United Kingdom for the financial year 1986-87 was £430 million in primary schools and £81 million in nursery schools.

There has also been a significant increase since 1966 in the number of day care places in day nurseries and playgroups and with registered childminders. In 1987

3.7 Pupils in independent schools: by sex and age [1]

Great Britain		Percentages	
	Pupils in independent schools as a percentage of all pupils [2]		
	1981	1986 [3]	1987
Boys aged:			
Under 11	4.1	4.7	4.8
11—15	6.5	7.1	7.5
16 or over	17.4	18.5	18.6
All ages	5.8	6.4	6.6
Girls aged:			
Under 11	3.9	4.5	4.7
11—15	5.7	6.3	6.8
16 or over	11.8	14.0	14.4
All ages	5.1	5.8	6.1
All pupils	5.4	6.1	6.4

1 Ages are as at December of the previous year for 1981. Thereafter ages are as at August for England and Wales and December for Scotland.
2 At January.
3 Includes estimates for Scotland.

Source: Department of Education and Science

3.8 Education and day care of children under five

United Kingdom   Thousands and percentages

		1966	1971	1976	1981	1985	1986[1]	1987[2]
Children under 5 in schools [3] (thousands)								
Public sector schools								
Nursery schools	— full-time	26	20	20	22	19	19	18
	— part-time	9	29	54	67	77	77	79
Primary schools	— full-time	220	263	350	281	319	306	309
	— part-time	—	38	117	167	221	228	231
Non-maintained schools	— full-time	21	19	19	19	20	20	21
	— part-time	2	14	12	12	15	15	16
Special schools	— full-time	2	2	4	4	4	4	4
	— part-time	—	—	1	1	2	2	2
Total		280	384	576	573	676	671	681
As a percentage of all children aged 3 or 4		*15.0*	*20.5*	*34.5*	*44.3*	*46.4*	*46.7*	*47.6*
Day care places [4] (thousands)								
Local authority day nurseries		} 21	23[3]	35	} 32	33	33	33
Local authority playgroups					5	6	5	5
Registered nurseries		} 75	296	401	} 23	27	29	33
Registered playgroups					433	470	473	477
Registered child minders [5]		32	90	86	110[6]	144	157	174
Total		128	409	522	603[6]	680	698	722

1 Data for 1985 have been used for Scotland for children under 5 in schools.
2 Data for 1988 have been used for Scotland for children under 5 in schools.
3 Pupils aged under 5 at December/January of academic year.
4 Figures for 1966 and 1971 cover England and Wales at end December

1966 and end March 1972 respectively. From 1976 data are at end March except for the Northern Ireland component which is at end December of the preceding year.
5 Includes child minders provided by local authorities.
6 Figures should be treated with caution.

Source: Department of Health and Social Security; Department of Education and Science; Scottish Education Department, Social Work Services Group; Welsh Office; Department of Health and Social Services, Northern Ireland; Northern Ireland Department of Education

half of day nursery places were provided by local authorities, while the majority of playgroup places were in registered playgroups. Places in day nurseries are generally available throughout the whole year and

therefore, along with childminders, provide the most suitable form of provision for families where both parents are working. Places in playgroups are normally only available for part of the day during the school term.

Qualifications and activities beyond age 16

Pupils throughout the United Kingdom have the option of leaving school at 16. However, the provisions for school-leaving dates in Scotland allow a large number of Scottish pupils to leave at age 15. The proportion of school pupils who stay on for one extra year tends to be higher in Scotland than in England and Wales. This is partly because school is the normal choice in Scotland for pupils seeking to gain entrance qualifications to higher education, whereas in England and Wales many young people attend further education establishments as an alternative to school.

Table 3.9 shows that between 1975/76 and 1986/87 the proportion of boys leaving school in the United Kingdom with at least 1 GCE 'O' level (grades A-C) or equivalent rose from 49 per cent to 53 per cent, while among girls leaving school it rose from 53 per cent to 60 per cent. These figures relate to school leavers only and it should be borne in mind that some pupils go on to further education establishments to further their academic qualifications.

3.9 School leavers – highest qualification [1] : by sex, 1975/76 and 1986/87

United Kingdom   Percentages and thousands

	Boys		Girls	
	1975/ 76	1986/ 87[2]	1975/ 76	1986/ 87[2]
Percentage with:				
2 or more 'A' levels/3 or more 'H' grades	14.3	15.0	12.1	14.7
1 'A' level/1 or 2 'H' grades	3.5	3.6	4.0	4.2
5 or more 'O' levels/grades (no A-levels): A-C grades[3]	7.2	9.5	9.4	11.8
1-4 'O' levels/grades: A-C grades[3]	23.9	24.7	27.0	29.2
1 or more 'O' levels/grades: D or E grades, or CSE grades 2-5	29.9	34.5	28.4	31.0
No GCE/SCE or CSE grades	21.2	12.7	19.1	9.1
Total school leavers (= 100%) (thousands)	423	442	400	425

1 See Appendix, Part 3: School-leaving qualifications.
2 Includes provisional data for Scotland.
3 Includes CSE grade 1.

Source: Department of Education and Science

3.10 School leavers attempting GCE O-level/CSE: by sex and subject

England and Wales   Percentages and thousands

	Boys			Girls			All		
	1970/71	1980/81	1986/87	1970/71	1980/81	1986/87	1970/71	1980/81	1986/87
Percentage of school leavers who attempted GCE O-level or CSE in:									
English	55	81	83	54	87	88	55	84	86
Mathematics	53	79	80	45	81	82	49	80	81
Science	40	62	64	36	63	66	38	63	65
Technology [1]	36	59	57	8	15	20	22	37	39
Modern Languages	26	29	32	32	46	49	29	37	40
History/Geography	44	62	63	42	60	58	43	61	61
Creative Arts	18	29	30	22	35	38	20	32	34
Total leavers (= 100%) (thousands)	315.3	396.9	387.7	298.1	381.0	372.2	613.4	777.9	759.8

1 Craft, Design, Technology and other sciences.   *Source: Department of Education and Science*

The number of school leavers attempting GCE O-level or CSE increased by 27 per cent between 1970/71 and 1980/81, from 613 thousand to 778 thousand before decreasing slightly to 760 thousand in 1986/87 (Table 3.10). About half the total number of attempts were by boys. Amongst all pupils, English and Mathematics remained the most popular subjects and by 1986/87, 80 per cent or more students sat these examinations compared to around 50 per cent in 1970/71. Boys are more likely to attempt examinations in Technology than girls whilst girls are more likely to attempt examinations in modern languages than boys.

Whereas Table 3.10 showed the attempts made at GCE 'O' level or CSE examinations in England and Wales,

Chart 3.11 shows the proportion of boys and girls in Great Britain who gained higher grade results at GCE 'O' level (grades A-C) or CSE (grade 1) or the Scottish equivalent qualification (SCE O-grade) in selected subjects. In 1986-87 girls were more likely than boys to have gained higher grade results in English, Biology, French and History, whilst boys were more likely than girls to have gained higher grade results at Mathematics, Physics, Geography and Chemistry. The greatest difference between the sexes was for Physics in which 22 per cent of boys gained a higher grade result compared to only 10 per cent of girls, and English in which 46 per cent of girls gained a higher grade result compared to only 35 per cent of boys.

3.11 School leavers with higher grade results at 'O' level or CSE[1,2] in selected subjects : by sex, 1980/81 and 1986/87

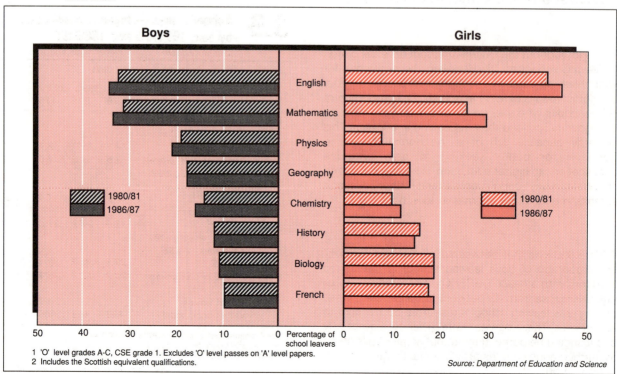

Great Britain

1 'O' level grades A-C, CSE grade 1. Excludes 'O' level passes on 'A' level papers.
2 Includes the Scottish equivalent qualifications.

Source: Department of Education and Science

In England and Wales a new single examination system was introduced for those aged 16 or over in 1988. The General Certificate of Secondary Education (GCSE) replaced GCE 'O' levels and CSEs with the first examinations having taken place in the summer of 1988. The GCE 'O' level examinations were originally considered suitable for the most able 20 per cent of pupils in each subject, while the CSE examinations were originally designed for the next 40 per cent of the ability range. However, by 1986/87 over 90 per cent of school leavers achieved at least one graded result at 'O' level/CSE and 55 per cent achieved at least one higher graded result ('O' level grades A-C or CSE grade 1). The GCSE examination is open to all pupils and the aim of the new system is to encourage pupils of all abilities to follow suitable courses and have these recognised with certificates which show their levels of achievement. The new GCSE examinations are intended to give a clearer and more precise definition than now exists of the levels of attainment of 16 year olds in relation to their knowledge, understanding, skills and competence which the examination courses are designed to develop. The GCSE has a seven-point scale of grades, which encompasses the grading scales of the GCE 'O' level and CSE examinations. (Further details can be found in the Government White Paper *Better Schools Cmnd 9469*). A further new examination is also being introduced; the Advanced Supplementary ('AS') level will run alongside GCE 'A' levels to offer greater breadth in the curriculum for students in the sixth form or equivalent. The first 'AS' level examination will take place in summer 1989.

Chart 3.12 shows that the proportion of 16 year olds who were in full-time education rose from 40 per cent in 1976 to 45 per cent in 1987. In 1982, 14 per cent of 16 year olds were on the Youth Opportunities Programme. However, between 1985 and 1987, 27 per cent were on the Youth Training Scheme (YTS), the programme which succeeded it (see Table 4.28). In 1987, 11 per cent of all 16 year olds were unemployed; this proportion is not comparable with the unemployment rates shown in Chapter 4 which use the working population as their base (see Appendix, Part 4: Unemployment rate).

3.12 Educational and economic activities of 16 year olds[1]

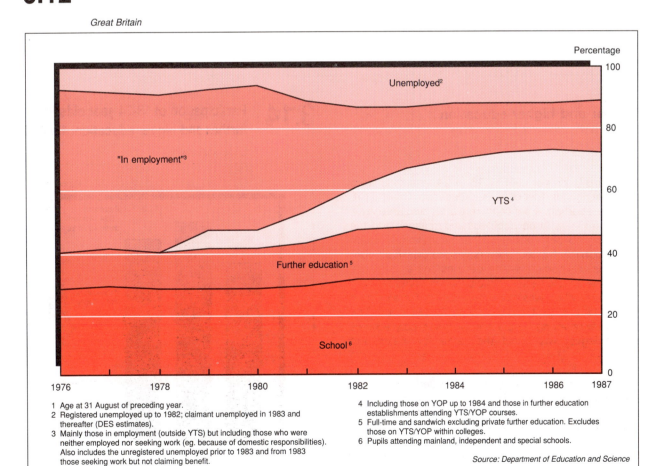

Great Britain

1 Age at 31 August of preceding year.
2 Registered unemployed up to 1982; claimant unemployed in 1983 and thereafter (DES estimates).
3 Mainly those in employment (outside YTS) but including those who were neither employed nor seeking work (eg. because of domestic responsibilities). Also includes the unregistered unemployed prior to 1983 and from 1983 those seeking work but not claiming benefit.
4 Including those on YOP up to 1984 and those in further education establishments attending YTS/YOP courses.
5 Full-time and sandwich excluding private further education. Excludes those on YTS/YOP within colleges.
6 Pupils attending mainland, independent and special schools.

Source: Department of Education and Science

The England and Wales Youth Cohort Study is designed to look at the activities of young people in the three years after finishing compulsory school education. The study aims to follow three cohorts, or groups, selected from those who were eligible to leave school in 1984, 1985 and 1986. The results of a survey of those who were eligible to leave school in 1985, which was carried out in Spring 1986 (see Appendix, Part 3: Youth Cohort Study for details of sample size) showed that those with qualifications were more likely to be in full-time education and less likely to be unemployed than those without them; 78 per cent of those with four or more higher grade qualifications ('O' level grades A-C or CSE grade 1) were in full-time education and only 1 per cent were unemployed (Chart 3.13). Among those with no graded qualifications the percentages in full-time education and unemployed were 3 per cent and 30 per cent respectively. The survey results showed that 39 per cent of respondents were in full-time education, 28 per cent on Youth Training Schemes (YTS), 22 per cent had full-time jobs and 10 per cent were unemployed.

In Scotland, the Scottish Young People's Survey provides details of the destinations of school leavers from the 1985/86 session. These results confirmed the trend found in England and Wales that those with qualifications were more likely to be in full-time education and less likely to be unemployed than those without them.

3.13 Educational and economic activities of 16-17 year olds: by highest qualification, 1986[1]

England & Wales

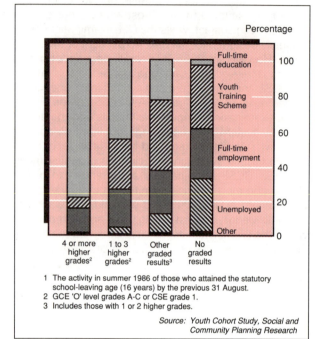

1 The activity in summer 1986 of those who attained the statutory school-leaving age (16 years) by the previous 31 August.
2 GCE 'O' level grades A-C or CSE grade 1.
3 Includes those with 1 or 2 higher grades.

Source: Youth Cohort Study, Social and Community Planning Research

Further and higher education

In 1986/87, 25 per cent of 18 to 24 year olds were participating in further or higher education (Chart 3.14). Of this proportion, 4 per cent were attending university, 6 per cent were in polytechnics and colleges and the remaining 15 per cent in further education. Though largely publicly funded, universities are classified non-profit making bodies serving persons and as such are part of the private sector. Participation in non-advanced further education was more common for females than males, 17 per cent compared to 12 per cent. The proportion of young people in universities, polytechnics and colleges was about the same for males and females.

The number of students who enrolled on further education courses in the United Kingdom fell by 182 thousand between 1975/76 and 1980/81 but rose by 174 thousand between 1980/81 and 1986/87 (Table 3.15). Female part-time and day release students and females who attended only in the evening accounted for almost three-quarters of this increase. Students aged 21 or over also accounted for an increasing proportion of all students who enrolled at further education establishments between 1980/81 and 1986/87. These

3.14 Participation of 18-24 year olds in further and higher education, 1986/87

United Kingdom

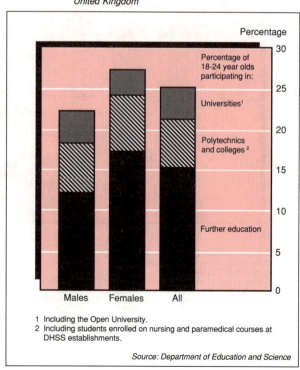

1 Including the Open University.
2 Including students enrolled on nursing and paramedical courses at DHSS establishments.

Source: Department of Education and Science

3.15 Further education [1] — all courses: by sex, type of course and age

United Kingdom   Thousands

	Males					Females				
	1970/71	1975/76	1980/81	1985/86[2]	1986/87[2]	1970/71	1975/76	1980/81	1985/86[2]	1986/87[2]
Student enrolments in further education establishments										
Type of course										
Full-time and sandwich	116	144	154	166	174	95	156	196	208	210
Day release	{559	477	{400	269	267	{198	257	{99	120	125
Other part-time day			53	104	111			126	196	207
Evening only	332	309	244	274	287	432	511	399	433	466
Total student enrolments	1,007	930	851	813	839[6]	725	924	821	958	1,007[6]
of which aged										
18 or under	467	407[5]	444	374	375	246	258[5]	320	339	337
19 or 20	{540	{157	123	99	96	{479	{79	59	75	75
21 or over		{366	254	340	368		{587	442	544	595
Student enrolments on courses in local authority adult education centres [3]	519	686	558	413	427	1,108	1,511	1,240	1,112	1,138
Student enrolments on other courses of adult education [4]	153	180	168	187	..	205	254	230	281	..

1 See Appendix, Part 3: Stages of education.
2 England, Wales and Northern Ireland only.
3 Previously known as Evening Institutes. In Northern Ireland this relates to students on non-vocational courses in FE establishments.
4 University Extramural Departments, Workers' Educational Association, Welsh National Council of the Young Men's Christian Association.
5 In 1980 measurement by age was changed from 31 December to 31 August.
6 Excludes 6,593 link students in FE colleges in Northern Ireland.

Source: Department of Education and Science; Welsh Office

students are less likely than the younger ones to be re-sitting examinations which they have already taken.

The number of students on full-time higher education courses in the United Kingdom rose by 15 per cent between 1980/81 and 1986/87 to stand at 613 thousand (Table 3.16). This increase has been entirely confined to polytechnics and colleges, with university numbers remaining almost constant. Students aged over 20 years have increased by about 20 per cent in this period, and over two-thirds of this increase is attributed to the increased number of female students over 20 years. In 1986/87, 54 per cent of full-time, higher education United Kingdom students were male compared to 58 per cent in 1980/81.

Between 1970/71 and 1986/87 the number of students in part-time higher education in the United Kingdom more than doubled to stand at 359 thousand (Table 3.17). The Open University accounted for 12 per cent

3.16 Higher education [1] — full-time students: by origin, sex and age

United Kingdom   Thousands

	Males					Females				
	1970/71	1975/76	1980/81	1985/86	1986/87	1970/71	1975/76	1980/81	1985/86	1986/87
Full-time students by origin										
From the United Kingdom										
Universities[2] — post-graduate	23.9	23.2	20.7	21.0	21.4	8.0	10.2	11.3	12.6	13.2
— first degree	{128.3	130.1	145.1	{134.3	134.5	{57.0	73.6	96.2	{99.9	101.4
— other[3]				1.5	1.6				1.2	1.2
Polytechnics and colleges	102.0	109.3	111.9	143.5	145.3	113.1	120.1	96.4	132.2	137.1
Total full-time UK students	254.2	262.6	277.7	300.4	302.8	178.2	203.8	203.9	245.9	252.9
From abroad	20.0	38.6	40.7	38.4	39.9	4.4	9.9	12.6	15.3	17.2
Total full-time students	274.2	301.2	318.4	338.7	342.8	182.6	213.7	216.5	261.3	270.1
Full-time students by age										
18 or under	28.7	31.7[4]	50.3	49.6	50.0	30.4	30.5[4]	41.6	43.3	43.8
19—20	99.0	104.6	117.8	130.1	128.9	82.3	90.0	89.7	109.9	109.5
21—24	104.6	108.7	95.6	97.5	104.0	44.5	59.8	53.5	68.0	73.6
25 or over	42.0	56.1	54.5	61.5	59.9	25.3	33.4	31.5	40.0	43.2

1 See Appendix, Part 3: Stages of education.
2 Origin is on fee-paying status except for EC students domiciled outside the United Kingdom who from 1980/81 are charged home rates but are included with students from abroad. From 1984 origin is based on students' usual places of domicile.
3 University first diplomas and certificates.
4 In 1980 measurement by age changed from 31 December to 31 August.

Source: Department of Education and Science

3.17 Higher education [1] — part-time students [2]: by type of establishment, sex and age

United Kingdom   Thousands

	Males					Females				
	1970 /71	1975 /76	1980 /81	1985 /86	1986 /87	1970 /71	1975 /76	1980 /81	1985 /86	1986 /87
Part-time students by establishment										
Universities	18.1	19.3	22.6	26.3	27.6	5.7	7.0	10.7	16.0	17.0
Open University [3]	14.3	33.6	37.6	41.7	42.6	5.3	22.0	30.1	36.0	37.1
Polytechnics and colleges										
— part-time day courses	69.8	80.2	110.5	112.2	116.1	6.7	15.4	30.8	49.9	59.0
— evening only courses	39.8	35.0	35.1	34.4	36.5	5.0	5.8	15.2	20.3	23.0
Total part-time students	142.0	168.1	205.7	214.6	222.8	22.7	50.2	86.8	122.2	136.1
Part-time students by age										
18 or under	..	..	11.8	8.9	8.6	..	..	3.2	2.8	3.1
19—20	..	..	33.9	29.9	29.0	..	..	7.5	9.0	9.7
21—24	..	..	48.3	46.4	46.5	..	..	16.0	20.8	22.8
25 or over	..	..	111.7	129.4	138.7	..	..	60.1	89.6	100.5

1 See Appendix, Part 3: Stages of education.
2 Excludes students enrolled on nursing and paramedical courses at DHSS establishments; some 95 thousand in 1985/86 and 1986/87.
3 Calendar year beginning in second year shown. Excludes short course

students up to 1982/83. In 1985/86 and 1986/87 there were respectively 6.4 and 6.3 thousand specialised short course students for whom data by sex were not available; these have been excluded.

Source: Department of Education and Science

of part-time students when it opened in 1970/71, but by 1986/87 this proportion had risen to 22 per cent. The increase in part-time higher education has taken place almost entirely among those aged over 25 years, with a particularly rapid increase for women. Women accounted for 38 per cent of part-time students in 1986/87 compared to only 14 per cent in 1970/71. Overall, women accounted for 42 per cent of students

in full-time and part-time higher education in 1986/87 compared to only 33 per cent in 1970/71.

The number of mature students in Great Britain starting higher education courses increased by 42 per cent between 1979 and 1986 to stand at 186 thousand (excluding those at the Open University), two thirds of which were part-time students. The increase in the

3.18 Higher education qualifications obtained [1]: by subject group of study, type of qualification and sex

United Kingdom   Thousands

	All Subjects			1986				
				Subject Group of Study				
	1981	1984	1985	Arts	Science [2]	Education	Other [3]	Total
Type of qualification								
Below degree level [4]								
Males	45	51	54	21	31	2	—	54
Females	17	22	25	17	8	3	—	27
Total	62	72	79	38	38	5	—	81
First degree [5]								
Males	76	77	80	35	37	2	4	78
Females	48	56	60	35	16	6	4	61
Total	124	133	139	70	53	8	8	139
Post-graduate [6]								
Males	24	24	26	10	12	5	—	27
Females	13	13	15	6	3	6	—	16
Total	37	37	41	16	15	11	—	43
All higher education qualifications								
Males	144	152	160	66	79	9	4	158
Females	78	91	99	58	27	15	4	103
Total	222	243	260	124	106	24	8	262

1 Includes estimates of successful completions of public sector professional courses (43 thousand in 1986-87). Excludes successful completions of nursing and paramedical courses at DHSS establishments (35 thousand in 1986-87) and the private sector.
2 Medicine, engineering, agriculture and science.
3 Open University and other not specified.
4 First university diplomas and certificates; CNAA diplomas and

certificates below degree level; BTEC/SCOTVEC higher diplomas and certificates; and HND/HNC. Data by sex for SCOTVEC and HND/HNC have been estimated.
5 University degrees, and estimates of CNAA degrees (and equivalent) and in university validated degrees (Great Britain only).
6 Universities, CNAA and PGCES.

Source: Department of Education and Science

3.19 Destination of first degree graduates: by sex, 1985/86[1]

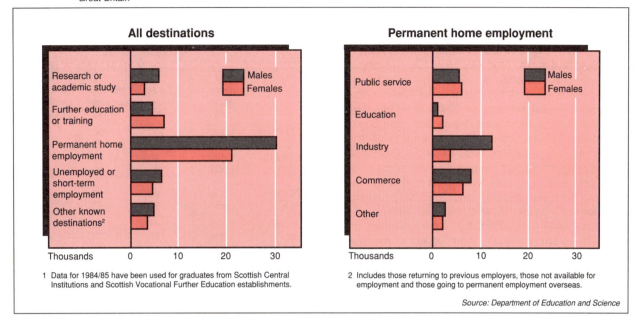

Great Britain

All destinations

- Research or academic study
- Further education or training
- Permanent home employment
- Unemployed or short-term employment
- Other known destinations[2]

Males
Females

Thousands   0   10   20   30

Permanent home employment

- Public service
- Education
- Industry
- Commerce
- Other

Males
Females

Thousands   0   10   20   30

1 Data for 1984/85 have been used for graduates from Scottish Central Institutions and Scottish Vocational Further Education establishments.

2 Includes those returning to previous employers, those not available for employment and those going to permanent employment overseas.

Source: Department of Education and Science

number of women mature students was greater than that for men regardless of the institution or academic level of study, or whether the course was full-time or part-time. In 1986, men accounted for 58 per cent of mature students compared to 67 per cent in 1979. The proportion of full-time mature students decreased from 37 per cent of all students in 1979 to 32 per cent in 1986. In the same period the proportion attending universities remained at about 17 per cent over the period, the others attending polytechnics and colleges.

The number of higher education qualifications awarded in the United Kingdom rose by 18 per cent between 1981 and 1986 to stand at 262 thousand (Table 3.18). For example, the number of first degrees awarded rose from 124 thousand in 1981 to 139 thousand in 1986. In 1986 44 per cent of first degrees and 37 per cent of post-graduate qualifications were awarded to women compared to 39 per cent and 35 per cent respectively in 1981. In 1986, 50 per cent of all higher education qualifications awarded to men were in Science and 42 per cent in the Arts. For women these percentages were 26 and 56 respectively.

In 1985/86, the destinations of 51.1 thousand male and 38.6 thousand female first degree graduates were known. Of these first degree graduates, 57 per cent entered permanent home employment (ie employment expected to last for more than 3 months including those remaining with or returning to a previous employer) compared with 45 per cent in 1980/81. Proportionately fewer women than men entered permanent home employment but more entered further education or training (Chart 3.19). Of the graduates known to have entered permanent home employment in 1985/86, women were most likely to have entered commerce or

public service, while men were most likely to have entered industry.

In 1986/87, 11 per cent of first degree graduates of known destination were unemployed or in short term employment around six months after graduation. The level of unemployment varies according to subject; in general it is lowest among graduates in medical/health and business/administration subjects and in education and engineering. Conversely, it is highest among graduates in humanities, creative arts, biological science, languages and social studies.

In 1986 the Department of Employment's Employment Market Research Unit (EMRU), in association with the Department of Education and Science, carried out a survey of 1980 graduates and diplomates. The first results, published in *Employment Gazette* September 1988, taken six years after graduation, showed that the vast majority of these graduates and diplomates were in employment while only a small minority were unemployed or in further study. At the time of the survey, 17 per cent of those who were in employment had entered teaching, but no other occupation accounted for more than 5 per cent. Graduates and diplomates were more likely to have entered service industries and less likely to have entered manufacturing than the employed labour force as a whole. For about a quarter of graduates and diplomates, a higher education qualification had been neither the minimum formal entry qualification for the job they were in at the time of the survey, nor had it been helpful in securing the job. The average salaries of both male and female graduates and diplomates was higher than the average non-manual earnings at the time.

Table 3.20 shows the value of the student maintenance grant in England and Wales, excluding those studying in London and those studying elsewhere who were living with their parents; students who live at home receive a lower grant. Although its value has increased significantly in cash terms since 1978/79, in real terms it has fallen. Most parents are required to contribute to the ordinary maintenance grant, depending on their level of income. Between 1980/81 and 1986/87 the average percentage contribution by parents rose from 13 per cent to 30 per cent, with most of this increase occurring between 1983/84 and 1985/86. Just over 100 thousand students who were in receipt of a mandatory award in 1986/87 were awarded the maximum grant because their parent's assessed contribution was nil. A smaller proportion of the parents of students at public sector establishments, ie polytechnics and colleges, are assessed to pay large contributions than the parents of students at university.

3.20 Student awards — real value and parental contributions

England & Wales

| | Ordinary maintenance grant [1] (£) | Index (September 1978 = 100) of the real value of the grant·deflated by | | Average assessed percentage contribution by parents [3] |
		Retail prices index	Average earnings index [2]	
1978/79	1,100	100	100	*16*
1979/80	1,245	97	97	*13*
1980/81	1,430	96	92	*13*
1981/82	1,535	93	89	*14*
1982/83	1,595	90	85	*19*
1983/84	1,660	89 [4]	81	*20*
1984/85	1,775	91	82	*25*
1985/86	1,830	88	78	*30*
1986/87	1,901	89	75	*30*
1987/88	1,972	89	..	..

1 Excludes those studying in London and those studying elsewhere living in the parental home. Prior to 1982/83 Oxford and Cambridge were also excluded.
2 The average earnings index is a Great Britain measure.
3 Assessed contributions to maintenance as a percentage of sum of maintenance fees. Of the students assessed for parental contributions in 1986-87 there were 105.2 thousand mandatory award holders (30 per cent) who were receiving the maximum grant because their parents assessed contribution was nil.
4 Since 1984/85 the rate of grant has included an additional travel allowance of £50. If this additional allowance were excluded, the index of the real value of the grant deflated by the retail prices index would be 88 in 1984/85, 86 in 1985/86 and 87 in 1986/87 and 1987/88.

Source: Department of Education and Science; Department of Employment

Educational standards of adults

Chart 3.21 shows the type of educational establishment last attended full-time by people aged 25-49 years and no longer in full-time education. The chart shows a marked tendency for education to be related to the socio-economic group of father. Of those whose fathers were, or had been, in professional occupations, 28 per cent had had a university education compared with about 12 per cent of those with fathers in the other non-manual groups and 2 per cent of those whose fathers were in manual occupations. Overall, 26 per cent continued their full-time education after leaving school, 6 per cent at university and the remainder at a polytechnic or college of further education.

The 1987 Labour Force Survey (LFS) included data on the qualifications of the population of Great Britain by age group (Table 3.22). There is evidence that the general level of attainment and the proportion of people who gain any sort of qualification is higher for those of the younger age-groups.

The LFS also confirmed that, for both men and women, the possession of a formal qualification is associated with a greater probability of having a job and a lesser

3.21 Educational establishment last attended full-time: by socio-economic group of father, 1985-1986

Great Britain

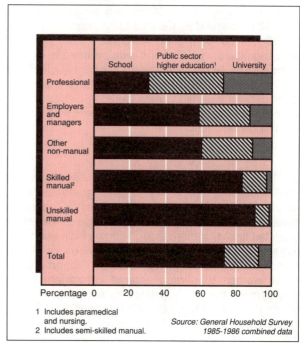

1 Includes paramedical and nursing.
2 Includes semi-skilled manual.

Source: General Household Survey 1985-1986 combined data

3.22 Qualifications [1] of the population aged between 25 and 59: by sex, 1987

Great Britain   Percentages and thousands

	Males aged					Females aged				
	25 −29	30 −39	40 −49	50 −59	All ages	25 −29	30 −39	40 −49	50 −59	All ages
Percentage of the population with a qualification:										
At degree level or equivalent	13	15	12	10	13	9	8	5	3	6
At least higher education below degree level	18	20	17	14	17	17	17	14	10	14
At least GCE 'A' level or equivalent or apprenticeship	55	56	50	42	51	32	29	22	17	25
At least GCE 'O' level or equivalent	69	66	58	48	60	61	50	38	25	42
At least CSE grades 2−5	77	68	58	48	62	72	54	38	26	46
Any qualification [2]	80	74	65	56	68	75	61	48	35	54
Total (= 100%) (thousands)	2,113	3,769	3,395	2,886	12,163	2,087	3,759	3,381	2,959	12,186

1 Percentages are based on data excluding those who did not know or preferred not to state their qualifications: however, the total includes such persons.

2 Includes foreign qualifications and other qualifications which are not listed in the Table.

Source: Labour Force Survey, 1987, Department of Employment

probability of being unemployed. Results published in *Employment Gazette* October 1988 showed that almost half of the unemployed possessed no formal qualifications, while the remainder reported that they did hold educational or vocational qualifications of some kind. Almost a fifth of the unemployed held an 'A' level or equivalent whilst a further twentieth held a higher education qualification above 'A' level.

Resources

3.23 Selected statistics of manpower employed in education

United Kingdom   Thousands and percentages

						Percentage who were graduates	
	1970/71	1975/76	1980/81	1985/86[1,2]	1986/87[2]	1980/81	1986/87[2]
Full-time teachers and lecturers							
Schools							
Public sector							
Primary schools [3]	203	240	222	202	203	16.5	26.2
Secondary schools	199	259	281	267	260	53.8	63.0
Non-maintained schools [4]	36	39	43	43	44	63.3	69.8
Special schools	10	17	19	19	19	21.7	32.7
Total	448	555	565	530	526	38.8	48.2
Establishments of further education [5]	69	86	89	92	93	42.8	46.7
Universities [6]	29	32	34	31	31	98.9	99.0
Total educational establishments [7]	546	677	693	657	657	42.2	50.0
Other employees (local authority only)							
Part-time teachers and lecturers [8,9]	. .	21	41	43	45	. .	. .
Full-time support staff	. .	253[10]	235	209	215	. .	. .
Part-time support staff [8]	. .	230[10]	242	229	239	. .	. .

1 Data for maintained schools in England and Wales are estimated.
2 Data for 1984/85 have been used for manpower in schools in Scotland.
3 Includes nursery schools.
4 Excludes independent schools in Scotland and Northern Ireland.
5 Includes former colleges of education.
6 Excludes Open University. There were 631 professors and lecturers and 5,301 part-time tutorial and counselling staff employed by the Open University at January 1987. Also excludes the independent University College of Buckingham.
7 Includes miscellaneous teachers in England and Wales (5.5 thousand in 1986/87) not shown elsewhere above.
8 Full-time equivalents.
9 Great Britain only. Figures for 1980 / 81 onwards include further education and unqualified teachers in England and Wales.
10 Great Britain data from the Department of Employment.

Source: Department of Education and Science

The resources required by the education system are closely linked to the size of the population of school age. The peak in births in the mid-sixties led to a peak in the number of school children from 1970 to the early 1980s (see Chart 1.3 in Chapter 1: Population), but these people have now passed through the education system unless they are in higher education or are mature students. Now the most striking feature in the school population is the steady decrease from this peak to the trough of those aged 9-10 years in 1987. These peaks and troughs require careful monitoring by the education authorities to plan where and when resources are required.

The number of full-time teachers employed in the United Kingdom fell by 7 per cent between 1980/81 and 1986/87 to 526 thousand (Table 3.23) reflecting the decreasing school population. Over the same period the percentage of teachers who were graduates rose from 39 to 48 per cent. The number of full-time lecturers in United Kingdom universities fell from 34 thousand in 1980/81 to 31 thousand in 1986/87. However, the number of lecturers in establishments of further education rose slightly from 89 thousand in 1980/81 to 93 thousand in 1986/87. The number of enrolments on teacher training courses have decreased from about 74 thousand in 1977 to about 40 thousand in 1986.

Table 3.24 shows the average number of pupils per teacher for schools in the United Kingdom, ie the pupil/teacher ratio. Averaged over all types of school this ratio has fallen from 22.0 in 1971 to 17.2 in 1987. Of public sector schools, secondary schools have the lowest pupil/teacher ratio whilst nursery and primary schools have about the same ratio.

3.24 Pupil/teacher ratios [1]

United Kingdom			Numbers
	1971	1981	1987 [2]
Public sector schools			
Nursery	26.6	21.5	21.2
Primary	27.1	22.3	21.8
Secondary	17.8	16.4	15.4
All public sector schools	23.2	19.0	18.3
Non-maintained schools	14.0 [3]	13.1 [4]	11.6
Special schools	10.5 [3]	7.4	6.4
All schools	22.0 [3]	18.2 [4]	17.2

1 See Appendix, Part 3: Pupil/teacher ratios.
2 Includes 1988 data for nursery schools in Scotland.
3 Excludes independent schools in Scotland.
4 Excludes independent schools in Northern Ireland.

Source: Education Statistics for the United Kingdom; Department of Education and Science

3.25 Composition of total net expenditure: by sector of education, 1986-87

United Kingdom

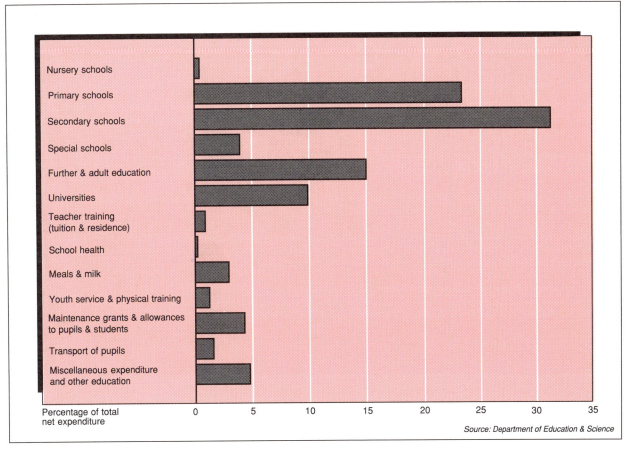

Source: Department of Education & Science

Secondary schools accounted for 31 per cent of the United Kingdom net expenditure on education in 1986-87 (Chart 3.25). The other main components were primary schools (23 per cent), further and adult education (15 per cent) and universities (10 per cent). Expenditure on components such as school meals and milk and transport of pupils, although small, add to the proportions given above for various types of educational establishment.

In 1986-87 government expenditure on education was £19.0 billion (Table 3.26). Capital expenditure accounted for 4 per cent of total education expenditure in 1986-87 compared to 15 per cent in 1970-71. Current expenditure on further and adult education rose from 10 per cent of total expenditure on education to 14 per cent between 1970-71 and 1986-87.

By September 1989, all Local Education Authorities outside inner London must submit schemes of local management of schools (LMS) involving: proposals for an open and fair system for calculating budgets for all their schools; delegation of budgets to all secondary schools and to primary schools with 200 or more pupils. The budget will cover the majority of running costs, including staff salaries.

3.26 Government expenditure on education

United Kingdom £ million and percentages

	1970 —71	1980 —81	1986 —87
Current expenditure (£ million)			
Schools			
Nursery	7	52	81
Primary	546	2,840	4,157
Secondary	619	3,695	5,620
Special	50	443	727
Further and adult education [1]	265	1,591	2,618
Training of teachers: tuition	60	78	142
Universities [1]	246	1,264	1,654
Other education expenditure	95	516	871
Related education expenditure	443	1,809	2,434
Total current expenditure	2,331	12,288	18,303
Capital expenditure (£ million)			
Schools	245	480	397
Other education expenditure	164	282	342
Total capital expenditure	409	762	739
Total government expenditure (£ million)	2,740	13,050	19,042
Of which, expenditure by local authorities	2,318	11,270	16,390
Expenditure as a percentage of GDP	*5.1*	*5.5*	*4.9*

1 Includes tuition fees

Source: Department of Education and Science; Central Statistical Office

Chapter 4: Employment

The labour force

- In Great Britain the civilian labour force is projected to rise by 0.9 million between 1987 and 1995, though the number aged under 25 is projected to fall by 1.2 million.   *(Table 4.3)*

- Economic activity rates amongst women under 60 years rose substantially between 1971 and 1987, and are projected to continue to rise up to 1995.   *(Table 4.5)*

Type of employment

- The number of employees in employment in the United Kingdom reached 22.1 million in 1988, an increase of 1.0 million on the low point reached in 1983, but lower than the previous peak of 23.2 million in 1979.   *(Table 4.10)*

- The number of self-employed people in the United Kingdom is estimated to have risen by over 1 million between 1979 and 1988, after remaining fairly flat during the 1970s.   *(Table 4.11)*

Time at work

- On average men in employment in the United Kingdom worked more hours per week than men in the rest of the European Community in 1986.   *(Table 4.19)*

Unemployment

- In 1987 the annual average rate of unemployment for men in the United Kingdom was 11.9 per cent compared to 7.3 per cent for women.   *(Chart 4.21)*

- The number of long-term unemployed claimants of benefit in the United Kingdom reached a peak of almost 1.4 million in January 1986, but fell to 948 thousand by July 1988.   *(Chart 4.23)*

Employment and training measures

- For the under 35s, and more especially those under 20, men were more likely than women to have received job-related training in 1987.   *(Table 4.29)*

4.1   Workforce and workforce in employment

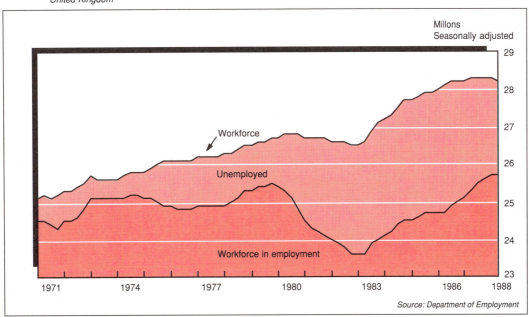

United Kingdom

Millons
Seasonally adjusted

Workforce

Unemployed

Workforce in employment

Source: Department of Employment

Glossary of terms

The economically active - people in employment plus the unemployed as measured by household surveys and censuses. The unemployed are conventionally defined in Great Britain labour force estimates as people without a job and seeking work in a reference week.

The economically inactive - people who are not economically active, eg full-time students who neither have, nor are seeking, paid work and those who are keeping house, have retired early or are permanently unable to work.

The total labour force - the economically active.

The civilian labour force - the total labour force less the armed forces (see Appendix, Part 4: The labour force).

Employees in employment - a count of civilian jobs, both main and secondary, which are as an employee paid by an employer who runs a PAYE tax scheme.

Self-employed persons - those who in their main employment work on their own account, whether or not they have any employees.

Work related government training programmes - those participants on government training programmes and schemes who in the course of their participation receive training in the context of a workplace but are not employees, self-employed or HM Forces.

The workforce in employment - employees in employment as measured by employer enquiries, self-employed, HM Forces and participants on work related government training programmes.

The workforce - the workforce in employment plus people claiming benefit at Unemployment Benefit offices.

The population of working age - males aged 16 to 64 years and females aged 16 to 59 years.

Civilian economic activity rate - the percentage of the population in a given age group which is in the civilian labour force.

The labour force

The composition of the population of working age in Great Britain is shown in Chart 4.2. Between 1971 and 1987 the proportion of males in Great Britain who were economically inactive has increased from 9 per cent to 12 per cent. At the same time the proportion of married females who were economically inactive has decreased sharply from 51 per cent to 34 per cent, while the proportion in employment has grown from 47 per cent to 60 per cent.

4.2 Population of working age: by economic status

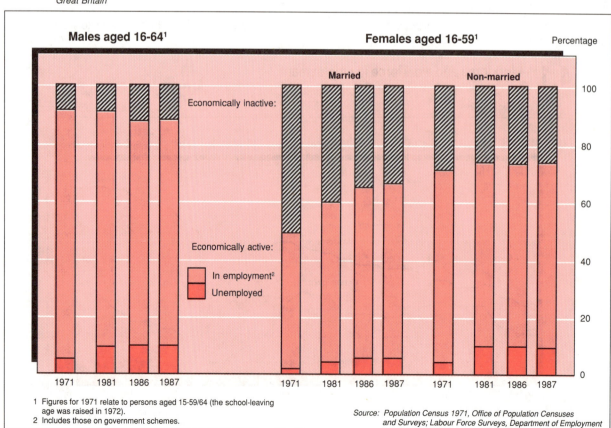

Great Britain

Males aged 16-64[1]   **Females aged 16-59[1]**   Percentage

Married   Non-married

Economically inactive:

Economically active:
  In employment[2]
  Unemployed

1971 1981 1986 1987   1971 1981 1986 1987   1971 1981 1986 1987

1 Figures for 1971 relate to persons aged 15-59/64 (the school-leaving age was raised in 1972).
2 Includes those on government schemes.

Source: Population Census 1971, Office of Population Censuses and Surveys; Labour Force Surveys, Department of Employment

4.3 Civilian labour force [1]: by age

Great Britain   Millions

	16 – 24	25 – 54	55 +	All aged 16 or over
Estimates				
1971	5.1	15.0	4.9	24.9
1976	5.1	16.1	4.5	25.7
1981	5.8	16.3	4.1	26.2
1983	5.9	16.4	3.7	25.9
1984	6.0	16.7	3.6	26.4
1985	6.1	17.0	3.5	26.6
1986	6.1	17.2	3.4	26.7
1987	6.2	17.6	3.4	27.2
Projections				
1988	6.1	18.0	3.4	27.5
1991	5.6	18.9	3.3	27.9
1995	5.0	19.8	3.3	28.1

1 The civilian labour force, which excludes HM Forces, includes those students who are economically active. Estimates for 1971 are based on the Census of Population and those for 1976-1987 are based on Labour Force Survey results adjusted to a mid-year basis and for the inclusion of non-private households. See Appendix, Part 4: Labour force.

Source: Department of Employment

The civilian labour force grew at an average rate of 140 thousand a year during the 1970s and reached 26.2 million in 1980 and 1981 (Table 4.3). It fell by over 300 thousand between 1981 and 1983, but the upward trend was then resumed and in 1987 it reached 27.2 million. The overall increase of 2.3 million between 1971 and 1987 was almost entirely attributable to an increase in the number of women in the civilian labour force. Relatively high birth rates in the 1960s (see Table 1.9) had the effect of increasing the number of 16 year old entrants to the civilian labour force during the second half of the 1970s. However, this effect reached its peak in 1981 after which the number of 16 year old entrants fell, and is projected to continue to do so until the early 1990s. Between 1987 and 1995 the civilian labour force is projected to grow by nearly 900 thousand. A rise of over 2 million is projected in the 25-54 age group but a fall of over 1 million is expected in 16-24 year old group.

The size of the civilian labour force is influenced partly by the size of the population of working age and partly by economic activity rates. The size of the population of working age increased continuously throughout the period 1971 to 1987 (Chart 4.4) rising by 7½ per cent in total, with both sexes growing by over 1 million. Over the same period the civilian labour force of working age grew by 12 per cent, and 87 per cent (2.5 million) of this growth was women. The population of working age is projected to rise at a declining rate up to the early 1990's and then to fall slightly before resuming a slow upward path.

4.4 Civilian labour force[1] of working age[2] and population of working age[2]: by sex

Great Britain

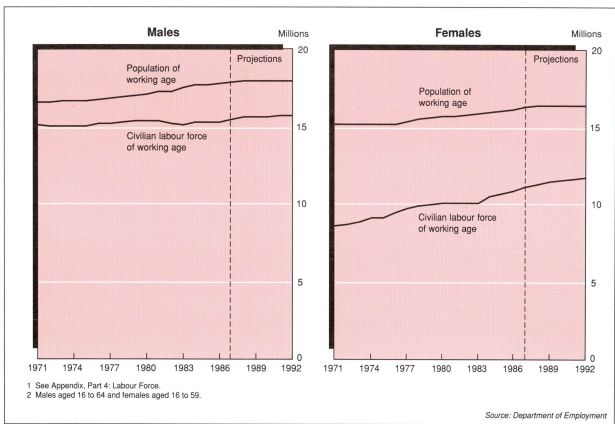

1 See Appendix, Part 4: Labour Force.
2 Males aged 16 to 64 and females aged 16 to 59.

Source: Department of Employment

The number of females in employment increased as did their economic activity at all ages between 1971 and 1987, except for those aged 60 or over (Table 4.5). The increase in activity rates has been partly due to an increase in the availability of part-time jobs and other social and economic changes encouraging women into the labour force (see Chart 4.9 below). Demographic factors have also influenced female economic activity rates; women with children are less likely to be economically active, especially those with children aged under 5. Thus, comparatively lower birth rates in the 1970s than in the 1960s and a rise in the average age at which women have children (affecting economic activity rates of younger women) have helped to increase female economic activity rates. In contrast, male activity rates have fallen in all age groups with the exception of the 16-19 year old group but especially in the older groups. While male rates are now expected to remain fairly constant until 1995, the activity rates of females are projected to keep on rising for all age categories except those aged 60 or over.

The 1987 Labour Force Survey estimated that of all those who were classed as economically inactive (not in employment nor unemployed on Great Britain labour force definition) in spring 1987, 238 thousand had not sought work in the week prior to interview because they believed that there were no jobs available, but nevertheless would like to have a job. These people are known as 'discouraged workers' and almost all of them were available for employment. The estimated number of discouraged workers who had not looked for work in the four weeks prior to interview in spring 1987 was just under 150 thousand, about a third lower than in 1986. This sharp fall followed a period from 1984 to 1986 during which the number had remained remarkably constant at about 220 thousand. The 1987 survey also identified around 90 thousand additional people who had looked for work in the last four weeks but not in the reference week itself because of a perceived lack of job opportunity; this was some 30 thousand fewer than in 1986.

4.5 Civilian labour force economic activity rates [1] and projections: by age and sex

Great Britain — Percentages

	16—19	20—24	25—44	45—54/59 [2]	55—59 60—64 [3]	60/65+ [4]	All aged 16 or over
Males							
1971	69.4	87.7	95.4	94.8	82.9	19.2	80.5
1976	70.5	85.9	95.7	94.9	80.4	14.5	78.9
1981	72.4	85.1	95.7	93.0	69.3	10.3	76.5
1983	69.6	84.1	94.5	90.2	59.4	8.1	74.2
1984	72.9	84.7	94.4	89.1	56.7	8.2	74.3
1985	73.7	84.9	94.4	88.9	54.4	8.2	74.0
1986	72.8	84.9	94.0	88.0	53.4	7.5	73.4
1987	75.0	85.7	94.2	87.3	54.6	7.6	73.7
Projections							
1988	75.4	86.2	94.4	87.7	56.4	7.3	74.0
1991	75.6	86.1	94.2	87.7	56.0	6.2	73.7
1995	75.6	86.1	94.0	87.7	55.4	4.9	73.3
Females							
1971	65.0	60.2	52.4	62.0	50.9	12.4	43.9
1976	68.2	64.8	60.0	66.5	54.3	10.3	46.8
1981	70.4	68.8	61.7	68.0	53.4	8.3	47.6
1983	66.8	68.2	62.2	68.1	50.6	7.5	47.0
1984	68.8	69.2	65.2	69.2	51.1	7.6	48.4
1985	70.7	68.7	66.4	69.4	51.8	6.8	48.8
1986	70.8	69.3	67.2	70.2	51.7	6.5	49.2
1987	73.2	69.5	68.6	70.7	52.6	6.4	50.0
Projections							
1988	74.0	70.1	69.8	71.1	54.1	6.6	50.8
1991	75.1	71.0	72.2	71.8	55.1	6.4	51.9
1995	76.5	71.9	74.6	72.2	56.0	6.1	53.0

1 The percentage of the resident population, or any sub-group of the population, who are in the civilian labour force.
2 45-54 for females, 45-59 for males.

3 55-59 for females, 60-64 for males.
4 60 or over for females, 65 or over for males.

Source: Department of Employment

4.6 Economic status of the population of working age: by sex and ethnic group, 1985-1987

Great Britain   Percentages and thousands

	Males					Females				
	Ethnic group					Ethnic group				
	White	West Indian or Guyan-ese	Indian/ Pakistani/ Bangla-deshi	Other[1]	All males[2]	White	West Indian or Guyan-ese	Indian/ Pakistani/ Bangla-deshi	Other[1]	All females[2]
Economically active										
(percentages)										
In employment										
Employees — full-time	64	55	45	46	63	31	41	21	26	31
— part-time	2	.. 6	.. 6	.. 6	2	25	15	7	15	24
— all[3]	66	57	48	49	65	56	56	29	41	55
Self-employed	11	.. 6	16	11	11	4	.. 6	4	.. 6	4
On government scheme	2	.. 6	.. 6	.. 6	2	1	.. 6	.. 6	.. 6	1
All in employment[4]	79	65	64	61	78	61	59	34	46	60
Out of employment	9	18	16	11	10	7	13	8	9	7
All economically active	88	84	80	72	88	68	73	42	55	67
Economically inactive										
(percentages)										
Long-term sick or disabled	4	.. 6	5	.. 6	4	3	.. 6	.. 6	.. 6	3
Looking after home	0	.. 6	.. 6	.. 6	0	20	13	44	26	20
Full-time student	3	6	11	22	4	3	7	7	11	3
Retired	2	.. 6	.. 6	.. 6	2	1	.. 6	.. 6	.. 6	1
Other inactive	3	.. 6	3	.. 6	3	6	.. 6	5	6	6
All economically inactive	12	16	20	28	12	32	27	58	45	33
Total of working age[5] (= 100%)(thousands)	16,534	173	393	226	17,485	15,048	191	369	196	15,964

1 Includes African, Arab, Chinese, other stated, and Mixed.
2 Includes ethnic group not stated.
3 Includes hours of work not stated.

4 Includes employment status not stated.
5 Males aged 16-64, females aged 16-59.
6 Sample size too small for reliable estimate

Source : Labour Force Survey , combined data for 1985 to 1987 inclusive, Department of Employment

Table 4.6 uses the combined results of the 1985, 1986 and 1987 Labour Force Surveys. It shows that the proportion of men of working age in Great Britain who were economically active was higher among the White population and the West Indian/Guyanese group than among those from the 'other' ethnic group, partly because the latter group contained a higher proportion of full-time students. Among women the variation was greater; only 42 per cent of those from the Indian/Pakistani/Bangladeshi ethnic group were economically active compared to 68 per cent in the White group and 73 per cent of those from the West Indian/Guyanese group. There was also some variation within the Indian/Pakistani/Bangladeshi ethnic group; the economic activity rate among women of Pakistani/Bangladeshi origin, at 18 per cent, was much lower than that among those from the Indian group, at 55 per cent.

Social Trends 19, © Crown copyright 1989   71

Unemployment rates for the ethnic minority groups were higher than for the White population (see also Table 4.26), and were highest among those of West Indian/Guyanese origin and for the Pakistani/Bangladeshi ethnic group. Among those in employment, males from the Indian/Pakistani/Bangladeshi ethnic group, especially Indian males (18 per cent), were far more likely to be self-employed than those from other groups.

Table 4.7 shows that in 1987 a higher proportion of women without dependent children under 16 worked full-time than women with dependent children under 16. Very young dependent children have a large effect on a woman's likelihood of being in employment. Although more than two-thirds of women with dependent children between the ages of 10 and 15 were in employment, less than one-third of women with children under 5 were working. The difference is especially marked in relation to full-time employment.

At June 1987 female part-time employees in employment in Great Britain accounted for 20 per cent of all employees compared to only 13 per cent at June 1971. Some of the reasons for this increase are illustrated by the results of the 1980 *Women and Employment Survey*, conducted by the Department of Employment and Office of Population Censuses and Surveys. This survey found that in the 1970s women tended to return to work more quickly after having a baby than in the 1960s and also that they tended to return to work between births, with the majority taking a part-time job upon returning to work. Using the results

of this survey, the 1984 report *Women and Employment: A Lifetime Perspective* found that the majority of women who took part-time employment after childbearing did so because of the need to combine paid work with domestic responsibilities. The convenient hours of part-time work enabled them to do so (for more details see *Women and Employment: A Lifetime Perspective*, J Martin and C Roberts, HMSO, London, 1984).

4.7 Women in employment[1]: by age of youngest dependent child, spring 1987

Great Britain — Percentages and thousands

	Percentage working			All women aged 16 and over (= 100%) Thousands
	Full-time	Part-time	All working[2]	
Women with youngest dependent child aged:				
Under 5 years	9.7	22.6	32.4	3,085
5 to 9 years	15.5	44.4	60.0	1,646
10 to 15 years	25.1	44.6	69.8	1,940
All ages (up to 15 years)	15.6	34.4	50.1	6,671
Women without dependent children				
under 16 years	29.0	14.6	43.8	15,872
All women	25.0	20.5	45.7	22,543

1 Employees and self-employed including those on government employment and training schemes.
2 Including those who did not state whether they worked full or part-time.

Source: Labour Force Survey, 1987, Department of Employment

Type of employment

Since 1983, when it was at its lowest for some years, the workforce in employment in the United Kingdom rose by 1.7 million to stand at 25.3 million at mid-1987, much the same as the 1979 peak (Table 4.8). About 24 per cent of the workforce was employed in the public sector at mid-1961, by mid-1983 it had risen to 30 per cent, but then fell to 25 per cent at mid-1987, excluding those on work related government training programmes. Most of the decrease in public sector employment since 1981 was accounted for by a fall in employment in public corporations, partly because of privatisation; over 0.2 million people were transferred to the private sector following the privatisation of British Telecom in November 1984 and in December 1986 0.1 million British Gas employees were re-classified to the private sector. Between mid-1981 and mid-1987 the workforce employed by public corporations fell by nearly a half. Within general government, local authorities and the National Health Service together accounted for 4.3 million employees (80 per cent of total general government) at mid-1987, even though the National Health Service employees have fallen in number from their 1983 peak.

4.8 Workforce in employment: by sector[1]

United Kingdom — Millions

	Public sector			Private sector	Work related government training programmes[2]	Workforce in employment
	General government	Public corporations	Total			
1961	3.7	2.2	5.9	18.6	—	24.5
1971	4.6	2.0	6.6	17.9	—	24.5
1976	5.3	2.0	7.3	17.5	—	24.8
1979	5.4	2.1	7.4	17.9	—	25.4
1981	5.3	1.9	7.2	17.2	—	24.3
1983	5.3	1.7	7.0	16.7	—	23.6
1984	5.3	1.6	6.9	17.1	0.2	24.2
1985	5.3	1.3	6.6	17.9	0.2	24.6
1986	5.3	1.2	6.5	18.0	0.2	24.7
1987	5.4	1.0	6.4	18.5	0.3	25.3
Males	2.2	0.9	3.1	11.2	0.2	14.5
Females	3.1	0.1	3.3	7.4	0.1	10.8

1 As at mid-year. See Appendix, Part 4: Sector classification.
2 See Appendix, Part 4: Workforce.

Source: Central Statistical Office

Social Trends 19, © Crown copyright 1989

Great Britain

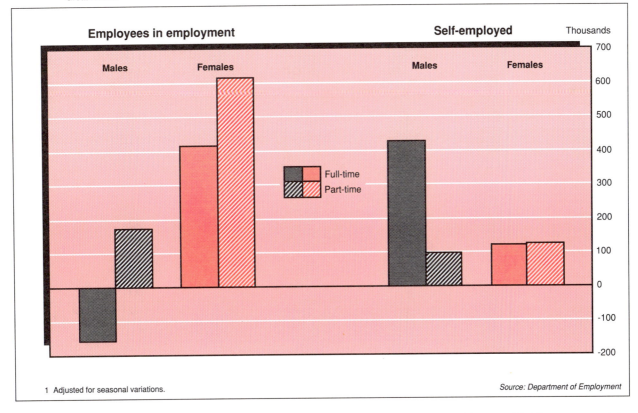

Employees in employment   **Self-employed**   Thousands

1 Adjusted for seasonal variations.

Source: Department of Employment

Chart 4.9 summarises the changes in employees and self-employed between June 1983 and June 1988. Over the period the number of employees in employment rose by over 1 million, with virtually all of the rise accounted for by females, both full-time and part-time. The increase in male part-timers only marginally exceeded the 157 thousand fall in full-time male employees. However the trend among the self-employed was quite different with 56 per cent of the growth during the period due to full-time males.

The number of employees in banking, finance, insurance, business services and leasing grew steadily between 1971 and 1988, accounting for nearly a third of the overall increase in services industries, while the number employed in transport and communications fell

4.10 Employees in employment: by industry [1]

United Kingdom   Thousands

	Standard Industrial Classification 1980	1971	1979	1981	1986	1988 Males	1988 Females	1988 Total
Manufacturing								
Extraction of minerals and ores other than fuels, manufacture of metal, mineral products, and chemicals	2	1,282	1,147	939	778	592	179	771
Metal goods, engineering, and vehicle industries	3	3,709	3,374	2,923	2,334	1,751	468	2,219
Other	4	3,074	2,732	2,360	2,125	1,214	893	2,108
Total manufacturing	2 – 4	8,065	7,253	6,222	5,236	3,557	1,541	5,097
Services								
Distribution, hotels, catering, and repairs	6	3,686	4,257	4,172	4,403	2,043	2,509	4,551
Transport and communication	7	1,556	1,479	1,425	1,340	1,080	293	1,372
Banking, finance, insurance, business services, and leasing	8	1,336	1,647	1,739	2,202	1,239	1,229	2,468
Other	9	5,049	6,197	6,132	6,541	2,509	4,311	6,820
Total services	6 – 9	11,627	13,580	13,468	14,486	6,870	8,342	15,212
Agriculture, forestry, and fishing	0	450	380	363	329	230	83	313
Energy and water supply industries	1	798	722	710	539	387	72	459
Construction	5	1,198	1,239	1,130	991	901	121	1,022
All industries and services	0 – 9	22,139	23,173	21,892	21,581	11,946	10,158	22,104

1 As at June each year.

Source: Department of Employment

4.11 Self-employed: by industry [1]

United Kingdom   Thousands

	Standard Industrial Classification 1980	1971	1979	1981	1986	1988 Males	1988 Females	1988 Total
Manufacturing								
Extraction of minerals and ores other than fuels, manufacture of metal, mineral products and chemicals	2	4	6	8	11	9	3	13
Metal goods, engineering and vehicle industries	3	36	42	46	63	70	7	77
Other	4	91	93	94	137	130	45	175
Total manufacturing	2–4	131	141	148	211	209	55	265
Services								
Distribution, hotels, catering and repairs	6	747	652	714	798	546	294	840
Transport and communication	7	66	88	101	113	157	8	166
Banking, finance, insurance, business services and leasing	8	152	148	191	278	249	75	324
Other	9	266	238	292	458	271	272	544
Total services	6–9	1,231	1,126	1,298	1,646	1,224	650	1,874
Agriculture, forestry and fishing	0	314	286	276	274	239	30	269
Energy and water supply industries	1	—	1	1	1	1	—	1
Construction	5	351	352	396	495	555	21	576
All industries and services	0–9	2,026	1,906	2,119	2,627	2,228	757	2,985

1 As at June each year.   *Source: Department of Employment*

over this period (Table 4.10). Part-time employment has accounted for much of the growth in the number of employees employed in the other service industries, particularly among women; in 1988, 82 per cent of female employees were employed in the service industries. The shift in employment, for employees, from the manufacturing to non-manufacturing sector can be seen in Chart 4.12.

The overall trend in self-employment in the United Kingdom complements that for employees; between 1971 and 1979 there was little change in the number of self-employed people, but then rose substantially between 1979 and 1988 from 1.9 million to 3.0 million (Table 4.11). Since 1979 self-employment has increased in both manufacturing and services industries and their respective shares of total self-employment have remained roughly constant; in 1988 manufacturing industries accounted for 9 per cent of total self-employment while service industries accounted for 63 per cent.

In 1979 only 19 per cent of the self-employed were females, though this proportion rose to 25 per cent in 1988. In 1988 the self-employed accounted for 12 per cent of the workforce in employment compared to only 8 per cent in 1971.

Between June 1971 and June 1988 the number of employees employed in manufacturing in Great Britain fell by 37 per cent (Chart 4.12). Over the same period the number of non-manufacturing employees rose by 2.8 million (20 per cent) to 16.6 million.

4.12 Manufacturing and non-manufacturing employees in employment

Great Britain

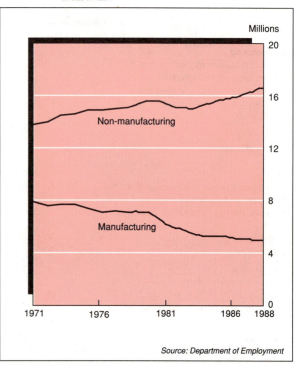

Source: Department of Employment

4.13 Change in employment: by occupation, 1987-1995

Great Britain

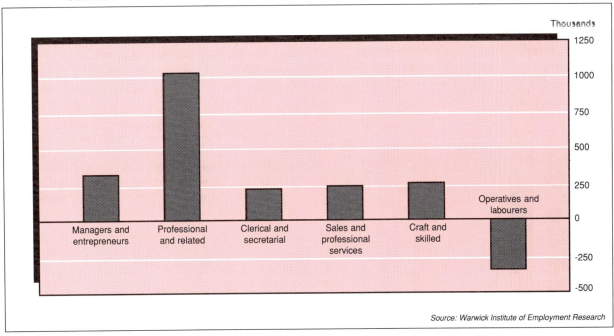

Source: Warwick Institute of Employment Research

Chart 4.13 shows the change in employment by occupational group between 1987 and 1995, as anticipated by the Warwick Institute of Employment Research. The expected rise in craft and skilled employment, 258 thousand, is forecast to be concentrated in construction occupations, while the predicted fall in less skilled jobs reflects continued automation.

4.14 Full-time [1] employees as a percentage of all in employment [2]: by industry, 1983 and 1987

Great Britain Percentages and thousands

	1983	1987
Industry Division (SIC 1980) *(percentages)*		
0 *Agriculture, forestry and fishing*	43.1	39.8
1 *Energy and water supply*	96.1	95.5
2 *Extraction of minerals and ores other than fuels; manufacture of metals, mineral products and chemicals*	92.7	91.2
3 *Metal goods engineering and vehicles*	92.3	90.2
4 *Other manufacturing*	83.3	80.5
5 *Construction*	67.9	58.3
6 *Distribution, hotels and catering, repairs*	51.9	48.1
7 *Transport and communication*	87.5	82.1
8 *Banking, finance, insurance, business services and leasing*	75.1	72.4
9 *Other services*	65.4	59.6
All industries [3] (thousands)	16,264	16,050

1 Based on respondent's own opinion, not on the number of hours worked.
2 Includes all employees, those self-employed and persons on Government employment and training schemes.
3 Includes workplaces outside the UK and other inadequately described.

Source: Spring 1983 and 1987 Labour Force Surveys, Department of Employment

In 1987 surveys of employers, jobcentres and Professional and Executive Recruitment Offices found that skill shortages were most common for professional engineers, experienced computer programmers, skilled machinists, fitter-mechanics and welders, accountants and nurses. Shortages were greatest in the South East and the Midlands. In March 1987 it was estimated that about 2½ per cent, or 5 thousand, of all vacancies at jobcentres in Great Britain had remained unfilled for more than two months because of skill shortages. Almost half of these were in the South East and Greater London. The main occupations affected were nursing, hairdressing, cooking and sewing/embroidery occupations.

The Labour Force Survey (LFS) provides data on employment on a different basis to the workforce in employment used above. The major difference is that the employee data included in the workforce in employment is collected from employers, and therefore an employee with more than one job with different employers is counted more than once. The LFS however is a household enquiry and can therefore provide more comprehensive labour market data including estimates of people with second jobs. Using the LFS the number of full-time employees fell by over 1 per cent between 1983 and 1987 at a time when the total number of persons in full-time and part-time employment grew by 6 per cent (Table 4.14). Only in the energy and water supply industry was the proportion of part-time employees the same in 1987 as it was in 1983. In all other industries the proportion of part-time employees increased. This implies that between 1983 and 1987 the industries which were contracting were

4.15 People with a second job: by sex and employment status, 1983 and 1987

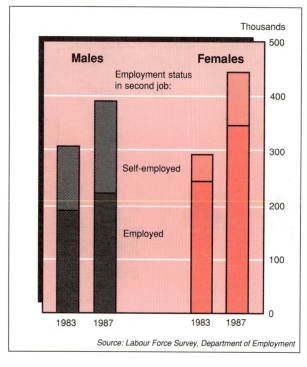

Great Britain

Source: Labour Force Survey, Department of Employment

relinquishing a higher proportion of full-time employees and those that were expanding were employing a higher proportion of part-time employees. For further details of which broad industry groups were contracting and which expanding see Table 4.10.

Chart 4.15, using data from the 1983 and 1987 LFS, shows that in 1987 there were more women with a second job than men, whereas the reverse was true in 1983. Nearly 300 thousand more people had second jobs in 1987 than in 1983, with 37 per cent of the increase due to people who were self-employed in their second job. The number of women with a second job increased by 82 per cent between 1983 and 1987.

Time at work

The New Earnings Survey (NES) figures in table 4.16 show that on average full-time manual male employees in Great Britain in April 1987 worked nearly 6 hours more per week than their non-manual counterparts with paid overtime hours accounting for two-thirds of this difference. However these figures take no account of unpaid overtime, which is more likely to occur in non-manual occupations. The difference of almost 3 hours in the average working week between manual and non-manual full-time female employees was half that of men; women worked far fewer paid overtime hours than men. Overall, weekly averages in April 1987 were nearly 42 hours for men compared to 37½ hours for women. Men were much more likely to work long hours, with

9 per cent of male employees working over 52 hours a week compared to just 1 per cent of female employees. For full-time manual males 5 industry groups recorded average usual paid overtime exceeding 5.9 hours per week: transport and communications; agriculture, forestry and fishing; extraction of minerals and ores other than fuels, manufacture of metals, mineral products and chemicals; metal goods, engineering and vehicles industries; and other manufacturing industries. While the NES figures quoted relate only to paid overtime of full-time employees, the 1987 Labour Force Survey found in spring 1987 that unpaid overtime averaged over 3½ hours a week for professionals in education, welfare and health or

4.16 Average weekly hours of full-time employees[1], April 1987

Great Britain

Percentages, thousands and hours

	Males			Females		
	Manual	Non-manual	All employees	Manual	Non-manual	All employees
Percentage of each group with total weekly hours in the range:						
32 or under	0.2	3.1	1.5	2.6	5.8	5.1
Over 32 but not over 36	2.0	20.3	10.3	13.2	27.4	24.2
Over 36 but not over 40	42.6	57.3	49.3	61.5	59.4	59.9
Over 40 but not over 44	16.2	9.3	13.1	11.0	4.8	6.2
Over 44 but not over 48	14.7	4.8	10.2	6.4	1.5	2.6
Over 48 but not over 52	9.6	2.2	6.2	3.0	0.6	1.1
Over 52	14.7	3.0	9.4	2.3	0.5	0.9
Sample size (= 100%) (thousands)	39	33	73	8	28	36
Average weekly hours						
Normal basic hours	39.1	37.2	38.2	38.1	36.2	36.7
Overtime hours	5.5	1.5	3.7	1.6	0.6	0.8
Total weekly hours	44.6	38.7	41.9	39.7	36.8	37.5

1 Hours of full-time employees on adult rates whose pay for the survey pay-period was not affected by absence and for whom normal basic hours were reported. Total weekly hours are the sum of normal basic hours and paid overtime hours.

Source: New Earnings Survey, 1987, Department of Employment

supporting management and among managers. Chart 10.2 shows trends in basic hours and actual hours worked.

During 1980 there was a large increase in the number of manual workers in manufacturing industries in Great Britain who worked short-time, and a corresponding decrease in those working overtime (Chart 4.17). Short-time working reached a peak in January 1981, coinciding with the trough in those working overtime; 610 thousand people were then working short-time and 1,016 thousand were working overtime. After 1981 the situation reversed, with the average number working short-time falling steadily to 28 thousand in 1985, while the average number working overtime rose to 1,329 thousand. However, in 1986 the average number working short-time rose slightly to 34 thousand, while the average number working overtime fell to 1,304 thousand. In 1987 the average number working short-time fell again to 25 thousand while the number working overtime rose to 1,359 thousand. Details of overtime hours and pay are given in Table 5.7 and its accompanying text.

There were 3.5 million working days lost through stoppages of work during 1987 in the United Kingdom caused by industrial disputes (Chart 4.18). While above the 1.9 million days lost recorded in 1986, the 1987 figure is substantially less than the annual average of 11.0 million days lost for the ten years 1977 to 1986. During the twelve months to June 1988, a provisional total of 2.1 million working days were lost, the lowest comparable June figure since 1967.

The number of stoppages recorded as being in progress in 1987 was 1,016 compared to 1,074 in 1986 and the ten year average of 1,615 for the period 1977 to 1986. However, comparisons involving the number of stoppages must be made with caution because of the

4.17 Operatives in manufacturing industries working short-time and overtime

United Kingdom

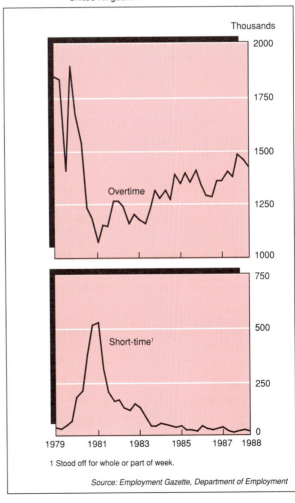

1 Stood off for whole or part of week.

Source: Employment Gazette, Department of Employment

4.18 Industrial disputes[1] — working days lost and number of stoppages

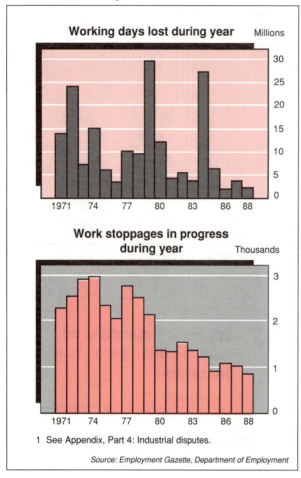

United Kingdom

Working days lost during year   Millions

Work stoppages in progress during year   Thousands

1 See Appendix, Part 4: Industrial disputes.

Source: Employment Gazette, Department of Employment

exclusion of some of the smallest stoppages from the statistics (see Appendix, Part 4: Industrial disputes).

Table 4.19 shows that in 1986 male employees in the United Kingdom usually worked more hours on average per week than their European counterparts, whereas women tended to work fewer hours than those elsewhere in the European Community. The UK male average hours at work rose by about 40 minutes between 1984 and 1986, while over the same period male employees in the Federal German Republic, France, Italy, Denmark and Greece worked on average less hours per week. Most of the rise in the United Kingdom is due to overtime as basic weekly hours are falling (see Chart 10.2).

4.19 Average hours usually worked per week [1, 2]: by sex, EC comparison, 1986

Hours

	Male	Female	All persons
United Kingdom	43.6	29.8	37.5
Belgium	38.5	32.7	36.4
Denmark	38.6	31.9	35.5
France	39.6	34.8	37.5
Germany (Fed. Rep.)	40.7	34.6	38.3
Greece	40.5	37.6	39.6
Irish Republic	41.2	36.2	39.3
Italy	39.5	35.8	38.2
Luxembourg	40.3	35.6	38.7
Netherlands [3]	40.5	28.5	36.3
Portugal	43.2	38.8	41.5
Spain	..	..	..

1 Employees only.
2 Excludes meal breaks but includes paid and unpaid overtime.
3 Figures relate to 1985.

Source: Statistical Office of the European Communities

Unemployment

Table 4.20 shows that the number of unemployed claimants in the United Kingdom rose until 1986, but fell in both 1987 and 1988. The number of claimants fell below 3 million in May 1987, the lowest it had been

in 4 years and by October 1988 was only a little above 2.1 million. Since 1986, there has been a proportionally larger fall in claimants, for both sexes, in the under 25 age groups.

4.20 Unemployed claimants [1]: annual averages

United Kingdom

Thousands

	1983	1984	1985	1986[2]	1987	1988[3]
Males						
Aged under 25	745.8	753.4	764.8	727.7	627.6	558.0
Aged 25 and over	1,475.5[5]	1,445.0	1,494.4	1,539.0	1,458.1	1,334.6
Females						
Aged under 25	461.3	479.2	479.6	460.8	385.6	339.7
Aged 25 and over	416.1	480.7	542.5	584.9	544.3	496.6
All claimants [4]	3,098.7[5]	3,158.3	3,281.3	3,312.4	3,015.6	2,729.0

1 See Appendix, Part 4: The unemployed.
2 Because of a change in the compilation of the unemployment statistics, figures from February 1986 (estimated for February 1986) are not directly comparable with earlier figures.
3 Year ending mid-1988.
4 Averages for January, April, July and October each year.
5 Comparisons of the 1983 figures and later years is affected by the provisions of the 1983 budget, whereby men mainly aged 60 and over no longer had to sign on at an Unemployment Benefit Office.

Source: Department of Employment

Social Trends 19, © Crown copyright 1989

4.21 Unemployment rate[1]: annual averages

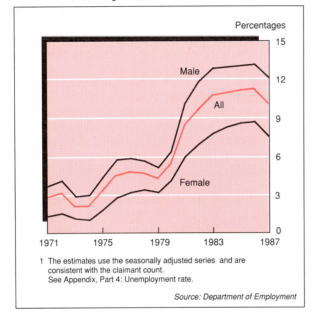

United Kingdom

1 The estimates use the seasonally adjusted series and are consistent with the claimant count. See Appendix, Part 4: Unemployment rate.

Source: Department of Employment

Chart 4.21 shows the seasonally adjusted series of unemployed consistent with the current coverage of the claimant count in the form of unemployment rates, ie expressed as percentage of the workforce - see Appendix, Part 4: Unemployment rate. It can be seen that unemployment rose very sharply in 1980 and 1981. The upward trend subsequently continued, although the rate of increase slowed down in the period up to 1986.

There was then a steady fall in the unemployment rate and in October 1988 it stood at 7.7 per cent. The male and female unemployment trends have followed a broadly similar pattern, with the male rate consistently higher than the female rate.

The Organisation for Economic Co-operation and Development (OECD) standardised rates of unemployment in selected countries are shown in Table 4.22. These rates are estimated by OECD to conform, as far as possible, to International Labour Organisation guidelines, and they are calculated as percentages of the total labour force. The term 'unemployed' covers all people who are without work, are available for work and are seeking employment for pay or profit. Between 1980 and 1982 the average unemployment rate rose in all the countries shown and in 1982 it was above 10 per cent in the United Kingdom, Spain, Belgium, Canada and the Netherlands. The unemployment rate also reached 10 per cent in Italy and in France in 1985. Between 1986 and 1988 the rate fell in all countries for which recent figures are available, but in Belgium, France and Spain remained above 10 per cent in 1988. The rate for the United Kingdom fell to some 8 per cent, in the Netherlands 9.4 per cent and Canada to 7.9 per cent.

4.22 Unemployment rates adjusted to OECD concepts [1]: international comparison

Percentages

	1976	1977	1978	1979	1980	1981	1982	1983	1984	1985	1986	1987	1988
United Kingdom	5.6	6.0	5.9	5.0	6.4	9.8	11.3	12.5	11.7	11.2	11.2	10.3	8.0 [2]
Belgium	6.4	7.4	7.9	8.2	8.8	10.8	12.6	12.1	12.1	11.3	11.2	10.9	10.2 [2]
France	4.4	4.9	5.2	5.9	6.3	7.4	8.1	8.3	9.7	10.2	10.4	10.6	10.6 [2]
Germany (Fed. Rep.)	3.7	3.6	3.5	3.2	3.0	4.4	6.1	8.0	7.1	7.2	6.5	6.5	6.6 [3]
Italy	6.6	7.0	7.1	7.6	7.5	7.8	8.4	9.3	9.9	10.1	..	..	..
Netherlands	5.5	5.3	5.3	5.4	6.0	8.5	11.4	12.0	11.8	10.6	9.9	9.6	9.4 [2]
Portugal	..	..	..	..	..	..	..	7.9	8.4	8.5	8.5	7.0	6.1 [4]
Spain	4.6	5.2	6.9	8.5	11.2	13.9	15.8	17.2	20.1	21.4	21.0	20.1	19.5 [4]
Australia	4.7	5.6	6.2	6.2	6.0	5.7	7.1	9.9	8.9	8.2	8.0	8.1	7.0 [2]
Canada	7.1	8.0	8.3	7.4	7.4	7.5	10.9	11.8	11.2	10.4	9.5	8.8	7.9 [2]
Finland	3.8	5.8	7.2	5.9	4.6	4.8	5.3	5.4	5.2	5.0	5.3	5.0	4.4 [2]
Japan	2.0	2.0	2.2	2.1	2.0	2.2	2.4	2.6	2.7	2.6	2.8	2.8	2.5 [3]
Sweden	1.6	1.8	2.2	2.1	2.0	2.5	3.2	3.5	3.1	2.8	2.7	1.9	1.6 [2]
United States	7.6	6.9	6.0	5.8	7.0	7.5	9.5	9.5	7.4	7.1	6.9	6.1	5.5 [2]

1 See Appendix, Part 4: Definition of unemployment – OECD concepts.
2 Latest month, August.
3 Latest month, July.
4 Latest month, May.

Source: Main Economic Indicators and Quarterly Labour Force Statistics, OECD

4.23 Unemployment [1]: by duration

United Kingdom

Weeks:
over/up to
- 8
- 8-26
- 26-52
- 52-104
- 104-156 [2]
- 156 [2]

1 There is a discontinuity in the data at October 1982. For more details see Appendix, Part 4: Unemployment—discontinuity.
2 Data are only available from April 1979.

Source: Department of Employment

The long-term unemployed, that is claimants unemployed for over one year, accounted for an increasing proportion of all claimants in the United Kingdom after 1979 (Chart 4.23). In July 1979 they accounted for some 25 per cent. This compares with nearly 41 per cent of all claimants in July 1988 although this proportion had been falling since 1987. The growth in long-term unemployment was concentrated among the longest duration groups. For example, the proportion of all claimants unemployed for more than five years increased from 2 per cent in July 1983 to 11 per cent in July 1988, when they numbered 263 thousand. However, the number of claimants who are long-term unemployed has begun to fall; in the year to July 1988 it fell by 290 thousand to under 1 million for the first time for more than five years, the largest annual fall on record.

Table 4.24 shows the duration of uncompleted spells of unemployment for those people who were unemployed in the United Kingdom in July 1988. Among unemployed males, 23 per cent had been unemployed for over three years and a further 22 per cent for between one and three years. The proportion of claimants who were long-term unemployed increased with age; 67 per cent of unemployed males aged 50 to 59 had been unemployed for more than a year, compared to 17 per cent of males aged 16 to 19 - although proportionally fewer of the latter group could have been unemployed for over 12 months.

The durations of unemployment for females also show comparatively high proportions of older women who were long-term unemployed. These figures are affected by women's entitlement to benefit; many married women cease signing on at an unemployment office after one year because they exhaust their entitlement to unemployment benefit and are often not subsequently entitled to income support (formerly supplementary benefit up to April 1988), for example if their husband is working.

4.24 Unemployed claimants: by sex, age, and duration, July 1988

United Kingdom

Percentages and thousands

	Duration of unemployment (weeks)						Total (= 100%) (thousands)
	Up to 13	Over 13, up to 26	Over 26, up to 52	Over 52, up to 104	Over 104, up to 156	Over 156	
Males aged:							
16—19	39.1	19.6	24.7	12.2	3.7	0.8	154.1
20—24	35.1	16.1	20.1	13.6	5.9	9.3	307.6
25—34	22.8	14.5	17.8	14.6	8.2	22.1	398.9
35—49	17.8	12.1	14.5	13.6	8.7	33.3	386.2
50—59	12.0	9.0	12.2	15.5	12.0	39.4	313.5
60 or over	25.4	19.6	29.0	11.3	3.5	11.3	46.1
All males aged 16 or over	23.5	13.8	17.3	14.0	8.0	23.4	1,606.3
Females aged:							
16—19	38.5	19.0	25.6	12.3	3.9	0.7	110.7
20—24	40.9	17.1	20.6	9.9	4.1	7.3	172.4
25—34	30.8	21.3	26.6	10.3	3.3	7.8	175.8
35—49	27.2	16.9	19.8	14.1	7.4	14.6	144.3
50 or over	13.2	10.1	14.0	14.8	11.4	36.5	116.2
All females aged 16 or over	30.8	17.2	21.6	12.0	5.7	12.6	719.4

Source: Department of Employment

4.25 Unemployed [1,2] people: by sex and reason for leaving last employment, spring 1987

Great Britain   Percentages and thousands

	Men	Women		All persons
		Married	Non-Married	
Percentage of unemployed who left last job in previous 3 years because:				
Made redundant	40	14	26	32
Temporary job ended	23	17	23	22
Resigned	10	10	15	11
Family/personal	4	40	14	14
Health reasons	5	7	8	6
Retired [3]	4	—	—	3
Other reasons/not stated	13	11	13	13
Total unemployed who left last job in previous 3 years (Thousands) (= 100%)	1,053	409	262	1,724
As percentage of all unemployed [4] (percentages)	61	61	53	60

1 Whose last employment ended less than 3 years previously.
2 ILO/OECD definition. See Appendix, Part 4: Definition of Unemployment — OECD concepts.
3 Includes early retirement.
4 Includes those who have never worked and also those who last worked more than 3 years previously.

Source: Labour Force Survey, 1987, Department of Employment

Table 4.25 shows that according to the Labour Force Survey the main reason unemployed men (using ILO/OECD definition) left their last job was because they had been made redundant. Including those whose temporary job ended this suggests that three-fifths of all males left their last job through no choice of their own. The pattern for non-married women was similar to that for men, but two-fifths of married women gave family or personal reasons as the main reason for leaving their last job.

The proportion of unemployed people (see Appendix, Part 4: GHS definition of unemployed) who reported a long-standing illness in the 1985 General Household Survey was higher than that for working people, but lower than that for those who were economically inactive. About 31 per cent of all people who were classified as unemployed said that they had a long-standing illness, and 16 per cent said that they had a long-standing illness which limited their activities. These rates were respectively 24 and 11 per cent among those who were working and 50 and 36 per cent among the economically inactive. Also the average number of GP consultations per person per year for the unemployed (4.2) was higher than that for those who were working (3.3), but lower than that for the economically inactive (5.8). Further details of GP consultations are given in Table 7.9 in *Social Trends 18*.

Table 4.26 uses combined data from the 1985-1987 Labour Force Surveys: people are classified as unemployed using the internationally recommended ILO/OECD definition based broadly, on a four week job search period (see Appendix, Part 4). The table shows lower unemployment rates for the White population than for other ethnic groups of the same sex and broad level of highest qualification held.

Problems of literacy have also been identified among the long-term unemployed. A survey of people attending a Restart Course in January 1987 indicated that a quarter had some form of literacy difficulty. To combat this problem the Training Agency offers training in basic literacy and numeracy skills as part of some of their training programmes. In 1986-87, 8,300 people were given such training on either the Wider Opportunities Training Programme or the Voluntary Projects Programme. The Community Programme and the Youth Training Scheme also offer similar training, though no information is available on the numbers involved.

4.26 Unemployment rates [1]: by ethnic group, sex and highest qualification, 1985–1987

Great Britain   Percentages

	Highest qualification			
	A-level or higher qualification [2]	Other qualification [2]	No qualification [2]	All [3]
Male [4]				
White	3	9	18	11
West Indian or Guyanese	.. [6]	24	25	24
Indian	.. [6]	13	21	15
Pakistani/Bangladeshi	.. [6]	.. [6]	31	28
Other [5]	.. [6]	18	24	17
Female [4]				
White	5	10	12	10
West Indian or Guyanese	.. [6]	24	.. [6]	18
Indian	.. [6]	19	20	18
Pakistani/Bangladeshi	.. [6]	.. [6]	.. [6]	.. [6]
Other [5]	.. [6]	20	.. [6]	16
All [4]				
White	4	10	15	11
West Indian	.. [6]	24	22	21
Indian	.. [6]	15	21	16
Pakistani/Bangladeshi	.. [6]	29	32	29
Other [5]	.. [6]	19	20	17

1 See Appendix, Part 4: Definition of unemployment — OECD concepts.
2 Higher qualifications are those at degree level or above, and those above A-level including teaching and nursing qualifications.
3 Includes those who did not state their highest qualification.
4 Males aged 16 – 64, females aged 16 – 59.
5 Includes African, Arab, Chinese, other stated and Mixed.
6 Sample size too small for reliable estimate.

Source: Labour Force Surveys. Combined data for 1985 to 1987 inclusive, Department of Employment

Employment and training measures

A number of employment and training measures have been developed in response to the rise in unemployment in the 1970s and 1980s, some of which have been phased out and replaced by other schemes. For example, the Community Programme, introduced at the end of 1982 to provide temporary work for those who had been out of work for long periods, replaced the Community Enterprise Programme. The total number supported by these measures rose sharply in the third quarter of 1981 to over 1.1 million, mainly because of the 875 thousand supported by the Temporary Short-Time Working Compensation Scheme which began in 1979 and ended in 1984 (details of short-time working in manufacturing industries are given in Chart 4.17). The underlying trend in the total number of people supported by Employment Department - Training Agency measures (see Appendix, Part 4: Employment and training measures) has been generally upwards since 1976 (Chart 4.27).

In 1986 the government introduced the Restart Programme, aimed at the long-term unemployed. Initially, all those who had been unemployed for at least 12 months were invited to an interview at a jobcentre and offered opportunities aimed at helping them back towards employment. However, in 1987 the Programme was extended to cover those who had been unemployed for 6 months or over. The opportunities offered include an interview for a job; a place on a government scheme, mainly the new Job Training Scheme which was introduced in 1987 to provide training and practical experience with an employer; a place on a Restart Course, which aims to give people the confidence and motivation to move on to other employment opportunities; a Jobstart allowance, which is a payment of £20 per week if a full-time job is taken which has a gross weekly wage of £90 or less; or a place in a Jobclub. Jobclubs help people who have been unemployed for 6 months or over by providing expert advice on finding jobs and free facilities, such as telephones and stationery. By September 1988, 1,221 Jobclubs had been opened. During 1987-88 almost 2.3 million people were interviewed under the Restart Programme and between April and September 1988 a further 1.1 million were interviewed.

On 1 September 1988 the government launched Employment Training with the slogan 'Training the workers without jobs to do the jobs without workers'. The aim of the scheme is to fill some 700 thousand job vacancies and continue the downward trend in unemployment. Employment Training represents an investment by the government of about £1.4 billion a year. Employment Training offers training at every level from basic skills to technician level skills.

4.27 Employment and training measures[1]: numbers of people supported

Great Britain

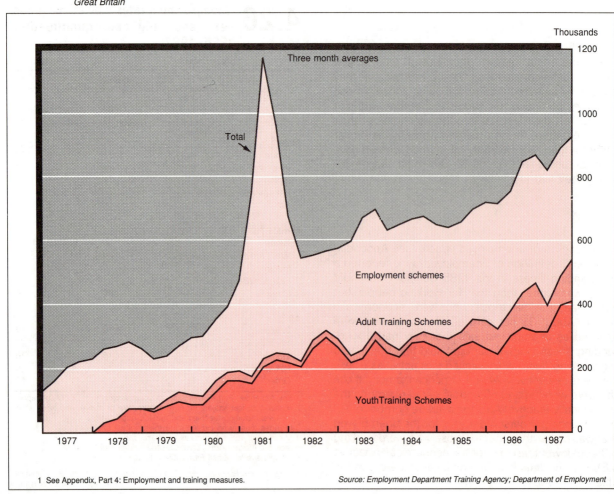

1 See Appendix, Part 4: Employment and training measures.

Source: Employment Department Training Agency; Department of Employment

4.28 Youth Training Scheme entrants and leavers

Great Britain   Thousands and percentages

	1983−84	1984−85	1985−86	1986−87	1987−88[1,2]
Entrants (thousands)					
Starts	370	397	406	420	397
Average number of training	161	267	264	296	376
Percentage of 16 − 17 year old labour market entrants					
who join YTS	45	58	58	59	. .
Percentage in training who are employees	. .	4 [4]	8	13	15
Leavers (thousands)	128	368	418	356	324
Percentage who gained a qualification	. .	27 [5]	21	21	29
Destination (percentages)					
Full-time work					
Same Employer	12 [3]	23	28	28 [6]	23
Different employer	37	32	25	29	34
Part-time work	. .	1	4	4	4
Full-time course at college/training centre	1	3	3	3	3
Different YTS Scheme	12	6	7	11	12
Other	3	2	4	3	3
Unemployed	34	32	28	23	21

1 The information on leavers in 1986 − 87 and 1987 − 88 is not representative of two year YTS as there were very few two year completers before April 1988.
2 Information for 1987 − 88 is subject to revision.
3 These figures are based on a sample of YTS trainees used in a survey of nine area offices (April 1983 to March 1984).
4 This figure is based on a sample of YTS trainees used in the nine area office survey (April 1984 to July 1984).

5 Based on an early sample follow-up survey in the period June 1984 to March 1985.
6 These figures include YTS1 leavers in the period April 1986 to September 1986. A small number of YTS1 leavers after September 1986 were not followed up.

Source: YTS Management Information System and the YTS Follow-up survey - unless otherwise stated

Estimates from Labour Force Surveys indicate that there was proportionally more job-related training for employees aged 16-19 years old in spring 1987 than for other age groups (Table 4.29). Job-related training for employees does not include government schemes such as YTS but does include day release and ad hoc tuition. Between spring 1985 and spring 1987 the percentage of 16-19 years old employees receiving job related training fell while over the same period it rose for all other age groups, for both sexes. In all age groups, apart from the oldest, men were more likely, or at least as likely, to receive job related training than women; this was especially noticeable in the younger age groups.

The Youth Training Scheme (YTS) was introduced in April 1983, providing up to 12 months training and planned work experience as an introduction to working life. In April 1986 the scheme was extended to provide two years of work-related training for 16 year old school leavers and one year for 17 year old school leavers, with opportunities for all trainees to gain recognised vocational qualifications or credits towards such qualifications. The estimated cost per place in 1987-88 was £2,600 and the estimated total cost of the scheme was £1,004 million. There was a 5 per cent reduction in the number of entrants on YTS between 1986-87 and 1987-88 Table 4.28. Over the same period the number of leavers who gained a qualification rose from 21 per cent to 29 per cent. In 1987-88 almost three-fifths of YTS leavers left for full-time work while one-fifth were unemployed.

4.29 Job-related training [1]: by sex and age

Great Britain   Percentages

	1985	1986	1987
Employees who received job-related training during 4 weeks prior to interview, as a percentage of all employees of working age [2] in band			
Males aged:			
16 − 19	29.3	26.9	25.5
20 − 24	17.9	17.7	18.1
25 − 34	12.6	13.1	14.4
35 − 49	8.7	9.3	9.9
50 − 64	3.4	3.8	4.2
Females aged:			
16 − 19	18.7	17.8	17.3
20 − 24	13.6	14.3	15.3
25 − 34	10.5	11.7	13.0
35 − 49	7.0	7.7	9.9
50 − 59	4.0	4.3	5.2

1 Includes on-the-job and/or off-the-job training, does not include people on government schemes.
2 People of working age are men aged 16 and under 65 and women aged 16 and under 60. Includes some employees still at school, who were not asked if they had received job-related training.

Source: Labour Force Surveys, Department of Employment

New Earnings Survey 1988

The results of the New Earnings Survey 1988 have been published in six separate parts, forming a comprehensive report on the survey. They are available from Her Majesty's Stationery Office, price £9.75 each net. Subscriptions for the set of six, including postage, £56.00.

The contents of the six parts are:

- *Part A*
  Streamlined analyses giving selected results for full-time employees in particular wage negotiation groups, industries, occupations, etc:
  Key results for particular wage negotiation groups.

- *Part B*
  Further streamlined analyses giving combined results for full-time adults of both sexes;
  Summary analyses for broad categories of employees irrespective of their particular industries, occupations;
  Other results for particular wage negotiationg groups;
  Description of survey method, classifications, terminology, etc.

- *Part C*
  Earnings and hours of particular industries.

- *Part D*
  Earnings and hours for particular occupations.

- *Part E*
  Earnings and hours in regions, counties and age groups.

- *Part F*
  Earnings and hours of part-time women employees.

HM Stationery Office
PO Box 276
London SW18 5DT
or
HMSO Bookshops

Chapter 5: Income and Wealth

Household income
- Real household disposable income per head rose on average by 3 per cent per year between 1981 and 1987. *(Chart 5.1 below and Table 5.2)*

- Although the difference has decreased, in 1987 a full-time female employee still earned, on average, only two-thirds of a full-time male employee's gross weekly earnings. *(Table 5.4)*

- The total number of claimants for social security benefits for the unemployed fell by 18 per cent in the year to November 1987. *(Table 5.9)*

Taxes
- The top 10 per cent of all taxpayers are estimated to pay 39 per cent of total income tax in 1988-89, a small reduction on the 41 per cent paid in 1987-88 but considerably more than the 35 per cent paid in 1981-82. *(Table 5.12)*

Income distribution
- When ranked in terms of disposable income, the top 20 per cent of households in 1986 received 42 per cent of total disposable income. In 1976, the households which then made up the top 20 per cent accounted for 38 per cent. *(Table 5.18)*

Lower incomes
- The proportion of individuals in households below half average income increased from 8 per cent in 1981 to 9 per cent in 1985. *(Table 5.20)*

Wealth
- A third of all the net wealth of the personal sector in the United Kingdom in 1987 was invested in dwellings. *(Table 5.22)*

- In early 1988 over a fifth of the adult population owned shares, nearly a three-fold increase over 1981. *(Chart 5.24)*

5.1 Real household disposable income per head

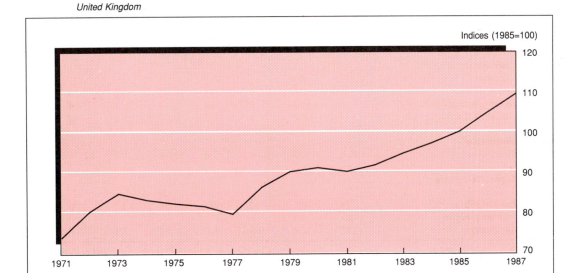

United Kingdom

Indices (1985=100)

Source: Central Statistical Office

Household Income

Real household disposable income per head in the United Kingdom is shown in Chart 5.1 and Table 5.2. This income rose in each year between 1981 and 1987. The average annual growth rate between the last peak in 1980 and 1987 was 2½ per cent. Total household disposable income in the United Kingdom rose from £36.5 billion in 1971 to £260.1 billion in 1987, a more than seven-fold increase (Table 5.2); however, after allowing for inflation the increase was 51 per cent. The increase from 1981 to 1987 was £99.7 billion, an increase of 22 per cent after allowing for inflation.

The share of total household income derived from wages and salaries fell from 68 per cent in 1971 to 60 per cent in 1986 and then rose slightly to 61 per cent in 1987. Conversely, the share of income from social security benefits increased steadily from 9 per cent in 1971 to 14 per cent in 1982 and then dropped slightly to 13 per cent in 1985, 1986 and 1987. This may be attributed partly to large increases in the number of unemployed during the early eighties, followed by a levelling out in 1983 to 1986 and a fall in 1987; see Unemployment section of Chapter 4. Another major factor has been the growing number of elderly people in the United Kingdom and this is also reflected in the increased proportion of household income from private

pensions and annuities. The proportion of total household income paid in income tax increased from 14 per cent in 1971 to 17 per cent in 1976, decreased to 14 per cent in 1979 and thereafter remained fairly steady at 15 per cent. The proportion paid in national insurance contributions remained at 3 per cent from 1971 to 1981 and then increased to 4 per cent from 1982 onwards. Chapter 6 gives details of how people spend their disposable incomes.

Earnings from employment are the main source of income for most people. One measure of changes in the level of earnings in Great Britain is the average earnings index and Chart 5.3 shows the percentage changes in this index over 12 months. The rate of increase in the index rose from about 10 per cent per year in early 1978 to levels exceeding 20 per cent per year during 1980. It then fell to below 6 per cent per year between February and August 1984, mainly because figures were affected by the dispute in the coal industry. The underlying trend rate of increase was still between 7½ and 8 per cent per year over this period. Between August 1984 and February 1987 the underlying trend remained at about 7½ per cent per year, but has since been rising gradually and stood at 9¼ per cent in September 1988.

5.2 Household income [1]: national totals

United Kingdom

	1971	1976	1981	1982	1983	1984	1985	1986	1987
Income *(percentages)*									
Wages and salaries [2]	68	68	64	62	62	61	60	60	61
Income from self-employment [3]	9	9	8	8	9	9	8	8	8
Rent, dividends, interest	7	6	6	6	6	6	7	7	7
Private pensions, annuities, etc	5	5	6	7	7	7	8	8	8
Social security benefits	9	10	13	14	14	14	13	13	13
Other current transfers [4]	2	2	2	2	3	3	3	3	3
Total household income (= 100%) (£ billion)	44.7	100.1	200.1	219.6	236.4	254.8	279.2	302.7	326.9
Direct taxes etc *(percentages of total household income)*									
Taxes on income	14	17	15	14	15	15	15	15	15
National insurance contributions [5]	3	3	3	4	4	4	4	4	4
Contributions to pension schemes	1	2	2	2	2	2	2	2	2
Total household disposable income (£ billion)	36.5	78.0	160.4	175.6	187.2	201.9	221.4	240.9	260.1
Real household disposable income per head									
(index numbers — 1985 = 100)	74	82	90	92	95	97	100	105	109
Annual change on previous year (percentages)	0.3	− 0.8	− 0.9	1.6	3.1	2.6	3.0	4.9	4.4

1 See Appendix, Part 5: The household sector.
2 Includes Forces' pay and income in kind.
3 After deducting interest payments, depreciation, and stock appreciation.

4 Mostly other government grants, but including transfers from abroad and from non-profit-making bodies.
5 By employees and the self-employed.

Source: Central Statistical Office

5.3 Average earnings index[1]

Great Britain

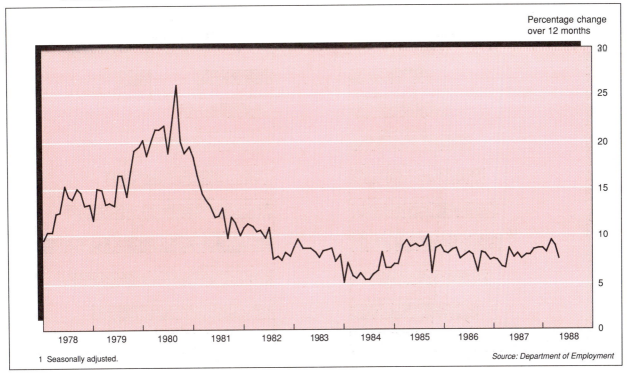

Percentage change over 12 months

1 Seasonally adjusted.

Source: Department of Employment

In the year to April 1987 the average gross weekly earnings of all full-time male employees in Great Britain receiving adult rates of pay increased by £16.50 to £224, approximately 8 per cent (Table 5.4). Over the same period manual males' wages rose by £11.10, about 6 per cent against a rise of £21.00, or 9 per cent for non-manual males.

The rates of earnings growth shown by the average earnings index in Chart 5.3 and the New Earnings Survey figures in Table 5.4 are not directly comparable. While the average earnings index in Chart 5.3 covers all employees, the New Earnings Survey figures used for Table 5.4 only cover full-time adult employees whose earnings during the survey periods were unaffected by absence.

5.4 Gross weekly earnings of full-time employees[1]: by sex

Great Britain

£ and percentages

	Males					Females				
	1971	1981	1985	1986	1987	1971	1981	1985	1986	1987
Manual employees										
Mean (£)	29.0	120.2	163.6	174.4	185.5	15.3	74.7	101.3	107.5	115.3
Median (£)	27.7	112.8	153.3	163.4	173.9	14.6	71.6	95.3	101.1	108.2
As percentage of median										
Highest decile	*147*	*151*	*155*	*155*	*157*	*143*	*143*	*150*	*150*	*153*
Lowest decile	*68*	*69*	*66*	*65*	*64*	*71*	*70*	*69*	*69*	*68*
Non-manual employees										
Mean (£)	38.5	160.5	225.0	244.9	265.9	20.0	97.5	133.8	145.7	157.2
Median (£)	34.0	147.0	202.4	219.4	235.7	18.2	87.7	122.0	131.5	142.2
As percentage of median										
Highest decile	*175*	*167*	*172*	*175*	*177*	*169*	*172*	*163*	*167*	*167*
Lowest decile	*60*	*60*	*58*	*57*	*56*	*65*	*68*	*66*	*65*	*64*
All employees										
Mean (£)	32.4	138.2	192.4	207.5	224.0	18.4	92.0	126.4	137.2	148.1
Median (£)	29.4	124.6	172.8	185.1	198.4	16.7	82.8	115.2	123.4	132.9
As a percentage of median										
Highest decile	*162*	*168*	*171*	*173*	*176*	*165*	*172*	*164*	*170*	*172*
Lowest decile	*65*	*64*	*61*	*60*	*59*	*66*	*68*	*66*	*65*	*64*

1 Figures relate to April each year and to full-time employees on adult rates whose pay for the survey pay-period was not affected by absence.

Source: New Earnings Survey, Department of Employment

5.5 Average gross weekly earnings of full-time employees[1]: by age and sex, April 1987

Great Britain

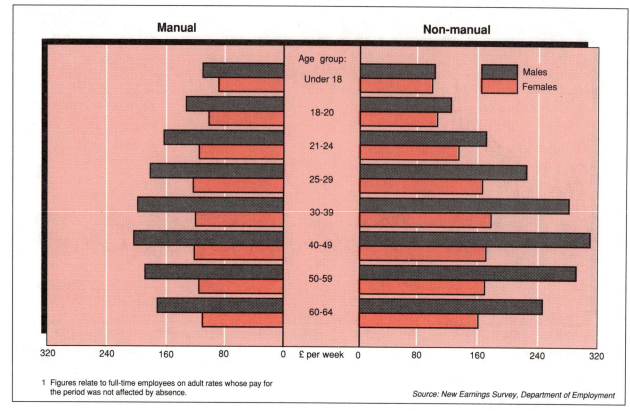

1 Figures relate to full-time employees on adult rates whose pay for the period was not affected by absence.

Source: New Earnings Survey, Department of Employment

The decile points referred to in Table 5.4 are those points on the earnings distribution which divide the observations into ten equal-sized groups. The fifth decile, or middle point is called the median. A common measure of the spread of earnings is the difference between the highest and lowest decile points as a proportion of the median. For manual males, in the year to April 1987, the spread increased by 3 percentage points; between 1971 and 1987 this difference changed by 14 percentage points. Similarly for non-manuals the change was 3 percentage points in the year to April 1987 and 6 percentage points between 1971 and 1987. These indicate a widening of the earnings distribution but they do not show what has happened to particular groups. This is analysed further in the discussion of Chart 5.6 below.

The average gross weekly earnings of all full-time female employees on adult rates in April 1987 was just over £148, nearly 8 per cent higher than in April 1986. On average manual female employees earned 73 per cent of the earnings of non-manual female employees, about the same as in 1986. Manual male employees earned, on average, 70 per cent of the earnings of their non-manual counterparts in 1987.

Average gross earnings vary over the working life of wage-earners and are affected by promotion, long service awards, changes in the amount of overtime working and the taking of less physically demanding jobs in later life. Earnings, on average, rise during the earlier years of work, then fall back (Table 5.5). For male employees average gross weekly earnings peak in the 40 to 49 year age group. For female employees the peak is between 30 and 39 years for non-manuals and between 25 and 29 years for manuals.

Chart 5.6 shows the percentage increase in earnings, adjusted for inflation, for various occupational groups over the periods 1973 to 1979 and 1979 to 1986. The New Earnings Survey, upon which the chart is based, codes the occupational descriptions on the survey forms into over 450 specific occupations, which are in turn placed into 18 broad occupational groups. The General Management group is too small to give reliable statistics and is therefore excluded from the chart. The occupation groups are shown in order of their average level of earnings in 1979. Over the period 1973 to 1979, the occupational groups which experienced a fall in real earnings were all towards the top of the earnings distribution. This resulted in a narrowing of the earnings distribution, which may have been caused at least partly by incomes policy, especially in the phases of a flat rate limit rather than a percentage increase limit and where there were cut-offs above specific salary levels. In the period from 1979 to 1980 the real earnings of all occupational groups increased, which was not the case in the earlier period; the highest percentage increases were for those in the highest earning occupation groups whilst the occupations which did least well are concentrated in the middle of the distribution. Thus while the earlier narrowing of the earnings distribution was reversed and the distribution widened in the 1980s, it was not the groups with the lowest average earnings that did least well.

5.6 Changes in real earnings for men: by occupation group,[1,2] 1973 to 1979 and 1979 to 1986

Great Britain

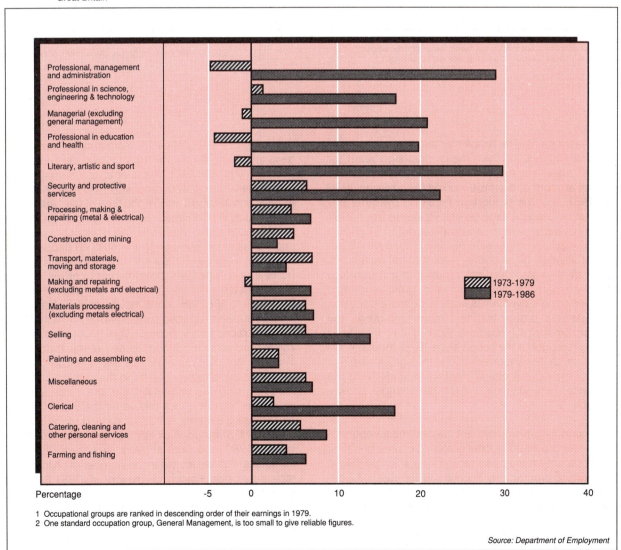

1 Occupational groups are ranked in descending order of their earnings in 1979.
2 One standard occupation group, General Management, is too small to give reliable figures.

Source: Department of Employment

5.7 Overtime: pay and hours worked by full-time employees [1], by sex

Great Britain

	Males					Females				
	1976	1981	1985	1986	1987	1976	1981	1985	1986	1987
Manual employees										
Average weekly overtime pay (£)	8.5	14.4	23.8	25.1	27.0	1.0	2.5	5.2	5.1	6.2
Overtime pay as a percentage of average gross earnings	*13*	*12*	*15*	*14*	*15*	*3*	*3*	*5*	*5*	*5*
Average weekly overtime hours [2]	5.3	4.4	5.4	5.4	5.5	0.8	1.0	1.5	1.4	1.6
Percentage receiving overtime pay	*54*	*46*	*54*	*54*	*55*	*14*	*15*	*24*	*23*	*25*
Non-manual employees										
Average weekly overtime pay (£)	2.3	4.6	8.6	9.0	9.2	0.4	1.1	2.4	2.7	3.1
Overtime pay as percentage of average gross earnings	*3*	*3*	*4*	*4*	*4*	*1*	*1*	*2*	*2*	*2*
Average weekly overtime hours [2]	1.3	1.3	1.6	1.5	1.5	0.3	0.4	0.5	0.6	0.6
Percentage receiving overtime pay	*18*	*18*	*22*	*22*	*21*	*8*	*10*	*15*	*16*	*16*

1 Figures relate to April each year and to full-time employees (more than 30 normal basic hours per week) on adult rates whose pay for the survey pay-period was not affected by absence.

2 Actual hours of overtime worked for which overtime earnings were paid.

Source: New Earnings Survey, Department of Employment

Basic earnings may be supplemented by earnings from overtime (Table 5.7). Overtime is most significant for manual male employees. For these employees the average amount of overtime worked fell between 1976 and 1981, and the proportion receiving overtime pay dropped by 8 percentage points. However, from 1981 to 1987 average overtime hours increased to 5½ hours per week and overtime earnings accounted for 15 per cent of average gross earnings for manual males. For non-manual males overtime represents a much less important part of their hours and gross earnings; however, unpaid overtime is likely to be more common amongst this group. For all female employees the average amount of overtime worked has increased steadily throughout the period since 1976, though it still plays a much less important part in their gross earnings than for males. It is one of the factors underlying the differences between male and female earnings shown in Table 5.4.

After income from employment the next most important source of household income is social security benefits. Social security remains by far the largest single public expenditure programme, accounting for about 32 per cent of public expenditure in the United Kingdom in 1987-88. Of all social security benefits retirement pensions are by far the largest component, accounting for 40 per cent of the total expenditure on social security benefits in Great Britain in 1987-88 (Table 5.8). In line with the growth in the number of elderly people in the population, the number of recipients of retirement pensions rose by more than 7 per cent between 1981-82 and 1987-88. Recipients of unemployment benefit fell from 1,220 thousand in 1981-82 to 845 thousand in 1987-88 and, at the time of the 1988 public expenditure White Paper, were expected to fall further to 755 thousand in 1988-89. This does not necessarily imply a fall in the number of unemployed people, since unemployment benefit is a contributory benefit paid for up to a year, after which entitlement ceases and the means-tested income support (or supplementary benefit up to 1987-88) alone may be paid. In April 1988, income support replaced supplementary benefit, family credit replaced family income supplement (FIS) and the social fund was introduced, all part of the *1986 Social Security Act;* for more details see the Low Income section of this chapter. The fall in the number of people receiving sickness benefit reflects the introduction of employers' statutory sick pay under the *Social Security and Housing Benefits Act 1982.* As part of the Act, the *Employers' Statutory Sick Pay Scheme* was introduced in April 1983; see Time at Work section of Chapter 4 for details. The steady fall in the number of child benefit recipients, from over 13 million in 1981-82 to a projection of just over 12 million in 1988-89 is due to the fall in the birth rate in the mid-seventies. Child benefit is a non-taxable, non-contributory benefit paid in respect of each child under 16, or under 19 if still at school.

5.8 Social security benefits: public expenditure and estimated numbers of recipients

Great Britain

£ million and thousands

	Expenditure[1] (£ million)				Recipients[1, 2] (thousands)			
	1981-82 outturn	1986-87 outturn	1987-88 estimated outturn	1988-89 plans	1981-82	1986-87	1987-88	1988-89
National insurance benefits								
Pension benefits								
Retirement pensions	12,126	17,771	18,725	19,312	9,015	9,575	9,690	9,735
Invalidity benefit	1,370	2,673	2,986	3,211	660	935	995	1,040
Industrial disablement benefit	315	440	446	439	195	200	200	205
Widow's benefits and industrial death benefit	738	886	894	928	490	430	410	395
Lump-sum payment to contributory pensioners	101	107	107	108	10,100	10,700	10,800	10,900
Other benefits								
Unemployment benefit	1,702	1,734	1,543	1,481	1,220	1,005	845	755
Sickness benefit[3]	680	179	166	167	445	100	90	90
Death grant[4]	17	18	.	.	600	640	.	.
Maternity allowance[5]	158	168	67	43	125	110	40	25
Non-contributory benefits								
Pension benefits								
Non-contributory retirement pension	39	45	44	44	50	40	35	35
War pension	479	589	589	592	345	280	265	255
Attendance allowance and invalid care allowance[6]	336	883	1,013	1,065	355	630	740	770
Severe disablement allowance[7]	130	285	306	307	180	265	265	265
Mobility allowance	173	514	596	663	210	435	495	540
Lump-sum payments to non-contributory pensioners	6	8	8	7	600	700	700	700
Other benefits								
Supplementary pensions[8]	1,418	1,178	1,260	.	1,740	1,835	1,875	.
Supplementary allowances[8]	3,422	6,789	6,829	.	1,985	3,285	3,285	.
Income support	.	.	.	8,584	.	.	.	4,925
Child benefit	3,372	4,513	4,608	4,528	13,145	12,175	12,090	12,015
Family income supplement	66	161	165	.	125	215	210	.
Family credit	.	.	.	409	.	.	.	470
One-parent benefit	76	148	160	169	470	615	635	665
Maternity grant[4]	16	14	.	.	640	560	.	.
Housing benefit — rent rebates and allowances	562	3,368	3,620	3,874	1,840	4,900	5,010	4,465
Social Fund[9]	.	.	33	164	.	.	.	.
Administrative and miscellaneous services	1,273	1,937	2,231	2,362	.	.	.	.

1 Some small items (other industrial benefits, guardian's allowance and child's special allowance) included in *Cm 288* are omitted.
2 Estimated average number receiving benefit on any one day, except for lump-sum payments, death grant, maternity grant and social fund payments which (because they are single payments) are the total number paid in each year. The child benefit figures relate to the number of qualifying children. See Appendix, Part 5: Social Security benefits.
3 Reflects the introduction of statutory sick pay from April 1983 and its extension to 28 weeks from April 1986.
4 Death grant and maternity grant were abolished in April 1987 and were replaced by payments from the Social Fund.
5 Reflects the introduction of payments through employers from April 1987.

6 Reflects the extension of invalid care allowance to married women which was announced in June 1986. Expenditure in 1986-87 includes substantial arrears.
7 Includes non-contributory invalidity pension.
8 In 1986-87 and 1987-88 the number of recipients includes those receiving housing benefit supplement (some 440,000 in 1987-88) who are also included in the housing benefit recipients.
9 Social Fund provision for 1988-89 is expenditure after repayment of loans.

Source: The Government's Expenditure Plans (Cm 288), HM Treasury; Government Actuary's Department

Not all of those who are entitled to social security benefits claim their entitlement. Take-up varies according to the type of benefit, for example, latest available figures indicate that, in 1984, 54 per cent of people entitled to FIS actually claimed it, compared with 77 per cent for housing benefit and very nearly 100 per cent for retirement pensions and child benefit.

The number of unemployed men claiming social security benefits in Great Britain fell between November 1986 and November 1987 from 2.1 million to 1.7 million

(Table 5.9). Over 18 per cent of the male claimants received only unemployment benefit in November 1987, while over 61 per cent received supplementary benefit alone. Approximately 6 per cent claimed both benefits. The remainder received no benefit because, for example, either they may not have paid enough national insurance contributions or they may have exhausted their right to unemployment benefit but have sufficient savings to be ineligible for supplementary benefit. The percentage of claimants receiving unemployment benefit at any point in time has fallen since 1981, while

5.9 Social security benefits for the unemployed [1, 2]

Great Britain

Percentages and thousands

	1961	1971	1976	1981	1985	1986	1987
Unemployed male claimants receiving *(percentages)*:							
Unemployment benefit only	47.2	40.9	30.0	28.2	18.1	20.2	18.3
Unemployment and supplementary benefits	9.4	13.6	10.9	11.4	8.0	7.5	6.2
Supplementary benefit only	21.9	27.1	42.4	46.0	61.8	59.3	61.4
No benefit	21.6	18.4	16.6	14.4	12.1	13.0	14.1
Total unemployed male claimants (= 100%) (thousands)	283	721	1,076	1,994	2,074	2,086	1,742
Unemployed female claimants receiving *(percentages)*:							
Unemployment benefit only	39.7	41.0	29.1	38.9	32.0	33.5	30.1
Unemployment and supplementary benefits	2.5	6.7	3.9	3.8	2.9	2.7	2.5
Supplementary benefit only	12.2	20.5	44.6	37.4	43.1	40.8	44.0
No benefit	45.5	31.8	22.4	20.0	22.0	23.0	23.4
Total unemployed female claimants (= 100%) (thousands)	101	138	380	709	949	955	766

1 At November each year except for 1976 when figures relate to August, 1981 when figures for February 1982 are quoted.
2 Prior to 1981 count of registered unemployed ; for 1981 count of registered unemployed claimants ; after then , count of unemployed claimants. See Appendix, Part 5: Unemployed claimants.

Source: Department of Health and Social Security

the percentage receiving supplementary benefit has increased, thus reflecting the increase in the number of long-term unemployed (ie those unemployed for over 52 weeks). The total number of female claimants also decreased between November 1986 and November 1987, from 955 thousand to 766 thousand.

Chart 5.10 shows the real values of unemployment benefit and the state retirement pension, ie after allowing for inflation as measured by the retail prices index. The rates shown are for a married couple claiming on the basis of the man's national insurance contributions. Increases were made, in November for the years 1981 to 1985, in July 1986 and in April for

years 1987 and 1988, between which the real value of the benefits were eroded by increasing prices. These benefit upratings are currently announced in the autumn and are based on the annual change in the retail prices index recorded in September. Thus, depending on the rate of inflation between September and the following April when the new rates are implemented, the uprating may under-or-over-compensate for the effects of increasing prices. In 1982 when the inflation rate was high but falling the uprating was larger than was needed to restore the November 1981 purchasing power, but in 1987 when the inflation rate was low but rising the uprating failed to restore the April 1986 purchasing power.

5.10 Real values[1] of unemployment benefit and retirement pension

United Kingdom

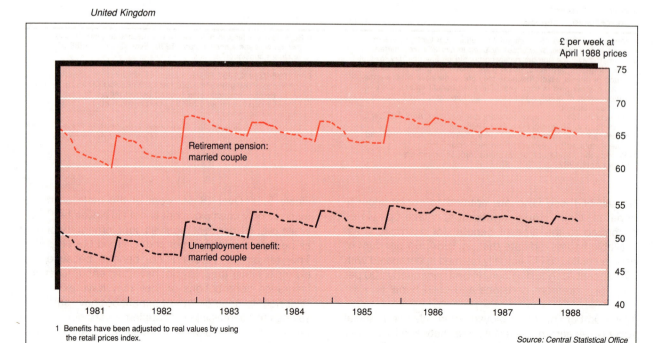

£ per week at April 1988 prices

1 Benefits have been adjusted to real values by using the retail prices index.

Source: Central Statistical Office

Taxes

5.11 Income tax payable: by range of total annual income [1], 1988-89 [2]

United Kingdom

| | Total annual income (£ million) | Tax payable at basic rate | | Tax payable at higher rate | | Total tax payable (£ million) | Average rate of tax payable (%) | Average amount of tax payable (£) |
		Number of tax units [3] (millions)	Amount [4] (£ million)	Number of tax units [3] (millions)	Amount (£ million)			
Annual income								
£2,500 but under £5,000	9,874	2.6	654	0	0	654	*7*	256
£5,000 but under £7,500	23,117	3.7	2,586	0	0	2,586	*11*	700
£7,500 but under £10,000	29,101	3.3	3,768	0	0	3,768	*13*	1,133
£10,000 but under £15,000	63,631	5.2	8,803	0	0	8,803	*14*	1,701
£15,000 but under £20,000	49,749	2.9	7,379	0	0	7,379	*15*	2,563
£20,000 but under £30,000	54,148	2.3	9,026	0.4	115	9,141	*17*	4,011
£30,000 and over	47,738	1.0	9,682	0.9	2,493	12,175	*26*	12,088
All ranges	277,358	20.9	41,898	1.2	2,608	44,506	*16*	2,128

1 Total income for income tax purposes including earned and investment income. All figures in the table relate to taxpayers only.
2 Based on a projection from the 1985-86 Survey of Personal Incomes.
3 A tax unit is a married couple or a single person over school-leaving age but not in full-time education.
4 Including the basic rate component of tax payable at higher rate.

Source: Inland Revenue

In the tax year 1988-89 it is estimated that some 20.9 million tax units (single people and married couples) will pay income tax of £44.5 billion (Table 5.11). Of these, 1.2 million tax units will have some of their income taxed at the higher rate of 40 per cent, while the remaining 19.7 million will pay at the basic rate of 25 per cent only. This progressive structure results in average rates of tax payable on total income ranging from 7 per cent for the 2.6 million taxpayers with incomes between £2,500 and £5,000 per year up to 26 per cent for the 1.0 million taxpayers with incomes above £30,000 a year.

Tax rates have been reduced considerably since 1978-79. The basic rate has been cut from 33 per cent to 25 per cent, the higher rates of tax which rose to a maximum of 83 per cent have been replaced by one 40 per cent rate, and the surcharge of up to 15 per cent on investment income has been abolished. Nonetheless income tax paid has risen as earnings and other sources of income have increased and the proportion of tax paid by the top taxpayers has steadily increased. In 1981-82,

the top 10 per cent of taxpayers paid 35 per cent of the total, the same proportion as in 1976-77, but by 1987-88 the proportion had increased to 41 per cent (Table 5.12). The 1988 Budget cuts which cut the top rate of tax from 60 per cent to 40 per cent have reduced that proportion to 39 per cent in 1988-89. The bottom 50 per cent of taxpayers pay only 17 per cent of total income tax.

In contrast to income tax, employee's contributions to national insurance (NI) have not in general decreased. For example, for a single person on average earnings who is not contracted out of the state-earnings related pension scheme, NI contributions increased from 7.7 per cent in 1981-82 to 9.0 per cent in 1983-84 and subsequently stayed at 9.0 per cent (Table 5.13). The average rate of income tax however fell from 23.7 per cent in 1981-82 to 19.0 per cent in 1988-89. In October 1985, reduced rates of NI contributions of 5 per cent and 7 per cent were introduced for the low paid and these have helped, for example, reduce the NI

5.12 Shares of total income tax liability

United Kingdom

Percentages and £ billion

	1976 -77	1981 -82	1982 -83	1983 -84	1984 -85	1985 -86	1986 -87[2]	1987 -88[2]	1988 -89[2]
Quantile groups of taxpayers									
Top 1 per cent	*11*	*11*	*12*	*11*	*12*	*14*	*14*	*15*	*13*
Top 5 per cent	*25*	*25*	*25*	*26*	*26*	*28*	*29*	*30*	*28*
Top 10 per cent	*35*	*35*	*36*	*36*	*38*	*39*	*40*	*41*	*39*
Next 40 per cent	*45*	*46*	*46*	*47*	*45*	*44*	*43*	*42*	*44*
Lower 50 per cent	*20*	*19*	*18*	*17*	*17*	*17*	*17*	*17*	*17*
All taxpayers (£ billion = 100%)	18.3	30.3	32.4	33.4	35.4	39.5	41.9	44.1	44.5

1 Counting married couples as one and combining their incomes.
2 Estimates are based on a projection of the 1985–86 Survey of Personal Incomes and are provisional.

Source: Inland Revenue

5.13 Percentage of income paid in income tax and national insurance contributions [1]: by marital status and level of earnings [2]

United Kingdom

Percentages

	1981–82	1982–83	1983–84	1984–85	1985–86	1986–87	1987–88	1988–89[3]
Single person								
Half average earnings [2]								
Tax	17.5	16.7	16.0	15.3	14.9	14.5	13.9	13.0
NIC	7.7	8.7	9.0	9.0	7.0	7.0	7.0	7.0
Average earnings [2]								
Tax	23.7	23.4	23.0	22.7	22.4	21.7	20.4	19.0
NIC	7.7	8.7	9.0	9.0	9.0	9.0	9.0	9.0
Twice average earnings [2]								
Tax	27.3	26.7	26.5	26.3	26.2	25.4	23.7	22.0
NIC	6.1	7.1	7.2	7.1	7.1	7.2	6.9	6.6
Married couple [4]								
Half average earnings [2]								
Tax	10.5	9.3	8.0	6.9	6.3	6.3	6.5	6.1
NIC	7.7	8.7	9.0	9.0	7.0	7.0	7.0	7.0
Average earnings [2]								
Tax	20.2	19.6	19.0	18.5	18.1	17.6	16.7	15.5
NIC	7.7	8.7	9.0	9.0	9.0	9.0	9.0	9.0
Twice average earnings [2]								
Tax	25.1	24.8	24.5	24.2	24.1	23.3	21.9	20.3
NIC	6.1	7.1	7.2	7.1	7.1	7.2	6.9	6.6

1 Employees' contributions. Assumes contributions at Class 1, contracted in, standard rate.
2 Earnings are average earnings for full-time adult male manual employees working a full week on adult rates.
3 1987-88 based projections.
4 Assuming wife not in paid employment.

Source: Inland Revenue

contribution rate for those on half average earnings. At the top of the income scale, average NI contributions have fallen slightly as a percentage of earnings because earnings have grown more quickly than the Upper Earnings Limit above which NI contributions are not paid.

The combined effect of changes in gross earnings, income tax, NI contributions and child benefit are illustrated in Table 5.14. Net earnings, after allowing for inflation, have increased at the median point of the earnings distribution by 18 per cent or more between 1981 and 1987 for each of the types of family shown. However the widening of the earnings distribution has caused the increases at the top of the distribution to be larger and at the bottom to be much less. For example, the married man with no children at the highest decile point has received an increase of 26 per cent, compared with 19 per cent at the median, and 12 per cent at the lowest decile point. Changes in the distribution of earnings do not necessarily indicate the movement in earnings of an individual. They are caused by several factors and one of the most important is the change in the structure of employment.

5.14 Real [1] weekly earnings [2] after income tax, national insurance contributions and child benefit: by selected family type

Great Britain

£ and percentages

	1971	1981	1985	1986	1987	Percentage change 1971–1981	Percentage change 1981–1987
Single man							
Lowest decile point	71.3	79.2	82.5	85.5	88.1	11.1	11.1
Median	105.5	111.5	126.9	133.2	139.6	11.4	18.7
Highest decile point	166.8	191.5	210.8	224.2	241.2	14.8	26.0
Single woman							
Lowest decile point	45.7	59.1	64.9	67.1	68.9	29.3	16.6
Median	63.8	81.7	89.1	93.3	97.7	28.1	19.6
Highest decile point	99.5	132.5	137.8	149.1	158.7	33.2	19.8
Married man [3], no children							
Lowest decile point	76.5	85.3	90.3	93.2	95.2	11.5	11.6
Median	110.6	123.6	134.6	140.8	146.7	11.8	18.7
Highest decile point	172.0	197.6	218.5	231.8	248.3	14.9	25.7
Married man [3], 2 children [4]							
Lowest decile point	88.6	98.4	105.0	107.8	109.7	9.8	11.5
Median	123.6	136.7	149.3	155.4	161.2	10.6	17.9
Highest decile point	185.0	210.6	233.2	246.4	262.8	13.8	24.8

1 At April 1987 prices.
2 Figures relate to April each year and to full-time employees on adult rates whose pay for the survey pay-period was not affected by absence.
3 Assuming no wife's earnings.
4 Aged under 11.

Source: Inland Revenue, from New Earnings Survey

5.15 Mortgage interest tax relief: by income range, 1987–88

United Kingdom

Annual income [2]	Number of tax units [1] receiving mortgage interest relief (thousands)	Average value of relief per mortgage (£ per annum)	Total cost of relief (£ million)
Under £5,000	690	360	250
£5,000 but under £10,000	2,010	440	880
£10,000 but under £15,000	2,640	520	1,360
£15,000 but under £20,000	1,700	540	910
£20,000 but under £25,000	750	600	450
£25,000 but under £30,000	370	830	310
£30,000 and over	590	1,090	640
All ranges	8,750	550	4,800

1 A tax unit is a married couple or a single person over school-leaving age who is not in full-time education.
2 Excludes non-taxable income such as certain social security benefits.

Source: Inland Revenue

Tax relief is available on a loan to purchase a property in the United Kingdom, provided that the house is used as the borrower's main residence. In 1987-88, 8.75 million tax units received a total of £4.8 billion in mortgage interest tax relief (Table 5.15). The average value of relief per mortgage increased with annual income up to £1,090 for those with incomes over £30,000 per year in 1987-88.

Table 5.16 shows how selected countries collect revenue in taxes and social security contributions. Over the ten years to 1985 the percentage of the total taxes and social security contributions paid in direct taxes by households in the United Kingdom fell from 39 per cent to 28 per cent. This was offset by increases in the proportion accounted for by corporations, social security contributions paid by employees and indirect taxes (see also Table 5.13).

5.16 Taxes and social security contributions as a percentage of total taxes and social security contributions: by category, international comparison

Percentages

	Direct Taxes		Social Security Contributions		Indirect taxes	Taxes on capital	Total
	Paid by households	Paid by corporations	Paid by employers	Paid by employees			
United Kingdom							
1975	39	6	11	7	36	1	100
1981	30	9	9	7	43	1	100
1985	28	13	9	9	41	1	100
Germany (Fed. Rep.)							
1975	27	4	18	20	32	—	100
1981	26	4	18	21	31	—	100
1985	25	5	18	21	30	—	100
United States							
1975	34	12	11	10	32	1	100
1981	39	9	12	10	28	1	100
1985	37	8	13	12	29	1	100
France							
1975	14	6	30	11	39	1	100
1981	15	6	29	14	36	1	100
1985	15	5	28	16	35	1	100
Japan							
1975	22	20	14	14	29	1	100
1981	24	18	15	14	28	1	100
1985	24	19	15	14	28	1	100
Sweden							
1975	46	2	18	1	32	—	100
1981	40	2	28	1	29	—	100
1985	39	3	24	1	33	—	100

Source: Central Statistical Office

Income distribution

This section details some of the distributive effects on personal and household income of the government's tax-benefit system.

Directly or indirectly most government revenue is raised from households, and its expenditure benefits households, one of the consequences of which is to even out the distribution of income. Initially households receive income from various sources: from their employment (that is, wages and salaries and income from self-employment); from occupational pensions; from their investments; and from other households (for instance gifts and alimony payments). Total income from these sources is defined as original income. The addition to original income of cash benefits paid by the state, such as retirement pensions and supplementary benefit, yields gross income, from which income tax payments and national insurance contributions are deducted to produce disposable income. Final income is obtained by deducting payments of indirect taxes, such as VAT and rates, and then adding the imputed benefits to households from government expenditure on certain services such as education and health.

The quintile group with the lowest original income derived over 96 per cent of gross income from cash benefits (Table 5.17). This is because a negligible number of adults in these households had worked in the previous year and over half were pensioners. Although the tax liability of this group was negligible, tax relief was still given at source on payments of premiums for life assurance policies, resulting in a net gain from the income tax system. In the second lowest quintile group over 47 per cent of the adults had retired but many more of these had occupational pensions to supplement their state pensions. This group was also far less reliant on non-contributory benefits, such as supplementary benefit. Over the three higher quintile groups, the number of economically active people increased. The top fifth had a strong reliance on earnings, usually with more than one salary coming in, thus over 89 per cent of their gross income was derived from earnings.

Indirect taxes include Value Added Tax paid in respect of goods purchased and customs and excise duties paid on commodities such as petrol and alcohol. Therefore

5.17 Redistribution of income through taxes and benefits, all households [1], 1986

United Kingdom   £ per year and numbers

	Quintile groups of households ranked by original income					All house-holds
	Bottom fifth	Next fifth	Middle fifth	Next fifth	Top fifth	
Average per household (£ per year[2])						
Earnings of main earner	10	1,420	5,980	9,400	16,050	6,570
Earnings of others in the household	—	80	710	2,760	6,720	2,050
Occupational pensions, annuities	50	770	720	480	620	530
Investment income	50	400	480	430	1,180	510
Other income	10	130	130	110	220	120
Total original income	130	2,800	8,030	13,180	24,790	9,790
+ Benefits in cash						
Contributory	1,750	1,880	740	380	270	1,000
Non-contributory	1,620	840	510	490	410	780
Gross income	3,500	5,520	9,280	14,060	25,470	11,570
— Income tax[3] and NIC[4]	— 10[6]	330	1,490	2,880	5,650	2,070
Disposable income	3,510	5,200	7,790	11,170	19,820	9,500
— Indirect taxes	880	1,540	2,280	2,900	4,250	2,370
+ Benefits in kind						
Education	370	450	650	850	850	630
National Health Service	910	870	730	710	720	790
Travel subsidies	50	60	50	50	100	60
Housing subsidy	130	80	50	30	20	60
Welfare foods	50	40	30	20	20	30
Final income	4,130	5,150	7,020	9,940	17,260	8,700
Average per household (numbers)						
Adults	1.4	1.7	1.9	2.2	2.6	2.0
Children	0.4	0.4	0.7	0.8	0.7	0.6
Economically active people[5]	—	0.6	1.2	1.8	2.2	1.2
Retired people	0.8	0.8	0.3	0.1	0.1	0.4
Number of households in sample	1,435	1,436	1,436	1,435	1,436	7,178

1 These estimates are based on the Family Expenditure Survey. See Appendix, Part 5: Redistribution of income.
2 Rounded to the nearest £10.
3 After tax relief at source on mortgage interest and life assurance premiums.
4 Employees' national insurance contributions.

5 Comprising employees, the self-employed and others not in employment but who were seeking or intending to seek work, but excluding those away from work for more than 1 year.
6 Negative average tax payments result largely from imputed tax relief on life assurance premiums paid by those with nil or negligible tax liabilities.

Source: Central Statistical Office, from Family Expenditure Survey

the amount of indirect tax paid by a household increases with expenditure and thus, in general, with disposable income.

The net effect of the tax-benefit system is to raise the final income of households in the lower part of the income distribution and reduce the income of those in the higher quintile groups. The bottom quintile group has an average annual original income of £130 and an average final income of £4,130, whereas the average original income of the top quintile group is £24,790 compared with an average final income of £17,260.

For the bottom 20 per cent of households in the United Kingdom the 1986 figures represent a continuing trend in the reduction of their share of total original, disposable and final incomes (Table 5.18). This group's share of original income fell sharply in the early eighties. This fall was partly but not wholly compensated by the payment of cash benefits and the group's share of disposable and final income also fell. In contrast, the top quintile group gained a larger share of the original, disposable and final incomes. The table also shows that benefits in kind and indirect taxes when taken together have little effect, since the shares of disposable and final income, especially in 1986, are very similar.

However in making these comparisons it should be borne in mind that the composition of each quintile group also may change over time. For example, in 1985 the lowest quintile group contained fewer retired households and more families with children than in 1976. They have different sources of income, different needs for cash benefits, different consumption patterns and make different demands on services. Thus at least part of the change in income shares is because the mix of households within each quintile group has changed.

The changing distribution of original income is similar to the widening distribution of earnings mentioned in the Household Income section of this chapter (Table 5.4, Chart 5.6), but it should be noted that economically inactive people were not included there and the household units here are distinct from the individuals used in that section.

5.18 Distribution of original, disposable and final household income

United Kingdom   Percentages

| | Quintile groups of households | | | | | |
	Bottom fifth	Next fifth	Middle fifth	Next fifth	Top fifth	Total
Original income[1]						
1976	0.8	9.4	18.8	26.6	44.4	100.0
1981	0.6	8.1	18.0	26.9	46.4	100.0
1985	0.3	6.0	17.2	27.3	49.2	100.0
1986	0.3	5.7	16.4	26.9	50.7	100.0
Disposable income[2]						
1976	7.0	12.6	18.2	24.1	38.1	100.0
1981	6.7	12.1	17.7	24.1	39.4	100.0
1985	6.5	11.3	17.3	24.3	40.6	100.0
1986	5.9	11.0	16.9	24.1	42.2	100.0
Final income[3]						
1976	7.4	12.7	18.0	24.0	37.9	100.0
1981	7.1	12.4	17.9	24.0	38.6	100.0
1985	6.7	11.8	17.4	24.0	40.2	100.0
1986	5.9	11.4	17.0	23.9	41.7	100.0

1 Households ranked by original income.
2 Households ranked by disposable income.
3 Households ranked by final income.

Source: Central Statistical Office, from Family Expenditure Survey

Lower Incomes

Poorer families, both in and out of work, are eligible for a number of benefits and in April 1988 some major changes to the benefit system were implemented. Child benefit continues to be paid to all families with children as a flat-rate non-taxable benefit in respect of each child, but elsewhere there are changes. Supplementary benefit, the main benefit for those not working and having insufficient means, was replaced by the much simpler income support, while family income supplement, payable to low income working families with children, was replaced by the new family credit. Housing benefit, which helps low income families with their rent and rates, was also revised.

One major difference between the new system and the old is that family credit and housing benefit are based on net rather than gross incomes. This has the effect of greatly reducing the scope of the 'poverty trap' which describes the situation in which an increase in gross earnings could be more than offset by consequential increases in tax and national insurance contributions, together with reductions in benefits. This improvement is illustrated in Chart 5.19.

Chart 5.19 shows the net income after housing costs of three different family types earning between £50 and £200 per week, before and after the April 1988 social security changes. It is assumed here that they have no other income other than the earnings of the head of household and social security benefits, for which the full entitlement is claimed, that they have only their personal tax allowances, that they live in local authority rented accommodation and are not contracted out of the state pension scheme. Average local authority rent and rates are deducted from their incomes and the value of free welfare milk and school meals are added, where relevant, to arrive at net income after housing costs.

In general net income after housing costs increases with gross income. But in April 1987 there were also some ranges of gross income over which net income after housing costs fell. For example, a married couple with three children with gross earnings of £73 would have net income after housing costs about £6.20 greater than a similar family with gross earnings of £126. In April 1988, because of the changes in the benefit structure, there are no longer any such ranges of income over which net income after housing costs falls as gross earnings rise.

5.19 Net income after housing costs[1]: by level of gross earnings[2] and type of family, April 1987 and April 1988

Great Britain

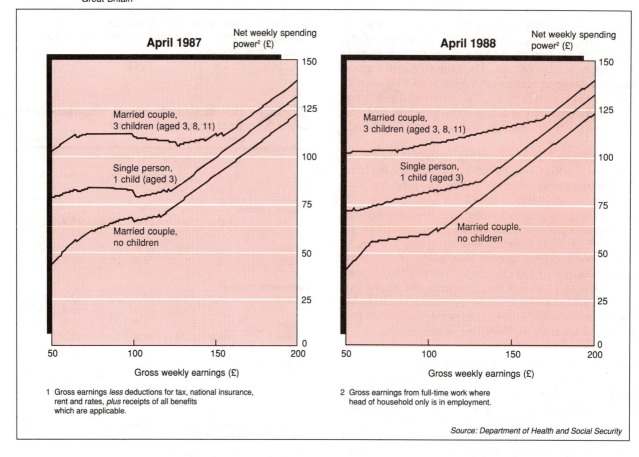

1 Gross earnings *less* deductions for tax, national insurance, rent and rates, *plus* receipts of all benefits which are applicable.

2 Gross earnings from full-time work where head of household only is in employment.

Source: Department of Health and Social Security

Tables 5.17 and 5.18 rank households by income and show the distribution of income by quintiles. Table 5.20 and Chart 5.21 provide an alternative perspective and compare income with the average income of all households. All incomes are before housing costs and are adjusted to take account of household size and composition. It is important to stress that the average income used in each case is not the same. In Table 5.20 the average is the average income for the year in question, whereas in Chart 5.21 the average is the average income for 1981 which is then inflated, using the retail prices index, to 1985 price levels, in order to maintain its real value.

5.20 Proportions of individuals in households with below average income [1]: by income threshold and economic status [2]

Great Britain

Percentages and thousands

	Percentage with incomes below half the average			Percentage with incomes below 80% of the average		
	1981	1983	1985	1981	1983	1985
Economic status of head of benefit unit						
Pensioner	6	5	7	66	60	66
Full-time worker	3	3	3	28	26	26
Sick or disabled	21	16	19	74	61	70
Single parents	27	16	19	86	86	90
Unemployed	42	38	47	75	81	84
Others	13	18	14	52	54	57
All economic types	8	8	9	42	41	43
Number of individuals (thousands)	4,440	4,290	4,990	22,220	22,250	23,340

1 Each individual is assumed to have the net equivalent income of the household in which they live. See Appendix, Part 5: Households below average income.
2 Individuals are classified according to the economic status of the head of their social security benefit unit. Where more than one

description applies they are allocated to the first named. See Appendix, Part 5: Households below average income.

Source: Households Below Average Income 1981 – 85, Department of Social Security

5.21 Proportions of individuals in households with below average income[1]: by constant income threshold[2] and economic status[3]

Great Britain

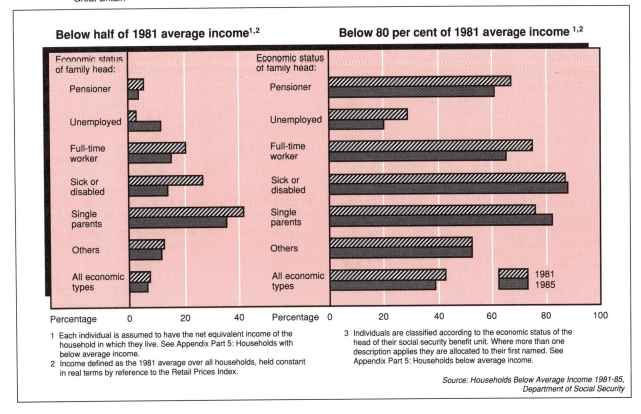

Below half of 1981 average income[1,2]

Economic status of family head:	
Pensioner	
Unemployed	
Full-time worker	
Sick or disabled	
Single parents	
Others	
All economic types	

Below 80 per cent of 1981 average income[1,2]

Economic status of family head:	
Pensioner	
Unemployed	
Full-time worker	
Sick or disabled	
Single parents	
Others	
All economic types	

1981
1985

Percentage 0 20 40 Percentage 0 20 40 60 80 100

1 Each individual is assumed to have the net equivalent income of the household in which they live. See Appendix Part 5: Households with below average income.
2 Income defined as the 1981 average over all households, held constant in real terms by reference to the Retail Prices Index.

3 Individuals are classified according to the economic status of the head of their social security benefit unit. Where more than one description applies they are allocated to their first named. See Appendix Part 5: Households below average income.

Source: Households Below Average Income 1981-85, Department of Social Security

Table 5.20 shows that the unemployed are the most likely to have incomes below half the average income, with 47 per cent having incomes below this threshold in 1985. Only 3 per cent of full-time workers received less than half the average income in each of the years 1981, 1983 and 1985, and almost three quarters had incomes over 80 per cent of the average in each of these years. The proportion of single parent families with incomes below 80 per cent of the average rose from 86 per cent in 1981 and 1983 to 90 per cent in 1985. For pensioners this proportion fell from 66 per cent in 1981 to 60 per cent in 1983, then rose to reach

66 per cent again in 1985; corresponding changes in the real value of the retirement pension are shown in Chart 5.10.

The average real income per head rose between 1981 and 1985. For all the household types shown in Chart 5.21 there was a lower proportion of people below half the 1981 average, uprated to 1985 prices, in 1985 than below half the 1981 average in 1981. This is also true for the 80 per cent of the 1981 average income threshold, with the exception of single parents and the unemployed.

Wealth

5.22 Composition of the net wealth[1] of the personal sector

United Kingdom

Percentages and £ billion

	1971	1976	1981	1986	1987
Net wealth *(percentages)*					
Dwellings (net of mortgage debt)	22.1	30.1	32.1	31.8	33.0
Other fixed assets	8.9	10.1	10.0	6.6	6.5
Non-marketable tenancy rights	9.9	12.7	11.4	8.0	7.8
Consumer durables	8.3	11.9	10.5	8.4	8.2
Building society shares	6.0	6.9	7.1	7.9	7.7
National Savings, bank deposits, etc	11.9	10.2	9.4	7.9	7.6
Stocks and shares	21.7	8.2	7.0	9.6	10.3
Other financial assets net of liabilities	11.1	9.9	12.6	19.7	19.1
Total (= 100%) (£ billion)	199.3	376.2	803.5	1,466.2	1,681.8

1 See Appendix, Part 5: Personal wealth.

Source: Central Statistical Office

5.23 Distribution of wealth

United Kingdom   Percentages and £ billion

	1971	1976	1981	1985[4]
Marketable wealth				
Percentage of wealth				
owned by:				
Most wealthy 1%[1]	31	24[3]	21	20
Most wealthy 5%[1]	52	45	40	40
Most wealthy 10%[1]	65	60	54	54
Most wealthy 25%[1]	86	84	77	76
Most wealthy 50%[1]	97	95	94	93
Total marketable				
wealth (£ billion)	140	263	546	863
Marketable wealth plus				
occupational and				
state pension rights				
Percentage of wealth				
owned by:				
Most wealthy 1%[1]	21	14	12	11
Most wealthy 5%[1]	37	27	24	25
Most wealthy 10%[1]	49	37	34	36
Most wealthy 25%[1,2]	69-72	58-61	55-58	57-60
Most wealthy 50%[1,2]	85-89	80-85	78-82	81-85

1 Of population aged 18 or over.
2 Estimates vary with assumptions. See Appendix, Part 5: Personal wealth.
3 Between 1979 and 1980 there was a change in methodology as described in *Inland Revenue Statistics 1986.*
4 Estimates for 1971, 1976 and 1981 are based on the estates of persons dying in those years. Estimates for 1985 are based on estates notified for probate in 1985/86.

Source: Inland Revenue

The proportion of national wealth held by the personal sector rose from 63 per cent in 1981 to 77 per cent in 1987. Over these years the value of the personal sector wealth rose from around £800 billion to nearly £1700 billion (Table 5.22).

An increasing proportion of this personal sector wealth has been tied up in dwellings, this increase being most noticeable when house prices rose sharply in the early seventies. In 1987 almost a third of all personal sector wealth was in dwellings. The increase in home ownership has therefore had a very significant effect on the distribution of wealth.

The proportion of wealth in national savings and bank deposits has fallen consistently since 1971, whereas the proportion invested in building society shares only began to fall in the year to 1987. A substantial fall in share prices and the lack of confidence during the early 1970s caused the proportion of wealth invested in stocks and shares to fall from nearly 22 per cent in 1971 to 7 per cent in 1981. However, during the eighties firmer market prices and a wider share ownership have increased the proportion invested in this area, thus accounting for over a tenth of all personal sector wealth in 1987.

For many adults their non-marketable rights in pension schemes, whether occupational schemes or the State pension scheme, have represented an increasingly important component of personal wealth over and above holding of marketable wealth. In 1985 the

wealthiest 1 per cent and 10 per cent of the adult population owned 20 and 54 per cent of the marketable wealth of the United Kingdom (Table 5.23). After the addition of pension rights these proportions declined to 11 and 36 per cent respectively. The substantial reductions in the percentage of the marketable wealth owned by the richest groups in the early 1970s may also be attributable to the fall in the value of stocks and shares.

As mentioned above stocks and shares have, in the 1980s, become a more popular method of investment for individuals. The privatisation of state-owned companies, incentives for employee share-ownership schemes and schemes, such as Personal Equity Plans, for making shares more attractive and easier to buy have all contributed to a wider share-ownership. As a result the percentage of the adult population owning shares increased from 6 per cent in the third quarter of 1984 to over 20 per cent in the first quarter of 1988 (Chart 5.24).

A survey sponsored by the Treasury and the Stock Exchange and carried out in January and February 1988 showed the significance of privatisation, as 8 per cent of the adult population owned shares only in privatised companies, including the Trustees Savings Bank Group (TSB). The substantial growth in share ownership began with the British Telecom privatisation in 1984 in which 2 million people bought shares. The TSB and British Gas flotations, in September and November 1986 respectively, provided further major boosts, attracting 3 million and 4½ million shareholders.

Although share ownership is most concentrated in the professional and managerial socio-economic groups where one third of individuals own shares, two thirds of share owners come from other groups.

5.24 Shareholders as a percentage of the adult[1] population

Great Britain

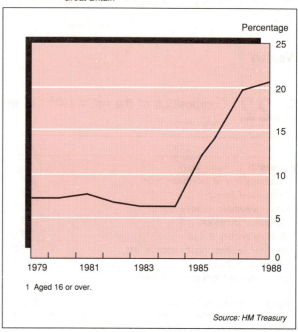

1 Aged 16 or over.

Source: HM Treasury

Chapter 6: Expenditure and Resources

Household expenditure

● Expenditure on TV and video in the United Kingdom doubled in real terms between 1976 and 1987, whilst expenditure on tobacco fell. *(Chart 6.1 below and Table 6.2)*

● In 1987, nearly a third of households in Great Britain had a microwave oven and just over half had two or more television sets. *(Table 6.5 and page 105)*

Prices

● Between 1981 and 1987, the rate of inflation in the United Kingdom was about a quarter of that in Portugal and Greece, but more than twice that of the Netherlands and the Federal Republic of Germany. *(Chart 6.11)*

● A married man on average earnings had to work 41 minutes to buy a pound of rump steak in 1987, compared with 55 minutes in 1971. *(Table 6.12)*

Consumer credit and household saving

● The amount of consumer debt outstanding (excluding mortgages) was £38 billion in current prices at the end of March 1988, having more than doubled in real terms since the end of 1981. *(Chart 6.13)*

● Household expenditure exceeded household disposable income in 1986 and 1987 for the first time since these aggregates have been calculated. *(Chart 6.16)*

Public income and expenditure

● General government expenditure amounted to 40.5 per cent of GDP in the United Kingdom in 1987, the lowest proportion since 1970. *(Chart 6.17)*

National resources

● Since 1981, growth in UK GDP has been rising and reached 4.3 per cent between 1986 and 1987. *(Chart 6.21)*

6.1 Household expenditure[1] on selected goods and services

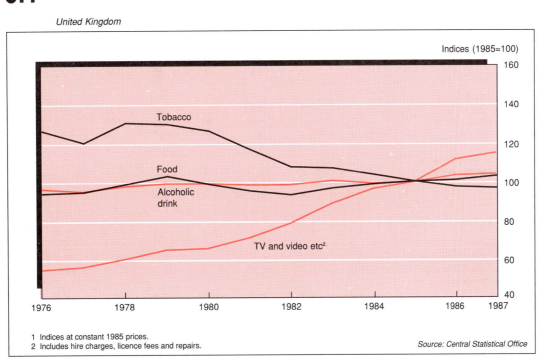

United Kingdom

Indices (1985=100)

Tobacco

Food

Alcoholic drink

TV and video etc[2]

1 Indices at constant 1985 prices.
2 Includes hire charges, licence fees and repairs.

Source: Central Statistical Office

Household expenditure

Whereas Chapter 5 discusses people's income, this section analyses how they spend it, and a later section in the chapter presents some statistics on consumer credit and saving.

Total household expenditure in the United Kingdom rose by 5 per cent between 1986 and 1987 at constant 1985 prices - that is, in real or volume terms (Table 6.2). This was a similar increase to that recorded between 1985 and 1986, but considerably higher than most year-on-year changes since the mid-1970s. The only categories for which expenditure has fallen in real terms over the last ten years or so have been tobacco, and books, newspapers etc. The category recording the fastest

growth since 1976 has been TV and video, for which the volume of expenditure has more than doubled - see also Chart 6.1. Other items for which the volume of expenditure has nearly doubled are clothing, post and telecommunications, and the purchase of vehicles. Expenditure by UK households abroad doubled in real terms between 1976 and 1981, and has grown by a further third since 1981.

The bottom half of Table 6.2 shows changes in the composition of household expenditure. The proportion of total expenditure which goes on food has fallen by more than five percentage points between 1976 and 1987, from 18.7 per cent to 13.4 per cent, and the

6.2　Household expenditure [1]

United Kingdom

	1976	1981	1982	1983	1984	1985	1986	1987 Indices/per-cent-ages	1987 £ million (current prices)
Indices at constant 1985 prices									
Food	96	99	98	100	99	100	103	104	33,643
Alcoholic drink	93	95	93	96	98	100	100	103	17,309
Tobacco	126	117	108	106	103	100	97	97	7,653
Clothing and footwear	68	80	83	88	94	100	107	115	17,788
Housing	84	92	93	96	98	100	103	107	38,862
Fuel and power	92	96	94	94	93	100	103	102	11,082
Household goods and services									
Household durables	82	85	88	95	97	100	106	109	8,539
Other	89	90	89	90	94	100	106	113	8,224
Transport and communication									
Purchase of vehicles	64	78	80	101	95	100	108	119	14,303
Running of vehicles	81	90	93	95	96	100	105	109	15,700
Other travel	86	93	90	93	96	100	105	117	8,356
Post and telecommunications	61	85	85	91	95	100	108	117	5,018
Recreation, entertainment, and education									
TV, video, etc	54	71	78	88	96	100	111	115	5,703
Books, newspapers, etc	109	110	104	100	99	100	102	103	3,529
Other	75	88	89	92	94	100	106	114	14,450
Other goods and services									
Catering (meals, etc)	90	88	87	92	96	100	107	115	18,066
Other goods	83	84	89	91	97	100	105	113	8,863
Other services	62	74	79	88	93	100	112	126	14,908
Less expenditure by foreign tourists, etc in the UK	87	74	73	85	91	100	96	101	7,194
Household expenditure abroad	47	94	94	96	96	100	112	128	6,668
Household expenditure	82	90	91	95	97	100	105	111	251,470
Percentage of total household expenditure at current prices									
Food	*18.7*	*16.1*	*15.6*	*15.2*	*14.9*	*14.3*	*14.0*	*13.4*	33,643
Alcoholic drink	*7.7*	*7.4*	*7.3*	*7.4*	*7.4*	*7.5*	*7.1*	*6.9*	17,309
Tobacco	*4.2*	*3.7*	*3.6*	*3.4*	*3.4*	*3.3*	*3.2*	*3.0*	7,653
Clothing and footwear	*7.8*	*6.8*	*6.6*	*6.7*	*6.9*	*7.1*	*7.1*	*7.1*	17,788
Housing	*13.7*	*15.0*	*15.7*	*15.4*	*15.3*	*15.3*	*15.4*	*15.5*	38,862
Fuel and power	*4.8*	*5.1*	*5.3*	*5.2*	*5.0*	*5.1*	*4.8*	*4.4*	11,082
Household goods and services	*7.7*	*7.0*	*6.7*	*6.7*	*6.7*	*6.8*	*6.7*	*6.7*	16,763
Transport and communication	*15.2*	*16.8*	*16.9*	*17.4*	*16.9*	*17.0*	*16.7*	*17.2*	43,377
Recreation, entertainment, and education	*9.3*	*9.4*	*9.4*	*9.3*	*9.4*	*9.4*	*9.5*	*9.4*	23,682
Other goods, services, and adjustments	*11.0*	*12.6*	*12.9*	*13.3*	*14.1*	*14.2*	*15.4*	*16.9*	41,311
Total	*100.0*	*100.0*	*100.0*	*100.0*	*100.0*	*100.0*	*100.0*	*100.0*	251,470

1 See Appendix, Part 6: Household expenditure.

Source: United Kingdom National Accounts, Central Statistical Office

6.3 Pattern of household expenditure: by household type and income level [1], 1986

United Kingdom — Percentages and £ per week

	Percentage of reported expenditure									Average total expenditure (£ per week) (=100 %)	Number of households in sample
	Food	Housing	Fuel and light	Alcohol	Tobacco	Clothing and footwear	Durable household goods	Transport and vehicles	Other goods, services, miscellaneous		
Pensioner households [2]											
Low income	26.5	21.5	13.5	2.3	2.1	5.8	4.6	4.3	19.3	57.32	757
Other	27.0	17.5	10.5	3.7	3.6	6.6	5.1	8.2	17.7	90.23	244
One-parent households											
Low income	27.3	8.2	12.7	2.6	6.3	12.1	5.7	6.1	19.0	71.65	110
Other	22.1	14.1	8.0	1.5	2.6	8.9	8.5	9.7	24.6	138.38	156
Other households with children											
Low and middle income	22.9	15.9	6.3	4.0	3.5	7.8	7.7	13.3	18.5	182.21	1,463
High income	18.1	15.6	4.3	4.0	1.5	8.7	8.6	14.6	24.5	335.33	611
One person households [3]											
Low income	19.8	23.3	10.0	4.3	3.6	5.9	6.0	8.2	18.9	68.38	434
Other	14.9	23.3	5.8	5.5	2.0	6.7	6.5	13.5	21.8	134.94	653
Other households without children											
Low income	23.6	17.7	8.9	5.4	4.3	6.1	5.8	13.2	14.9	118.17	89
Middle income	19.7	17.4	5.9	5.0	2.9	6.7	7.7	14.3	20.3	175.10	1,880
High income	16.5	14.5	3.9	5.7	1.8	8.1	8.7	18.8	21.9	325.96	781
All households	19.6	16.8	5.9	4.6	2.6	7.6	7.8	14.3	20.9	178.10	7,178
Low income	24.1	20.0	11.7	3.4	3.3	6.4	5.2	7.3	18.7	67.83	1,436
Middle income	20.7	17.6	6.2	4.6	3.0	7.3	7.6	13.4	19.6	164.59	4,306
High income	17.1	15.0	4.1	4.9	1.7	8.3	8.6	17.1	23.3	328.89	1,436

1 The income distribution used is that of disposable household income - low income is defined here as the lowest 20 per cent of this income distribution, middle income as the next 60 per cent and high income the highest 20 per cent.

2 Pensioner households are defined as those households solely containing one or two persons of pensionable age.

3 Excludes pensioners.

Source: Central Statistical Office, from Family Expenditure Survey

proportions on alcoholic drink and tobacco have also fallen slightly. Expenditure on housing increased from 13.7 per cent of total expenditure in 1976 to 15.7 per cent in 1982, but has since steadied. In 1976, expenditure on food took the highest proportion of total expenditure but has now slipped to third place, overtaken by transport and communication and housing.

Table 6.3 shows the expenditure patterns of different types of households at different income levels, using data from the 1986 Family Expenditure Survey (FES). The low income group is defined here as the 20 per cent of households with the lowest incomes and high income as the 20 per cent with the highest incomes. Thus, according to the FES, 11 per cent of all households in the UK in 1986 were pensioner households on low incomes (in the FES, 757 out of 7178 households). Housing costs are shown net of any assistance which the household might be getting through the Housing Benefit scheme.

As one would expect, low income households tend to allocate a higher proportion of their expenditure to necessities such as food, housing and fuel and light than those with higher incomes. These three items accounted for over half the expenditure of low income households, compared with just over a third of the expenditure of those with high incomes. High income households spent the same proportion on transport and vehicles as they did on food, whereas amongst pensioner households and one parent households transport expenditure was relatively small. Alcohol formed an above average proportion of the expenditure of households without children, and a below average proportion for pensioner and one parent households. The proportion of expenditure allocated to tobacco tended to fall as income rose, except amongst pensioner households, though the actual amount spent tended to rise.

6.4 Percentage of food purchases made from large supermarket chains: by type of household, January–June 1987

Great Britain   Percentages

	Bread, cereals, biscuits and cakes	Beef, lamb and pork	Other meat and meat products	Fish	Dairy products	Fresh fruit and vege-tables	Sweets and choco-late	Groceries and other food	All food
High income households [1]	65	52	66	52	51	59	33	74	61
Pensioner households mainly dependent on state benefits [2]	46	32	44	45	38	31	26	61	43
All other households [3]	55	38	52	50	43	42	32	64	50
All households	58	39	52	49	43	42	31	62	50

1 Those households with income in the top 4 per cent of the income distribution.
2 At least three-quarters of household income derived from state benefits.

3 These households equate to those covered by the retail prices index.

Source: Family Expenditure Survey

Table 6.4 uses data collected for the first time in the 1987 Family Expenditure Survey to show which types of households tend to shop for which types of food at large supermarket chains. Overall, half of all food purchases are made at supermarkets: groceries and bread, cereals, biscuits and cakes are the most likely items to be bought at supermarkets, and sweets and chocolate are the most likely to be bought at other types of retail outlet. High income households make the highest proportion of their food purchases in supermarkets, buying three-fifths of their food there compared to just over two-fifths bought by pensioner households. However, even pensioner households buy 61 per cent of their groceries in supermarkets.

Table 6.3 showed that the proportion of expenditure allocated to durable household goods increases as household income increases, and this is reflected in the pattern of ownership of durable goods shown in Table 6.5. Ownership of virtually all the durable goods shown increases steadily as household income increases. The one exception is black and white televisions where the reverse pattern can be observed. For many of the goods shown, the contrast between households with incomes

above £350 per week and below £60 per week is very striking. For example, ownership of videos ranged from 7 per cent of the lowest income group to 65 per cent of the highest income group, and ownership of dishwashers from 1 per cent to 22 per cent. The General Household Survey collected data on ownership of microwave ovens for the first time in 1986, and found that overall nearly a quarter of households interviewed possessed one.

The General Household Survey (GHS) has monitored the availability of certain durable goods since 1972. During this time the proportion of households with each of the durable goods covered has risen, with the sole exception of black and white televisions for which availability has fallen as colour televisions have reduced in price and increased in popularity, though a quarter of all households with incomes under £60 per week had only black and white sets in 1986. Preliminary results from the 1987 GHS indicate that these trends have continued. The consumer durables which have only recently been developed have shown the greatest increases in availability; the percentage of households with videos rose from 38 per cent to 46 per cent

6.5 Households with durable goods: by usual gross weekly household income, 1986

Great Britain   Percentages

	Usual gross weekly household income (£)								
	0– 60.00	60.01– 100.00	100.01– 120.00	120.01– 140.00	140.01– 180.00	180.01– 250.00	250.01– 350.00	350.01 or more	All house-holds [1]
Percentage of households with:									
Deep-freezer	39	58	65	68	76	80	87	91	72
Washing machine	53	75	79	80	85	89	94	95	82
Tumble drier	11	21	27	33	35	41	48	55	36
Microwave oven	5	7	14	15	24	24	33	39	23
Dishwasher	1	1	1	2	2	4	6	22	7
Telephone	63	71	74	74	81	88	94	98	83
Television									
Colour	68	83	87	88	91	93	96	97	88
Black and white only	26	14	9	9	8	6	3	2	10
Video	7	15	21	24	37	48	56	65	38
Home computer	2	6	11	11	16	22	26	33	17

1 Includes households which cannot be allocated to income bands because they did not provide income information.

Source: General Household Survey, 1986

6.6 Household expenditure patterns : EC comparison, 1986

Percentages

	Food, beverages, tobacco	Clothing and footwear	Rent, fuel and power	Furniture, furnishings, household equipment	Medical care and health expenses	Transport and communication	Recreation, entertainment, education, culture	Misc. goods and services	Total
United Kingdom	18.9	7.2	20.3	6.8	1.3	16.3	9.7	19.5	100.0
Belgium [1]	21.3	8.1	18.3	10.4	10.6	12.2	6.5	14.1	100.0
Denmark	23.5	6.0	25.1	6.8	1.8	17.4	9.6	9.8	100.0
France	20.5	7.2	18.7	8.5	8.9	16.4	7.2	12.6	100.0
Germany (Fed. Rep)	17.0	8.1	19.0	8.4	14.2	14.5	8.9	9.8	100.0
Greece	39.9	8.6	11.6	8.2	2.9	15.0	4.5	9.3	100.0
Irish Republic [1]	43.2	6.4	12.4	6.5	2.6	13.0	9.1	6.9	100.0
Italy	24.5	9.1	14.9	8.6	5.5	12.6	8.4	16.3	100.0
Luxembourg [1]	23.3	6.6	21.0	9.2	6.7	16.9	3.4	12.9	100.0
Netherlands	19.1	7.3	19.4	7.5	12.7	10.9	9.5	13.6	100.0
Portugal [2]	37.9	9.2	5.3	8.9	4.4	15.5	5.6	13.1	100.0
Spain	27.2	7.2	15.2	7.1	3.4	13.9	6.7	19.2	100.0

1 Percentages add to more than 100 because of a statistical adjustment
    to total expenditure
2 1985.
3 1983.

Source: Statistical Office of the European Communities

between 1986 and 1987, and the percentage with microwave ovens rose from 23 per cent to 30 per cent. However, the percentage of households with some of the more well-established durables such as telephones, televisions and washing machines showed little if any increase in 1987. For the first time in 1987 the GHS asked those with televisions how many sets they had. Just over half the households in Great Britain, 51 per cent, had 2 or more sets and 47 per cent had one only.

Care has to be taken in comparing the household expenditure patterns of the member countries of the European Communities (Table 6.6), mainly because of the differences between countries in their provision of services free at the time of use. Medical care and health expenses are the most important examples of such differences. In countries such as the UK and Denmark where health care is provided, in the main, free at the time of use, the proportion of household expenditure on this item is naturally very low. Where health care is paid for directly by households, who are subsequently reimbursed by the social security administration, such as in France, Germany and the Netherlands, the proportions are much higher.

Nevertheless, there are some interesting contrasts to be drawn from the table. Rent (which includes an imputation for the rent of owner-occupied housing), fuel and power range from 5 per cent of expenditure in Portugal where rents are very low, to 25 per cent in Denmark, with countries in the north of Europe tending to spend a higher proportion than those in the south. Food generally accounts for less than 25 per cent of expenditure in most countries, but rises to 38 per cent in Portugal, 40 per cent in Greece and 43 per cent in the Irish Republic. These comparisons are still valid if the differences in expenditure on medical care are discounted.

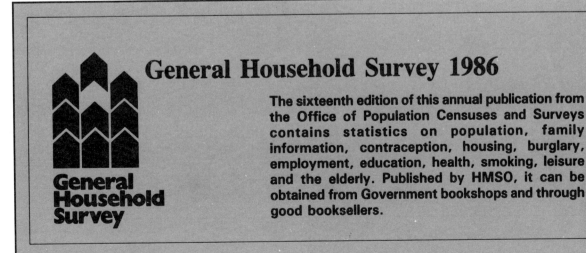

General Household Survey 1986

The sixteenth edition of this annual publication from the Office of Population Censuses and Surveys contains statistics on population, family information, contraception, housing, burglary, employment, education, health, smoking, leisure and the elderly. Published by HMSO, it can be obtained from Government bookshops and through good booksellers.

Prices

The rate of growth in retail prices in the United Kingdom, sometimes known as the rate of inflation, is generally measured by the retail prices index (RPI). This index monitors the change from month to month in the cost of a representative 'basket' of goods and services of the sort bought by a typical household. Prices rose rapidly during 1979 and 1980 (Chart 6.7). However the year-on-year increases then declined during 1981 and 1982 and reached a low point of 3.7 per cent per year in May and June 1983, compared with the peak of 21.9 per cent in May 1980. Since 1983 prices rose again slightly in 1985, fell to a new low point of 2.4 per cent per year in July and August 1986 and since have been gradually rising again.

The RPI can also be regarded as a measure of changes in the purchasing power of a given net income. It is affected by changes in indirect taxes, such as VAT and petrol duty, but not by changes in national insurance contributions or in income tax, other than through changes in tax relief on mortgage interest payments. Thus, for example, if there is a cut in income tax the RPI will remain unchanged, though households' purchasing power will increase. The Tax and Price Index (TPI), also shown in Chart 6.7, was developed as a supplement to the RPI, to take account of changes in households' purchasing power arising not only from changes in prices but also from changes in income tax and national insurance (NI) contributions. It therefore indicates the extent by which the gross income - ie before tax and NI contributions - of most taxpayers would need to change to maintain the purchasing power of their net income. For non-taxpayers, the RPI remains the appropriate measure of changes in purchasing power.

Between April and August 1988 the year-on-year increases in the TPI were about 2 percentage points lower than the RPI because of the increases in personal tax allowances and the reduction of income tax rates in the 1988 Budget. The increase in the TPI has been lower than that for the RPI since the 1983 Budget, indicating that changes in income tax liability have increased the purchasing power of taxpayers.

The composition of the 'basket' of goods and services on which the RPI is based - that is, the relative importance or 'weight' attached to each of the various goods and services it contains - is revised every year using the latest available information on household spending patterns from the Family Expenditure Survey. Thus, for example, out of a total weight of 1,000, food accounted for 350 in 1961 but only 167 in 1987 (Table 6.8), reflecting the fall in the proportion of expenditure accounted for by food already observed in Table 6.2. The weights for 1987 reflect the implementation of changes in the coverage and construction of the RPI which were proposed in 1986 by the RPI Advisory Committee. Four of the subgroups - durable household goods; transport and vehicles; miscellaneous goods; services - were considerably rearranged to produce seven new subgroups shown at the bottom of Table 6.8.

It is possible to see from Table 6.8 how price changes for the various categories of goods and services within the 'basket' have varied within the overall RPI percentage change. Between 1986 and 1987, the RPI increased by 4.2 per cent: however, within this increase, housing costs rose by 8.6 per cent whereas the price of fuel and light fell by 0.9 per cent.

6.7 Retail prices index and tax and price index

United Kingdom

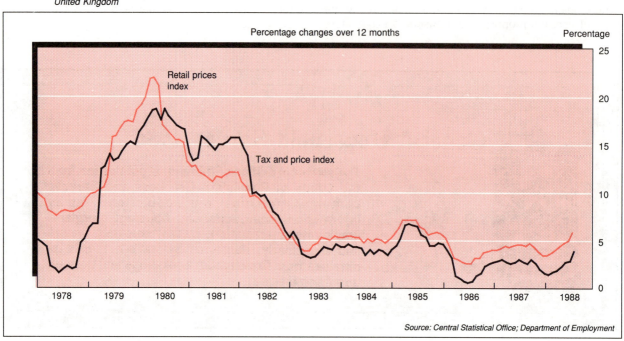

Percentage changes over 12 months

Source: Central Statistical Office; Department of Employment

6.8 Index of retail prices: rates of change

United Kingdom

Weights and percentages

| | Weights 1961 | Average annual percentage change | | | | | | | | | Weights 1987[1] |
		1961 −71	1971 −76	1976 −81	1981 −82	1982 −83	1983 −84	1984 −85	1985 −86	1986 −87[1]	
General index											
All items	1,000	4.6	14.5	13.4	8.6	4.6	5.0	6.1	3.4	4.2	1,000
All items, excluding housing	913	. .	. .	12.8	7.9	4.9	4.3	4.9	3.0	3.3	843
Food	350	4.7	17.4	11.7	7.9	3.2	5.6	3.1	3.3	3.1	167
Meals bought and consumed outside home [2]	. .	4.5[4]	17.0	15.1	7.5	6.5	7.4	5.8	6.3	6.4	46
Alcoholic drink	71	4.9	11.6	14.0	11.4	7.5	5.8	6.3	4.5	4.1	76
Tobacco	80	3.8	12.0	15.9	15.4	6.7	10.9	8.9	9.8	3.2	38
Housing	87	5.8	13.3	17.3	12.6	2.5	9.2	12.9	5.7	8.6	157
Fuel and light	55	5.4	16.4	15.8	14.0	7.4	2.9	4.3	1.3	− 0.9	61
Clothing and footwear	106	2.9	11.9	8.4	1.1	2.0	− 0.1	3.9	2.8	1.8	74
Durable household goods	66	3.3	11.0	10.5	2.8	2.7	2.5	2.8	1.1	. .	. .
Transport and vehicles	68	4.3	14.6	14.2	6.5	6.6	2.3	4.8	− 0.6	. .	. .
Miscellaneous goods	59	5.1	13.1	13.3	8.3	6.1	5.5	7.5	4.3	. .	. .
Services	58	5.8	14.9	13.5	10.2	3.4	4.2	6.7	5.0	. .	. .
Household goods	. .	. .	. .	. .	. .	. .	. .	. .	. .	. .	73
Household services	. .	. .	. .	. .	. .	. .	. .	. .	. .	. .	44
Personal goods and services	. .	. .	. .	. .	. .	. .	. .	. .	. .	. .	38
Motoring expenditure	. .	. .	. .	. .	. .	. .	. .	. .	. .	. .	127
Fares and other travel costs	. .	. .	. .	. .	. .	. .	. .	. .	. .	. .	22
Leisure goods	. .	. .	. .	. .	. .	. .	. .	. .	. .	. .	47
Leisure services	. .	. .	. .	. .	. .	. .	. .	. .	. .	. .	30
Pensioner indices [3]											
All items, excluding housing											
One-person households	.	4.8[5]	15.5	12.8	9.3	4.5	5.0	4.9	3.2	2.3	.
Two-person households	.	4.8[5]	15.5	12.8	9.1	4.5	5.1	4.9	3.2	2.5	.

1 A new structure of weights was introduced in January 1987 which involved a considerable rearrangement of some component sections and so for some groups 1986-87 annual percentage changes cannot be calculated.
2 Described as 'Catering' in 1987.
3 Pensioner indices relate to those households in which at least three-quarters of the total income was derived from pensions and supplements to them. See Appendix, Part 6: Retail prices.
4 Not separately identified until 1968. The figure relates to the period 1968-71.
5 The figures relate to the period 1962-71.

Source: Department of Employment

The RPI does not cover households with very high incomes, that is those in the top 4 per cent of incomes, nor those consisting of retired people mainly dependent on state pensions and benefits. For many years special price indices have been calculated for the 'pensioners', separately for one and two person households, because of their different expenditure patterns. Between 1986 and 1987, the pensioner indices increased by only 2.3 and 2.5 per cent respectively, compared with the overall increase of 4.2 per cent in the RPI.

As the RPI increases, so the volume of goods and services which can be purchased with a given sum of money, ie purchasing power, decreases. Chart 6.9 illustrates the erosion of the purchasing power of the pound since 1951: £1.00 in 1987 could purchase what it required only the equivalent of 10 pence to buy in 1951.

Purchasing power of a currency varies not only over time, as shown in Chart 6.9, but also between countries. Chart 6.10 shows the purchasing power of the pound in the European Community (EC) by comparing the ratios of purchasing power parities to official exchange rates. The purchasing power parity between the United

6.9 Purchasing power of a 1951 pound

United Kingdom

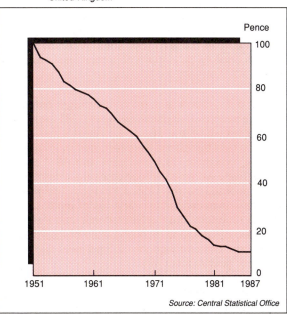

Source: Central Statistical Office

6.10 Purchasing power of the pound in the European Community[1]

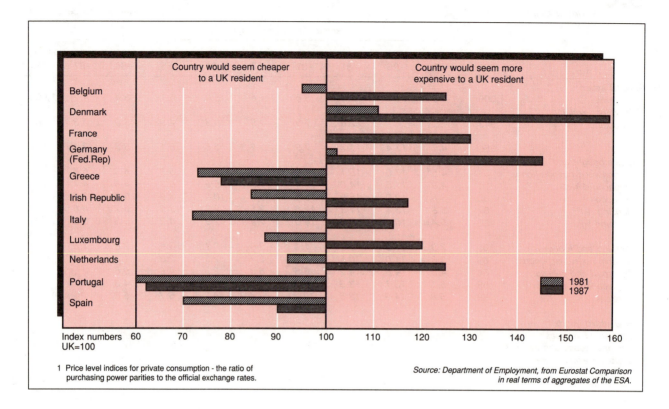

Country would seem cheaper to a UK resident | Country would seem more expensive to a UK resident

Belgium
Denmark
France
Germany (Fed.Rep)
Greece
Irish Republic
Italy
Luxembourg
Netherlands
Portugal
Spain

1981
1987

Index numbers UK=100   60   70   80   90   100   110   120   130   140   150   160

1 Price level indices for private consumption - the ratio of purchasing power parities to the official exchange rates.

Source: Department of Employment, from Eurostat Comparison in real terms of aggregates of the ESA.

Kingdom and another country is the number of units of that country's currency required to buy the equivalent of consumer goods and services costing £1.00 in the United Kingdom - in other words, to give the consumer the same purchasing power in that country as in the United Kingdom. If this is greater than the official exchange rate, then the price level index shown in the chart would be greater than 100 and the country would seem more expensive to a UK resident. Conversely if the index is less than 100 the country would seem cheaper. Thus, in both 1981 and 1987 Greece, Portugal and Spain would have seemed cheaper to someone coming from the United Kingdom. However, to obtain the same basket of goods and services costing £1.00 in the United Kingdom in 1987, one would have had to pay nearly 60 per cent more in Denmark and nearly 45 per cent more in the Federal Republic of Germany. Movements in these indices are affected by changes both in price levels in these countries and in exchange rates.

Chart 6.11 shows the annual average percentage change in consumer prices between 1981 and 1987 in each country of the EC. The highest rates of price inflation over this period were recorded by Portugal and Greece, which at 19.4 per cent and 19.7 per cent respectively were nearly four times the rate of 5.3 per cent recorded by the United Kingdom. Belgium and Denmark experienced similar rates of increase to the United Kingdom, but the Netherlands and the Federal Republic of Germany recorded rates of less than half that of the United Kingdom - 2.3 per cent and 2.2 per cent per year respectively.

An alternative way to analyse price levels and changes over time is to relate them to earnings by calculating

how long someone would have to work to earn enough to pay for certain goods and services. This is done in Table 6.12, which takes as its base the net income of a married man on average earnings with two children and whose wife was not earning. In this table, an increase in the length of time necessary to work to pay for a particular item will indicate that the percentage price increase for that item was higher than the percentage increase in the family's net income.

6.11 Change in consumer prices: EC comparison, 1981-1987

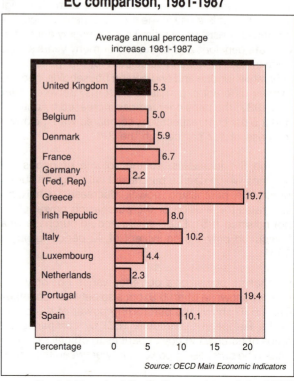

Average annual percentage increase 1981-1987

Country	Percentage
United Kingdom	5.3
Belgium	5.0
Denmark	5.9
France	6.7
Germany (Fed. Rep)	2.2
Greece	19.7
Irish Republic	8.0
Italy	10.2
Luxembourg	4.4
Netherlands	2.3
Portugal	19.4
Spain	10.1

Percentage   0   5   10   15   20

Source: OECD Main Economic Indicators

6.12 Length of time necessary to work to pay for selected commodities and services

Great Britain   Hours and minutes

	Married couple with husband only working [1]												
	1971		1981		1983		1984		1985		1986		1987
	Hrs mins		Hrs mins		Hrs mins		Hrs mins		Hrs mins		Hrs mins		Hrs mins
1 large loaf (white sliced)		9		8		7		7		7		7		6
1lb of rump steak		55		58		53		51		47		45		41
500gr of butter (home produced)		19		20		19		17		17		16		14
1 pint of fresh milk		5		4		4		4		4		4		4
1 dozen eggs (medium size)		22		17		13		16		14		14		15
100gr of coffee (instant)		22		19		23		22		23		22		20
1 pint of beer		14		12		12		12		12		12		12
20 cigarettes		22		20		21		21		21		22		20
Motor car licence	40	30	27	14	27	25	26	47	27	47	25	38	23	35
Colour television licence	19	55	13	21	14	50	13	41	16	07	14	52	13	41
Weekly gas bill [2]		56	1	01	1	19	1	19	1	20	1	15	1	10
Weekly electricity bill [2]	1	05	1	16	1	15	1	09	1	06	1	03		58
1 gallon of petrol (4 star)		33		36		34		33		34		26		24
Weekly telephone bill [2]		50		43		40		38		..		37		35

1 Length of time necessary for married man on average hourly male adult earnings for all industries and services, with non-earning wife and two children under 11, to work so that his net income pays for the various goods.

2 For an average household in the second quarter of the year, excluding the highest-paid and pensioners mainly dependent on state benefits. The amounts consumed may also vary over time for these items.

Source: Department of Employment; HM Treasury

Between 1986 and 1987 the length of time the husband would have needed to work to pay for all the items shown, except eggs, either fell or remained the same, indicating in general that earned incomes rose faster than prices. Since 1971, the time taken to earn enough to buy a pound of rumpsteak has fallen by 14 minutes, but the time taken to pay for 20 cigarettes has remained virtually unchanged.

Changes between years in the length of time necessary to pay for each item reflect both changes in prices and incomes. For most of the items shown in the table, the calculation is based on a fixed amount, for example 1 pint of beer. However, for some items, such as a weekly gas bill, the amount consumed may also vary over time and changes between years for these items will also reflect this.

Consumer credit and household saving

Consumer credit in Great Britain has increased very substantially since 1981: in cash terms the amount of outstanding debt rose three-fold since the end of 1981 to reach nearly £40 billion by mid-1988 (Chart 6.13). The amount outstanding at the end of 1987 amounted to 14 per cent of annual household disposable income (see Table 5.2) compared to 8 per cent in 1981. When adjusted for the effect of inflation as measured by the RPI, the amount of outstanding debt grew by about 3 per cent a quarter between the end of 1981 and 31 March 1988. This credit excludes borrowing for house purchase; for information on mortgage debt see Chapter 8. The growth in consumer credit has been accompanied by growth in retail sales; the volume of retail sales, that is the value of sales adjusted to remove the effects of price inflation, rose by nearly 30 per cent between 1981 and 1987.

The high proportion of household expenditure financed through credit and the amount of consumer debt in recent years has been partly a result of the growing number of people who use credit cards as a method of payment for goods and services. Data compiled by the Committee of London and Scottish Bankers show that at the end of 1987 there were 13.1 million Visa cards and 11.4 million Access cards in issue, increases of 8 per cent and 15 per cent respectively on the previous year. At the end of 1975 there were only 3.3

6.13 Consumer credit: amount outstanding

Great Britain

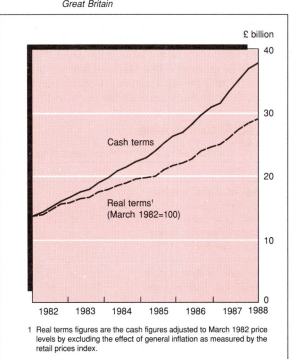

1 Real terms figures are the cash figures adjusted to March 1982 price levels by excluding the effect of general inflation as measured by the retail prices index.

Source: Central Statistical Office

6.14 Composition of consumer credit

United Kingdom

Percentages and £ billion

	1981	1982	1983	1984	1985	1986	1987
Bank credit card lending	11.7	12.6	13.7	14.9	15.8	17.0	16.3
Other lending from the monetary sector [1]	65.0	66.2	64.6	63.2	62.2	61.0	61.9
Non-monetary sector credit companies [2]	8.8	8.2	9.8	9.9	10.8	12.2	12.4
Insurance companies	2.2	2.0	1.9	3.1	2.9	2.7	2.3
Retailers	12.2	11.0	10.0	9.0	8.4	7.2	7.1
Amount of credit outstanding at the end of year (= 100%) (£ billion)	13.4	16.0	18.9	22.3	26.1	30.7	36.8

1 Banks and all other institutions authorised to take deposits under the Banking Act 1987.

2 Finance houses and other credit companies.

Source: Central Statistical Office

million Visa cards and 3.1 million Access cards in issue. Between 1986 and 1987 the total value of transactions in which these cards were used increased by 26 per cent to reach £16.6 billion, while the number of transactions increased by 16 per cent to 522 million.

The bulk of consumer credit in the United Kingdom is financed by banks and other institutions authorised to take deposits under the Banking Act 1987 (Table 6.14). However the importance of this source of credit has fallen somewhat since 1981, as has credit extended by retailers. On the other hand, lending through bank credit cards and by credit companies has increased in importance. Lending by credit companies includes much of the traditional hire purchase lending as well as credit extended through retailers' credit cards where the schemes are financed by credit companies.

Evidence from the Family Expenditure Survey indicates that in 1985, about 8 per cent of household expenditure was on credit, and that this proportion fell with age from 11 per cent among households headed by a person aged 18 to 29 to 3 per cent among households headed by a person aged 60 or over. (For further details on credit expenditure on selected items by age of head of household see Table 6.18, page 109, Social Trends 18.)

The proportion of adults in Great Britain with a Building Society account increased from 15 to 64 per cent between 1968 and 1986 (Table 6.15). Over the same period the proportion with a National Savings account fell from 37 to 7 per cent, while the proportion with a Trustees Savings Bank account fell from 18 to 12 per

cent. Between 1978 and 1983 the proportion of adults with a bank account rose from 50 to 61 per cent, but remained at about this level in 1986.

Following the Building Societies Act 1986, from the beginning of 1987 building societies have been able to offer a full range of retail banking services, and with the parallel growth of bank deposit accounts with cheque books the traditional distinction between the accounts offered by these institutions has become less clear-cut. New developments in telecommunications and information technology are also changing the face of banking services. Cash withdrawals via computer terminals are now widespread, and debit cards have been introduced which can be used to debit payments for goods in high street stores direct from a customers account. These developments have resulted partly from the need to reduce paperwork because of the increasing cost of processing cheques.

Chart 6.16 shows household saving as a percentage of household disposable income. In 1986 and 1987 this

6.15 Account holding

Great Britain

Percentages and numbers

	1968	1978[1]	1986
Percentage of adults[2] holding:			
Bank current account	..	50	60
Bank deposit account	23	26	..
Bank account earning interest			
With cheque book	.	.	10
Other	.	.	24
National Savings Bank account	37	18	7
Trustee Savings Bank account	18	17	12
Building Society account	15	43	64
Sample size (numbers)	3,082	2,903	2,455

1 Fieldwork took place between November 1978 and February 1979.
2 Aged 16 or over.

Source: The Building Societies Association

6.16 Household saving[1]: as a percentage of household disposable income

United Kingdom

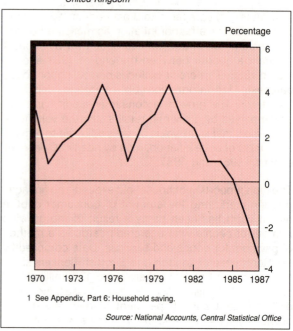

1 See Appendix, Part 6: Household saving.

Source: National Accounts, Central Statistical Office

percentage was negative, indicating that the total of all households' current expenditure exceeded their disposable income and underlining the effect of the growth in credit outstanding observed above. Household savings are not measured directly in the UK National Accounts but have to be derived as a residual by deducting the savings of other sectors from the total for the economy as a whole, which could affect the reliability of this series, but all the available evidence appears to confirm this turning point in the savings ratio. However, at the same time life assurance premiums paid, which form part of household expenditure but which are in effect a form of savings, have grown strongly and if they were taken into account the savings ratio would remain positive.

Public income and expenditure

So far in this chapter, attention has been focussed on spending by individuals and households. In this section expenditure by the government is examined. The government's own consumption is measured by public spending on goods and services. However, the government also has to make interest payments and transfer payments such as grants and loans and these also contribute to the amount which the government has to raise by taxation and borrowing. This wider measure is known as general government expenditure (GGE) and is widely used for analysing overall trends in public spending. Growth in GGE may be compared to growth in the economy as a whole by expressing it as a percentage of gross domestic product (GDP). Chart 6.17 shows that many of the peaks in this percentage coincide with periods of war, in particular the two World Wars (1914 to 1918 and 1939 to 1945). A peak of around 60 per cent was reached during World War II. Although GGE fell back as a percentage of GDP at the end of each World War, in both cases it never dropped as far as its pre-war levels. During the early 1950's the percentage rose a little at the time of the Korean War (1951 to 1952) and there was a small peak in 1968 and a larger one in the mid 1970s. In 1982 the percentage reached its highest level since the mid 1970s but since then has fallen each year to reach 40.5 per cent in 1987, the lowest level since 1970. Government spending on goods and services alone as a percentage of GDP has followed the same pattern as GGE: in the early years of the century and also during the two World Wars the two were virtually identical indicating the relative unimportance of transfer payments at those times.

6.17 General government expenditure as a percentage of GDP

United Kingdom

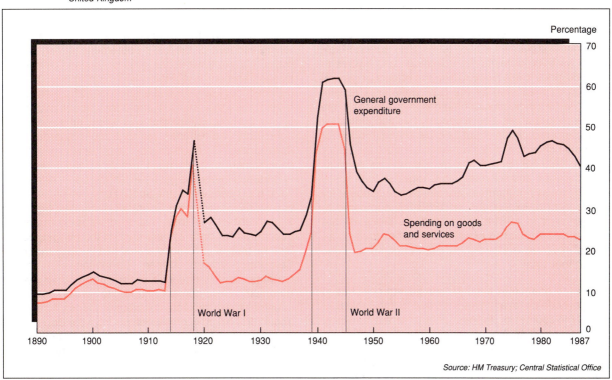

Source: HM Treasury; Central Statistical Office

6.18 Public expenditure in real terms [1]: by function

United Kingdom £ billion

Function	1981-82 outturn	1983-84 outturn	1984-85 outturn	1985-86 outturn	1986-87 outturn	1987-88 estimated outturn	1988-89 (plans)
Defence	16.1	17.6	18.8	18.5	18.1	18.1	17.6
Overseas services, including overseas aid	2.0	2.9	3.0	2.7	3.0	3.3	2.7
Agriculture, fisheries, food and forestry	2.1	2.8	2.6	3.0	2.2	2.4	2.4
Industry, energy, trade and employment	9.4	7.7	9.7	7.2	7.2	6.0	6.2
Arts and libraries	0.8	0.9	0.9	0.9	1.0	1.0	1.0
Transport	6.5	6.0	6.1	5.8	5.7	5.6	5.7
Housing	5.4	5.0	4.8	4.2	3.8	3.5	3.8
Other environmental services	5.1	5.4	5.4	5.1	5.0	5.0	4.6
Law, order and protective services	5.7	6.2	6.7	6.5	6.9	7.5	7.7
Education and science	18.5	18.7	18.6	18.1	19.2	20.1	20.1
Health and personal social services	20.2	20.9	21.4	21.3	22.3	23.3	23.6
Social security	37.7	41.4	42.9	44.1	45.8	45.9	45.9
Other expenditure [2]	4.1	3.1	3.3	3.3	3.6	4.4	7.1
Privatisation proceeds	— 0.6	— 1.3	— 2.3	— 2.8	— 4.4	— 4.8	— 4.6
Planning total	133.0	137.2	141.8	137.7	139.2	141.3	143.9
Of which expenditure by:							
Local authorities [3]	34.0	37.9	38.2	36.4	37.9	39.3	39.1
Nationalised industries	4.5	2.6	4.2	1.8	0.4	0.4	0.6
Other public corporations	1.4	1.1	1.2	0.9	0.8	0.6	0.7

1 Real terms figures are the cash outturns or plans adjusted to 1986-87 price levels by excluding the effect of general inflation as measured by the GDP deflator.
2 Includes miscellaneous expenditure, local authority current expenditure not allocated to function, the Reserve and, in 1987-88, an adjustment for the difference between the Treasury's overall view of likely outturn and the sum of the other items shown.
3 Excludes finance for public corporations.

Source: The Government's Expenditure Plans (Cm 288), HM Treasury

For the purposes of planning and control, the Government uses the public expenditure planning total. By controlling expenditure within this cash total, the Government seeks to achieve its wider medium term objective specified in terms of GGE. Table 6.18 summarises, in real terms, the public expenditure planning total by function for the United Kingdom. The main differences between the planning total and GGE are that gross debt interest is excluded from the planning total and the market and overseas borrowing of public corporations is included. Although public expenditure is planned in cash terms, the figures in Table 6.18 have been obtained by adjusting cash figures to 1986-87 price levels by excluding the effects of general inflation as measured by the GDP deflator. Thus the table gives an indication of changes in real terms in the various programmes. Social security has accounted for the highest proportion of public expenditure throughout the period shown, and is planned to account for 32 per cent in 1988-89. Health and personal social services and education and science follow: together with social security these programmes are planned to account for 62 per cent of expenditure in 1988-89, compared to 57 per cent in 1981-82. Privatisation proceeds are treated as an offset to expenditure rather than as an item of revenue, and are therefore deducted to arrive at the final total.

In order to finance its expenditure, government has to raise revenue by taxation and borrowing and Table 6.19 shows the sources of revenue for both central and local government. The proportion of central government income raised through persernal income tax rose from 28 per cent to 32 per cent between 1961 and 1971 but then fell back to 26 per cent in 1981 and has remained around that level since. The other major source of revenue is taxes on expenditure: these fell from 35 per cent of central government income in 1961 to 32 per cent in 1971 and 30 per cent in 1981. However the proportion rose again slightly to 32 per cent in 1986 and 33 per cent in 1987. The central government borrowing requirement has fallen from a peak of over 11 per cent of income in 1983 to about 2½ per cent in 1987.

The United Kingdom made a gross contribution, after taking account of the UK's abatement of VAT, of just over £4 billion towards the 1987 European Community budget and in total, the 1987 Community budget provided for expenditure of a little over £25 billion. Chart 6.20 shows that in 1981 and 1986, about two-thirds of the Community budget was spent on support for agriculture and fisheries, mainly through guaranteeing farm prices. The Regional Fund, which promotes development of declining industrial regions, reduced in importance in the budget between 1981 and 1986 from 13 to 8 per cent whilst the Social Fund, which supports social policy in Member Countries, increased from 5 to 7 per cent of the total. Aid to developing countries accounted for only 2½ per cent of the budget, but in fact the bulk of assistance is provided through the Lomé Convention to 66 African, Caribbean and Pacific countries and is financed outside the budget by the European Development Fund, to which member countries make separate contributions. The UK received about £2.3 billion in gross receipts from the Community budget in 1987, and receipts in respect of agriculture and fisheries amounted to nearly three-fifths of this total.

6.19 Central government and local authority income: by source

United Kingdom   Percentages and £ million

	1961	1971	1981	1985	1986	1987	1987 (£ million)
Central government *(percentages)*							
Taxes on income							
Paid by persons[1]	27.9	31.9	26.1	24.1	25.7	26.0	40,428
Paid by corporations[2]	10.7	7.4	8.2	11.3	9.6	9.8	15,173
Taxes on expenditure							
Customs and Excise duties (including VAT)	32.0	25.9	24.4	26.5	28.6	29.2	45,412
Other indirect taxes	3.2	6.2	6.1	3.1	3.5	3.8	5,920
Social security contributions							
Paid by employees	7.2	6.6	6.5	8.0	8.4	8.7	13,494
Paid by employers[3]	6.3	7.1	8.3	8.4	9.0	9.4	14,657
Transfer payments[4]	—	0.1	0.2	0.2	0.2	0.2	298
Rent, interest, dividends, royalties and other current income	6.7	8.0	7.5	8.0	7.0	7.0	10,802
Taxes on capital [5]	3.3	3.3	1.3	1.5	1.9	2.2	3,361
Borrowing requirement	2.9	3.1	9.8	8.1	5.7	2.6	4,009
Other financial receipts	− 0.2	0.4	1.6	0.8	0.4	1.1	1,754
Total (= 100%) (£ million)	7,941	20,413	105,841	145,819	147,965	155,308	155,308
Local authorities *(percentages)*							
Current grants from central government							
Rate support grants and other non-specific grants	23.3	33.3	38.7	32.4	32.7	32.3	15,491
Specific grants	7.3	3.7	8.8	16.5	16.2	16.2	7,806
Total current grants from central government	30.6	37.0	47.5	48.9	48.9	48.5	23,297
Rates	30.8	27.0	31.9	32.5	34.4	34.7	16,648
Rent	9.3	9.1	10.3	7.3	6.9	6.2	2,988
Interest, dividends and other current income	7.2	6.3	6.7	6.1	6.2	6.1	2,956
Capital grants from central government	1.7	2.3	1.0	1.6	1.8	1.9	904
Borrowing requirement	17.6	17.8	0.8	3.6	1.5	2.1	1,011
Other financial receipts	2.8	0.6	1.8	0.0	0.3	0.5	220
Total (= 100%) (£ million)	2,702	7,725	32,001	41,933	44,272	48,024	48,024
Total general government income (excluding intra-sector transactions[6]) (£ million)	9,725	23,673	120,981	158,820	160,789	169,825	169,825

1 Includes surtax.
2 Includes profits tax and overspill relief.
3 Includes employers' contributions to the redundancy fund.
4 Payments in lieu of graduated contributions / state scheme premiums.
5 Death duties, capital transfer tax, capital gains tax and

development land tax. Also includes other capital receipts.
6 Some of these intra- sector transactions are included in the lines on borrowing requirements and on interest, dividends and other current income.

Source: United Kingdom National Accounts , Central Statistical Office

6.20 European Community expenditure: by sector

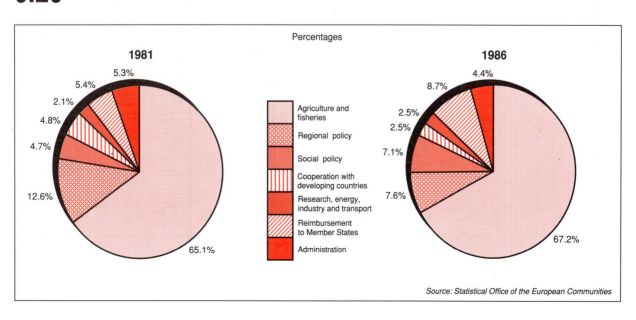

Percentages

1981
5.3%
5.4%
2.1%
4.8%
4.7%
12.6%
65.1%

1986
4.4%
8.7%
2.5%
2.5%
7.1%
7.6%
67.2%

- Agriculture and fisheries
- Regional policy
- Social policy
- Cooperation with developing countries
- Research, energy, industry and transport
- Reimbursement to Member States
- Administration

Source: Statistical Office of the European Communities

National resources

The final section of this chapter broadens the scope of expenditure and resources further, to that of the nation as a whole. The gross domestic product (GDP) of a country represents the total value of the goods and services produced by its residents in a given time period, usually a year. It therefore measures the level of economic activity within the national economy, and changes in GDP over time are used to indicate whether an economy is growing or contracting. To make such comparisons it is usually necessary to eliminate the effects of price changes, since it is changes in the volume of activity which are of most interest. Further details of the concepts used in national income accounting can be found in the CSO publication 'The United Kingdom National Accounts - Sources and Methods'.

Chart 6.21 shows movements in GDP in volume terms over the last twenty years; price changes have been eliminated by valuing each year's production at the price levels which prevailed in 1985. The picture is one of general growth over the period: the only periods during which the UK economy contracted were between 1973 and 1975 in the wake of the first sharp increase in the price of oil, and during the world-wide recession of 1979 to 1981. Since 1981 growth in GDP has been generally rising and reached 4.3 per cent between 1986 and 1987. Provisional estimates for the first half of 1988

indicate that strong growth has continued. In the first quarter of 1988 GDP was 4.4 per cent higher than in the first quarter of 1987, and in the second quarter it was 4.0 per cent higher than the equivalent period in 1987.

GDP is also commonly used to compare the levels of economic activity between countries; however, to do this it is usually expressed in 'per head' terms to allow for differences in the sizes of population of different countries. Chart 6.22 compares the average annual percentages changes in GDP per head at constant prices - ie in volume terms - in the twelve countries of the European Community between 1976 and 1986. During the course of this period, all of the EC countries experienced a fall in GDP per head at constant prices in one or more of the years between 1979 and 1983, at the time of the world-wide recession. However, over the period as a whole, they all showed positive growth. The annual rate of change in the United Kingdom (1.6 per cent) was similar to the growth in Belgium, France and Greece, but below the rate in the Federal Republic of Germany (2.1 per cent) which was the highest among the larger EC countries. The Netherlands and Spain showed the slowest annual growth rates of all the EC countries, at 0.9 per cent and 1.0 per cent respectively.

6.21 Volume index of gross domestic product at 1985 market prices

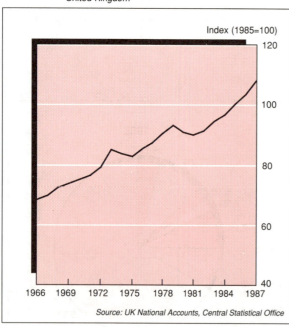

United Kingdom

Index (1985=100)

Source: UK National Accounts, Central Statistical Office

6.22 Change in gross domestic product per head at constant prices: EC comparison, 1976-1986

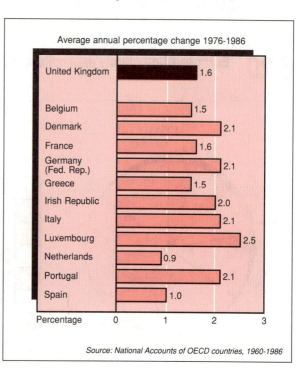

Average annual percentage change 1976-1986

United Kingdom	1.6
Belgium	1.5
Denmark	2.1
France	1.6
Germany (Fed. Rep.)	2.1
Greece	1.5
Irish Republic	2.0
Italy	2.1
Luxembourg	2.5
Netherlands	0.9
Portugal	2.1
Spain	1.0

Source: National Accounts of OECD countries, 1960-1986

Chapter 7: Health and Personal Social Services

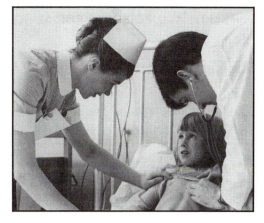

The nation's health
● In 1951 the death rate from lung cancer in women was 9 per million population but by 1987 it had risen to almost 41 per million population. *(Chart 7.6)*

● By the end of October 1988, more than 1,000 people in the UK had died from AIDS. *(Page 120)*

Diet
● Between 1961 and 1987 the consumption of brown and wholemeal bread had increased over 2½ times. *(Chart 7.11)*

Social habits and health
● The reduction in the prevalence of cigarette smoking apparent since 1972 continues slowly. *(Table 7.14)*

Accidents
● In 1987, 38 per cent of all fatal accidents took place in the home compared with 42 per cent which involved road vehicles. *(Table 7.18)*

Prevention
● The proportion of children in Great Britain vaccinated against measles rose from 45 per cent in 1976 to 71 per cent in 1986. *(Table 7.23)*

Health services
● More patients are being treated in fewer hospital beds. The number of patients treated per bed per year in the UK has increased from 12 in 1971 to 21 in 1987. *(Table 7.24)*

Personal social services
● The number of elderly residents in local authority and voluntary or private homes in Great Britain rose by 40 per cent between 1976 and 1986. *(Chart 7.32)*

● In 1985 about one adult in eight in the UK was an informal carer looking after an elderly or disabled person. *(Page 134)*

Resources
● Medical/dental staff and nursing/midwifery staff increased between 1976 and 1986 by about 20 per cent and 18 per cent respectively. *(Table 7.36)*

7.1 Expectation of life at birth: by sex

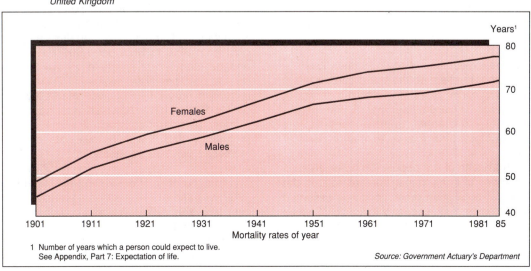

United Kingdom

1 Number of years which a person could expect to live. See Appendix, Part 7: Expectation of life.

Source: Government Actuary's Department

The nation's health

7.2 Expectation of life: at birth and specific ages

United Kingdom   Years

		Males							Females						
		1906	1931	1951	1961	1971	1981	1985	1906	1931	1951	1961	1971	1981	1985
Expectation of life [1]															
At birth		48.0	58.4	66.2	67.9	68.8	70.8	71.5	51.6	62.4	71.2	73.8	75.0	76.8	77.4
At age	1 year	55.0	62.1	67.5	68.6	69.2	70.7	71.3	57.4	65.1	72.1	74.2	75.2	76.6	77.0
	10 years	51.4	55.6	59.1	60.0	60.5	62.0	62.5	53.9	58.6	63.6	65.6	66.5	67.8	68.2
	15 years	46.9	51.1	54.3	55.1	55.6	57.1	57.6	49.5	54.0	58.7	60.6	61.6	62.8	63.3
	20 years	42.7	46.7	49.5	50.4	50.9	52.3	52.8	45.2	49.6	53.9	55.7	56.7	57.9	58.4
	30 years	34.6	38.1	40.2	40.9	41.3	42.7	43.2	36.9	41.0	44.4	46.0	47.0	48.2	48.6
	40 years	26.8	29.5	30.9	31.5	31.9	33.2	33.7	29.1	32.4	35.1	36.5	37.3	38.5	38.9
	45 years	23.2	25.5	26.4	26.9	27.3	28.5	29.0	25.3	28.2	30.6	31.9	32.7	33.8	34.2
	50 years	19.7	21.6	22.2	22.6	23.0	24.1	24.6	21.6	24.1	26.2	27.4	28.3	29.2	29.6
	60 years	13.4	14.4	14.8	15.0	15.3	16.3	16.6	14.9	16.4	17.9	19.0	19.8	20.8	21.0
	65 years	10.8	11.3	11.7	11.9	12.1	13.0	13.2	11.9	13.0	14.2	15.1	16.0	16.9	17.2
	70 years	8.4	8.6	9.0	9.3	9.5	10.1	10.3	9.2	10.0	10.9	11.7	12.5	13.3	13.6
	75 years	6.4	6.4	6.7	7.0	7.3	7.6	7.9	7.1	7.4	8.0	8.7	9.4	10.2	10.4
	80 years	4.9	4.8	4.8	5.2	5.5	5.7	5.9	5.4	5.4	5.8	6.3	6.9	7.4	7.6

1 Further number of years which a person could expect to live.
  See Appendix, Part 7: Expectation of life.   *Source: Government Actuary's Department*

In the United Kingdom diseases such as cholera and typhoid have been virtually eradicated by improvements in public health and sanitation. Other diseases such as poliomyelitis and diphtheria have been largely controlled by vaccination over the last twenty to thirty years. In addition the World Health Organisation (WHO) declared that smallpox had been eradicated from the world at the beginning of this decade.

The effect of improvements since the turn of the century, not only in health care, but also in areas like health education, housing, and nutrition is reflected in the increased longevity shown in Table 7.2. This shows the further number of years that a man or woman might expect to live when he or she has reached a certain age, on the assumption that the death rates prevailing at the time continue unchanged into the future. The mortality rates which underline the figures are based on total deaths occurring in the three year period of which the year shown is the middle year (except in the case of 1906 for which a longer period is used). Thus for example, the 1985 rates are based on deaths in 1984, 1985 and 1986.

Until 1979, the expectation of life had been lower at birth than at age 1, reflecting the toll of higher infant mortality rates of earlier years. However, the decline in infant mortality to its current level means that there is little room for substantial improvement in the expectation of life at birth relative to that at age 1.

The improving health of the population has increased people's chances of living longer; for example, in the principal official population projections it is assumed that the expectation of life at birth will rise to 75 years for a male and 80 years for a female by the year 2011. In 1951 their life expectancies were 66 and 71 years respectively.

Survival in the perinatal period and infancy is closely related to birthweight (Table 7.3). Therefore, birthweight is an important factor in the analysis of infant and perinatal mortality. Since 1975, through the co-operation of district medical officers, the Office of Population Censuses and Surveys (OPCS) has obtained birthweight information for live and still births from birth notification forms. Information on infant and perinatal mortality by birthweight is obtained by linking each infant death record with its birth record. Since 1986 almost 100 per cent of birth notifications had a stated birthweight, although some babies dying soon after birth are not weighed, and the group for which birthweight is not stated may include an excess of babies of low birthweight.

It can be seen from Table 7.3 that the highest rates of perinatal and infant deaths occur in infants who weigh less than 2,500 grams (about 5.5lbs) at birth. The proportion of these low birthweight births has been around 7 per cent for the past 20 years. Between 1983 and 1986 there was a steady fall in mortality among such infants. The perinatal mortality rate fell by 10 per cent from 95.8 to 86.4 per 1,000 live and still births and the infant mortality rate fell by over 9 per cent from 69.4 to 65.3 per 1,000 live births. There has also been increased survival in heavier infants over the same period. Studies have shown an association between the number of cigarettes smoked by the mother during pregnancy and lower birthweights of babies and increased perinatal mortality.

The total number of deaths in the United Kingdom in 1987 was about 644 thousand, a decrease of 2½ per cent from the 1986 level, and compared to a level of 633 thousand in 1951 (see Table 1.13 Death rates by age and sex). Chart 7.4 illustrates that in 1987, 4.1 per cent of men were likely to die due to accidents or

7.3 Perinatal[1] and infant[2] mortality rates: by birthweight

England & Wales

Rates

	Perinatal mortality rates[1]					Infant mortality rates[2]				
	1982	1983	1984	1985	1986	1982	1983	1984	1985	1986
Birthweight (grams)										
Under 1,500	380.0	381.0	366.9	356.1	345.5	331.3	332.3	315.4	302.2	302.4
1,500-1,999	108.8	106.9	94.7	93.7	85.0	68.0	65.3	60.9	54.8	61.1
2,000-2,499	29.3	29.7	30.4	28.3	27.3	21.6	22.1	20.7	21.4	19.7
Under 2,500	94.1	95.8	92.6	88.9	86.4	67.4	69.4	66.8	64.9	65.3
2,500-2,999	7.5	7.5	7.3	7.2	6.6	9.0	8.9	8.3	8.1	8.0
3,000-3,499	3.2	2.8	2.8	2.9	3.0	5.6	5.0	4.7	4.5	4.8
3,500-3,999	2.1	2.2	2.1	1.8	2.0	4.0	3.9	3.6	3.6	3.9
4,000 and over	3.3	2.9	2.8	3.1	2.7	4.2	3.7	3.0	3.8	3.7
Not stated	..	228.2	242.0	195.0	187.1	..	260.1	220.4	167.1	181.1
All weights	11.2	10.4	10.1	9.8	9.5	10.6	10.0	9.3	9.2	9.4

1 Stillbirths and deaths of infants under 1 week of age per thousand live and stillbirths.

2 Deaths of infants under 1 year of age per thousand live births.

Source: Office of Population Censuses and Surveys

violence compared to 2½ per cent of women. Deaths due to respiratory diseases and cancer were slightly more likely amongst men than women, although since 1951 deaths amongst men from respiratory diseases had fallen from 15 per cent of all deaths to 11 per cent, whilst deaths from cancer had risen from 16 per cent of all deaths to 26 per cent. This trend was also reflected in the female population. Deaths due to infectious diseases are now comparitively very few. *Social Trends 18* included a similar chart (7.4) on selected causes of death which included details of age groups. The leading cause of death among both men and women is diseases of the circulatory system; it is responsible for more deaths among women than among

men and accounts for about twice as many deaths as cancer. Circulatory diseases include all types of heart disease, and in 1987 there were over 209 thousand deaths from heart disease in the United Kingdom. Chart 7.5 shows the mortality rate from one particular type of heart disease - coronary artery disease - between 1951 and 1987. In 1951 the rate for men was 248 and for women 175 per million population; by 1987 this had risen to 359 and 270 respectively.

Most of those who die each year from heart disease are elderly, but the number of deaths particularly of men between the ages of 35 to 64 is still significant. There are thought to be three main risk factors. These are

7.4 Selected causes of death[1]: by sex, 1951 and 1987

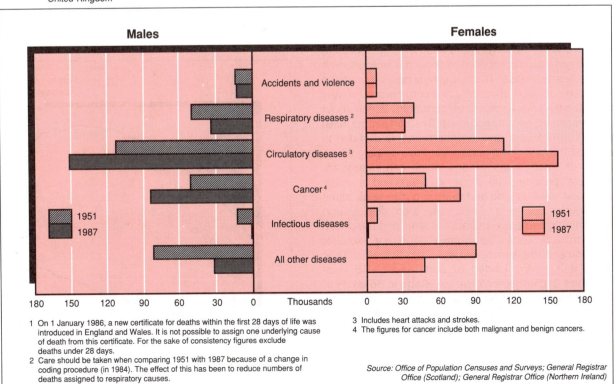

United Kingdom

1 On 1 January 1986, a new certificate for deaths within the first 28 days of life was introduced in England and Wales. It is not possible to assign one underlying cause of death from this certificate. For the sake of consistency figures exclude deaths under 28 days.

2 Care should be taken when comparing 1951 with 1987 because of a change in coding procedure (in 1984). The effect of this has been to reduce numbers of deaths assigned to respiratory causes.

3 Includes heart attacks and strokes.

4 The figures for cancer include both malignant and benign cancers.

Source: Office of Population Censuses and Surveys; General Registrar Office (Scotland); General Registrar Office (Northern Ireland)

7.5 Mortality rates from coronary artery disease: by sex

United Kingdom

Source: Office of Population Censuses and Surveys

raised blood cholesterol concentration levels, high blood pressure and cigarette smoking. Secondary factors such as diabetes and a family history of heart disease are also relevant. In Great Britain, between 1 April 1985 and 5 April 1986, there were 38.8 million days per year of certified incapacity for sickness and invalidity benefit where the cause of incapacity was ischaemic heart disease.

In April 1987 the first major national heart disease prevention campaign *'Look after your heart'* was launched. An evaluation of advertising during the first year of the campaign, showed that knowledge of the main risk factors for coronary heart disease grew, though among the lower socio-economic groups there are still large gaps in knowledge about the factors which cause heart disease. The campaign has secured the active co-operation of industry and commerce. One way has been through a scheme of 'contracts', which about 75 companies, employing almost 2 million people, have signed. Employers and organisations undertake to support the principles underlying the campaign by a series of practical innovations which can include for example, providing no smoking areas and a wider choice of suitable food and drink in public restaurants and works canteens. They may also display and disseminate campaign material to staff and the public and introduce *'Look after yourself'* courses in exercise, nutrition and stress management. In its first year, *'Look After Your Heart'* funded or part funded 118 local initiatives and under-took the trial stage in 36 areas of a *'Heartbeat Award Scheme'* for hotels, resturants, cafes and canteens. The Department of Health and the Health Education Authority are consulting widely about the future shape of the *'Look After Your Heart'* programme.

Chart 7.6 shows that between 1951 and 1987 the rate of deaths from lung cancer in the United Kingdom rose rapidly in both men and women. In 1951 the death rate for men was 51 per million population but for women it was only 9 per million population. By 1987 the rate for women had risen to almost 41 and that for men had doubled to 102. (Further information on smoking habits is contained in Table 7.14) However since 1979 the death rate from lung cancer among men has dropped from 111 to 102 per million population but among women it has risen from 32 to 41 per million population. Lung cancer is the second largest cancer killer of women in this country, and accounted for almost 12 thousand female deaths in 1987; breast cancer accounted for some 15 thousand deaths.

According to the Commission of the European Communities about 85 per cent of cases of lung cancer are linked with smoking. The EC intends to strengthen national activities in the fight against smoking through the elimination of trade barriers and help with education programmes and 1989 has been declared the European Information on Cancer Year; there was also a European Cancer Prevention Week in May 1988. This Europe Against Cancer Programme is operating in 4 key areas: cancer prevention, health information and education, training for the health professions and cancer research.

Table 7.7 shows age standardised mortality rates of those under 65 years of age in various countries of Western Europe. Of the countries show in the table, the highest rates of diseases of the circulatory system and ischaemic heart disease are in the Republic of Ireland, closely followed by Finland. Rates for lung cancer and cervical cancer are highest in Denmark although the UK also has a high rate of deaths from cervical cancer (5.21 per 100,000 population). Sweden has the lowest rate of deaths from cerebro-vascular diseases (eg strokes etc) and malignant neoplasms (ie cancer).

7.6 Mortality rates from lung cancer: by sex

United Kingdom

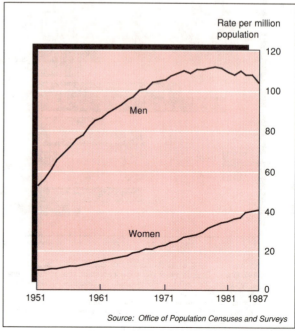

Source: Office of Population Censuses and Surveys

Rates

	Rate per 100,000 population							Rate per 1,000 live births	
	Diseases of the circulatory system	Ischaemic heart disease	Cerebro-vascular diseases	Malignant neoplasms (all causes)	Lung cancer	Cancer of the cervix	Road traffic accidents (all ages)	Suicides (all ages)	Infant [1] mortality	Maternal [1] mortality
United Kingdom [2]	104.53	74.99	16.19	95.44	24.47	5.21	10.01	8.53	9.1 [5]	0.07
Belgium	82.04	30.40	13.99	98.33	26.17	2.82	18.72	22.65	10.7	0.09
Denmark	85.22	58.81	12.17	104.00	26.49	5.95	12.18	28.19	7.9 [3]	0.08
Finland	120.78	82.73	20.00	74.07	18.26	1.35	10.27	24.75	5.9 [2]	0.02
France	54.19	21.35	13.28	99.50	17.47	2.14	29.15	21.30	8.3 [3]	0.14
Germany (Fed. Rep.) [3]	82.60	44.70	13.45	88.82	17.21	3.34	11.79	18.63	8.5 [2]	0.11
Greece	65.92	31.24	17.37	75.10	18.22	1.55	20.57	3.84	14.1 [3]	0.09
Irish Republic [4]	127.05	89.25	19.41	97.66	23.54	3.10	15.52	9.25	9.6 [6]	0.12
Luxembourg [3]	91.24	45.04	21.50	104.58	22.98	1.81	21.17	14.27	8.1 [2]	0.00
Netherlands	76.44	48.13	11.17	89.85	23.83	2.67	10.64	12.52	8.0 [3]	0.10
Norway	82.27	58.61	11.45	74.80	12.94	3.56	9.82	14.52	8.5 [3]	0.02
Portugal [3]	76.13	24.86	31.24	78.07	10.00	2.24	25.47	9.86	15.9 [2]	0.10
Sweden [3]	73.73	50.83	10.47	69.78	10.90	2.43	9.23	17.22	6.7	0.05

1 Crude death rates.
2 1986.
3 1985.
4 1983.

5 1987
6 1984

Source: Office of Population Censuses and Surveys; European Regional Office of World Health Organisation

Contrary to popular belief, Sweden does not have the highest rate for suicides; Denmark at 28.19 per 100,000 population is the highest and the UK (8.53) the lowest after Greece (3.84). According to the WHO the total number of new cases of cancer world wide in 1980 was estimated to be 6.35 million. These cases were almost equally divided between the sexes and the developed and developing countries. In 1980 stomach cancer was judged to be the most common cancer in the world. Breast cancer, which accounts for 9 per cent of all new cancers and cervical cancer (7.3 per cent of all new cancers) are among the five most common malignant tumours in the world. This is all the more striking since they are confined to half the population, ie women. Together these two sites are responsible for one third of all new cases of cancer among females.

The UK has the lowest death rate from road traffic accidents of all the EC countries shown, and only slightly higher than Norway and Sweden.

Table 7.8 shows the notifications of selected infectious diseases in the United Kingdom between 1951 and

1987. Notifications of whooping cough dropped rapidly between 1951 and 1961, but there have been occasional epidemics since then because whooping cough has a three to four year cycle. The last epidemic peaked in 1986 at a lower level than the previous, 1982-3, epidemic because of increased up-take of vaccination. However about 30 per cent of 2 year old infants are still not vaccinated against whooping cough or measles (see Table 7.23). In England and Wales there were 3 deaths from whooping cough and 10 from measles in 1986. Notifications of respiratory tuberculosis had fallen by 80 per cent between 1961 and 1987. The availability of modern antibiotics has contributed by reducing the time patients are infectious, but the main means of control are early detection of new cases and effective surveillance of contacts. Since 1951 notifications of malaria have risen five-fold even though the condition is almost always preventable by the use of drugs. There was a slight increase in cases of acute meningitis between 1986 and 1987 (5 per cent). In England and Wales in 1987 there was a total of 1,080 cases of meningococcal meningitis, an increase of 210 on the year before.

7.8 Notifications of selected infectious diseases

United Kingdom

Thousands and numbers

	1951	1961	1971	1976	1981	1982	1983	1984	1985	1986	1987
Notifications (thousands)											
Infective jaundice	..	..	17.9	7.6	11.0	12.0	7.6	7.0	5.4	4.3	4.4
Whooping cough	194.9	27.3	19.4	4.4	21.5	70.9	21.6	6.2	24.2	39.9	17.4
Measles	636.2	788.8	155.2	68.4	61.7	105.6	114.9	67.6	104.8	90.2	46.1
Notifications (numbers)											
Tuberculosis											
Respiratory	..	22,893	10,778	9,123	6,817	6,696[2]	6,138[2]	5,579[2]	5,292[2]	5,421[2]	4,514[2]
Other	..	3,432	2,958	2,635	2,473	1,906[2]	1,764[2]	1,450[2]	1,404[2]	1,489[2]	1,271[2]
Malaria	217	107	268	1,243	1,328	1,241	1,180	1,480	1,763	1,744	1,264
Acute meningitis	1,802	858	2,295	2,317	1,629	1,496	1,445	1,542	1,815	2,514	2,644
Typhoid fever	214[1]	105[1]	136	216	195	173	189	160	182	167	148
Paratyphoid fever	1,218[1]	347[1]	109	78	82	80	80	75	80	93	67

1 Great Britain only.
2 Categories overlap and therefore some cases will be included in both respiratory and other tuberculosis.

Source: Office of Population Censuses and Surveys; Scottish Health Service, Common Services Agency; Department of Health and Social Services, Northern Ireland

Chart 7.9 and Table 7.10 show the number of cases of those who have Aquired Immune Deficiency Syndrome (AIDS) continues to increase. At the end of June 1988 the number of cases of AIDS, in the UK, reported to the Communicable Disease Surveillance Centre (CDSC) and the Communicable Disease (Scotland) Unit (CD(S)U) was 1598, (including 28 under 16 years of age), of whom 897 had died; by the end of October these figures had risen to 1862 and 1002 respectively. Of the 1598 cases reported by June 1988, 97 per cent were men and of these 85 per cent were homosexual/bisexual and 7 per cent were haemophiliacs. There have also been 34 new cases of AIDS thought to have been acquired through heterosexual contact during the past year. However, around 180 cases of AIDS have now been reported among hetrosexual adults, assuming that most intravenous drug abusers and adult haemophiliacs are hetrosexual. There were 16 reported AIDS cases in children born to infected mothers; 8 of these have died.

The Human Immunodeficiency Virus (HIV) which is the cause of AIDS is transmitted through penetrative sexual activity, injection into the blood stream of blood from someone else who is already infected and from an infected mother to her baby. Many haemophiliacs became infected by HIV in the early 1980's from receiving contaminated Factor VIII, a substance in the blood essential to normal clotting. Since 1985 all blood has been screened for HIV antibody and blood products have, where possible, been heat treated so that the risk of HIV contamination is now minimal. The actual number of people who are HIV antibody positive (9242 cases up to the end of September) is thought to be much higher than those reported due to the fact that many of those infected are not tested, perhaps because they are asymptomatic and quite unaware of their infection. The government set up a working group chaired by Professor Sir David Cox to estimate the number of people currently infected and to make medium term forecasts. The working group reported in November 1988 and the government has accepted its recommendations.

It is likely that almost all those infected with HIV will, within 15 years, develop AIDS. The disease appears to be inevitably fatal although the development and use of new drugs may extend the lifespan and improve the quality of life of the sufferers. As yet the development of an effective vaccine or cure seems unlikely for several years. Health education and other preventive activities to secure changes in sexual and drug misusing behaviour offer the only effective way to limit the spread of the disease. The government has made action against AIDS a high priority and has developed a comprehensive strategy to prevent the further spread of HIV infection and to provide diagnostic and treatment facilities, counselling and support services for those infected or at risk. The main elements of the strategy are public eduction, research, infection control, monitoring and surveillance, provision of services, and international co-operation. The Health Education Authority has been responsible for public education since October 1987. The sum of £30 million has been committed to this work from March 1986 to March 1989. A further £31 million has been committed over five years to fund a directed programme of research, co-ordinated by tne Medical Research Council, aimed at developing anti-viral drugs for HIV and HIV-related diseases.

In October 1988, the WHO had received reports of 124.1 thousand cases of AIDS from about 130 countries, a figure which the Organisation believes represents under half the actual number of cases of the disease world wide.

7.9 AIDS: new cases and deaths reported[1]

United Kingdom

1 Cases data shown are the numbers of new cases reported each quarter to the Communicable Disease Surveillance Centre and Communicable Disease (Scotland) Unit; the deaths data show the number of these cases who were known to have died up to mid-1988.

Source: Public Health Laboratory Service, Communicable Disease Surveillance Centre; Communicable Disease (Scotland) Unit

7.10 AIDS — total cases and deaths reported [1]: by sex and by patient characteristic/presumed risk group, June 1988

United Kingdom   Numbers

	Cases		Deaths	
	Males	Females	Males	Females
Homosexual/bisexual	1,315	0	738	0
Intravenous drug abuser	20	7	14	3
Homosexual and intravenous drug abuser	27	0	12	0
Haemophiliac	107	1	67	1
Recipient of blood — abroad	10	9	7	5
— UK	9	3	7	3
Heterosexual — possibly infected abroad	36	14	11	6
— UK [2]	4	6	3	4
Child of at risk/infected parent	6	10	2	6
Other/undetermined	12	2	6	2
Total	1,546	52	867	30

1 Data shown are cases and deaths reported to the Communicable Disease Surveillance Centre and Communicable Disease (Scotland) Unit up to the end of June 1988.
2 No evidence of being infected abroad.

Source: Public Health Laboratory Service, Communicable Disease Surveillance Centre; Communicable Diseases (Scotland) Unit

Diet

The nutritional value of a persons diet depends upon the overall mixture of foods that is eaten during the course of weeks, months or years and upon the needs of the individual eating them. No single food can be 'good or bad' in isolation. Thus it is consistent overeating and not the occasional over indulgence that results in obesity; conversely, it takes a consistent reduction in energy intake or increase in energy expenditure and not sporadic bouts of starvation to effect permanent weight loss. Similarly, there is no likelihood of a heart attack from eating too much fat at a single meal unless such practices are repeated for long periods. Even then, there is such variation in individuals' needs for energy and for other nutrients that it is difficult to predict for any individual the exact effects of any particular diet on health either in the short or the long term. However it appears likely that the statistically high levels of heart disease in this country are strongly associated with the high fat, low fibre diet which is habitual for many people. It is nevertheless good nutritional practice to develop basic eating patterns that are as conducive to good health as possible. This involves eating one or more balanced meals per day, with a variety of foods which can be chosen from among the cereals, vegetables, pulses, fruit, meat, poultry or fish, oils and fats, and dairy products. For example, the diet is much more likely to contain enough Vitamin C if fruit, fruit juice or vegetables are eaten every day than if they are eaten only at irregular intervals. Such guidelines are especially important for people whose needs are high and whose appetites may be small, such

as young children, pregnant women and elderly people. Further information on diet is contained in the *Manual of Nutrition* available from HMSO.

Table 7.11 shows that there have been some significant changes in the pattern of food purchases for consumption in the home among households in Great Britain since 1961. Consumption of butter fell by almost two thirds between 1961 and 1987, and butter consumption in 1987 reached its lowest level in the post-war period. However, the consumption of margarine, especially soft margarine, increased steadily between 1961 and 1982 since when it has decreased slightly. Purchases of other fats, which include low fat and dairy spreads and cooking oils, have increased rapidly in recent years. The decline in the per capita consumption of milk and cream shows some signs of being arrested with purchases of lower fat milks continuing to increase at the expense of whole milk. The consumption of eggs has declined by over a third since 1961 while purchases of fruit products have risen, reflecting in particular, increased consumption of fruit juices. The household consumption of bread has shown little variation in the 1980's with the decline in standard white loaves being offset by increased purchases of other breads, particularly wholemeal and soft grain breads. Between 1961 and 1987 the consumption of brown and wholemeal bread has increased over 2½ times, whereas the consumption of standard white loaves has halved.

7.11 Purchases[1] of selected foods for home consumption

Great Britain — Indices of average quantities per person[2] per week, 1980 = 100

Type of food	1961	1971	1976	1980	1981	1982	1983	1984	1985	1986	1987
Type of food											
Milk and cream	114	113	111	100	97	96	94	94	90	91	89
Cheese	79	93	97	100	100	98	103	99	101	107	105
Eggs	126	123	111	100	100	95	96	87	85	82	78
Beef and veal	112	98	94	100	86	87	81	77	80	81	83
Mutton and lamb	150	120	93	100	94	80	86	74	73	67	59
Pork	47	74	70	100	92	97	85	80	84	88	77
Poultry	36	73	90	100	109	102	104	108	102	107	119
All other meat and meat products	98	105	98	100	102	103	103	99	100	100	98
Fish and fish products	119	107	95	100	103	105	107	102	102	108	106
Butter	153	137	127	100	91	78	81	71	70	56	53
Margarine	86	82	80	100	107	113	107	107	98	107	104
All other fats	76	87	82	100	97	104	99	100	104	123	117
Fresh potatoes	138	120	86	100	102	100	97	97	100	95	92
Other fresh vegetables[3]	101	99	92	100	98	95	94	92	90	99	94
Other vegetables and vegetable products[3]	61	78	92	100	105	107	107	105	114	121	120
Fresh fruit	83	96	88	100	96	90	94	91	89	98	97
Other fruit and fruit products	88	92	88	100	109	113	125	122	118	144	148
Bread, standard white loaves	165	137	121	100	100	99	95	92	89	76	73
Bread, brown and wholemeal	58	55	65	100	100	97	106	118	132	165	151
Cakes, biscuits, etc	128	123	105	100	100	103	99	97	95	99	99
Sugar	162	141	109	100	99	92	88	82	75	72	67
Tea	139	117	108	100	97	99	100	88	85	85	83
Instant coffee	30	81	94	100	96	94	98	100	100	102	96

1 Includes also the household consumption of "free" foods,
 eg garden and allotment produce etc.
2 Irrespective of age.

3 Includes tomatoes

Source: National Food Survey, Ministry of Agriculture, Fisheries and Food

Chart 7.12 shows the fat and fatty acid content of the average British diet. Total fat intake has fallen by approximately 10 per cent since 1959. This is in line with reductions in energy intake: fat as a proportion of energy has stayed constant. Between 1969 and 1986 the average intake of saturated fat has fallen by 28 per cent whilst that of polyunsaturated fat has risen by 30 per cent. The sources of fat in the national household diet are fats and oils, including butter and margarine, meat and meat products and milk. In Britain fat has for many years provided about 40 per cent of the energy value of the diet and the Department of Health has recommended that those adults and children over 5 for whom fat provides more than 35 per cent of energy intake should adjust their diet until this level is reached. High intakes of saturated fatty acids can increase cholesterol in the blood in susceptible individuals; high concentrations of cholesterol in the blood are associated with an increased risk of coronary heart disease. Information on deaths from coronary artery disease is shown in Chart 7.5.

The total fibre content of the average diet in the UK has not changed much over the past century, apart from increases during World War II, but a greater proportion now comes from fruit and vegetables and less from cereals as a result of changing eating habits. There has, however been a recent increase in the consumption of wholemeal bread, as mentioned above, and also of breakfast cereals containing bran.

Obesity is not easy to measure directly. Weight is partly accounted for by height and can only be used as an indicator if the height effect is removed. The most common measure of weight, adjusted for height, is the Body Mass Index (also known as the Quetelet Index) which is calculated by dividing squared height in metres into weight in kilos. Whatever point on the Body Mass Index (BMI) range of values is identified as the threshold of obesity it is bound to seem rather arbitrary. Nevertheless, as a rough guide, the Royal College of Physicians has suggested that those with a BMI over 25 could be regarded as overweight and those with a BMI over 30 as obese. Chart 7.13 shows the percentage of the population between the ages of 16-64 who are overweight or obese by these standards. The overall results for men and women aged 16 to 64 show that more men had a BMI above 25 (39 per cent) than women (32 per cent). However, more women than men had a BMI above 30. The proportion of women who were overweight or obese tends to rise steadily with age. Among men, the proportions tend to stabilise in early middle age. The range of observed values for BMI stretches above 40 but only 0.1 per cent of men and 0.4 per cent of women were found to be above this threshold.

7.12 Fat and fatty acid[1] content of the average British diet

Great Britain

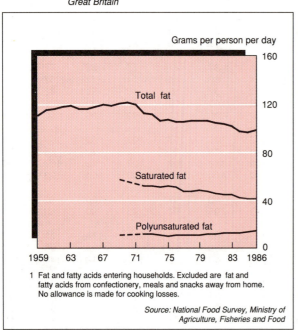

1 Fat and fatty acids entering households. Excluded are fat and fatty acids from confectionery, meals and snacks away from home. No allowance is made for cooking losses.

Source: National Food Survey, Ministry of Agriculture, Fisheries and Food

7.13 Percentage of population overweight and obese: by age and sex, 1980

Great Britain

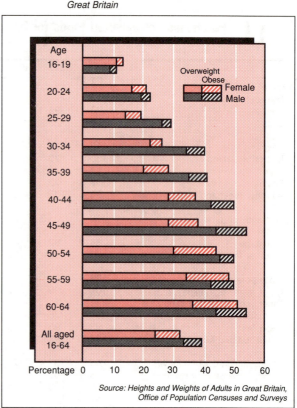

Source: Heights and Weights of Adults in Great Britain, Office of Population Censuses and Surveys

Social habits and health

The proportion of people interviewed in the General Household Survey (GHS) who smoked cigarettes has continued to fall (Table 7.14). In 1986, 33 per cent of people aged 16 or over were cigarette smokers, and a somewhat lower proportion of women than men smoked (35 per cent of men and 31 per cent of women were cigarette smokers). The reduction in the prevalence of cigarette smoking apparent since 1972 continues slowly. Although, since 1972 there has been a narrowing of the gap between men and women in the proportion smoking cigarettes, the prevalence has, in general, remained higher among men than among women. However among 16-19 year olds, 30 per cent of both men and women were cigarette smokers. In 1986 the prevalence of cigarette smoking among both men and women continued to be considerably higher in the manual occupation groups. In the non-manual groups there was little difference between the sexes in the extent of cigarette smoking. However, men smoke pipes and cigars as well and overall, 44 per cent of men were smokers in 1986 compared with 31 per cent of women.

A survey carried out by the Office of Population Censuses and Surveys (OPCS) in 1986 into the smoking habits of secondary school children found that 7 per cent of boys and 12 per cent of girls aged between 11 and 15, in England and Wales, were regular cigarette smokers (defined as usually smoking one or more cigarette a week). These figures were 10 per cent and 14 per cent respectively in Scotland.

The annual cost to the National Health Service (NHS) of smoking related diseases is estimated to be £500 million. In 1987-88 over £0.2 million was spent on grants to voluntary organisations for anti-smoking campaigns and on publishing tar and nicotine levels and a further £1.1 million was spent by the Health Education Authority. National 'No Smoking Day' is held annually in March. In 1987 it was estimated that 800 thousand people gave up on that day and 50 thousand may have done so permanently.

A survey of adults' alcohol consumption in England and Wales was conducted by the Office of Population Censuses and Surveys (OPCS) in 1987. It showed little change in overall reported alcohol consumption from the last such survey in 1978 (Chart 7.15). The heaviest consumption of alcohol is in the 18-24 age group and consumption generally decreases with age. Average weekly consumption by those aged 18 or over in both surveys was 9.5 units of alcohol (a unit is half a pint of beer or the approximate equivalent in other types of drink). There was a small rise in women's consumption between 1978 and 1987 to an average of nearly five units a week but the recorded fall in men's consumption over the period was not statistically significant. Consumption of alcohol is difficult to measure from social surveys, which consistently record less consumption than would be expected from Customs and Excise statistics of alcohol released for home consumption. The Customs' data supports the evidence of little change in total consumption between 1978 and 1987 but they indicate that consumption was not stable over this period; average alcohol consumption peaked in 1979, fell until 1982 and has since been rising slowly again.

The cost to the NHS of treating alcohol related illnesses is about £110 million per year. The total cost to society of alcohol misuse has been estimated at nearly £2 billion per year. A survey carried out in two Accident

7.14 Adult [1] cigarette smoking: by sex and socio-economic group

Great Britain | | | | | | | | | | | Percentages and numbers

	Males						Females					
	1972	1976	1980	1984	1986	1986 sample size (numbers)	1972	1976	1980	1984	1986	1986 sample size (numbers)
Socio Economic Group												
Professional	33	25	21	17	18	547	33	28	21	15	19	491
Employers and managers	44	38	35	29	28	1,628	38	35	33	29	27	1,678
Intermediate and junior non-manual	45	40	35	30	28	1,468	38	36	34	28	27	2,582
Skilled manual and own account non-professional	57	51	48	40	40	3,327	47	42	43	37	36	2,758
Semi-skilled manual and personal service	57	53	49	45	43	1,305	42	41	39	37	35	1,849
Unskilled manual	64	58	57	49	43	419	42	38	41	36	33	511
All persons [2]	52	46	42	36	35	8,874	42	38	37	32	31	10,304
Average weekly cigarette consumption per smoker	120	129	124	115	115		87	101	102	96	97	

1 Persons aged 15 or over in 1972, but 16 or over in later years.
2 Includes members of the armed forces, people in inadequately described occupations and all people who have never worked.

Source: General Household Survey

7.15 Average number of units of alcohol consumed weekly: by age and sex, 1978 and 1987

England and Wales

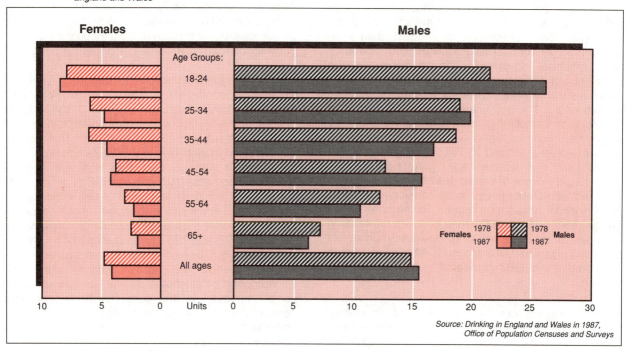

Source: Drinking in England and Wales in 1987,
Office of Population Censuses and Surveys

and Emergency Departments in North West England, over a 2 week period in 1986, showed that 13 per cent of all patients treated had positive levels of alcohol in the blood. On Saturday night two thirds of the 55 patients in the Accident and Emergency Departments surveyed had positive blood alcohol levels.

Table 7.16 shows that although there were nearly 6 times as many new drug addicts reported in 1985 as in 1973, there has been a fall of almost a third between 1985 and 1987. The vast majority of new and former addicts are reported as addicted to heroin, either alone

or with other drugs (nearly 90 per cent in the years 1985 to 1987). These data relate to notifications under the *Misuse of Drugs (Notification of and Supply to Addicts) Regulations 1973,* which require doctors to send to the Chief Medical Officer at the Home Office particulars of persons whom they consider to be addicted to any of the 14 controlled drugs listed, see Part 12 of the Appendix. The number of addicts who are formally notified is probably only a small proportion of the number of misusers. Many will not have sought medical treatment and will not therefore have been notified. Some research carried out on behalf of the Department

7.16 New and former addicts notified: by type of drug

United Kingdom   Numbers

	New addicts					Former addicts				
	1973	1981	1985	1986	1987	1973	1981	1985	1986	1987
Type of drug										
Heroin	508	1,660	5,930	4,855	4,082	339	674	2,160	2,549	2,730
Methadone	328	431	669	659	627	371	434	495	738	661
Dipipanone	28	473	223	116	113	13	239	160	224	118
Cocaine	132	174	490	520	431	43	68	193	295	246
Morphine	226	355	326	343	250	64	180	189	294	238
Pethidine	27	45	34	33	37	8	11	10	26	11
Dextromoramide	28	59	104	97	101	6	20	63	100	88
Levorphanol	1	2	3	0	0	0	0	2	0	0
Hydrocodone	0	0	1	0	0	0	0	2	0	0
Oxycodone	0	0	1	2	1	0	0	1	1	0
Phenazocine	1	2	3	2	4	1	2	3	2	4
Piritramide	0	0	0	0	0	0	1	0	0	0
Hydromorphone	0	0	0	0	0	0	0	0	0	0
Opium	0	0	14	23	17	0	0	0	10	6
Total notified addicts [1]	806	2,248	6,409	5,325	4,593	599	1,063	2,410	2,810	3,100

1 As an addict can be reported as addicted to more than one notifiable drug, the figures for individual drugs cannot be added together to produce totals.

Source: Home Office

of Health and Social Security in 1981 in two urban areas in England suggested that the number of notified addicts was about one fifth of the actual number of drug addicts in the local population at that time. More recent small scale studies show considerable variations in such 'multipliers'. There is sporadic information on usage of other drugs, particularly cannabis, cocaine and amphetamines; legally prescribed drugs such as astamesapam can also be misused. However the drug scene varies across the country and can change rapidly. The only data on solvent abuse available to the Department of Health are those on deaths collected by a continuing study undertaken by St George's Hospital Medical School, London. In 1986 this study reported that there were 93 deaths from solvent abuse notified in the United Kingdom, more than 11 times the number in 1976.

Table 7.17 shows that there were around 700 thousand new cases of sexually transmitted diseases seen at NHS genito-urinary medicine clinics in 1986. Some of the increase results from people concerned about AIDS presenting themselves for testing. Their counselling is a major new burden for the clinics. These figures cannot be taken as giving the true incidence of sexually transmitted disesases as some patients will be recorded more than once for different courses of treatment and some receive treatment other than at NHS genito-urinary medicine clinics. They do, however, provide a useful indication of trends, as NHS genito-urinary medicine clinics are believed to cover about 90 per cent of all patients needing treatment. Non-specific gential infection includes cases of chlamydia, urethitis, proctitis, and cervicitis, though these different conditions cannot be distinguished from the statistics. These are far more common in males than in females (the rates for England

7.17 Sexually transmitted diseases: new cases seen at hospital clinics

United Kingdom   Thousands

		1971	1981	1986
Cases (in all stages) dealt with for the first time at any centre				
Syphilis	Male	2	3	2
	Female	1	1	1
Gonorrhoea	Male	43	37	28
	Female	20	21	18
Herpes simplex	Male	3[1]	7	11
	Female	1[1]	5	9
Non-specific genital infection	Male	65	99	119
	Female	14[2]	33	56
Other conditions requiring treatment	Male	50	88	131
	Female	61	110	175
Other conditions not requiring treatment	Male	50	77	95
	Female	28	45	59
Total	Male	213	311	384
	Female	125	215	319

1 England & Wales only.
2 Figure excludes Scotland.

Source: Department of Health; Scottish Health Service Common Services Agency; Welsh Office; Department of Health and Social Services, Northern Ireland

were 740 and 364 per 100,000 population respectively in 1986) but the female rate is increasing faster than that for males. This table does not distinguish cases of HIV infection and AIDS; details of the number of cases and of deaths from AIDS are shown in Chart 7.9 and Table 7.10. Details of cervical cancer are shown in Table 7.22.

Accidents

The first table in this section (7.18) summarises the main causes of accidental deaths in Great Britain since 1971. It excludes those deaths where it was not known whether the death was accidental or inflicted on purpose. The total number of accidental deaths in 1987 was 7 per cent lower than in 1986 and 32 per cent down on the 1971 total. Between 1971 and 1987 accidental deaths in the home or in residential accommodation fell by 29 per cent. In 1987, 38 per cent of all fatal accidents took place in the home compared with 42 per cent which involved road vehicles.

Table 7.19 shows the types of home accidents which were treated in hospital during 1987. These data were obtained from the Home Accident Surveillance System (HASS), a survey of home accident cases treated at the accident and emergency departments in a rolling sample of 20 hospitals in England and Wales, conducted by the Consumer Safety Unit, Department of Trade and Industry. Other industrialised nations are

7.18 Accidental deaths

Great Britain   Numbers

	1971	1981	1986	1987
Total accidental deaths	19,246	15,132	14,057	13,041
Cause of death				
Railway accident	212	95	99	112
Road accident[1]	7,970	4,880	5,565	5,473
Other transport accident	219	143	235	135
Other accident				
At work[2]	860	. .[3]	370	. .
At home or in residential accommodation[2]	7,045	. .[3]	5,460	4,980
Other	2,940	10,014	2,328	2,341
Total	10,845	10,014	8,158	7,321

1 These figures are not comparable with those issued by the Department of Transport; see Appendix, Part 7: Road accident deaths.
2 See Appendix, Part 7: Accidental deaths.
3 Data not available due to 1981 registration officers industrial dispute.

Source: Office of Population Censuses and Surveys; General Register Office (Scotland)

7.19 Home accidents treated in hospital: by age and sex, 1987

England & Wales   Percentages and numbers

	Age Group										
	Males					Females					All persons
	0–4	5–14	15–64	65–74	75 or over	0–4	5–14	15–64	65–74	75 or or over	
Type of accident *(percentages)*											
Falls	49.2	37.7	22.6	40.2	67.9	47.5	42.1	33.9	59.9	75.8	39.3
Cutting/piercing	6.1	16.2	30.0	25.7	8.7	5.2	12.2	21.0	11.9	4.1	17.2
Struck by object/person [1]	17.4	26.7	20.7	13.7	6.8	16.0	24.9	20.1	11.4	6.7	18.9
Burning	6.5	2.9	3.5	3.5	3.6	6.3	3.4	4.8	3.2	2.1	4.4
Foreign body	5.5	4.6	5.9	4.5	2.0	7.1	4.1	3.5	1.6	0.9	4.6
Poisoning	6.8	0.7	0.2	0.2	0.0	7.8	0.9	0.2	0.2	0.1	1.9
Over exertion	0.7	0.6	1.8	1.4	0.8	1.7	0.7	1.4	0.6	0.3	1.2
Other/unknown	7.7	10.8	15.4	10.8	10.2	8.2	11.7	15.2	11.3	10.0	12.6
Sample size (= 100%) (numbers)	14,015	8,686	25,863	1,988	1,659	10,877	7,019	26,752	3,546	6,177	107,253 [2]

1 Also falling object.
2 Includes 671 cases where age was unknown.

Source: Home Accident Surveillance System 1987,
Consumer Safety Unit, Department of Trade and Industry

now setting up similar systems, largely based on the HASS model. Amongst these is the European Home and Leisure Accident Surveillance System (EHLASS) which was introduced by the Council of the European Community in 1986, and 58 European hospitals participated in the scheme in 1988. Hospitals in Northern Ireland and Scotland have now joined the HASS scheme, which has been extended to cover leisure accidents.

Between 1966 and 1986 the number of fatal home accidents in England and Wales was reduced from just under 7½ thousand to 4½ thousand and is now amongst the lowest in Europe. The majority of home accidents involve falls. In 1987, 60 per cent of accidents amongst women between the ages of 65-74 involved falls and this increased to 76 per cent for those aged 75 or over. The figures for men in the same age groups were 40 and 68 per cent respectively. There is also a high incidence of falls amongst children under 5, and they are the most common home accident amongst those in the 5-14 age group. It is also interesting to note that girls under 5 are more than twice as likely to suffer from over exertion than are boys.

During 1987, 69 thousand people were killed or seriously injured (KSI) in road accidents in Great Britain. Of these 29 thousand were car users (drivers or passengers), 19 thousand were users of two wheeled vehicles (motor cycles or pedal cycles) and 17½ thousand were pedestrians (see also Table 9.13). The KSI rate per thousand population amongst those aged 15-19 was three times that for the rest of the population. (Chart 7.20). The KSI rate for users of two wheeled vehicles aged 15-19 was 6½ times the rate for users of other age groups, and among car users the KSI rate for 15-19 year olds was about 2½ times the rate for other age groups.

About a fith of the people killed in road accidents in 1986 were involved in accidents where at least one of the drivers or riders had a blood alcohol level over the legal limit. The number of breath tests administered following accidents has increased over the last 10 years from 37 thousand (of which nearly 12 thousand were positive) in 1977 to 65 thousand (of which just over 11 thousand were positive) in 1987.

7.20 Road users killed or seriously injured: by age and type of user, 1987

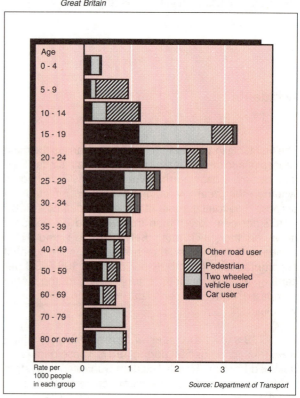

Great Britain

Source: Department of Transport

Social Trends 19, © Crown copyright 1989

The Department of Transport estimated that the average cost of a fatal road accident in Great Britain in 1987 was just over £555 thousand compared with just over £522 thousand in 1986. This includes the value of lost output, an allowance for pain, grief and suffering as well as the costs of medical and ambulance services, police and insurance administration and damage to property.

Table 7.21 presents provisional data on injuries as a result of work activities reported to the Health and Safety Executive. In 1987-88 there were over 188 thousand reported injuries to people arising from work activity. This includes employees and the self-employed (though not those working alone) injured while at work, and members of the public injured in the course of someone else's work. All fatal injuries, over 500, are believed to be reported but many other injuries reportable under the regulations, possibly as many as 50 per cent, are not reported. Among injuries not reportable and, therefore excluded from the statistics, are injuries giving rise to 3 or fewer days off work and fatal injuries to the self-employed working on their own. Also excluded are road traffic accidents involving people travelling in the course of their work, and injuries to fishermen, seamen and employees of aviation concerns, all covered by separate legislation. In 1987, 14 fishing vessels were lost with a consequent loss of 5 lives. Additionally there were 47 deaths of crew members on merchant vessels.

Fatal injuries to employees in all industries, expressed as a rate per 100 thousand, have been on a downward trend since 1965. In recent years this is thought to be due to the large changes in the pattern of employment, with the growth of the service sector and the decline in manufacturing and energy industries. A third of the 150 thousand reports of over 3 day injuries to employees in 1987-88 were sprains and strains, of which half affected the back. The self-employed are an important part of the work force particularly in construction, where, as many of them are sub-contractors, fatal injuries are reportable. Provisional figures for 1987-88 show that 141 employed and self-employed workers in construction suffered fatal injuries, an increase of 32 over the provisional figure for 1986-87.

7.21 Reported injuries [1] as a result of work activities: by severity of injury and industry, 1987–88

Great Britain   Numbers and rates

	Agriculture, forestry and fishing [2]	Energy and water supply	Manu-facturing industries	Construc-tion	Distri-bution, hotels and catering; repairs	Transport and communi-cation	Banking, finance etc	Other services	All indus-tries [3]
Employees									
Fatal injuries	18	33	96	100	17	48	5	23	340
Non-fatal major injuries	477	1,372	6,944	2,587	1,775	1,097	185	4,314	18,904
Over 3 day injuries [4]	1,319	16,067	51,283	16,316	11,412	11,694	1,068	42,997	153,080
Total injuries reported	1,814	17,472	58,323	19,003	13,204	12,839	1,258	47,334	172,324
Fatal, non-fatal and major injuries per 100,000 employees	160.5	293.9	139.6	270.7	40.6	85.7	8.1	66.6	89.8
Self-employed									
Fatal injuries	29	—	4	41	5	4	—	—	83
Non-fatal major injuries	78	2	70	450	23	5	6	33	668
Over 3 day injuries [4]	121	4	92	790	30	8	5	40	1,091
Total injuries reported	228	6	166	1,281	58	17	11	73	1,842
Non-employed									
Fatal injuries	8	2	—	16	10	3	—	63	102
Non-fatal major injuries	115	62	479	587	794	82	44	11,942	14,174
All reported injuries									
Fatal injuries	55	35	100	157	32	55	5	86	525
Non-fatal major injuries	670	1,436	7,493	3,624	2,592	1,184	235	16,289	33,746
Over 3 day injuries [4]	1,440	16,071	51,375	17,106	11,442	11,702	1,073	43,037	154,171
Total	2,165	17,542	58,968	20,885	14,066	12,941	1,313	59,412	188,442

1 Injuries reported to all enforcement authorities including local authorities under the Reporting of Injuries, Diseases and Dangerous Occurrences Regulations (1985).
2 Excludes sea-fishing.
3 Includes some injuries where the industry is unclassified.
4 Injuries to people at work, not classified as fatal or major, which leave them incapacitated for their normal work for more than three days.

Source: Health and Safety Executive

Prevention

7.22 Cervical cancer and screening

Great Britain   Thousands and percentages

	1976	1981	1982	1983	1984	1985	1986	1987 [1]
Deaths	2.4	2.2	2.1	2.2	2.1	2.2	2.2	2.1
Smears taken	2,923	3,442	3,378	3,669	3,911	4,455	4,468	4,754
Smears as a percentage of women aged 15 or over	*13.3*	*15.2*	*14.8*	*16.0*	*17.0*	*19.3*	*19.2*	*20.4*

1 1987 figures for England relate to the financial year ending.
  31 March 1988

Source: Department of Health; Scottish Health Service,
Common Services Agency; Welsh Office

Table 7.22 shows the number of cervical cancer smear tests carried out in Great Britain between 1976 and 1987. In 1976 just over 2.92 million smears were taken and by 1987 this had increased to over 4.75 million, an increase of almost 63 per cent. Although these figures relate to the number of smears examined and not to numbers of women - some women have more than one smear test - an indication of the increased proportion of women having smear tests can be seen from the fact that between 1976 and 1987, smears taken expressed as a percentage of women aged 15 or over had risen from over 13 per cent to almost 20½ per cent. There was a gradual decline in the number of deaths from cervical cancer between 1976 and 1981 but since then the numbers have remained stable. Within 5 years the cervical cancer screening programme, involving computerised call and recall systems, will have invited, for cervical smear tests, all women in the age range 20-64 years who are registered with a General Practitioner; around 13 million women are so registered in England. Programmes for cervical cancer screening on similar lines are being implemented in Scotland, Wales and Northern Ireland. The United Kingdom is the first industrialised country in the world to announce the implementation of such a nationwide programme. It should be noted that cervical cancer, which has been linked in research to smoking and to the number of sexual partners, commonly has a long detectable pre-cancerous stage during which the condition is curable: over 85 per cent of smears with a positive result in 1987 indicated that the condition was at this stage. Breast cancer is much more common and there are about 7 times the number of deaths per year than from cervical cancer. Breast cancer is the major premature killer of women in the United Kingdom. Around 90 per cent of breast lumps are benign, but still 15 thousand women die each year from this disease, although the survival rate is improving and over 60 per cent are now alive 5 years after being treated. The National Health Service is setting up a national breast cancer screening service over the 3 years. This service will also provide a computerised call and recall system to screen women in the age group 50-64. The Forrest Report, published in 1986, concluded that this screening should eventually reduce the deaths from breast cancer by at least one third. Within 3 years it is expected that there will be about 100 screening centres around the United Kingdom, each covering a population of about 45 thousand women aged 50-64 years.

The proportion of infants vaccinated against diphtheria, poliomyelitis and tetanus rose from 73 per cent to 85 per cent between 1976 and 1986, compared with the 1990 target level of 90 per cent (Table 7.23). The proportion of those vaccinated against measles was below the 1990 target level in 1986 (71 per cent), but it had risen steadily from 45 per cent in 1976, which was the fastest vaccination increase. In England in 1987, 76 per cent had been vaccinated against measles. By the end of 1986, 87 per cent of girls aged 14 had been vaccinated against rubella.The considerable drop in the proportions of infants vaccinated against whooping cough in the mid 1970's, due to anxiety about the side effects of the vaccine, has still not been completely made up. Of infants born in 1984 only 66 per cent had been vaccinated against whooping cough by the end of 1986. In October 1988, a combined measles, mumps and rubella vaccination was introduced, with the aim of achieving the high up-take rates needed to eliminate these diseases, which are more than just minor inconveniences: 10 children died from measles in 1986. Notifications of measles and whooping cough are shown in Table 7.8.

Very rarely vaccinations can result in harmful side effects. The *Vaccine Damage Payments Act 1979* provides for a specified lump sum payment to those children found, on balance of probability, to be severely disabled as a result of vaccination against specified diseases. Initially the scheme applied retrospectively to those affected by vaccination since 1948. However from May 1984 a statutory time limit has applied. Claims must now be made within 6 years of either the date of vaccination or within 6 years of the child's second birthday. By June 1988, 3316 claims had been received and 845 awards made.

7.23 Vaccination and immunisation of children

Great Britain   Percentages

Percentage vaccinated [3]	1971 [1]	1976	1981	1986	1987 [2]	1990 target up-take
Diphtheria	80	73	82	85	87	90
Whooping cough	78	39	46	66	73	..
Poliomyelitis	80	73	82	85	87	90
Tetanus	80	73	82	85	87	90
Measles	46	45	54	71	76	90
Rubella (girls only) [4]	..	..	84[2]	87[2]	86	95

1 England & Wales only.
2 England only. 1987 figures relate to the financial year ending
  31 March 1988.
3 Children born two years earlier and vaccinated by the end of the
  specified year. For example, 1986 data are the percentages of children
  born in 1984 and vaccinated by the end of 1986 and 1981 data are the
  percentages of children born in 1979 and vaccinated by the end of 1981.
4 Percentage of schoolgirls aged 14 years who were vaccinated by the year.

Source: Department of Health; Scottish Health Service,
Common Services Agency; Welsh Office; Department
of Health and Social Services, Northern Ireland

Health services

7.24 National Health Service hospital summary: all specialties

United Kingdom

	1971	1976	1981	1984	1985	1986	1987 [1]
All in patients							
Discharges and deaths (thousands)	6,437	6,525	7,179	7,666	7,884	7,959	8,088
Average number of beds available daily[2] (thousands)	526	484	450	429	421	409	392
Average number of beds occupied daily (thousands)							
Maternities	19	16	15	14	13	13	13
Other patients[3]	417	378	350	333	327	316	304
Total—average number of beds occupied daily	436	394	366	347	341	330	317
Patients treated per bed available (number)	12.3 [3]	13.6	16.0	17.8	18.7	19.4	20.6
Average length of stay (days)							
Medical patients	14.7 [4]	12.1	10.2 [4]	9.1	8.7	8.5	..
Surgical patients	9.1 [4]	8.6	7.6 [4]	6.9	6.7	6.5	..
Maternities	7.0 [4]	6.7	5.6 [4]	4.9	4.7	4.5	..
Percentage of live births in hospital [4]	*89.8*	*97.6*	*98.9*	*99.0*	*99.1*	*99.1*	*99.2*[8]
Private in-patients[5] (thousands)							
Discharges and deaths	115	95	98	79	71	..	..
Average number of beds occupied daily	2	2	1	1	1	..	..
Day case attendances (thousands)	..	565 [4]	863	1,081	1,166	1,288	1,207
New out-patients[6] (thousands)							
Accidents and emergency	9,358	10,463	11,342	12,279	12,492	12,682	12,797
Other out-patients	9,572	9,170	9,816	10,376	10,604	10,758	10,350
Average attendances per new patient (numbers)[7]							
Accidents and emergency	1.6	1.6	1.4	1.4	1.3	1.3	1.3
Other out-patients	4.2	4.0	4.4	4.3	4.3	4.3	4.2

1 1987 figures for England relate to the financial year ending 31 March 1988.
2 Staffed beds only.
3 Out of the 233 thousand in-patients in England in 1987, 86 thousand were mental illness/handicap patients who occupied 40 per cent of available beds.
4 Great Britain only.
5 England and Wales only.

6 The 1971 and 1976 figures for out-patients in Scotland include ancillary departments.
7 Patients attending out-patient clinics in England solely for attention of a minor nature and not seen by a doctor, eg to have a dressing changed are no longer counted.
8 United Kingdom.

Source: Department of Health; Scottish Health Service, Common Services Agency; Welsh Office; Department of Health and Social Services, Northern Ireland

The National Health Service (NHS) celebrated its fortieth birthday on 5 July 1988.

More patients are being treated in fewer hospital beds; between 1971 and 1987 the throughput of in-patients in NHS hospitals in the United Kingdom increased by nearly 26 per cent even though the daily number of available beds fell by 25 per cent (Table 7.24). Average length of stay also reduced over this period while the proportion of babies that were born in hospital increased to over 99 per cent. Day case attendances increased by nearly 40 per cent between 1981 and 1987.

Between September 1986 and September 1987 there was an overall fall of 3 per cent in the number of people waiting for hospital admission in the United Kingdom (Table 7.25). The most notable decreases in waiting lists were for gynaecology (almost 8½ per cent), general surgery (6½ per cent) and orthopaedics (almost 3 per cent). However there has been a slight rise in the number of people on waiting lists for ophthalmology in the United Kingdom and for urology in Great Britain. In England over 430 thousand in-patients were treated from the waiting lists between June and September 1987. If patients were treated strictly in turn, the notional time taken to clear the list would have been

21 weeks but the median waiting time of those treated was in fact only 7 weeks. This was because the most urgent cases were treated first.

7.25 Hospital in-patient waiting lists [1]: by specialty

United Kingdom   Thousands

Specialty	1976	1981	1985	1986	1987
General surgery[2]	200.5	169.1	174.0	180.3	168.4
Orthopaedics	109.8	145.1	154.1	160.5	155.9
Ear, nose, or throat	121.7	115.4	128.7	132.2	127.6
Gynaecology	91.8	105.6	107.1	106.6	97.6
Oral surgery	26.5	35.5	55.1	56.3	52.5
Plastic surgery	44.7	49.2	46.0	46.1	46.8
Ophthalmology	41.2	43.4	55.2	64.6	69.3
Urology[3]	22.0	29.1	38.9	42.7	44.5
Other	42.5	44.2	43.4	41.3	43.3
All specialties	700.8	736.6	802.6	830.6	805.9

1 Waiting lists of NHS hospitals only, as at 30 September each year.
2 Includes the Northern Ireland figures for 'Urology'.
3 Great Britain only.

Source: Department of Health; Scottish Health Service, Common Services Agency; Welsh Office; Department of Health and Social Services, Northern Ireland

7.26 In-patient operations performed [1] and average number of beds used daily [1], by age, 1985 [2]

Great Britain   Thousands and percentages

	Operations performed				Average number of beds used daily			
	Total	Percentage aged			Total	Percentage aged		
	All ages	0 — 14	15 — 74	75 years and over	All ages	0 — 14	15 — 74	75 years and over
Type of operation and procedure								
Neurosurgery	73.3	7.6	85.5	6.9	2.1	14.2	78.0	7.9
Eye	135.4	15.4	53.4	31.2	2.1	6.8	55.3	37.9
Ear Nose and throat	271.2	46.0	51.9	2.0	2.5	35.6	60.4	4.1
Oral surgery	99.9	16.2	81.8	2.0	0.8	13.6	81.1	5.2
Cardio-thoracic surgery	119.7	6.3	80.0	13.7	2.8	6.7	79.2	14.0
Abdominal	529.4	7.9	77.7	14.4	12.5	4.1	71.5	24.4
Urinary operations (including male genital organs)	275.5	16.2	64.3	19.6	4.7	7.1	64.2	28.6
Obstetric and gynaecology (excluding assisted delivery)	504.9	0.3	97.5	2.2	5.7	—	94.1	5.8
Orthopaedic	363.1	12.6	70.4	17.0	12.7	6.8	57.5	35.7
Arteries, veins and lymphatic system	85.0	1.1	91.2	7.7	1.5	1.5	81.0	17.4
Skin (including plastic surgery)	121.8	19.6	71.4	9.0	2.4	12.6	67.8	19.6
Other surgery and procedures	224.3	5.7	83.0	11.4	4.4	7.5	69.4	23.0
All operations and procedures	2803.5	12.6	75.9	11.5	54.2	7.0	70.3	22.7

1 Estimated.
2 Excluding psychiatric and maternity hospitals.

Source: Department of Health; Scottish Health Service, Common Services Agency; Welsh Office

During the same quarter, 151 thousand day case patients from the waiting list were treated and 13 weeks would have been required to clear the waiting list if no new patients were added. A major initiative was launched at the end of 1986 to make improvements in the time people wait for hospital treatment and this was backed by a waiting list fund of £25 million for 1987-88. This enabled some additional 100 thousand in-patients/day cases and 44 thousand out-patients to be treated. Health Authorities used the money to remove bottle-necks, for example by employing extra staff, buying new equipment, increasing operating theatre sessions or using spare capacity in neighbouring authorities or the independent sector. There are of course wide differences in the average length of time people have to wait for a hospital bed according to the condition requiring treatment. Neither are waiting times uniform between regions or districts since factors such

as population density, the age structure of the population and the facilities within the region can vary. Health authorities are encouraged to consider the use of non-NHS health care facilities where this would be a cost effective way of providing services to NHS patients. In 1986 patients from 121 health authorities received treatment from non-NHS health care institutions.

Table 7.26 provides a breakdown of the 2.8 million in-patient operations performed and average number of beds used in Great Britain during 1985. The most commonly performed operations were abdominal, obstetric and gynaecological. Of the operations involving ear, nose and throat, 46 per cent were on children and 20 per cent of skin operations also involved children. Those aged 75 or over constituted just over 31 per cent of those who had operative procedures on

7.27 Family practitioner services

United Kingdom

	General medical and pharmaceutical services						General dental services		
	Number of doctors[1] in practice (thousands)	Average number of patients per doctor (thousands)	Prescriptions dispensed[2] (millions)	Average cost per prescription (£)	Average number of prescriptions per person	Average prescription cost per person (£)	Number of dentists[3] in practice (thousands)	Average number of persons per dentist (thousands)	Average number of courses of treatment per dentist (thousands)
1961	23.6	2.25	233.2	0.41	4.7[4]	1.9[4]	11.9	4.4	1.4
1971	24.0	2.39	304.5	0.77	5.6	4.3	12.5	4.5	2.0
1981	27.5	2.15	370.0	3.46	6.6	23.0	15.2	3.7	2.2
1985	29.7	2.01	393.1	4.77	7.0	33.4	17.0	3.3	2.2
1986	30.2	1.99	397.5	5.11	7.0	36.0	17.3	3.3	2.2
1987	30.7	1.97	413.6	5.47	7.3	40.0	17.6	3.2	2.2

1 Unrestricted principals only. See Appendix, Part 7: Unrestricted principals.
2 Prescriptions dispensed by general practitioners are excluded. The number of such prescriptions in the United Kingdom is not known

precisely but in Great Britain during 1987 totalled some 29.4 million.
3 Principals plus assistants.
4 Estimated.

Source: Departments of Health and Social Security

the eye. Nearly 20 per cent of those who had urinary operations and 17 per cent of those who had orthopaedic operations were also elderly.

The number of General Practitioners in the United Kingdom increased by 3½ per cent between 1985 and 1987, almost twice as big an increase in two years as during the whole of the 1960s (Table 7.27). The growth rate in both 1986 and 1987 was 1.8 per cent. The national average number of patients per doctor was 1,970, a drop from 1,990 in 1986. The number of dentists increased by 2 per cent between 1986 and 1987 reducing the average number of persons per dentist to 3,230 in 1987 compared with 4,410 in 1961. The number of prescriptions dispensed rose between 1981 and 1987 by about 10½ per cent. The average net cost of a prescription (as opposed to charges paid by patients) rose to £5.47 compared with £5.11 in 1986. Prescription charges rose from 20 pence per item in 1976 to £2.80 per item from 1 April 1988. The average prescription cost per person in 1987 was £39.86.

The number of beds available in registered nursing homes and private hospitals in England and Wales rose by nearly 28 per cent between 1985 and 1986, continuing the increase shown since 1971 (Table 7.28). The average daily bed occupation of private patients in NHS hospitals was one thousand in 1986, a decrease of 9 per cent since 1985 and down 58 per cent since 1971. Private out-patient attendances increased by 9 per cent from 1985 and by 200 per cent since 1971. The overall scale of the private sector in relation to the NHS is still relatively small; in 1986 only 16 per cent of all beds in England and Wales in health care institutions were in private hospitals and nursing homes.

Chart 7.29 shows that the number of people covered by private medical insurance has increased by nearly 8 per cent since 1984 - from 5.0 million to 5.3 million in 1987. Tax concessions have been given since 1980 on employer-paid medical insurance premiums for people earning less than £8,500 per year. In 1987 the revenue from subscriptions reached over £715 million, and the benefits paid to almost £587 million. By the end of 1987 over 9 per cent of the population of the United Kingdom was covered by private medical insurance. It should be noted that up to 1984 the figures in the chart relate only to the three main provident associations - British United Provident Association, Private Patients Plan and Western Provident Association. These together accounted for about 92 per cent of all private medical insurance subscription income in 1985. From 1984 onwards the Department of Health and Social Security has collected statistics for all companies who offer private insurance schemes, including profit making concerns.

7.28 Private health services

England & Wales	1971	1981	1985	1986
Registered nursing homes and private hospitals				
Beds available (thousands)	25.3	33.5	51.0	65.1
Private patients in National Health Service hospitals				
Average daily bed occupation (thousands)	2.4	1.5	1.1	1.0
Discharges and deaths (thousands)	114.9	98.3	70.8	65.4
Average duration of stay (days)	7.9	5.6	5.5	5.4
Private out-patients attendances (thousands)	87.0	181.8	240.6	261.6

Source: Department of Health; Welsh Office

7.29 Private medical insurance: persons insured

United Kingdom

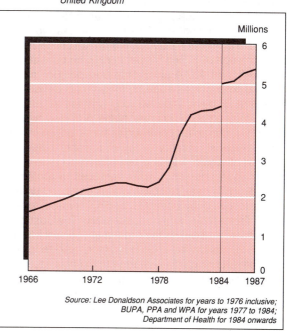

Source: Lee Donaldson Associates for years to 1976 inclusive; BUPA, PPA and WPA for years 1977 to 1984; Department of Health for 1984 onwards

According to the General Household Survey (GHS), the socio-economic group most likely to be covered by private medical insurance in Great Britain in 1986 was the professional group (24 per cent) followed by employers and managers (22 per cent) (Table 7.30). It is interesting to note that there were about the same proportions of young employers and managers covered as young professionals but for those aged 75 or over, the professional group were more than twice as likely to be covered than employers and managers.

7.30 Percentage of persons covered by private medical insurance: by socio-economic group and age, 1986

Great Britain   Percentages

| | Age | | | |
	16–44	45–64	65 and over	All ages
Socio-economic group				
Professional	23	27	27	24
Employers and Managers	25	25	12	22
Intermediate and junior non-manual	9	12	4	9
Skilled manual and own account non-professional	4	3	1	3
Semi-skilled manual and personal service	2	2	1	2
Unskilled manual	3	1	0	1
All persons [1]	9	10	4	8

1 Includes members of the armed forces, people in inadequately described occupations and all people who have never worked.

Source: General Household Survey

Personal social services

In recent years there has been a steady decrease in the number of children in care of local authorities but figures on cases where the local authority makes provision for a child removed on the authority of some other person or body show that the total number of children and young people removed to a place of safety in England and Wales during the year ending March 1987 was just under 8.4 thousand, 37 per cent more than in 1977, (Chart 7.31). About 42 per cent of these children were under the age of 5, and 53 per cent were between the ages of 5 and 15. A child or young person may be removed to a place of safety, for varying periods not exceeding 28 days, under various statutes. A 'place of safety' may be a community home provided by local authority, a controlled community home, police station, or any hospital, surgery or other suitable place, the occupier of which is willing temporarily to receive the child or young person. A child removed to a place of safety is not in care; removal to a place of safety need not be followed by care proceedings where for any reason these prove to be unnecessary. The Justice of the Peace who approves the order must be satisfied that one of the following criteria is met; risk to proper development or health, ill treatment, exposure to moral danger, being beyond the control of parent or guardian or not receiving proper education. A child may also be removed by the police in certain circumstances.

The National Society for the Prevention of Cruelty to Children estimated from a sample drawn from areas including about 9 per cent of the children in England and Wales, that a total of 25,700 children's names were added to registers in 1987, of which 8,000 were registered due to physical abuse, 7,100 due to sexual abuse and 7,200 were 'at risk'. The Department of Health is carrying out a pilot survey of children and young persons who were on child protection registers in England during the year ending 31 March 1988.

7.31 Children removed to a place of safety

England & Wales

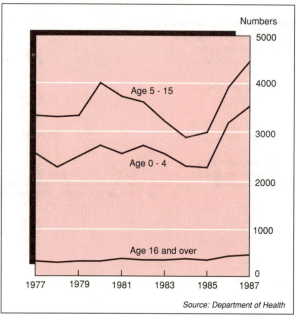

Source: Department of Health

In 1986, there were just over 231 thousand elderly residents in local authority and voluntary or private homes in Great Britain compared with just over 165 thousand residents in 1976 (Chart 7.32). In England in 1986 provision represented a rate of 58 residents in homes for every one thousand persons aged 75 or over compared with 50 places in 1982. The number of residents in private homes increased sharply at an average rate of over 21 per cent per year over the period 1982 to 1986. For local authority homes the numbers have remained constant and 51 per cent of residents were provided by local authorities in 1986. At the end of March 1986 there were over 21 thousand places in local authority day centres in England specifically for the elderly. There were over 17 thousand other places in mixed centres some of which were also taken up by elderly people. Combining these figures gives a rate equivalent to 12.7 day places for every 1 thousand persons aged 75 and over. Over the first part of the past decade there was an upward trend in the rate of provision of places but in the past five years the rate has levelled off and fell slightly in 1986. More information on the number of elderly in the population is contained in Chapter 1.

There are nearly 9 million people aged 65 or over in the United Kingdom and about a third of them live on their own. One of the most common problems encountered by elderly people is restricted mobility. The 1985 General Household Survey found that 13 per cent of people, aged 65 or over, living in private households were unable to walk down the road alone and 16 per cent could not do their own shopping. Of those women in the 80-84 age range, a third could not shop alone and this rose to nearly two thirds for those aged 85 or over. The survey also showed that 31 per cent of those aged 85 or over could not bath without assistance, 65 per cent could not cut their own toe nails, 32 per cent were unable to wash clothing by hand and 29 per cent were unable to cook a main meal. In addition 10 per cent of all elderly people were unable to open screw tops.

According to a survey on the prevalence of disability among adults undertaken by the Office of Population Censuses and Surveys (OPCS) between 1985 and 1988, there were just over 6 million adults in Great Britain with one or more disability. The severity scale used for these results ranges from 1 to 10 (category 1 least severe, category 10 most severe). For example, those in category 1 might have difficulty hearing someone talking in a normal voice in a quiet room, someone in category 5 might have mild cerebral palsy resulting in impaired intellectual functioning, and an example of someone in category 10 might be a person suffering from severely impaired mobility in the aftermath of a stroke. Just over 2 million were in the bottom two categories and 2.7 million in category 5 or higher.

Almost 14 per cent of adults living in private households have at least one disability according to the definitions used in the survey. Chart 7.33 shows that disability, and the severity of disability, above the relatively low threshold of disability used in the survey, increase with age. The rate of disability amongst elderly people aged

7.32 Elderly people in residential accomodation[1]

Great Britain

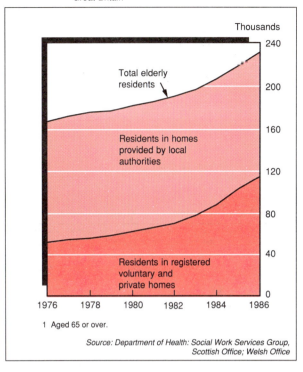

1 Aged 65 or over.

Source: Department of Health: Social Work Services Group, Scottish Office; Welsh Office

75 or over is 63 per cent for women compared to 53 per cent for men, indicating that elderly women are more likely to be disabled than elderly men. About 7 per cent of disabled people live in some kind of communal establishment. Just under 70 per cent of all

7.33 The prevalence of disability among adults: by age, sex and by severity category

Great Britain

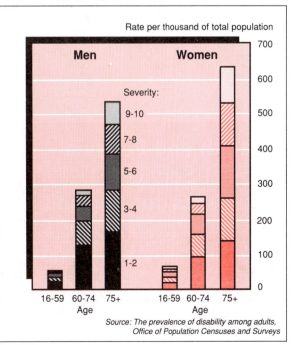

Source: The prevalence of disability among adults, Office of Population Censuses and Surveys

7.34 Carers aged 16 or over: by sex, 1985

United Kingdom		Percentages and numbers	
	Men	Women	All aged 16 or over
Percentage of people aged 16 or over			
Caring for someone in the same household [1]	4	5	4
Caring for someone in another private household only	7	10	9
All Carers	11	15	13
Caring for at least 20 hours per week	3	4	4
Sample size (= 100%) (numbers)	11,267	13,424	24,691

1 Includes people who were both caring for someone in the same household and someone in another private household.

Source: General Household Survey Informal Carers Report, 1985;
Continuous Household Survey (Northern Ireland), 1985

In 1985 about one adult in 8 in the United Kingdom was looking after an elderly or disabled person, representing about 6 million informal carers overall; 4 per cent of adults were caring for someone living with them, and 9 per cent looked after people living elsewhere (Table 7.34). The peak age for caring is 45-64 and in this age group about 1 in 4 women and 1 in 6 men were carers (Chart 7.35). Overall, women are more likely to be carers than men but the difference is not very marked, 15 per cent compared with 11 per cent. About 4 per cent of all adults devote at least 20 hours per week to caring. In Great Britain, those caring for someone in the same household number about 1.7 million. Nearly one quarter of informal carers have no help with caring, and the most common form of care is practical help with household tasks.

disabled adults were aged 60 or over and nearly half were aged 70 or over. Among the disabled living in communal establishments, half were aged 80 or over and 41 per cent of the most severely disabled adults (ie in the two highest severity categories) were aged 80 or over.

The majority of disabled adults had more than one type of disability. The most common type was difficulties in movement, followed by hearing and personal care disabilities. In communal establishments, mental complaints, particularly senile dementia, were most common. For disabled adults living in private households, musculo-skeletal complaints, notably arthritis were the most commonly cited cause of disability. Ear and eye complaints, and diseases of the circulatory system were also common.

7.35 Percentage of persons aged 16 or over who were carers: by sex and age, 1985

United Kingdom

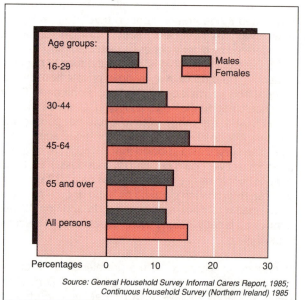

Source: General Household Survey Informal Carers Report, 1985;
Continuous Household Survey (Northern Ireland) 1985

Resources

7.36 Manpower in the health and personal social services [1]

United Kingdom

Thousands

	1976	1981	1983	1984	1985	1986
Regional and District Health Authorities						
Medical and dental (excluding locums)	43.8	49.7	51.2	51.4	52.1	52.4
Nursing and midwifery (excluding agency staff)	429.6	492.8	502.0	500.8	505.2	506.0
Other staff [2]	454.4	485.4	484.7	473.3	462.7	448.8
Total Regional and District Health Authorities	927.8	1,027.9	1,037.9	1,025.5	1,020.0	1,007.2
Family practitioner services	48.7	54.3	56.8	58.2	59.3	57.3
Dental Estimates Board and Prescription Pricing Authority/Prescription Pricing Division [3]	4.4	4.7	4.6	4.6	4.5	4.0
Personal social services	228.2	251.0	262.9	266.3	272.2	280.7

1 Figures for family practitioner services are numbers, all other figures are whole-time equivalents. See Appendix, Part 7: Manpower.
2 Includes professional and technical, administrative and clerical, ancillary, works, maintenance and ambulance staff.
3 In Northern Ireland the Central Services Agency.

Source: Department of Health; Scottish Health Service, Common Services Agency; Welsh Office; Department of Health and Social Services, Northern Ireland

Table 7.36 analyses staffing levels in the various health and personal social services in the United Kingdom. Between 1976 and 1983 total manpower in the regional and district health authorities increased by 12 per cent but then fell by almost 2½ per cent over the next three years. However, medical/dental staff and nursing/midwifery staff increased between 1976 and 1986, by about 20 per cent and 18 per cent respectively. Other staff increased up to 1981 by 7 per cent and then fell by 8 per cent between 1981 and 1986. This was mainly a consequence of contracting out services such as laundry, catering and domestic. Part of the 10 per cent increase in midwifery and nursing services between 1979 and 1981 was due to the reduction of the working week from 40 to 37½ hours during 1980–81. In England, the fall in overall hospital and community health service manpower (that is excluding family practitioner service staff) continued into 1988; total directly employed manpower in the NHS in England fell by about 2 per cent between 31 March 1986 and 31 March 1988. Personal Social Services staff in the United Kingdom rose by nearly a quarter between 1976 and 1986.

Table 7.37 shows that in the six years to 1987–88 public spending on health in the United Kingdom increased by about 40 per cent in cash terms. The health service has continued to receive additional demands for treatment, particularly from the growing number of very elderly people (the highest expenditure per person is generally incurred by those aged 75 years or over). Among other pressures on services is the need to combat the spread of AIDS/HIV infection, drug and alcohol misuse.

7.37 Public expenditure on health

United Kingdom

£ million

	1982-83 outturn	1987-88 estimated outturn	1988-89 plans[1]
Current expenditure			
Hospital and community health services	10,228	14,109	14,980
Family practitioner services	3,181	4,724	5,067
Central health and other services	407	705	720
Capital expenditure			
Hospital and community health services	837	969	993
Family practitioner services	9	22	15
Central health and other services	22	40	43
Total public expenditure on health	14,685	20,569	21,818

1 Figures do not include subsequent in-year additions in 1987–88 and 1988–89.

Source: The Government's Expenditure Plans (Cm 288), HM Treasury

THE NATIONAL FOOD SURVEY

The Annual Report of the National Food Survey Committee presents detailed analyses of household food consumption, expenditure and nutritional levels in Great Britain. Data is analysed at both national and regional level as well as according to household composition, the income group of the household and by other classifications.

Household Food Consumption and Expenditure

The next report 'Household Food Consumption and Expenditure 1987', will be published by HMSO in January 1989.

MINISTRY OF
AGRICULTURE, FISHERIES AND FOOD

Housing and Construction Statistics

Quarterly in two parts £3.90 per part
Annual Subscription £30.00 (including postage)

Annual Volume £25.00

HMSO

Chapter 8: Housing

The housing stock
- More people own their own homes — the number of owner-occupied dwellings more than doubled between 1961 and 1987 in the United Kingdom from just over 7 million to 14.5 million. *(Chart 8.1 below)*

- Almost 180 thousand new private houses were completed in 1987, the highest since 1973 and representing 84 per cent of all completions (public and private sectors). *(Chart 8.2)*

Homelessness
- Local authorities in England and Wales accepted responsibility for 118 thousand homeless households (and households threatened with homelessness) in 1987. *(Table 8.4)*

Housing action
- Between 1981 and the end of 1987, over 1 million local authority dwellings in the United Kingdom had been sold to their tenants. *(Table 8.9)*

Costs and mortgages
- The ratio of house prices to average earnings in 1987 stood at 3.8, nearly as high as the previous peak in 1979 though still far short of the 1973 peak. *(Chart 8.16)*

- The numbers of building society mortgage repossessions in the United Kingdom increased in 1987 to 22.9 thousand. The proportion of all loans which were over 6 months in arrears at the end of 1987 also rose, but fell again in the first half of 1988. *(Table 8.19)*

Characteristics of occupants
- Although the private rented sector has been decreasing in general, it is still an important source of housing for young people; one in five households with heads aged 24 or under lived in rented furnished accommodation in Great Britain in 1986. *(Table 8.20)*

8.1 Stock of dwellings: by tenure[1]

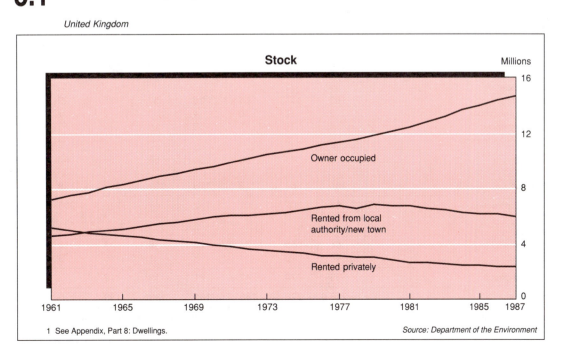

United Kingdom

1 See Appendix, Part 8: Dwellings.

Source: Department of the Environment

The Housing Stock

The housing stock in the United Kingdom totalled over 22¾ million dwellings at the end of 1987, an increase of about a third since 1961 (Chart 8.1 on the previous page). More people own their own homes; the number of owner-occupied dwellings more than doubled, from just over 7 million in 1961 to over 14½ million in 1987. The share of the total stock accounted for by the owner-occupied sector increased from 43 to 64 per cent over this period, rented dwellings declined by about 15 per cent. There was a substantial increase in the local authority and new town housing stock from 4.5 million dwellings in 1961 (26 per cent of all dwellings) to 6.8 million in the period 1978 to 1979 (32 per cent of all dwellings), there has subsequently been a fall to just under 6 million in 1987 as many tenants have bought their homes (see Table 8.9 below).

Chart 8.2 illustrates the contributions of housebuilding completions by both the public and private sectors to the overall increase in housing stock over the period 1961 to 1987. Total housing completions rose from just over 300 thousand at the beginning of the 1960s to a peak of nearly 426 thousand in 1968, but then fell and were down to 182 thousand in 1982, since then they have picked up to over 210 thousand a year. Private house completions reached a peak of 226 thousand in 1968, fell by half by 1981 before increasing to almost 180 thousand in 1987 the highest since 1973. The proportion of the total accounted for by private house completions increased from 53 per cent in 1968 to 84 per cent in 1987.

Housebuilding completions in the public sector peaked in 1967 at 211 thousand (51 per cent of all housebuilding completions) but had fallen to 34 thousand (16 per cent) by 1987.

The annual net gain in the UK dwelling stock has declined from an annual average of over 250 thousand in the 1960s to 230 thousand in the 1970s and in the

8.2 Housebuilding completions: by sector

United Kingdom

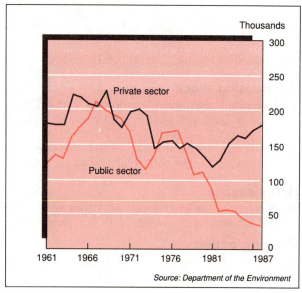

Source: Department of the Environment

first half of the 1980s it fell to under 200 thousand a year (Table 8.3). Increases in the housing stock as a result of new construction have been partially offset by demolitions. Since the second world war over 1½ million dwellings have been demolished under the slum clearance programme, with most of the households in them having been rehoused in local authority accommodation. The programme has contracted significantly in recent years, with only about 12 thousand dwellings demolished in the United Kingdom in 1987 compared to an average of about 65 thousand a year over the period 1961 to 1970.

The latest information on the condition of the housing stock in England is available from the *English House Conditions Survey, 1986,* published by HMSO in November 1988.

8.3 Average annual change in dwelling stock [1]

United Kingdom

Thousands

	1961 —1970	1971 —1980	1981	1982	1983	1984	1985	1986	1987
New construction									
Local authorities	152	111	58	36	37	35	29	24	21
New town corporations	9	12	10	4	2	2	1	1	1
Housing associations	4	16	19	13	16	17	13	13	12
Government departments	5	2	1	—	—	—	—	—	1
Total public sector	170	141	88	54	55	55	44	38	34
Private sector	198	161	119	128	151	163	159	170	178
Total new construction	368	302	207	182	207	218	203	208	212
Other changes									
Slum clearance	− 65	− 55	− 38	− 26	− 18	− 14	− 13	− 12	− 12
Other [2]	− 44	− 19	− 4	5	− 1	− 5	6	4	1
Total other changes	− 109	− 74	− 42	− 21	− 19	− 19	− 7	− 8	− 11
Total net gain	258	228	165	161	188	199	196	201	201

1 See footnote 1 to Chart 8.1.

2 Comprises net gains from conversions and other causes, and losses other than by slum clearance.

Source: Department of the Environment

Homelessness

8.4 Homeless households — local authorities' actions: by priority need category[1]

England & Wales — Percentages and thousands

Priority need category	1981	1985	1986	1987
(percentages)				
Household with dependent children	70[2]	66	65	64
Household member pregnant	13	14	14	14
Household member vulnerable because of:				
Old age	8	8	7	7
Physical handicap	2	3	3	3
Mental illness	2	2	2	2
Other reasons	2	4	6	6
Homeless in emergency	3	3	3	4
All categories (thousands)	69	91	101	107
In addition, number accommodated who were not in priority need (thousands)	5	7	9	11

1 Households for whom local authorities accept responsibility to secure accommodation under the *1977 Housing (Homeless Persons)* and *Housing Acts 1985* which define 'priority need'.
2 Results for 1981 are not fully comparable with those for later years because of a change in the reporting system.

Source: Department of the Environment; Welsh Office

8.5 Homeless households[1] — local authorities' actions: by reason[2] for homelessness, 1981 and 1987

England & Wales

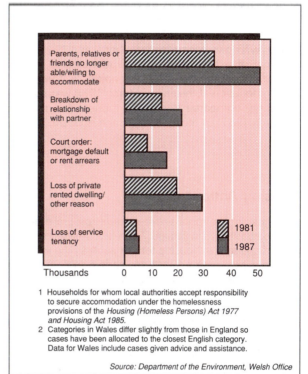

1 Households for whom local authorities accept responsibility to secure accommodation under the homelessness provisions of the *Housing (Homeless Persons) Act 1977 and Housing Act 1985.*
2 Categories in Wales differ slightly from those in England so cases have been allocated to the closest English category. Data for Wales include cases given advice and assistance.

Source: Department of the Environment, Welsh Office

Local authorities in England and Wales accepted responsibility for 118 thousand homeless households (and households threatened with homelessness) in 1987 compared to 110 thousand in 1986; 91 per cent of those in 1987 were found to be 'in priority need' for reasons such as the presence of dependent children (Table 8.4). Local authorities have a statutory duty to provide accommodation for homeless households in priority need.

The most frequent single reason for a household becoming homeless is that parents, relatives, or friends are no longer able or willing to accommodate them; this accounted for over 40 per cent of cases in England and Wales both in 1981 and 1987 (Chart 8.5). Almost a fifth were the result of a breakdown of a relationship with a partner. Homelessness arising from mortgage default or rent arrears, was 13 per cent in 1987, compared with 11 per cent in 1981.

In addition to the homeless households in England and Wales for which local authorities accepted responsibility in 1987, some 57 thousand non-priority cases were given advice and assistance, and a further 62 thousand enquirers were judged not to be homeless (Table 8.6). However recording practices vary considerably between authorities. At the end of 1987 about 25 thousand accepted homeless households were in temporary accommodation, of which 10 thousand were in bed and breakfast accommodation; 5 thousand in hostels (including women's refuges); and 10 thousand in short-life or other temporary accommodation. The number of households in temporary accommodation in England

and Wales at the end of 1987 was more than double that at the end of 1984, whilst the number in bed and breakfast accommodation at the end of 1987 was over treble that at the end of 1984.

8.6 Homeless households — local authorities' actions[1]: temporary accommodation and enquiries made

England & Wales — Thousands

	1984	1985	1986	1987
Enquiries by result				
Accepted — in priority need	80	91	101	107
— not in priority need	7	7	9	11
Given advice and assistance only	45	51	55	57
Found not to be homeless	57	63	65	62
Total enquiries	189	213	231	236
Transfers from other local authorities	1	1	1	1
Households in temporary accommodation at end of year				
Bed and breakfast	3	5	9	10
Hostels, including women's refuges	4	5	5	5
Short life tenancies and other accommodation	5	6	8	10
Total in temporary accommodation	12	16	21	25

1 Under the homelessness provisions of the *Housing (Homeless Persons) Act 1977* and *Housing Act 1985.*

Source: Department of the Environment; Welsh Office

Subsequent data show that the numbers of homeless acceptances in England have continued to rise: in the second quarter of 1988 local authorities in England accepted responsibility for 28 thousand households (7 thousand by London authorities) compared to 27 thousand in the second quarter of 1987. Over 25½ thousand of these households belonged to one or other of the 'priority need' categories; 64 per cent had dependent children. About 42 per cent were homeless because parents or relations or friends were no longer able or willing to accommodate them, and 19 per cent because of a breakdown of the relationship with a partner. The number of households in temporary accommodation at the end of March 1988 was over 28 thousand, compared to over 23 thousand at the end of March 1987. Of these, 11 thousand households, 7½ thousand of which were in London, were in bed and breakfast accommodation in March 1988 around the same numbers as at the end of March 1987. Estimated total expenditure on bed and breakfast accommodation provided by English local authorities in 1986-87 was £97 million.

Since December 1987, over £74 million has been allocated to local authorities with the greatest homelessness pressures to encourage them to make the best use of their existing stock by getting empty council properties back into use. Local authorities estimate that this will provide over 7,500 extra units of accommodation, planned to be available in 1987-88 and in 1988-89. Nearly half of this allocation went to Greater London.

Housing Action

Changes in the public expenditure programme on housing as shown in Table 8.7 can be considered in the light of changes in housing tenure, such as the increase in owner-occupation. Data are shown in cash terms (that is, not adjusted for price inflation), as that is how the Government's expenditure programmes are planned. Public expenditure provision for housing covers expenditure by central government on renovation and repair and some new building of homes for rent (mainly through the Housing Corporation), by local authorities and by new towns. It also includes local authority support of private sector home improvement and central government current expenditure subsidies to local authorities and new towns and the Housing Corporation. Capital receipts, which are shown separately in the table, accrue mainly from the sale of council housing and reduce net public expenditure. Mortgage interest tax relief is classified as a reduction in taxes rather than an item of public expenditure.

8.7 Public expenditure on housing

United Kingdom   £ million

	1982–83 outturn	1983–84 outturn	1984–85 outturn	1985–86 outturn	1986–87 outturn	1987–88 estimated outturn	1988–89 plans
Current expenditure							
Subsidies	1,389	1,136	1,136	1,153	1,249	1,143	1,107
Administration costs	152	183	188	214	227	260	261
Gross capital expenditure	4,722	6,062	5,877	5,427	5,305	5,709	5,769
Total gross expenditure	6,263	7,381	7,201	6,794	6,782	7,112	7,136
Capital receipts	− 2,463	− 3,016	− 2,809	− 2,742	− 3,003	− 3,430	− 2,973
Total net expenditure	3,800	4,365	4,392	4,052	3,779	3,682	4,163

Source: The Government's Expenditure Plans (Cm 288), HM Treasury

Housing and Construction Statistics

Quarterly in two parts £3.90 per part

Annual Subscription £30.00 (including postage)

Annual Volume £25.00

HMSO

8.8 Allocation of local authority housing

England & Wales   Percentages and thousands

	1971	1976	1981 —82	1982 —83	1983 —84	1984 —85	1985 —86	1986 —87
New tenants *(percentages)*								
Displaced through slum clearance, etc	..	12[3]	5	4	4	3	3	2
Homeless [1]	..	9	16	17	17	19	22	24
Key workers	..	2	9	8	9	8	8	7
Other priorities	..	7						
Ordinary waiting list	..	70	67	68	66	66	63	62
On non-secure tenancies [2]	.		3	3	4	4	4	4
Total	100	100	100	100	100	100	100	100
Lettings (thousands)								
To new tenants	257	287	265	271	260	255	261	257
To tenants transferring or exchanging	173	189	173	192	192	199	198	194
Total	430	476	438	463	452	454	459	451
Of which:								
New, acquired, or modernised stock	107	131	56[4]	41[4]	43[4]	44[4]	37[4]	33[4]
Relets	323	346	382	422	409	410	422	418

1 Because of differences of definition these data are not comparable with those in Tables 8.4 and 8.6, and Chart 8.5.
2 As defined in Schedule 1, *Housing Act 1985*. Non-secure tenancies granted in Wales are included under the other categories listed.
3 Relets Enquiry discontinued after 1977; data from 1979-80 are based on the Housing Investment Programme returns, and therefore are not strictly comparable with earlier years.
4 The number becoming available for letting within the year.

Source: Relets Enquiry — Local Authority Housing, and Housing Investment Programme returns, Department of the Environment

New lettings to local authority tenants in England and Wales, which include new tenants and tenants transferring or exchanging, remained fairly stable over the period 1983-84 to 1986-87, with 451 thousand lettings in 1986-87, though within this total fewer lettings of new, acquired, or modernised stock, have been largely balanced by relets (Table 8.8). Most new tenants of local authority housing continued to be households from ordinary waiting lists; the proportion was 62 per cent in 1986-87 compared to 67 per cent in 1981-82. However, over recent years there has been a gradual increase in the proportion of homes let to homeless households and a decrease in the proportion of lettings to people displaced by slum clearance. (The contraction of the slum clearance programme is shown in Table 8.3.) Nearly a quarter of all new tenants in 1986-87 were formerly homeless. In 1986-87, 4 per cent of new tenants, mainly homeless households, did not have the security of tenure which was introduced for most council housing under the *Housing Act 1980*.

The *Housing Act 1980* and its Scottish equivalent gave tenants of local authorities and of other public bodies the right to buy their homes if they had been tenants for more than three years. The *Housing and Building Control Act 1984* reduced this qualifying period to two years, increased the maximum discount available for 'right to buy' sales from 50 per cent under the 1980 Act to 60 per cent, and established the right to shared ownership. Sales of local authority and new town dwellings in the United Kingdom increased from about 93 thousand in 1980 to over 228 thousand in 1982, before falling back again to 109 thousand in 1986 (Table 8.9). Total sales in 1987 reached over 142 thousand, the highest for four years, and an increase of nearly a third over 1986. Total sales between 1980 and the end of 1987 reached over one million.

8.9 Sales [1] of dwellings owned by local authorities and new towns

England & Wales, and United Kingdom   Numbers

	Local authorities	New towns	Total sales
England & Wales			
1971	17,215	3,155	20,370
1976	5,795	100	5,895
1977	13,020	365	13,385
1978	30,045	575	30,620
1979	41,740	855	42,595
1980	81,485	4,225	85,710
1981	102,735	3,800	106,535
1982	202,055	5,315	207,370
1983	141,455	4,835	146,290
1984	103,175	4,310	107,485
1985	92,295	3,110	95,405
1986	88,737	2,414	91,151
1987	105,567	3,119	108,686
United Kingdom			
1980	86,310	6,350	92,660
1981	118,530	5,645	124,175
1982	221,780	6,675	228,455
1983	162,750	7,225	169,975
1984	124,120	6,250	130,370
1985	110,680	4,605	115,285
1986	105,005	4,015	109,020
1987	136,200	5,330	141,530

1 Including leases, sales to housing associations and sales of dwellings previously municipalised. Data are rounded to the nearest five.

Source: Department of the Environment

The General Household Survey (GHS) found that nearly two-fifths of households in rented local authority or new town accommodation who were not buying their accommodation during the period 1985 to 1986 gave financial reasons as the main reason for not doing so. A further quarter gave being too old or too old coupled with financial reasons as their main reason for not buying their accommodation. A quarter gave the condition or unsuitability of their accommodation as a reason for not buying (Table 8.10).

Results from the GHS also indicated that over the period 1981 to 1987 there had been a reduction in the percentage of local authority tenant households who had considered buying and had taken active steps to do so, from 10 per cent in 1981 to 7 per cent in 1987. There was a slight increase over the same period in those who had considered buying but had taken no active steps, from 11 per cent to 14 per cent.

Under the Government's low cost home ownership initiatives, local authorities and new towns sold sufficient land to private housebuilders in England between April 1979 and March 1988 for them to build almost 62 thousand houses (Table 8.11; see Appendix for details). 'Building under licence' schemes by private builders in partnership with local authorities resulted in 21 thousand homes for sale, and local authorities in Great Britain also built for sale over 8 thousand low cost homes. Measures intended to make existing housing stock available at low cost include homesteading, improvement for sale, and voluntary sale of vacant public sector property. (The Appendix, Part 8, gives details of all these initiatives.) By March 1988, just under 8 thousand dwellings had been sold by local authorities and new towns in Great Britain for homesteading, and nearly 2 thousand had been improved for sale.

On average between 1975 and 1981, 100 thousand renovation grants a year were paid to private owners and tenants and to housing associations in Great Britain (Table 8.12). There was then a sharp increase to 161 thousand in 1982, 311 thousand in 1983 and 341 thousand in 1984. This rise was stimulated by temporary measures which made intermediate and repairs grants to private owners and tenants available

8.10 Households in local authority and new town rented accommodation: reasons for not buying, 1985-86

Great Britain   Percentages and numbers

Reasons for not buying	Percentage of those who were no longer considering buying [1]	Percentage of those who had not considered buying [2]
Too old or too old and financial reasons	26	26
Financial reasons (old age not mentioned)	38	36
Accommodation in poor repair/lacks amenities	11	7
Accommodation is unsuitable for other reasons	14	17
Does not like people in the area	7	5
Other environmental reasons	6	6
Accommodation is not for sale	1	8
Does not know whether accommodation is for sale	—	4
Other reasons	21	18
Sample size (= 100%) (numbers)	540	4,405

1 Households in local authority rented accommodation who had considered buying their accommodation in the last 2 years but who were not considering buying at the time of interview.
2 Households in local authority rented accommodation who had not considered buying their accommodation in the last 2 years.

Source: General Household Survey, combined data for 1985 and 1986

at an increased maximum rate of 90 per cent for certain applications approved by local authorities after 12 April 1982 and submitted to them before 1 April 1984. The number of grants paid in 1986 and 1987, although down on 1983 and 1984, remained higher than in earlier years at 177 and 173 thousand respectively.

In 1978 the Government introduced measures to improve the standard of insulation in the housing stock as part of the energy conservation programme. A programme of insulation work in the public sector was undertaken with a view to providing basic insulation in public sector dwellings. In April 1980 the separate allocations to local authorities for insulation work were discontinued: authorities now decide how much of their

8.11 Low cost home ownership [1]: by type of initiative

Great Britain   Numbers

Initiative type	1979—80	1980—81	1981—82	1983—84	1984—85	1985—86	1986—87	1987—88
Local authority sales [2]								
Built for sale	917	1,855	990	990	1,020	785	655	448
Building under licence [3]	..	..	2,300	5,180	3,445	2,295	2,670	1,797
Improvement for sale	—	15	145	285	365	365	230	139
Homesteading	400	950	1,560	970	850	660	360	761
Sales of shared ownership	605	985	830	865	1,410	765	900	737
Sales of land for housing — dwelling equivalent [3,4]	..	7,290	7,980	11,410	8,325	6,645	5,612	3,933
Mortgage indemnities [3,5]	—	—	140	2,585	1,050	650	655	388

1 See Appendix, Part 8: Low cost home ownership.
2 Excludes new towns.
3 England only.
4 Assumes 23 dwellings per hectare.

5 Agreements whereby the local authority indemnifies the building society, insurance company, etc. in the event of default by the mortgagor, thus reducing the calls on local authority lending.

Source: Department of the Environment

8.12 Renovations [1]: by tenure

Great Britain and
United Kingdom

Thousands of
dwellings

	Renovations [1] by tenure: Great Britain				
	Local auth-orities[2]	Housing assoc-iation grant aided[3]	Grants for private owners and tenants[4]	Total	Total United Kingdom
1971	89	5	103	197	197
1972	137	4	146	287	288
1973	188	3	200	391	393
1974	121	4	246	371	373
1975	62	5	102	169	171
1976	75	14	82	171	173
1977	94	20	71	185	201
1978	106	15	70	191	214
1979	111	20	80	211	239
1980	100	18	95	212	238
1981	79	14	94	187	211
1982	108	22	139	269	295
1983	126	18	293	437	463
1984	123	21	320	464	492
1985	157	13	200	370	395
1986	207	14	163	385	420
1987	234	13	160	407	441

1 See Appendix, Part 8: Renovations.
2 England figures are of work approved up to 1977 and of work completed from 1978. Scotland figures are of work approved, and include figures for Scottish Special Housing Association. Wales figures are of work completed but from 1977 to 1983 inclusive local authorities figures for Wales were not collected.
3 Grants approved under specific housing association legislation. Figures for England and Wales are of work approved up to 1977 and work completed from 1978. Figures for Scotland are of work approved. Excludes hostel bedspaces from 1985.
4 Includes grants paid to housing associations under private owner legislation. England and Scotland figures from the fourth quarter 1980 and figures for Wales from the second quarter 1981 include a number of grants to tenants in both public and private sectors.

Source: Department of the Environment

block capital allocations to devote to such work. It should be noted that, in addition to the work carried out under the public sector programme, insulation of

8.13 Energy conservation

Great Britain

Thousands and £m

	Work completed for local authorities under the energy conservation programme [1]		Grants paid under the homes insulation scheme [2]	
	Dwellings (thousands)	Expenditure (£m)	Dwellings (thousands)	Amount (£m)
1978	139.1	5.6	94.4	3.8
1979	632.2	31.3	421.6	16.5
1980	454.7	28.2	332.6	15.3
1981	184.5	11.2 [3]	368.8	23.6
1982	271.6	16.0	400.3	27.3
1983	263.2	24.4	387.9	27.6
1984	152.2 [3]	17.8	345.2	23.6
1985	79.1	15.8	410.9	28.6
1986	82.6	10.8	397.6	27.3
1987	66.8	8.0	335.4	21.7

1 The 'energy conservation programme' began in April 1978.
2 The 'homes insulation scheme' was introduced in September 1978 for private owners and tenants and extended to public sector tenants in November 1979; figures for Wales prior to 1984, included in these data, are for private sector only.
3 From April 1981 cost figures for energy conservation programme for Wales no longer collected. Numbers of dwellings not collected from April 1981 to December 1983, inclusive.

Source: Housing and Construction Statistics, 1977—1987
Great Britain, Department of the Environment

public sector dwellings occurs as an inextricable part of renovation work. The Homes Insulation Scheme which was introduced in September 1978 made provision for grant assistance toward the cost of installing basic loft insulation in uninsulated private sector dwellings. In 1979 the scheme was extended to make grants available to public sector tenants. In July 1984 grant aid was extended to include the insulation of dwellings with inadequate existing loft insulation (ie less than 30mm). Between 1978 and 1987, 3.5 million grants worth over £215 million were paid (Table 8.13).

Costs and mortgages

Expenditure on housing by UK households according to the economic activity of head of household in 1986, is given in Table 8.14. Not surprisingly households with the highest household income generally incurred higher expenditure on housing. It should be noted that mortgage payments include capital repayments, and are shown after allowing for relief at the basic tax rate, which since 1983 has been deducted from interest charges at source by lending bodies. Mortgage interest relief at source (MIRAS) was introduced in April 1983 starting with the major lenders, the Building Societies. There remains a small percentage of mortgagors who continue to pay their mortgage interest gross of tax. Households buying their homes with mortgages, especially those with new mortgages, tend to pay out

more each week for housing than other households; however they are acquiring a capital asset at the same time.

The Green Paper *'Paying for Local Government' (Cmnd. 9714)* published in January 1986 sets out proposals for a phased replacement of domestic rates by the Community Charge which each authority would set and which would be paid by every adult resident in its area. These proposals are to be implemented in April 1989 in Scotland and in April 1990 in England and Wales. Households containing several adults are likely to pay more in Community Charge than in domestic rates, while households with only one adult are likely to pay less

8.14 Expenditure on housing: by tenure and household income [1], 1986

United Kingdom £ and numbers

	Gross normal weekly household income[1]						
	Up to £100	Over £100, up to £150	Over £150, up to £200	Over £200, up to £250	Over £250, up to £300	Over £300	All households
In process of purchase (£ per week)							
Mortgage payments (net of tax relief)	23.94	23.06	26.94	29.75	32.14	42.54	34.93
Rates and water charges[2]	5.56	6.51	7.49	8.01	9.39	11.28	9.45
Maintenance and insurance of structure	5.30	5.74	5.28	5.99	19.23	11.59	10.53
Ground rent	0.18	0.15	0.25	0.16	0.16	0.20	0.19
Total	34.98	35.46	39.96	43.91	60.92	65.61	55.10
Owned outright (£ per week)							
Rates and water charges[2]	5.26	7.96	8.91	9.41	9.37	11.47	7.99
Maintenance and insurance of structure	4.36	6.33	7.12	6.79	7.14	11.48	6.72
Ground rent	0.36	0.40	0.34	0.41	0.28	0.52	0.39
Total	9.98	14.69	16.37	16.61	16.79	23.47	15.10
Local authority tenants (£ per week)							
Rent, rates, and water charges [2]	6.83	15.35	21.19	23.44	25.73	25.31	12.86
Maintenance and insurance of structure	0.42	1.00	1.55	1.19	2.24	4.07	0.99
Total	7.25	16.35	22.74	24.63	27.97	29.38	13.85
Privately rented unfurnished (£ per week)							
Rent, rates, and water charges[2]	12.60	19.99	26.71	23.14	21.11	27.11	18.43
Maintenance and insurance of structure	0.55	1.18	0.80	0.20	0.59	0.63	0.67
Total	13.15	21.17	27.51	23.34	21.70	27.74	19.10
Privately rented furnished (£ per week)							
Rent, rates, and water charges[2]	15.69	27.22	28.47	37.04	47.65	60.63	31.05
Maintenance and insurance of structure	0.96	0.10	0.86	1.36	1.66	0.98	0.88
Total	16.65	27.32	29.33	38.40	49.31	61.61	31.93
Number of households in sample	1,988	861	838	754	696	1,753	6,890

1 Excluding imputed rent for owner-occupiers.
2 Net of rebates.

Source: Central Statistical Office, from Family Expenditure Survey

Housing benefit is the main source of assistance with housing costs available to people on low incomes and can be received in the form of rent rebates or allowances and rate rebates. The number of rent rebates and allowances has shown slight fluctuations between 1984 and 1987 with just over half the recipients also receiving supplementary benefit (Table 8.15). The number of rate rebates has remained largely stable between 1984 and 1987. During the period a number of changes to the standard housing benefit scheme were introduced which took some householders out of standard housing benefit and offset an otherwise upward movement in

8.15 Householders [1] receiving housing benefit: by type of rebate

Great Britain Thousands and percentages

	1984		1985		1986		1987	
	Certificated[2]	Standard[3]	Certificated[2]	Standard[3]	Certificated[2]	Standard[3]	Certificated[2]	Standard[3]
Type of rebate (thousands)								
Rent rebate and allowance	2,520	2,230	2,590	2,140	2,670	2,170	2,690	2,140
Of which (percentages)								
pensioners [4]	45	60	40	65	35	65	35	65
Rate rebate	3,210	3,620	3,310	3,540	3,450	3,380	3,430	3,420
Of which (percentages)								
pensioners [4]	45	70	45	70	40	70	40	70
Owner-occupiers	20	45	20	40	20	40	20	40
Local authority tenants	60	45	60	45	60	50	60	50
Private tenants	15	10	20	10	20	10	20	10

1 Householders are people responsible for paying rent or rates. Percentage breakdowns are given to the nearest 5 per cent. See Appendix, Part 8: Housing benefit.
2 Householders who are themselves, or whose partners are, in receipt of supplementary benefit. Figures are taken from the quarterly supplementary benefit statistical enquiries in August.

3 Estimates for householders not in receipt of supplementary benefit are based on the standard housing benefit statistical enquiries relating to September/October.
4 Certificated householders are given pensioner status if the supplementary benefit claimant is over pension age. Standard housing benefit householders are given pensioner status if they or their partners are over pension age.

Source: Department of Social Security

Social Trends 19, © Crown copyright 1989

numbers. Mortgage interest tax relief which relates to interest on mortgages of up to £30 thousand is a further source of assistance for owner-occupiers. This topic is discussed more fully in Chapter 5 (see Table 5.15). It is estimated that the cost of mortgage interest relief in the United Kingdom for 1987-88 was £4,850 million with an average cost per mortgage of £580.

Chart 8.16 clearly shows the two periods during the 1970s when house prices rose very rapidly in the United Kingdom, 1971-73 and 1978-79, and it was during these two periods that the ratio of house prices to gross earnings (as measured by the New Earnings Survey) rose significantly above its long term average figure of 3.5. The house price to earnings ratio rose sharply from 3.5 in 1971 to 5.0 in 1973 as a result of a four-fifths increase in house prices over the period. In 1979 the ratio peaked again following a 29 per cent rise in house prices since 1978. The 1987 figures show that house prices are continuing to increase more rapidly than earnings, and the ratio, now at 3.8, has almost reached the 1979 peak again, though far short of the previous peak in 1973.

Average price increases of new dwellings purchased with a building society mortgage remain much higher in the South East, particularly in Greater London, than elsewhere in the United Kingdom and much lower in Northern Ireland. There is, however, a narrowing of the gap between prices in London and adjoining regions with major house price rises being recorded in all regions on the edge of the South East between the 2nd quarter of 1987 and the 2nd quarter of 1988; especially in the West Midlands (26 per cent) East Midlands (24 per cent) East Anglia (31 per cent) and the South West (24 per cent). More information on regional differences can be found in the CSO publication *Regional Trends* and in the Department of the Environment publication *Housing and Construction Statistics.*

Although total mortgage advances continued to increase, the amount of building society advances dropped slightly in 1987 (Table 8.17). Building society mortgages still account for the majority of loans but the banks and insurance companies are taking an

8.16 Dwelling price to earnings ratio[1]

United Kingdom

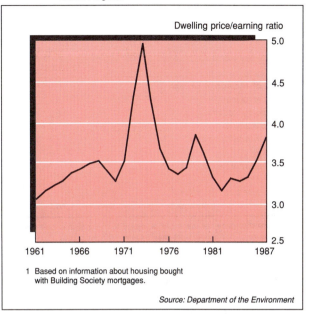

1 Based on information about housing bought with Building Society mortgages.

Source: Department of the Environment

increasing share of the mortgage market. The amount advanced in bank mortgages increased by over a third in 1987 compared to 1986 and advances have more than trebled during the period 1983 to 1987. Insurance companies have also increased their volume of business. In the past three years advances have more than doubled and mortgage advances are now ten times greater than in 1971. Advances by local authorities have dropped steadily since reaching a high point in 1982. The majority of local authority mortgages were for sales of dwellings under the 'right to buy' scheme (see Table 8.9) and the high point corresponds with the peak in the sale of dwellings. The average amount lent by building societies in 1987 was £27,600. Average loans made by banks, insurance companies, and local authorities were £36,600, £34,200 and £12,700 respectively. For first time buyers with building society mortgages the average loan in 1987 was £25,500.

8.17 Mortgages: by selected institutional sources[1]

United Kingdom

£ million

	Gross advances					Net advances [2]					
	Building societies	Banks [3]	Local authorities	Insurance companies	Total	Building societies	Banks	Local authorities	Insurance companies	Other public sector	Total [4]
1971	2,758	..	232	149	3,139	1,600	90	107	14	12	1,823
1976	6,117	..	320	229	6,666	3,618	80	67	45	60	3,870
1981	11,991	..	633	374	12,998	6,331	2,265	272	88	353	9,309
1982	15,339	..	1,046	383	16,768	8,147	5,078	555	6	351	14,137
1983	19,263	4,582	529	579	24,953	10,928	3,531	− 305	124	21	14,299
1984	24,034	3,917	429	605	28,985	14,572	2,043	− 195	259	− 20	16,659
1985	26,491	6,157	273	648	33,569	14,711	4,224	− 502	200	− 9	18,624
1986	36,937	9,248	176	1,108	47,469	19,541	4,670	− 506	435	− 7	24,133
1987	35,349	13,193	156	1,537	50,235	15,210	10,030	− 464	769	− 7	25,538

1 Loans for house purchase, improvement and 'topping up' loans; small amounts of commercial lending by building societies also included. Local authority figures are net of Housing Association Grant.
2 Net of repayments of principal and, for local authorities, housing association grant.

3 Excluding bridging finance.
4 Includes miscellaneous financial institutions from 1983.

Source: Department of Trade and Industry; Bank of England; Central Statistical Office; Department of the Environment

8.18 Source of mortgage or loan: by socio-economic group of head of household, 1986

Great Britain

Percentages and numbers

Source of mortgage or loan	Pro-fessional	Employers and managers	Inter-mediate and junior non-manual	Skilled manual and own account non-pro-fessional	Semi-skilled manual and personal service	Un-skilled manual	All heads of households
Source of mortgage or loan							
(percentages)							
Building society	80	76	84	80	77	82	80
Local authority	2	4	3	9	12	9	6
Insurance company	3	5	4	3	3	2	4
Bank	15	15	9	8	6	5	11
Other source	1	2	1	1	3	2	1
Sample size (= 100%)[1]							
(numbers)	367	960	809	1,227	336	56	3,755

1 Because mortgages or loans can be raised from more than one source, the sum of the percentages may exceed 100 per cent.

Source: General Household Survey, 1986

In 1986 9 out of 10 households in Great Britain with mortgages had either a building society or bank mortgage (Table 8.18). Of households headed by people in the professional group only 6 per cent had a mortgage from any other source. Local authorities were the second major source for households headed by semi-skilled manual workers, an eighth of households in this group had a local authority mortgage. For unskilled manual workers the major source for a mortgage is a building society. Four-fifths of this type of household have a building society mortgage compared with a tenth with a local authority mortgage, and even fewer have a bank mortgage.

The number of building society mortgage repossessions in the United Kingdom increased in 1987 to 22.9 thousand and the proportion of all loans which were over six months in arrears at the end of 1987 rose again after a slight drop in 1986 (Table 8.19), leaving the end 1987 figure at virtually the same level as at the end of 1985. Factors affecting the growth of arrears and repossessions in the early and mid-1980s were increasing unemployment, extension of building society lending criteria, competition in the mortgage market, and easier availability of credit. In 1984 and 1985 the figures were also affected by the dispute in the coal industry. However the first six months of 1988 showed a decrease in the number of loans in arrears with a drop of around 10 per cent compared with the first half of 1987. The number of properties taken into possession also showed a considerable change with a drop of more than 15 per cent over the figures for 1987.

8.19 Building societies mortgages: balances, arrears[1] and possessions

	All mortgages			Loans in arrear at end-period (thousands)		Properties taken into possession in period (thousands)
	Number of mortgages (thousands)	Balance due on mortgages (£ million)	Average mortgage balance (£)	By 6—12 months	By over 12 months	
1971	3,915	10,332	2,639	..	..	..
1976	4,624	22,565	4,880	..	..	..
1981	5,505	48,875	8,878	18.7 [2]	..	4.2 [3]
1982	5,664	56,697	10,011	23.8	4.8	6.0
1983	5,949	67,476	11,343	25.6	6.5	7.3
1984	6,354	81,889	12,887	41.9	8.3	10.9
1985	6,705	96,776	14,676	49.6	11.4	16.8
1986	7,071	115,695	16,611	45.3	11.3	21.0
1987	7,197	130,870	18,183	48.2	13.0	22.9
1988 [4]	7,280	142,794	19,615	45.8	12.0	9.8

1 Building Societies Association estimates as at 31 December in each year except 1988, 30 June.
2 Figure should be treated with caution.

3 Change in method of estimation.
4 At end June 1988.

Source: The Building Societies Association

Characteristics of occupants

8.20

Tenure of households [1]: by age of head, 1971 and 1986

Great Britain   Percentages and numbers

	Owner-occupied		Rented						Sample size (= 100%) (numbers)	
			Local authority/ new town		Unfurnished private [2]		Furnished private			
	1971	1986	1971	1986	1971	1986	1971	1986	1971	1986
Age of head of household *(percentages)*										
24 or under	31	35	21	30	24	17	23	18	503	461
25-29	52	65	24	20	17	10	7	5	848	819
30-44	56	73	29	18	13	7	2	2	3,118	2,850
45-59	48	70	35	23	16	7	1	1	3,475	2,326
60-69	48	56	32	35	19	9	1	—	2,186	1,711
70-79	46	51	31	36	22	12	1	—	1,338	1,465
80 or over	43	45	31	39	24	16	1	—	430	553
All households	49	62	31	26	17	9	3	2	11,898	10,185

1 Excludes those living in caravans or houseboats.
2 Includes those renting from a housing association and those
 renting with a job or business.

Source: General Household Survey, 1971 and 1986

Table 8.20 shows that households with heads aged between 30 and 59 accounted for most of the increase in the proportion of owner-occupiers in Great Britain between 1971 and 1986. The generally lower proportions of owner-occupiers in older age groups compared with those aged between 30 and 59 reflect the lower proportions of previous generations that became owner-occupiers and the fact that most of those local authority tenants who have bought their

homes under the 'right to buy' arrangements have been aged under 60. Even if the proportion of new generations becoming owner-occupiers stabilises, the overall proportion of owner-occupiers will rise as, for example, those in the 30 to 44 age group in 1986 move into the 55 to 69 age group in 2010.

Elderly households are more likely than households in general to live in local authority or unfurnished privately rented property. The private rented sector is also a

8.21

Accommodation type and tenure of households: by socio-economic group of head of household [1], 1986

Great Britain   Percentages and numbers

	Pro- fessional	Employers and managers	Inter- mediate and junior non- manual	Skilled manual and own account non-pro- fessional	Semi- skilled manual and personal service	Unskilled manual	All heads of households
Accommodation type *(percentages)*							
Detached house	44	38	18	13	8	5	19
Semi-detached house	31	29	32	38	30	27	33
Terraced house	15	19	26	35	36	36	29
Purpose built flat/maisonette	6	8	16	11	21	25	14
Converted flat or maisonette/rooms	4	4	7	3	4	6	4
With business premises/other	1	3	1	1	—	—	1
Tenure of households *(percentages)*							
Owner-occupied							
Owned outright	23	30	30	23	20	19	25
Owned with mortgage	67	53	38	40	19	10	38
Total owner-occupiers	90	83	68	63	39	29	63
Rented							
Local authority/new town	3	8	20	29	47	59	27
Unfurnished private [2]	2	4	8	6	10	10	7
Furnished private	2	1	3	1	2	2	2
Rented with job or business	4	4	1	1	3	—	2
Total rented	10	17	32	37	61	71	37
Total households in sample [3] (= 100%) (numbers)	541	1,800	2,101	3,041	1,723	554	9,760

1 Excludes households headed by members of the armed forces, full time
 students, and those who have never worked.
2 Includes those renting from a housing association.

3 Excludes those living in caravans or houseboats, and cases where
 tenure is not known.

Source: General Household Survey

comparatively important source of housing for young people; for example, households with heads aged 24 or under were the only group with a substantial proportion (18 per cent) living in furnished private rented accommodation in 1986. Households in the private rented sector are more mobile within their particular sector than other households, and most of the movers are in the age groups with household heads aged under 45.

Non-manual heads of household are likely to be buying their homes - 67 per cent of professional, and 53 per cent of employer or manager heads of household in Great Britain in 1986 were owner-occupiers with a mortgage (Table 8.21). By contrast, among unskilled manual heads of household only 10 per cent were owner-occupiers with a mortgage, while 59 per cent were local authority or new town tenants. This tenure pattern is not just a result of differences in current income level (although it may be linked to stability of income), as owner-occupation is higher in the non-manual groups than in manual ones even if people with the same incomes are compared.

Three-quarters of professional households occupy a detached or semi-detached house, five times as many as occupy a terraced house. Of unskilled manual workers' households over a third occupy a terraced house, just over a quarter a semi-detached house, and a quarter occupy a purpose built flat or maisonette. Nearly three-quarters of skilled manual workers occupy either a semi-detached or terraced house.

Digest of Environmental Protection and Water Statistics

The Digest highlights trends in the main area of environmental protection and water supply. Produced annually by the Department of the Environment the Digest brings together in a convenient form statistics from a wide variety of reports and papers.

Areas covered include air quality, radioactivity, noise, blood lead concentrations, solid waste, landscape and nature conservation, and water quality, supply and use.

Number 10, 1988.   £8.00

Chapter 9: Transport and the Environment

Transport

- Cars, taxis and motorcycles accounted for more than four-fifths of all passenger transport in Great Britain in 1987, compared to about half in 1961. *(Chart 9.1 below and Table 9.3)*

- The number of private cars licensed in the United Kingdom has increased almost three-fold between 1961 and 1987 whilst two-wheeled motor vehicles licensed have halved in this period. *(Table 9.6)*

- In 1987 about one-third of all households in Great Britain did not have regular use of a car or van compared with two-thirds in 1961. *(Chart 9.7)*

- Men are more likely to pass their motor vehicle driving test than women. *(Table 9.8)*

- For each kilometre someone travels, the likelihood of being injured on a pedal-cycle is second only to the likelihood on a motorbike. *(Table 9.13)*

The environment

- Emissions from power stations accounted for 70 per cent of total sulphor dioxide emissions in the United Kingdom in 1986, having remained fairly constant since 1976; emissions from other industries have halved in the same period. *(Table 9.15)*

- Natural sources of radiation provide almost nine-tenths of the total dose of radiation per head in the United Kingdom; almost all the dose from man-made sources arises from medical diagnosis and treatment. *(Chart 9.18)*

- The number of prosecutions for water pollution rose by 27 per cent between 1986 and 1987. *(Table 9.19)*

- The number of domestic noise complaints to Environmental Health officers in England and Wales rose seven-fold in the 10 years to 1986-87. *(Chart 9.21)*

9.1 Road and rail passenger transport use

Great Britain

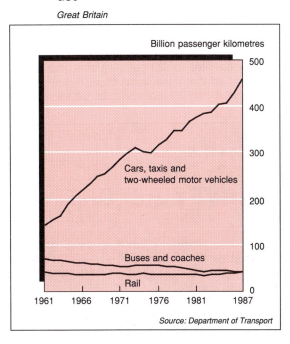

Billion passenger kilometres

Cars, taxis and two-wheeled motor vehicles

Buses and coaches

Rail

Source: Department of Transport

9.2 Air pollution: smoke and sulphur dioxide

United Kingdom

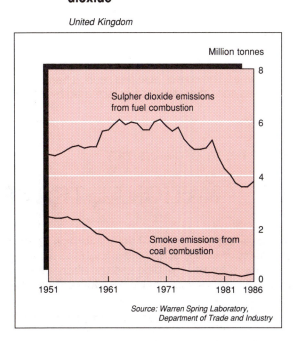

Million tonnes

Sulpher dioxide emissions from fuel combustion

Smoke emissions from coal combustion

Source: Warren Spring Laboratory, Department of Trade and Industry

Transport

9.3 Passenger transport: use and prices

Billion passenger kilometres and price indices

	1961	1971	1976	1981	1985	1986	1987
Use (Great Britain)							
Billion passenger kilometres travelled by:							
Air [1]	1	2	2	3	4	4	4
Rail [2]	39	36	33	34	36	37	39
Road							
Buses and coaches	67	51	53	42	42	41	41
Cars, taxis, and two-wheeled motor vehicles[3]	142	284	314	374	409	434	457
Bicycles	10	4	4	4	5	4	4
Total	259	377	406	457	496	520	545
Price indices (1985 = 100) (United Kingdom)							
Implied cost to the consumer [4] of:							
Air fares [5]	. .	29	54	86	100	99	95
Railway fares	. .	20	45	84	100	105	110
Bus and coach stage service fares	. .	18	36	78	100	107	111
Purchase of new and second-hand cars, motorcycles, and other vehicles	. .	22	42	85	100	108	120
Vehicle running costs	. .	19	40	80	100	94	97
All transport and travel	. .	21	41	82	100	101	106
Retail prices index (all items)	14	21	42	79	100	103	108

1 Domestic scheduled journeys only, including Northern Ireland and the Channel Islands.
2 British Rail, *plus* London Regional Transport, Strathclyde PTE, and Tyne and Wear PTE.
3 Based on statistics of vehicle-kilometres derived from traffic counts and estimates of average number of persons per vehicle derived from the National Travel Survey.
4 Based on national accounts estimates of consumers' expenditure. See Appendix, Part 9: Passenger transport prices.
5 Includes non-scheduled and international flights.

Source: Department of Transport; Central Statistical Office

Since 1961 there has been a decline in the use of public transport, while the use of private road vehicles has trebled (Chart 9.1 and Table 9.3). In 1987 cars, taxis, and motorcycles accounted for 84 per cent of all passenger kilometres travelled in Great Britain compared to 55 per cent in 1961. A quarter of all travel in 1961 was by bus or coach but by 1986 the share had fallen to less than a tenth. The amount of rail travel declined in the sixties and seventies but has since increased back to its 1961 level, although its share of total travel has fallen from 15 per cent in 1961 to just over 7 per cent in 1987.

The lower part of Table 9.3 shows transport costs to the consumer. The cost of new and second hand cars, motorcycles and other vehicles has increased by 20 per cent between 1985 and 1987 compared with an increase of only 8 per cent in the retail prices index. Rail fares together with bus and coach fares increased by slightly more than the retail prices index in this period, whilst the cost of air fares and vehicle running costs fell in this period.

According to the National Travel Survey (NTS), 27 per cent of all journeys made in 1985-86 were to or from work, or in the course of work (Table 9.4). These accounted for 32 per cent of mileage travelled. Journeys for social or entertainment purposes, holidays and day trips accounted for 33 per cent of all journeys and 42 per cent of the mileage travelled. Although shopping accounted for 20 per cent of all journeys it only

DEPARTMENT OF TRANSPORT

NATIONAL TRAVEL SURVEY REPORT

The only comprehensive, national source of travel information — linking different kinds of travel with the characteristics of travellers and their families. The NTS provides a picture of personal travel, particularly in terms of people and the distance they travel. It emphasises those characteristics of people and their households that have most effect on their extent of travel.

AN ANALYSIS OF PERSONAL TRAVEL

9.4 Number of journeys and distance travelled per person per week: by purpose [1] and age, 1985–86

Number of journeys and miles travelled

	To or from work	In course of work	Education	Escorting Work	Escorting Education	Shopping	Other personal business	Social or entertainment	Holidays/ day trips/ other	All purposes
Number of journeys										
0–15 years	0.1	—	2.6	0.2	0.2	1.8	1.0	3.0	0.7	9.8
16–59 years										18.0
Males	6.5	1.2	0.3	0.5	0.1	2.3	2.0	4.3	0.8	18.0
Females	3.7	0.3	0.3	0.3	0.5	3.1	1.8	3.8	0.7	14.5
60 years and over	0.8	0.1	—	0.1	—	2.9	1.4	2.5	0.8	8.6
All ages	3.1	0.4	0.7	0.3	0.2	2.6	1.6	3.5	0.8	13.2
Distance travelled (miles)										
0–15 years	0.5	0.1	8.1	1.1	0.6	8.5	4.5	21.9	11.4	56.6
16–59 years										
Males	54.8	28.2	1.9	2.0	0.6	11.3	12.1	37.6	14.8	163.2
Females	19.8	3.7	1.8	1.7	1.5	14.8	9.8	32.0	15.2	100.2
60 years and over	4.5	2.2	—	0.6	0.1	11.5	7.5	19.2	12.5	58.2
All ages	22.2	9.5	2.8	1.4	0.7	11.8	8.8	28.7	13.1	99.5

1 See Appendix, Part 9: Journey purpose.

Source: National Travel Survey, Department of Transport

accounted for 12 per cent of mileage travelled. In 1985-86, people were making 13 journeys per week compared with 11 in 1965 and the average journey length has increased from about 6½ miles in 1965 to 7½ miles in 1985-86. The average journey distance travelled by women to or from work was less than the distance travelled by men partly because fewer women than men worked and partly because women working both full-time and part-time tended to take jobs closer to home: the average journey to and from work for women was 5 miles compared to 8 miles for men.

Table 9.5 compares the various types of transport used by men and women to get to and from work. The differing patterns of travel to work between men and women are of course dependent on the distance that they have to travel to work. Women are more likely than men to travel to work by bus or on foot, whilst men are more likely than women to travel by car, motorcycle or bicycle. A similar percentage of men and women travel to work by train. In 1985-86, 67 per cent of all journeys to and from work were by car, van, or lorry as the main mode of transport, compared to 54 per cent in 1972-73. There was a downward trend in the use of buses which fell from 23 per cent in 1972-73 to 11 per cent in 1985-86. These general trends are reflected in both male and female journeys to work and show the changing patterns of transport use described at the beginning of this chapter.

At the end of 1987 the total number of vehicles licensed in the United Kingdom was 22.6 million (Table 9.6). The number of licensed private cars increased between 1961 and 1987 from 6.3 to 17.8 million with most of this increase taking place during the 1960s, the number almost doubling between 1961 and 1971. On the other

9.5 Transport to and from work: by main mode [1] of transport and sex

Great Britain

Percentages and thousands

	Rail	Bus	Car, van, lorry	Motor cycle	Bicycle	Walk[2]	Other	Number of journeys in sample (= 100%) (thousands)
Females								
1972-73	6	38	39	1	5	8	4	19,622
1975-76	5	30	46	1	6	10	3	32,262
1978-79	4	30	47	1	4	10	4	26,037
1985-86	6	19	59	1	4	7	3	30,925
Males								
1972-73	5	15	61	4	7	5	2	40,171
1975-76	5	11	66	4	7	5	2	61,096
1978-79	4	13	66	3	6	6	2	48,823
1985-86	5	7	72	3	6	4	2	53,269

1 The mode used for the greater part of the journey.
2 Excludes walks under 1 mile.

Source: National Travel Survey, Department of Transport

9.6 Motor vehicles currently licensed and British Rail passenger carriages

United Kingdom   Thousands

	1961	1971	1976	1981	1985	1986	1987
Type of vehicle							
Private and light goods [1]:							
Private cars	6,306	12,125	14,104[9]	15,287	16,858	17,396	17,805
Other vehicles	623	1,199	1,396	1,513	1,717	1,779	1,856
Motorcycles, scooters, and mopeds [2]	1,842	1,033	1,235	1,386	1,160	1,076	986
Public transport vehicles [3]	94	108	115	112	122	127	132
Goods [1,4]	675	697	669	578	600	608	631
Other vehicles [5,6,7]	687	697	701	908	1,169	1,186	1,203
All motor vehicles	10,227	15,859	18,220	19,784	21,626	22,172	22,613
British Rail passenger carriages [8]	..	18.3	17.1	16.2	14.1	13.7	13.0

1 The revised 'Private and light goods' and 'Goods' taxation classes became effective from 1 October 1982. Retrospective counts prior to 1982 have been estimated.
2 Also includes Northern Ireland figures for three wheelers (under 406 kilos) and pedestrian controlled vehicles.
3 Includes taxis. Tram cars are included in 1961.
4 Includes agricultural vans and lorries, showmen's goods vehicles, and vehicles licensed to draw trailers. Also includes Northern Ireland figures for general haulage tractors.
5 Includes agricultural tractors, combine harvesters and other agricultural machinery, mowing machines, digging machines,

mobile cranes, and works trucks, three wheelers, pedestrian controlled vehicles, general haulage contractors, and vehicles exempt from taxation.
6 Prior to 1976 includes personal and direct export vehicles, 11 thousand in 1987.
7 From 1981 includes exempt tax classes 61 and 62, which were not included in previous censuses, and electric vehicles which have been exempt from tax since 1980.
8 Position at end March.
9 From 1978 the census has been taken on 31 December, previous censuses were taken on 30 June.

Source: Department of Transport

hand, the number of motorcycles, scooters, and mopeds fell from 1.8 million in 1961 to 1.0 million in 1971, though it had increased again to 1.4 million by 1981 before falling back to 1.0 million by 1987. The number of British Rail passenger coaches decreased by 24 per cent between the years 1976 and 1987, most of this decrease occurring between 1981 and 1987. This is in contrast to an increase of 15 per cent in the distance travelled by rail passengers between 1981 and 1987, half of which is attributed to increased British Rail use. These figures represent the better use of resources and the tighter control of stock by British Rail.

Chart 9.7 illustrates how the rapid growth in car ownership during the 1960s has subsequently slowed down. In 1961, 31 per cent of households had the regular use of one or more cars. This proportion had increased to over 50 per cent by 1969 but only to 64 per cent by 1987. However, amongst car owning households, the proportion with at least two cars has continued to rise steadily - from 2 per cent of all households in 1961 to 19 per cent in 1987. Conversely the proportion of households without the regular use of a car has fallen from 69 per cent in 1961 to 36 per cent in 1987. The number of cars currently registered with a company address in Great Britain has risen by 18 per cent since 1983 to 2.2 million in 1987.

A much higher proportion of high income households than low income households had cars according to the National Travel Survey (NTS) in 1985-86. Amongst the 25 per cent of households with the lowest incomes only 20 per cent of households owned a car, while in the highest 25 per cent, 93 per cent owned a car. Car ownership is also related to socio-economic group According to the NTS, 86 per cent of households with heads in the professional or managerial groups had cars, while at the other extreme only 38 per cent of non-skilled manual workers had cars in 1985-86.

Table 9.8 shows that the pass rates of men in driving tests have changed little between October 1980 and April 1985, whilst those for women have increased slightly. In April 1985, 51 per cent of men taking their driving test for the first time and 56 per cent of those taking a subsequent test passed, while for women these proportions were only 39 and 49 per cent respectively. The pass rate decreases with age for all applicants at both first and subsequent tests. In both October 1980 and April 1985, 54 per cent of those taking motor car driving tests were female and between these dates, the share of males taking two wheeler driving tests fell from 92 per cent to 87 per cent.

9.7 Households with and without regular use of a car[1]

Great Britain

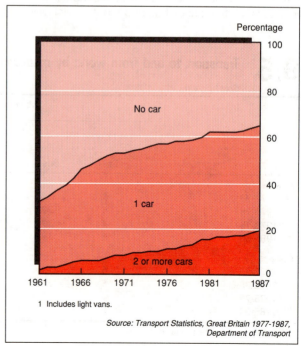

1 Includes light vans.

Source: Transport Statistics, Great Britain 1977-1987, Department of Transport

9.8 Driving tests: pass rates at first and subsequent tests [1]

Great Britain   Percentages

	First test				Subsequent test			
	Males		Females		Males		Females	
	Oct 1980	Apr 1985	Oct 1980	Apr 1985	Oct 1980	Apr 1985	Oct 1980	Apr 1985
Age group								
Under 21	53	53	40	44	61	59	52	56
21—40	47	50	37	36	54	55	48	49
41—50	42	40	21	22	31	40	34	35
Over 50	39	36	14	17	27	34	20	32
All aged 16 or over	51	51	37	39	55	56	46	49

1 Figures shown are based on all tests conducted during a two day
  period in the months shown for licence groups A to E (motor cars,
  motor cycles and mopeds).

Source: Department of Transport

In April 1985, by far the most common group of faults which led to, or contributed to failure in motor car driving tests was the 'omission of precautions before starting the engine; improper use of accelerator/clutch/brakes/gears and steering; lack of control on moving off'. In 11 per cent of tests the examiner had to take emergency action, either oral (4 per cent of tests) or physical (7 per cent of tests).

Table 9.9 looks at car ownership in various countries compared to that of the United Kingdom. In the United Kingdom, the number of cars per thousand population rose by almost a half between 1971 and 1987, with the greater part of that increase between 1971 and 1981. Greece had the largest rise in the number of cars per

thousand population, an increase of 4½ times between 1971 and 1987, whilst the USA had the smallest increase, a quarter over the same period. However, the USA had by far the greatest number of cars per thousand population of the countries compared throughout the period covered in the table. Care should be taken in making international comparisons because definitions and coverage of statistics can vary greatly between countries.

Some of the British Rail (BR) passenger business and performance indicators are presented in Table 9.10. The rail network in Great Britain comprises an inter-city network, local stopping services, commuter services, and freight and parcel services. The efficiency of the rail system may be measured, in part, by the punctuality

9.9 Car ownership [1]: international comparison

	Number of cars per 1000 population		
	1971	1981	1986
United Kingdom	224	281	323
Belgium	223	325	343
Denmark	231	267	303
France	261	367	386
Germany (Fed. Rep.)	247	385	441
Greece	30	93	137
Irish Republic	141	226	201
Italy	210	322	393
Japan	100	211	237
Luxembourg	300	377	432
Netherlands	212	324	346
Portugal	74	136	167
Spain	81	211	249
Sweden	291	348	389
USA	448	538	562
Yugoslavia	43	115	128

1 Includes all licensed cars.

Source: Annual Bulletin of Transport Statistics, United Nations; World Road Statistics, International Road Federation

9.10 British Rail: performance indicators

	1976	1981	1986–87	1987–88
Loaded train kilometres per member of staff (thousand)	2.07	2.21	2.67	2.86
PSO [1] plus PTE [2] grant per passenger kilometre (pence) [3]	3.04	3.74	2.67	2.43
Passenger receipts per passenger kilometre (pence) [3]	4.74	4.71	4.91	4.89
Percentage of trains arriving within 5 minutes of scheduled time	93	90	90	90
Percentage of trains cancelled	0.8	1.1	1.2	1.1

1 The PSO (Public Service Obligation) grant is paid by central government
  through the Department of Transport.
2 The PTE (Passenger Transport Executive) grant is paid by some local
  governments to subsidise services in their areas.
3 Adjusted for general inflation by the GDP market price deflator
  (1987-88 prices).

Source: Transport Statistics, Great Britain 1977– 1987 Department of Transport

of the passenger train service and by the number of passenger train cancellations as well as by the use people make of trains (see Tables 9.3 and 9.6). Two of BR's objectives are to achieve a 'punctuality' standard of 90 per cent of all passenger trains arriving on time or less than 5 minutes late and a 'cancellations' standard of only 1.per cent of current timetable services. It is evident that the first of these criteria has been met in recent years but the number of cancellations does not yet meet the objective set. The number of loaded train kilometres per member of staff has risen by 29 per cent from 1981 to 1987 whilst the Public Service Obligation (PSO) and Passenger Transport Executive (PTE) grants per passenger kilometres have decreased by 35 per cent in real terms, and the passenger receipts per passenger kilometre have increased by 4 per cent in the same period. In 1985-86, over half of the total distance travelled on British Rail or London Regional Transport was for work or education, a third for leisure purposes and only an eighth for personal business.

Chart 9.11 reflects the increasing popularity of air travel by United Kingdom residents who made a total of 19.3 million visits abroad by air in 1987, compared to 11.4 million in 1981 and 5.9 million in 1971. From a low starting point, the greatest proportional increase over the period 1971 to 1987 was in air travel to Australia and New Zealand. The number of such visits increased almost eight fold to 201 thousand in this period but still only represented 1 per cent of all visits by air. In 1987 air travel to the EC represented about two thirds of all air travel abroad.

Sea travel has also been increasing in popularity, but to a lesser extent than air travel. In 1987, United Kingdom residents made a total of 8.1 million visits abroad by sea, compared to 7.7 million in 1981 and 3.6 million in 1971. In 1987 sea travel to the EC represented about 93 per cent of all sea travel. (Table 10.16 and Charts 10.15 and 10.17 in Chapter 10: Leisure contain information on holidays abroad by residents of Great Britain.)

9.11 Air and sea travel — visits abroad[1] by United Kingdom residents: by destination

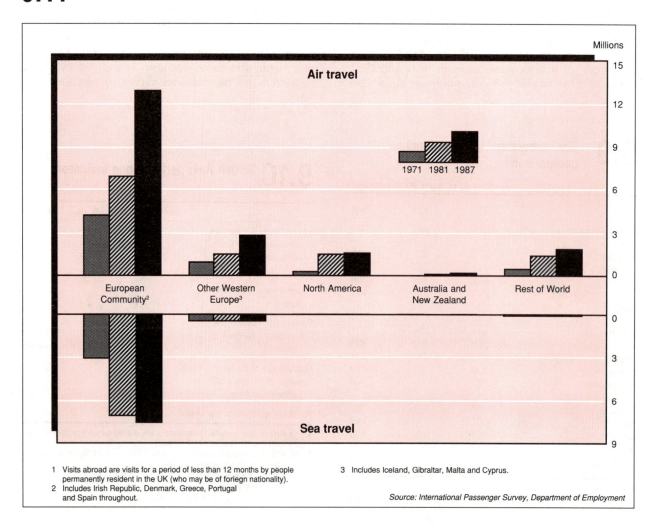

1 Visits abroad are visits for a period of less than 12 months by people permanently resident in the UK (who may be of foriegn nationality).
2 Includes Irish Republic, Denmark, Greece, Portugal and Spain throughout.

3 Includes Iceland, Gibraltar, Malta and Cyprus.

Source: International Passenger Survey, Department of Employment

Chart 9.12 shows that in 1987, 3.9 million accompanied passenger cars were carried by roll-on/roll-off ferries. Since 1970 accompanied car traffic has grown by almost 2½ times reflecting the growth in motoring holidays abroad and day tripping. The number of accompanied passenger cars carried by hovercraft services more than doubled between 1971 and 1979 to 374 thousand vehicles before declining dramatically to 204 thousand in 1984, though by 1987 it had recovered to 238 thousand. In contrast, the number of accompanied buses and coaches using the roll-on/roll-off ferry service increased about twelve-fold between 1971 and 1987 to 179 thousand.

Construction of the Channel Fixed Link between the United Kingdom and France began in 1987. When completed (planned for Spring 1993) it is intended to provide a direct rail link between London, Paris and Brussels and eventually with Glasgow, Birmingham and Manchester. A toll area, frontier controls, shops, and other facilities are planned at the United Kingdom shuttle terminal, with access for road vehicles from the M20 motorway and local roads.

9.12 Roll-on roll-off ferry traffic: accompanied passenger cars, foreign and coastwise traffic[1]

Great Britain

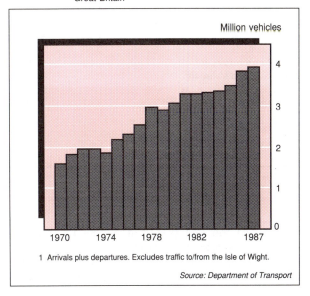

1 Arrivals plus departures. Excludes traffic to/from the Isle of Wight.

Source: Department of Transport

Table 9.13 shows transport casualty rates per billion passenger kilometres by mode of travel. Air transport is the least likely mode for a casualty to occur whilst two wheeled motor vehicles are the most likely, followed by pedal cycles. The rate of two-wheeled motor vehicle casualties decreased fairly steadily between 1976 and

9.13 Casualty rates: by mode of transport

Rate per billion passenger kilometres

	1976	1981	1982	1983	1984	1985	1986	Average 1976–86
Air [1]								
Deaths	1.1	—	—	—	—	0.7	—	0.3
Total casualties	1.1	0.1	—	0.3	—	1.3	0.2	0.5
Rail [2]								
Deaths	0.3	0.2	0.3	0.1	0.7	0.0	0.4	0.3
Total casualties	10.4	5.4	8.5	5.6	10.4	10.5	14.4	10.6
Road [3]								
Bus or coach [4]								
Deaths	1.3	0.5	0.8	0.9	0.9	0.8	0.6	0.8
Total casualties	242	235	243	246	249	244	232	240
Car [4]								
Deaths	8.2	6.1	6.3	5.1	5.3	4.8	5.2	5.9
Total casualties	482	392	388	331	348	351	372	382
Two-wheeled motor vehicles [4]								
Deaths	98	162	156	138	138	133	127	156
Total casualties	13,525	9,876	10,274	9,213	9,117	9,432	8,713	10,245
Pedal cyclists [4]								
Deaths	75	78	59	65	69	57	68	68
Total casualties	5,807	6,327	5,627	6,115	6,188	5,400	6,532	6,024
Sea [5]								
Deaths	1.2	1.0	2.1	1.5	0.5	3.0	0.6	1.8
Total casualties	..	..	..	34.6	29.8	56.9	43.0	41.1 [6]

1 World passenger carrying services of UK airlines for fixed wing craft over 2300 kg. Casualties exclude cabin crew. Passenger kilometres relate to revenue passengers only.
2 The rail casualty data refer to passengers and staff in train accidents only in Great Britain. They exclude other movement accidents, eg boarding, or alighting from trains, non-movement accidents such as falling over packages on platforms, and confirmed suicides and trespassers.

3 A road accident death is defined as 'sustained injuries which caused death within 30 days after the accident'.
4 Drivers and passengers in Great Britain.
5 Passenger carrying services of UK registered vessels. Casualties exclude crew.
6 Average for 1983 to 1986 only.

Source: Department of Transport

9.14 Consumers' expenditure per head [1] on transport

United Kingdom   £ per week at 1985 prices and percentages

	1963	1971	1976	1981	1984	1985	1986	1987
Net purchase of motor vehicles, spares and accessories	1.45	2.54	2.43	2.85	3.37	3.54	3.80	4.10
Maintenance and running of motor vehicles	1.74	3.10	3.72	4.12	4.48	4.63	4.85	5.04
Railway fares [2]	0.48	0.47	0.43	0.46	0.49	0.50	0.52	0.54
Bus and coach fares [2]	1.33	0.99	0.91	0.69	0.65	0.67	0.61	0.62
Other travel and transport[3]	0.47	0.77	0.88	1.26	1.36	1.42	1.60	1.89
All transport and vehicles	5.47	7.88	8.36	9.38	10.36	10.77	11.39	12.19
Expenditure on transport and vehicles as a percentage of total consumers' expenditure	*11.3*	*14.2*	*13.8*	*14.2*	*14.6*	*14.7*	*14.8*	*15.1*

1 Average weekly expenditure per head of population.
2 Includes purchase of season tickets.
3 Includes purchase and maintenance of other vehicles and boats.

Source : Central Statistical Office ; Office of Population Censuses and Surveys

1986, while the rate of bus and coach casualties remained at about the same level. In the last few years, the death rates for cars and two-wheeled motor vehicles have been below the 1976-86 average, but in general it is difficult to discern trends because the year to year rates fluctuate so much. Data averaged over the period 1976-86 show that 60 per cent of air casualties resulted in death compared to 4 per cent for sea transport, 3 per cent for rail transport, 2 per cent for cars and two-wheeled motor vehicles, 1 per cent for pedal cyclists and only 0.3 per cent for buses and coaches.

Between 1963 and 1987 the proportion of consumers' expenditure allocated to transport and vehicles increased from 11.3 to 15.1 per cent (Table 9.14). In 1963, 32 per cent of transport and vehicle expenditure was absorbed in the maintenance and running of motor vehicles; by 1987 this had increased to 41 per cent. Conversely, the proportion that went on bus and coach fares fell from 24 per cent in 1963 to 5 per cent in 1987. These figures reflect the changing patterns of transport use and costs shown earlier in Chart 9.1 and Table 9.3.

The Environment

There has been a growing concern over recent years about environmental problems and while this section gives a certain amount of information more detail is available from the Department of the Environment's *Digest of Environmental Protection and Water Statistics.*

9.15 Air pollution: by source

United Kingdom   Million tonnes and thousand tonnes

	1951	1956	1961	1966	1971	1976	1981	1986
Smoke: emissions from coal combustion (million tonnes)								
Domestic	1.31	1.32	1.13	0.88	0.55	0.33	0.24	0.24
Industry [1]	1.11	1.00	0.43	0.18	0.06	0.04	0.03	0.03
All sources	2.42	2.32	1.56	1.06	0.61	0.37	0.27	0.27
Sulphur dioxide: emissions from fuel combustion (million tonnes)								
Domestic	0.87	0.78	0.79	0.68	0.46	0.28	0.21	0.20
Power Stations	1.02	1.29	1.98	2.29	2.80	2.69	2.71	2.60
Other Industry [2]	2.88	3.06	2.93	2.96	2.57	2.02	1.30	0.93
All sources	4.77	5.13	5.70	5.93	5.83	4.99	4.23	3.74
Emissions of lead from vehicles (thousand tonnes)	..	..	..	..	7.3	7.6	6.7	2.9
Carbon monoxide from all sources (million tonnes)	..	..	..	..	..	4.86	5.07	5.60
Nitrogen dioxide from all sources (million tonnes) [3]	..	..	..	..	..	1.86	1.86	1.94
Hydrocarbons from all sources (million tonnes)	..	..	..	..	..	1.89	1.95	2.07

1 Includes collieries, commercial/public services, agriculture, and miscellaneous. Excludes fuel conversion industries (eg power stations) where smoke emissions are relatively low.

2 Includes commercial/public services, agriculture, road and rail transport, and refineries.
3 Expressed as nitrogen dioxide equivalent.

Source: Warren Spring Laboratory, Department of Trade and Industry

To try and gauge public concern the Department of the Environment (DoE) commissioned National Opinion Polls Market Research Limited (NOP) to carry out a survey in England and Wales in September 1986. A random sample of the population were asked how worried they felt about each of a list of environmental issues. More than four out of five respondents were either 'very worried' (the majority) or 'quite worried' about chemicals put into rivers and the sea and about getting rid of nuclear waste. Also of general concern were the destruction of wildlife, dirty beaches and bathing water and pollution from insecticides, fertilisers and chemical sprays. Fewer people (some two out of five) were generally worried about the lack of access to open spaces and countryside, ugly new buildings and noise (see Chart 9.14 in *Social Trends 18* for more details).

Fumes and smoke from factories and car exhaust fumes were of concern to about three-fifths of respondents to the DoE/NOP survey. Chart 9.2 and Table 9.15 show air pollution by source in the United Kingdom and it can be seen that improvements in emissions of most pollutants have taken place over the past 30 years. For example, emissions from domestic coal-burning fires, the major contributor to emissions of smoke in the United Kingdom, have fallen substantially in the last 20 to 25 years so that in 1986 the amount emitted was about a fifth of the amount in 1961. This reduction was due to the existence of smoke control areas and the gradual switch by consumers away from coal towards gas and electricity.

After being relatively stable throughout the 1960's and early 1970's total emissions of sulphur dioxide (SO_2) from fuel combustion in the United Kingdom fell by 39 per cent between their 1970 peak and 1986. However both smoke and sulphur dioxide emissions rose slightly between 1984 and 1986. In 1986 power stations accounted for 70 per cent of all SO_2 emissions. Even

given the reduction in United Kingdom SO_2 emissions they are still considerably higher than most other European Community countries (Table 9.15 and Table 9.16).

Chart 9.17 shows the acidity deposited in rain in the United Kingdom in 1986. It is based on the amount of hydrogen ions found per square metre; the more ions found the lower the pH and the greater the acidity. The chart shows that more acid rainfalls in areas of high rainfall, even though the areas of highest acidity of rain (that is acidity per unit of rainfall) are just to the east of the industrial centres of the North and Midlands.

Reflecting increasing interest in the environment over two-thirds of the respondents to the DoE/NOP survey referred to earlier in this section were either 'very worried' or 'quite worried' about acid rain which affects lakes, soils, forest, crops and the stonework of historic buildings. Rainfall is naturally slightly acid because atmospheric carbon dioxide dissolves in it to form carbonic acid, and other naturally occurring atmospheric constituents can increase its acidity. Man-made contamination is mainly by sulphuric and nitric acids formed from sulphur dioxide and oxides of nitrogen emitted during the burning of coal, oil, and natural gas. Unburnt hydrocarbons from car exhausts and other pollutants are also contributory factors.

9.17 Acidity deposited in rain [1], 1987

United Kingdom

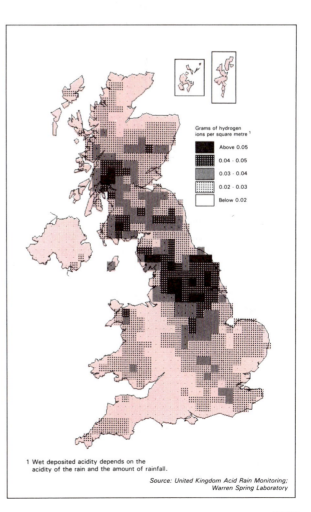

Grams of hydrogen ions per square metre [1]

- Above 0.05
- 0.04 - 0.05
- 0.03 - 0.04
- 0.02 - 0.03
- Below 0.02

1 Wet deposited acidity depends on the acidity of the rain and the amount of rainfall.

Source: United Kingdom Acid Rain Monitoring; Warren Spring Laboratory

9.16 Air pollution — sulphur dioxide emissions: EC comparison [1]

Million tonnes

	1975	1980	1985
United Kingdom	5.1	4.7	3.5
Belgium	. .	0.9	0.6 [5]
Denmark	0.4	0.4	0.3
France	3.2	3.6	1.7
Germany (Fed. Rep.)	3.5 [2]	3.2 [3]	2.6
Greece	. .	0.8	0.7
Irish Republic	0.2	0.2	0.1
Italy	. .	3.8	3.2 [5]
Luxembourg	. .	— [4]	— [4]
Netherlands	0.3	0.4	0.2
Portugal	0.2	0.3	0.3
Spain	3.0	3.3	2.9

1 Definitions and measurement methods may differ from country to country.
2 1976.
3 Annual average of 1978 and 1982.
4 Emissions for Luxembourg were about 20,000 tonnes in 1980 and 1985.
5 1983.

Source: OECD Environmental Data Compendium; Department of Environment

Despite an increase in petrol consumption of over a third since the early 1970s, emissions of lead by petrol driven vehicles in 1986 had dropped by 65 per cent from the peak year of 1973 when 8.4 thousand tonnes were emitted. This is a result of a reduction in the permitted lead content from 0.84 grams per litre in 1972 to 0.40 grams in January 1981 and to 0.15 grams in December 1985; by the end of January 1986 virtually all petrol sold conformed with the low lead specification. The week beginning 31 October 1988, was the United Kingdom's Nation Lead-Free Petrol Week. Almost two-thirds of cars on the road are potentially capable of using unleaded petrol; although some would need a minor adjustment. By October 1988 some 2,300 garages were selling unleaded petrol, and with increasing availability it is expected that uptake will increase from the level of about 2 per cent of total petrol consumption as at that date.

9.18 Radiation exposure of the UK population: by source, 1988

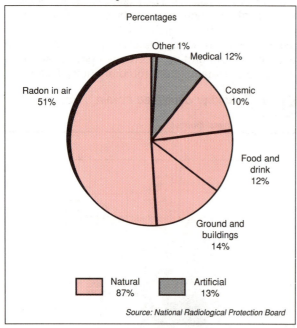

United Kingdom

Percentages

Other 1%
Medical 12%
Cosmic 10%
Radon in air 51%
Food and drink 12%
Ground and buildings 14%

Natural 87%   Artificial 13%

Source: National Radiological Protection Board

Public concern about radiation levels from artificial sources is frequently expressed in the United Kingdom. Chart 9.18 shows however that there are many natural sources of radiation which provide by far the greater proportion of the total dose of radiation per head in the

United Kingdom. For example: cosmic rays from outer space pass through the atmosphere and cause irradiation on earth; the ground and building materials contain naturally-occurring radioactive materials (uranium, thorium and potassium); our bodies are slightly radioactive because the food and drink we consume contains tiny quantities of natural radioactive material. With the dose from nuclear weapons fallout, nuclear waste disposal and other artificial sources below 1 per cent of the total, most of the non-natural exposure from radiation comes from medical uses.

One natural source of radiation, radon gas, is produced during the radioactive decay of the uranium in earth materials. The gas is present in rocks and soils, and levels are higher in some parts of the country than in others because the uranium content varies from place to place and because some rocks and soils allow air to move more freely through them than others. Although in the open air radon is diluted to low levels, it can find its way into enclosed spaces such as houses and build up to higher levels. Throughout most of the country, radon levels in houses are not remarkable, but NRPB studies have shown that in the south west of England and to a lesser extent elsewhere, there are houses with relatively high concentrations. The Government has established an action level of 20 millisievert (mSv) per annum for existing houses and a design level of 5 mSv per annum for new houses. It is estimated that a few thousand houses are built each year in which the doses to occupants may exceed the design level; a few tens of thousands of existing houses are likely to exceed the action level. A programme of detection, prevention and remedy is underway throughout the United Kingdom. According to the National Radiological Protection Board (NRPB) the overall annual dose from radiation in the United Kingdom is estimated to be about 2.5 mSv per head on average.

Pollution of water from farm wastes have been of concern to Water Authorities because of the severe polluting nature of silage and slurry. Table 9.19 shows that although only 19 per cent of incidents reported concerned farm waste in 1987, 60 per cent of the prosecutions involved farms. Further information on farm waste pollution can be found in *Water Pollution from Farm Waste* published by the Water Authorities Association. Between 1986 and 1987 prosecutions increased overall by 27 per cent, while in the same period incidents increased by only 5 per cent.

9.19 Water pollution: incidents reported [1] where pollution was found [2] and prosecutions: by cause

England & Wales   Numbers

	1986 [3]		1987 [3]	
	Incidents	Prosecutions [4]	Incidents	Prosecutions [4]
Farm	3,495	140	3,870	192
Industry	7,729	105	7,575	115
Sewage	4,137	—	4,177	7
Other	4,286	5	5,017	4
TOTAL	19,647	250	20,639	318

1 To water authorities
2 For one authority (Welsh Water) cases where no pollution was found are included.

3 Certain authorities supplied data for financial rather than calendar years.
4 May relate to incidents which took place in the previous year.

Source: Water authorities

9.20 Quality of popular coastal bathing waters [1]: by Water Authority area

England, Wales and Northern Ireland   Numbers

	1986		1987	
	Number tested	Numbers failing to comply with EEC Bathing Water Directive coliform standards [1]	Number tested	Number failing to comply with EEC Bathing Water Directive coliform standards [1]
Water Authority area				
Northumbrian	19	10	19	10
Yorkshire	21	3	22	2
Anglian	28	8	28	10
Thames	2	1	2	2
Southern	65	24	65	27
Wessex (South Coast)	27	3	27	1
South West	103	25	109	13
Wessex (Bristol Channel)	11	4	11	5
Welsh	47	24	47	19
North West	30	26	30	20
England & Wales	353	128	360	109
Northern Ireland	5	2	14	3

1 See Appendix, Part 9: Quality of popular coastal bathing waters.

2 Failure to meet standards does not necessarily imply a danger to health.

Source: Water Authorities and Department of Environment (NI)

Table 9.20 shows how many popular coastal bathing waters, in England, Wales and Northern Ireland, identified under the EEC *Bathing Water Directive*, met the Directives bacteriological standards in 1986 and 1987. There were improvements in bathing water quality in half the water authority areas in England and Wales between the two years: although the number of waters tested in 1987 was marginally higher than 1986, the number of waters failing the standards fell, with just over half as many waters failing in the south west in 1987 as had failed in 1986.

There has been mounting evidence that chlorofluorocarbons (CFCs) are damaging the Earths ozone layer, the thin shield of gas in the upper atmosphere that protects the Earth from harmful ultraviolet radiation. In September 1987 concerned countries signed the Montreal Protocol, which sought to reduce production and use of CFCs. CFCs are mainly used as foaming agents to make insulation for the construction industry and packaging for food; as refrigents; as solvents; and as propellants for aerosols. Even given reductions by some manufacturers, the chemical industry is currently producing CFCs six times more quickly than the atmosphere can break them down; every atom of chlorine released into the stratosphere can destroy many thousands of molecules of ozone.

The number of complaints about noise received by Environmental Health Officers in England and Wales rose almost four-fold in the ten years to 1986-87. Chart 9.21 shows those categories which are controlled by section 58 of the *Control of Pollution Act* 1974. In 1986-87 over three-fifths of such complaints received were due to domestic noise.

9.21 Noise — complaints received by Environmental Health Officers: by source[1]

England & Wales

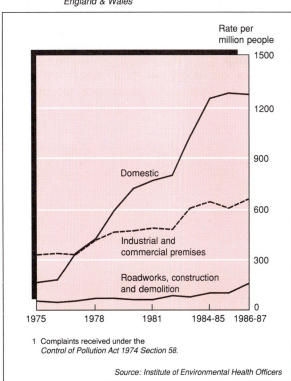

1 Complaints received under the *Control of Pollution Act 1974 Section 58.*

Source: Institute of Environmental Health Officers

9.22 Land: by agricultural and other uses, 1982 and 1987

United Kingdom   Percentages and thousand hectares

| | Agricultural land | | | Forest and wood-land [2] | Urban land and land not otherwise specified [3] | Total land (=100%) (thousand hectares) | Inland water (thousand hectares) |
	Crops and fallow	Grass and rough grazing	Other [1]				
Total land area *(percentages)*							
1982	21	57	1	9	12	24,088	323
1987	22	55	1	10 [4]	12 [4]	24,086 [4]	328 [4]

1 Land on agricultural holdings comprising farm roads, yards, buildings, gardens, ponds, derelict land, etc.
2 All forest land and private woodlands including woodland on agricultural holdings.

3 Land which is neither agricultural nor wooded, ie built-up areas, recreation areas, etc.
4 1986 data.

Source: Ministry of Agriculture, Fisheries and Food

Between 1982 and 1987 there was little change in the use of land in the United Kingdom (Table 9.22). There were marginal increases in the land used for crops and fallow, forest and woodland and inland water, while the amount of agricultural land used as grass and rough grazing fell by 2 percentage points (around 392 thousand hectares) over the five years.

Chart 9.23 shows the designated areas in the United Kingdom in 1988. Highlighted on the map are national parks, areas of outstanding natural beauty and defined heritage coasts. In 1988 there were 134 designated land areas covering 4,388 thousand hectares. In addition, there were 5,552 statutory protected land areas covering 2,206 hectares in 1988, such as Sites of Special Scientific interest, and 2,153 non-statutory protected land areas covering 135.1 thousand hectares. These latter areas are looked after by organisations such as the Royal Society for Nature Conservation, Nature Conservation Trusts, Royal Society for the Protection of Birds and the Woodland Trust. Table 11.6 shows membership of selected environmental groups.

9.22 Designated land areas [1], 1988

United Kingdom

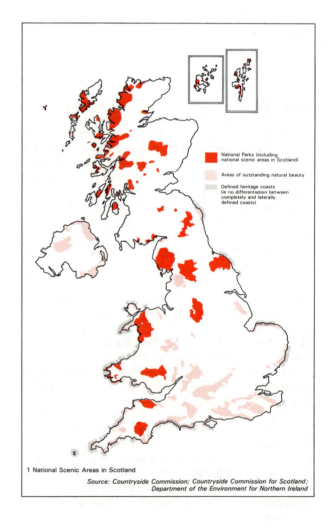

National Parks (including national scenic areas in Scotland)

Areas of outstanding natural beauty

Defined heritage coasts (ie no differentiation between completely and laterally defined coasts)

1 National Scenic Areas in Scotland

Source: Countryside Commission; Countryside Commission for Scotland; Department of the Environment for Northern Ireland

Chapter 10: Leisure

Availability of leisure time

- Retired men have the most leisure time per week and women in full-time employment have the least.
  (Chart 10.1 below)

- In the United Kingdom 99 per cent of full-time manual employees were entitled to four or more weeks holiday in 1987. This is double the most common holiday entitlement of 1961. *(Chart 10.2)*

Social and cultural activities

- In 1987 the average weekly time spent watching television in the United Kingdom was 25.5 hours. People aged over 65 watched more than 37.5 hours per week while those aged under 15 watched for around 19 hours. *(Table 10.4 and page 163)*

- Between 1983 and 1987 the proportion of households with a video cassette recorder in Great Britain increased from one in five to one in two. *(Chart 10.6 and page 165)*

- In 1987, there were around 75 million visits to the cinema in the United Kingdom, a 29 per cent increase on the trough of 58 million in 1984. *(Chart 10.7)*

Holidays

- About four out of ten adult residents of Great Britain did not take a holiday away from home in 1987, the same proportion as in 1971. The proportion taking two or more holidays each year increased from about one in seven in 1971 to one in five in 1987. *(Chart 10.15)*

Resources

- Households in the United Kingdom spent an average 16 per cent of their gross normal weekly income on leisure items in 1986. *(Table 10.20)*

10.1 Leisure time in a typical week, 1987

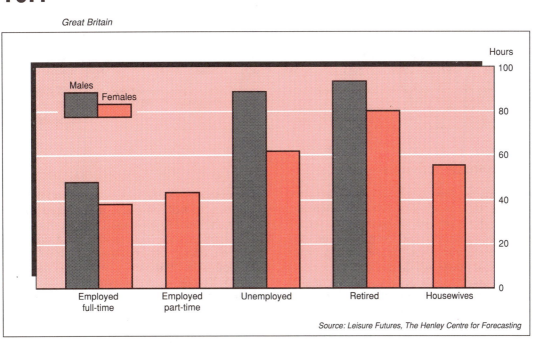

Great Britain

Source: Leisure Futures, The Henley Centre for Forecasting

Availability of leisure time

Chart 10.1 (on the previous page) illustrates the amount of leisure time available to people during a typical week in 1987. Of all the categories of people shown in the chart, the retired not surprisingly had the most leisure time per week at 93 hours for men and 80 hours for women. Unemployed males had 88 hours leisure time and unemployed females 62 hours; housewives had 55 hours leisure time. On average, female employees had less leisure time than males, generally because they spent more time on essential activities such as house cleaning, everyday cooking and essential shopping, although they spent less time on employment.

The trend over the past 25 years or so has been towards a reduction in working hours and an increase in holiday entitlement (Chart 10.2). In the 1960s a basic 40 hour working week became more common, and since then there has been a slow but continuous fall in normal basic hours of work. Over the period 1961 to 1987 the normal basic weekly hours worked by full-time manual employees fell from 42.8 to 38.9 hours and actual weekly hours worked from 45.5 to 43.0 hours. (Table 4.16 contains further details of average weekly working hours.) Average holiday entitlement with pay has been steadily increasing since the 1960s: in 1961, 97 per cent of full-time manual employees had a basic entitlement of only 2 weeks. By 1970 over half had an entitlement of 3 weeks or more and this had risen to 98 per cent by 1980. There were relatively few changes in holiday entitlements during the period of income policies between 1975 and 1978, but subsequently there was a general move towards a 4 week minimum, and by 1987, 99 per cent of full-time manual employees were entitled to 4 weeks or more, and 22 per cent to 5 weeks or more.

The rest of this chapter looks at what people do with their leisure time.

10.2 Weekly hours of work and paid holidays: full-time manual employees

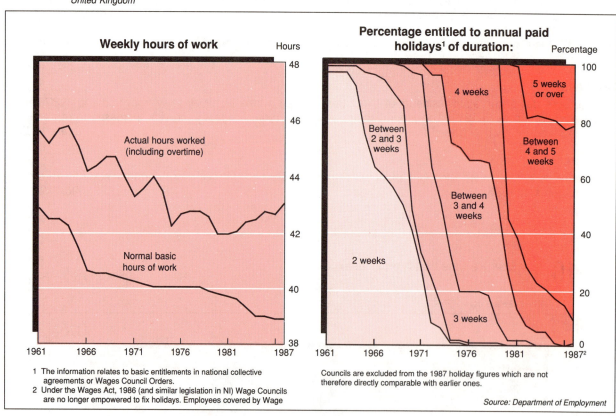

United Kingdom

1 The information relates to basic entitlements in national collective agreements or Wages Council Orders.
2 Under the Wages Act, 1986 (and similar legislation in NI) Wage Councils are no longer empowered to fix holidays. Employees covered by Wage Councils are excluded from the 1987 holiday figures which are not therefore directly comparable with earlier ones.

Source: Department of Employment

Social and cultural activities

Participation in many of the social and cultural activities shown in Table 10.3 varies little between men and women except for the almost exclusively female activities of needlework and knitting and the predominantly male activity of DIY. According to the General Household Survey (GHS) going to the cinema tends to be a young person's activity; about a quarter of 16 to 19 year olds went to the cinema in the four weeks before interview in 1986, 28 per cent of women and 24 per cent of men. Women are more likely to read books than men; nearly two-thirds of women read books in an average four-week period compared with just over half of men, and males aged 16 to 19 were the least likely to have read a book during the survey reference period. Men go out for a drink more than women, 65 per cent compared with 47 per cent, and for both sexes the participation rates decline over age 20 to 29 after increasing from age 16 to 19. Among other activities which decline in popularity with age are listening to records/tapes and dancing. Between 1983 and 1986 going out for a meal increased in popularity for men and women of all ages.

10.3 Participation [1] in selected social and cultural activities: by sex and age, 1986

Great Britain   Percentages and numbers

	Males					Females				
	16-19	20-29	30-59	60 or over	All aged 16 or over	16-19	20-29	30-59	60 or over	All aged 16 or over
Percentage in each age group engaging in each activity in the 4 weeks before interview										
Open air outings										
Seaside	4	6	8	4	6	9	9	9	5	8
Country	1	2	3	3	3	2	3	3	3	3
Parks	3	3	4	2	3	4	6	5	2	4
Entertainment, social, and cultural activities										
Going to the cinema	24	16	6	1	8	28	16	7	1	8
Visiting historic buildings	6	9	11	7	9	8	11	11	7	10
Going to the theatre/ opera/ballet	2	5	5	3	4	4	7	8	4	6
Going to museums/art galleries	3	5	4	3	4	2	5	4	2	4
Amateur music/drama	6	5	4	3	4	7	3	3	2	3
Going to fairs/amusement arcades	4	4	5	2	4	7	6	6	2	5
Going out for a meal [2]	41	56	50	35	47	50	57	51	35	47
Going out for a drink [2]	71	87	68	41	65	72	73	52	18	47
Dancing	19	13	9	5	9	32	18	11	5	12
Home-based activities										
Listening to records/tapes [2]	96	88	71	42	69	96	88	70	35	65
Gardening [2]	19	30	54	56	47	9	28	47	39	39
Needlework/knitting [2]	4	3	3	3	3	28	43	54	46	48
House repairs/DIY [2]	29	52	64	41	54	15	33	34	15	27
Reading books [2]	46	50	53	52	52	68	64	65	62	64
Sample size (= 100%) (numbers)	704	1,611	4,409	2,167	8,891	674	1,841	4,755	3,048	10,318

1 Annual averages of participation of people aged 16 or over.
2 The high participation levels are partly attributable to the fact that these items were prompted (see Appendix, Part 10: General Household Survey).

Source: General Household Survey, 1986

Generally people spend far more time watching television than listening to radio (Table 10.4). In 1987 the average weekly time spent watching television was 25 hours and 25 minutes per head, which meant that people aged 65+, viewing for 37 hours and 41 minutes per week, watched about 50 per cent more television than the average viewer. In 1987, people were watching, on average, more television than in 1984. The peak increase was between 1984 and 1985 and the amount of viewing decreased for all age groups except the over 65s between 1986 and 1987. The average time people spent listening to the radio was 8 hours and 52 minutes per head per week. Over 90 per cent of the population in the UK watched some television each

10.4 Television and radio: average viewing and listening per week, by age

United Kingdom   Hours and minutes and percentages

	Television viewing				Radio listening			
	1984	1985	1986	1987	1984	1985	1986	1987
Age groups (hours:mins per week)								
4-15	16:10	19:59	20:35	19:14	2:46	2:24	2:12	2:07
16-34	18:16	21:36	21:10	20:03	11:42	11:42	11:24	11:18
35-64	23:24	28:04	27:49	27:25	9:59	9:43	9:56	10:16
65+	29:50	36:35	36:55	37:41	8:01	8:04	8:27	8:44
Reach [1] (percentage)								
Daily	74	79	78	76	46	43	43	43
Weekly	90	94	94	93	81	78	75	74

1 Percentage of UK population aged 4+ who viewed television for at least three consecutive minutes or listened to radio for at least half a programme over a day (averaged over 7 days) or a week.

Source: Broadcasting Audience Research Board; British Broadcasting Corporation; Audits of Great Britain

10.5 Radio and television audiences[1] throughout the day, 1988[2]

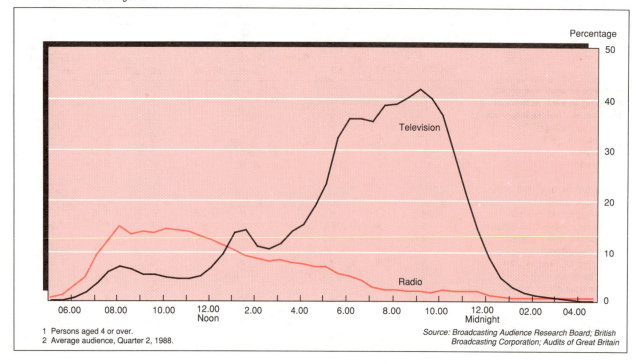

United Kingdom

Percentage

1 Persons aged 4 or over.
2 Average audience, Quarter 2, 1988.

Source: Broadcasting Audience Research Board; British Broadcasting Corporation; Audits of Great Britain

week in 1987, but the proportion who listen to some radio each week has been falling gradually in the last few years to 74 per cent in 1987.

The amount of time spent watching television increases with age in each year shown in Table 10.4, while radio listening consistently peaks at ages 16 to 34. In 1987 young people under 34 spent about half an hour per week less listening to the radio than they did in 1984, while people over 34 were spending half an hour more in 1987 than in 1984.

Not surprisingly, audiences for radio and television vary considerably at different times during the day (Chart 10.5). Between 8 am and 8.30 am an average 14.4 per cent of the UK population aged 4 or over listened to the radio in the second quarter of 1988, while 41.7 per cent watched television between 9 pm and 9.30 pm. Despite daytime television, radio is still more popular during the morning with television attracting more viewers from about 1.00 pm. Figures from the BBC Broadcasting Research Department show that the size of the potential audience of those people available to view in the daytime is very large. At the lunchtime peak it represents around half of the total UK population - about 26 million people. Even during mid-mornings and mid-afternoons it amounts to well over 20 million people.

At September 1988 television licence evasion involved an estimated 1.36 million households, approximately 6½ per cent of households in the United Kingdom. During the year to September 1988, 167 thousand people were convicted for television licence fee evasion compared to 162 thousand during the year to September 1987. In 1988 the maximum fine for licence

evasion was £400; the licence fee for a colour television in 1988 was £62.50.

Since 1979 video has been transformed from a specialised branch of communications technology to a mass domestic market. Chart 10.6 illustrates the substantial increase from 18 to 38 per cent in the proportion of households in Great Britain with a video

10.6 Households with a video cassette recorder: by household type, 1983 and 1986

Great Britain

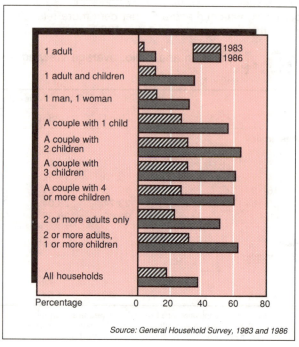

1 adult
1 adult and children
1 man, 1 woman
A couple with 1 child
A couple with 2 children
A couple with 3 children
A couple with 4 or more children
2 or more adults only
2 or more adults, 1 or more children
All households

Percentage 0 20 40 60 80

Source: General Household Survey, 1983 and 1986

cassette recorder (VCR) over the period 1983 to 1986, and preliminary GHS results indicate that in 1987 the figure had risen to 46 per cent. Availability of VCRs varies widely by composition of household; for example 64 per cent of households consisting of a couple with 2 children had the use of a VCR compared to 35 per cent of one-parent families and only 11 per cent of single-person households. The corresponding figures in 1983 were 31, 11 and 4 per cent respectively. Availability of VCRs had more than doubled for most household types between 1983 and 1986, and this corresponds with a reduction in the prices of blank and pre-recorded cassettes and the boom in rented video film availability.

According to the GHS, 17 per cent of all households had a home computer in 1986 compared with 9 per cent in 1984 - more data on household durables are available in Table 6.5.

Between 1955 and 1987 annual cinema admissions in the United Kingdom fell from 1,181 million to around 75 million. The downward trend is repeated in all countries shown on Chart 10.7, although the UK showed the most dramatic decline, with audiences cut by 94 per cent in 32 years, compared with a 48 per cent fall in the USA over the same period. Increased

10.7 Cinema audiences: selected countries

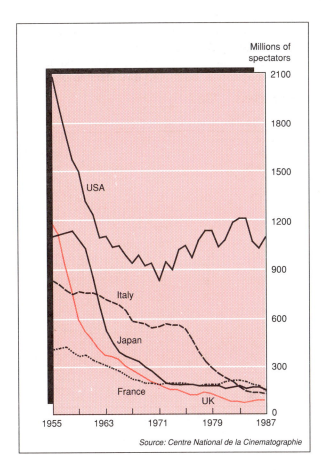

Source: Centre National de la Cinematographie

television ownership and viewing are obviously the main causes of decreasing cinema attendances, although the wider availability of video cassette recorders (see Chart 10.6) does not appear to have turned people away from the big screen since the three years to 1987 marked a 29 per cent rise in cinema attendances in the UK. (The Chart shows the number of spectators in each country; see Table 1.20 for relative population sizes.)

Chart 10.8 gives a comparison between UK sales of long-play albums (LPs), cassettes, singles and compact discs for the five years to 1987. While vinyl discs, particularly singles, have decreased in popularity, cassette sales have more than doubled since 1983, and compact disc sales have shown a massive 60-fold growth from 0.3 million units in 1983 to 18.2 million in 1987. In the USA CD sales growth is even more impressive from 0.8 million units in 1983 to 102.1 million in 1987, a 130-fold increase. Lower priced CD players, and the introduction of mid-price and budget discs have made the medium much more widely accessible and it is projected that CD trade deliveries may have secured a 40 per cent share of the total long-play market within three or four years.

Table 10.9 shows that in 1987 The Sun was the most popular daily newspaper, with a readership of 11.3 million people in Great Britain. Between 1971 and 1987 readership of The Sun rose by 33 per cent while that of the Daily Mirror fell by 34 per cent. In 1987 men were more likely than women to read each of the daily newspapers, while adults in social class A were the group most likely to read 'any daily newspaper' (74 per cent). In 1987 a new daily newspaper the London Daily

10.8 Trade deliveries of LPs, cassettes, compact disc and singles[1]

United Kingdom

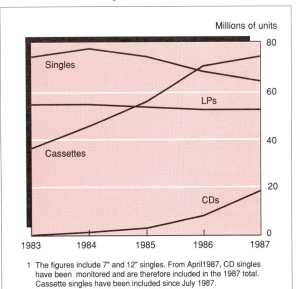

1 The figures include 7" and 12" singles. From April1987, CD singles have been monitored and are therefore included in the 1987 total. Cassette singles have been included since July 1987.

Source: British Phonographic Industry Year Book

10.9 Reading of national newspapers: by sex and social class[1], 1987

Great Britain

	Percentage of adults reading each paper in 1987		Percentage of adults in each social class reading each paper in 1987						Readership[2] (millions)		Readers per copy (numbers)
	Males	Females	A	B	C1	C2	D	E	1971	1987	1987
Daily newspapers											
The Sun	28	23	5	10	20	32	37	27	8.5	11.3	2.8
Daily Mirror	23	18	4	8	16	27	29	19	13.8	9.1	2.9
Daily Mail	11	10	14	14	14	9	6	5	4.8	4.5	2.5
Daily Express	10	9	9	12	13	10	6	6	9.7	4.3	2.5
The Star	11	7	2	2	6	12	15	9	—	3.9	3.2
The Daily Telegraph	7	5	28	16	8	3	1	2	3.6	2.8	2.4
The Guardian	4	3	9	10	4	1	1	1	1.1	1.5	3.1
The Times	4	2	16	8	3	1	1	1	1.1	1.2	2.7
Today	3	2	1	2	3	3	3	1	—	1.1	3.3
The Independent	3	1	6	6	3	1	1	—	—	0.9	2.8
Financial Times	3	1	8	5	2	1	—	—	0.7	0.8	3.5
Any daily newspaper [3]	73	63	74	67	67	70	72	59	..	68.0	
Sunday newspapers											
News of the World	30	27	9	12	23	36	40	30	15.8	12.8	2.6
Sunday Mirror	22	19	5	10	17	27	27	18	13.5	9.1	3.1
The People	20	17	3	8	16	23	25	17	14.4	8.1	2.8
Sunday Express	14	13	24	22	18	12	8	7	10.4	6.1	2.7
The Mail on Sunday	12	11	16	16	16	11	7	4	—	5.1	2.9
The Sunday Times	9	7	35	22	10	3	3	2	3.7	3.6	2.9
The Observer	6	5	14	14	7	3	2	2	2.4	2.3	3.0
Sunday Telegraph	5	4	19	11	7	3	2	1	2.1	2.2	3.0
Any Sunday newspaper [4]	76	71	78	75	74	76	76	64	..	74.0	

1 See Appendix, Part 10: Social class.
2 Defined as the average issue readership and represents the number of people who claim to have read or looked at one or more copies of a given publication during a period equal to the interval at which the publication appears.
3 Includes the above newspapers plus the *Daily Record*.

4 Includes the above newspapers plus *The Sunday Post* and *Sunday Mail*.

Source: National Readership Surveys, 1971 and 1987, Joint Industry Committee for National Readership Surveys; Circulation Review, Audit Bureau of Circulation

News was launched and the (London) Evening News was re-launched, but both had ceased publication before the end of the year. The Independent, launched in 1986, had a daily readership of nearly 1 million people in 1987.

Table 10.10 shows the readership of those general and women's magazines read by the highest proportions of the population in Great Britain. In 1971 and in 1987 the TV Times and the Radio Times were the most popular general magazines, both with a readership of around

10.10 Reading of selected magazines: by sex and social class[1], 1987

Great Britain

	Percentage of adults reading each magazine in 1987		Percentage of adults in each social class reading each magazine in 1987						Readership[2] (millions)		Readers per copy (numbers)
	Males	Females	A	B	C1	C2	D	E	1971	1987	1987
General magazines											
TV Times	19.5	21.4	21	22	22	20	20	17	9.9	9.2	3.0
Radio Times	19.2	20.7	26	26	23	18	17	16	9.5	8.9	2.9
Reader's Digest	16.0	14.5	20	20	18	15	12	9	9.2	6.8	4.3
Smash Hits	4.6	5.8	5	5	5	6	6	3	—	2.3	4.8
Weekly News	3.5	4.4	—	2	3	4	5	5	4.5	1.8	2.4
Exchange and Mart	5.7	1.9	3	3	4	5	4	2	—	1.7	7.7
Women's magazines[3]											
Woman's Own	3.4	17.7	8	10	12	11	11	9	7.2	4.8	3.8
Woman	1.9	13.7	6	7	9	8	7	7	8.0	3.6	3.1
Woman's Weekly	2.1	12.9	7	7	8	8	7	8	4.7	3.4	2.6
Family Circle	1.7	10.1	8	9	7	6	5	3	4.4	2.7	3.9
Good Housekeeping	2.0	9.2	15	12	7	4	3	2	2.7	2.6	6.4
Woman's Realm	1.2	7.9	4	4	5	5	5	5	4.6	2.1	3.0

1 See Appendix, Part 10: Social class.
2 See Table 10.9, footnote 2.
3 The social class analysis for women's magazines includes male readers.

Source: National Readership Surveys, 1971 and 1987, Joint Industry Committee for National Readership Surveys; Circulation Review, Audit Bureau of Circulation

10.11 Public libraries: percentage of stocks and issues by major type[1], 1986-87

United Kingdom

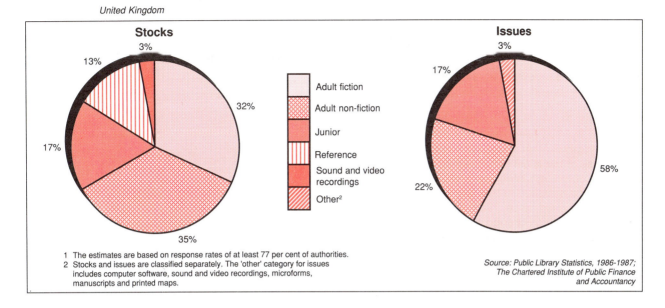

1 The estimates are based on response rates of at least 77 per cent of authorities.
2 Stocks and issues are classified separately. The 'other' category for issues includes computer software, sound and video recordings, microforms, manuscripts and printed maps.

Source: Public Library Statistics, 1986-1987; The Chartered Institute of Public Finance and Accountancy

9 million people. In 1987, slightly more women than men read these magazines. However, there was less variation in the proportion of adults in each social class reading the TV Times, than the Radio Times where the proportion ranged from 16 per cent in social class E to 26 per cent in social class A. Although Reader's Digest remained the third most popular general magazine, between 1971 and 1987 its readership fell by around a quarter.

Between 1971 and 1987 readership of all the most popular women's magazines fell. In 1987 the monthly magazines, Family Circle and Good Housekeeping, had on average more readers per copy than the other magazines shown in the table which are published weekly. Readership is not confined solely to women; among those magazines shown in the table 14 per cent of all readers in 1987 were men.

Public libraries in the United Kingdom held 135 million books in stock at the end of March 1987. During the year 1986-87, over 520 million issues were made. Adult fiction books accounted for almost 58 per cent of all issues but only 32 per cent of all stock (Chart 10.11).

The Public Lending Right (PLR) system enables payments to be made from central government funds to UK authors whose books are lent out from public libraries. Payments are annual and are proportionate to the number of times that the book is lent out during the year, and continue until 50 years after the author's death. According to a 1988 report published by the Registrar of Public Lending Right, 46 per cent of PLR payments are made to authors aged 60 and over, and only 7 per cent to those aged under 40. In 1988-89 about a third of the £3,500,000 distributed under PLR will go to authors of general and romantic adult fiction. One third of the money goes in payments of less than £600. No author can receive more than £6,000.

Table 10.12 shows the most popular tourist attractions in Great Britain. In recent years Blackpool Pleasure Beach has been the most popular attraction among those without an admission charge, with an estimated 6½ million visitors each year. In 1987 Madame Tussaud's in London was the top attraction for which there was an admission charge, with 2.4 million visitors. Next were Alton Towers Leisure Park and the Tower of

10.12 Attendances at the most popular tourist attractions

Great Britain   Millions

	1981	1986	1987
Attractions with free admission			
Blackpool Pleasure Beach	7.5	6.5	6.5
British Museum	2.6	3.6	3.7
National Gallery	2.7	3.2	3.6
Science Museum	3.8	3.0	3.2
Albert Dock, Liverpool	..	2.0	3.1
Tate Gallery	0.9	1.1	1.7
Bradgate Park	1.2	1.2	1.2
Duthie Park Winter Gardens, Glasgow	.	1.1	1.1
Pleasureland, Southport	.	.	1.1
Stapeley Water Gardens, Cheshire	.	1.0	1.0
Victoria and Albert Museum[1]	1.4	1.0	0.9
Attractions charging admission			
Madame Tussaud's	2.0	2.4	2.4
Alton Towers	1.6	2.2	2.3
Tower of London	2.1	2.0	2.3
Natural History Museum[2]	3.7	2.7	1.6
Blackpool Tower	.	1.4	1.5
London Zoo	1.1	1.2	1.3
Kew Gardens	0.9	1.1	1.3
Magnum Leisure Centre, Irvine	..	1.3	1.1
Thorpe Park	0.6	1.1	1.1
National Railway Museum	1.3	0.9	0.7

1 Voluntary admission charges apply.
2 Admission charges were introduced in April 1987.

Source: British Tourist Authority

London with 2.3 million visitors. Admissions to the Natural History Museum fell by around 40 per cent between 1986 and 1987 but attendances appear to have increased again in 1988. The Victoria and Albert museum now operates a scheme of voluntary entry charges.

Some of the most popular attractions to have opened since 1981 are outside London; the Jorvik Viking Centre in York, the Mary Rose Exhibition in Portsmouth, and the National Museum of Photography in Bradford as well as the Burrell Collection in Glasgow and the Albert Dock development in Liverpool. Innovative displays making use of the latest film and tape technology and computer controlled animated exhibits have made a significant contribution to the success of many of the attractions opened since 1981. The Museum of the Moving Image which opened on London's South Bank in September 1988 had attracted around 67 thousand visitors in its first six weeks.

According to the British Tourist Authority a record 15.4 million overseas visitors came to Britain in 1987. Nearly 20 per cent more visitors came from North America than in 1986, and historic properties gained most from this influx, showing a 9 per cent increase in visitors over the previous year. The overall rise in visitors at museums was 4 per cent, a significant improvement on the drop of 3 per cent between 1985 and 1986, in spite of the effects of the introduction of entry charges in some places.

Table 10.13 from the General Household Survey shows those sports in which at least 3 per cent of all adults in Great Britain took part in the most popular quarter of 1986. Walking was the most popular sporting activity; over a fifth of all adults went for at least one walk of 2 miles or more in the most popular quarters of both 1977 and 1986. Between 1977 and 1986 participation increased in swimming by around one third, and in snooker, billiards and pool by four-fifths (to 11 per cent). Over the same period participation in keep fit and yoga, squash, and cycling also increased, but still only 3 or 4 per cent of adults participated in each of these sports in 1986. In 1986 men were more likely than women to participate in all types of sports except for keep fit and yoga, which were predominantly female activities, and indoor swimming where the participation rates were very similar, 11 per cent for men and 12 per cent for women.

In 1987 estimated attendances at greyhound racing meetings were only just over half their level in 1971 (Table 10.14) although they were 10 per cent up on 1986. The Royal Automobile Club estimated that there were just over 4 million spectators at motor sports events in 1987, an increase of 50 thousand on 1982

10.13 Participation in the most popular[1] sporting activities

Great Britain   Percentages

		1986		
	1977	Males	Females	Total
Percentage engaging in each activity in the 4 weeks before interview (most popular quarter)				
Walking — 2 miles or more[2]	22	24	22	23
Swimming (Indoor)	13	11	12	11
(Outdoor)		7	6	7
Snooker/billiards/pool	6	19	3	11
Darts	10	11	4	7
Keep fit/yoga	1	1	6	4
Golf	4	6	1	4
Fishing	4	6	1	3
Football	3	7	—	3
Squash	2	4	1	3
Cycling	1	4	2	3
Tennis	3	4	2	3

1 Activities are listed in descending order of participation rates for all adults aged 16 or over in the most popular quarter for each activity in 1986.
2 Includes rambling and hiking.

Source: General Household Survey

but a drop of 26 per cent from 1986. The 1988 British Grand Prix at Silverstone was attended by 189 thousand spectators while the Open Golf Championship at Royal Lytham and St Annes had just under 207 thousand attendances over its 9 days. In 1987 attendances at Test and County cricket matches, at just over 700 thousand spectators were lower than those recorded in both 1971 and 1982 (the dates chosen for Table 10.14). Spectator attendances at Rugby Union matches in England more than trebled between 1982 and 1987, and Scottish Football League matches showed a 40 per cent increase over the same period. Attendances at Football League matches in England and Wales fell by over 36 per cent between 1971 and 1987; with almost all of this decline occurring between 1971 and 1982.

10.14 Spectator attendance[1] at selected sporting events

     Thousands

	1971	1982	1987
Greyhound racing	8,800	5,300	4,800
Horse racing	4,200	3,700	4,349
Motorcycle sports[2]	..	3,000	3,750
Motor sports[3]	..	4,000	4,050
Football League (England & Wales)	28,704	18,766	18,273
Scottish Football League	4,520	2,844	4,003
Rugby Football League[4]	1,170	1,668	1,380
Rugby Football Union (England)	700	750	2,500
English basketball[5]	2	257	280
Scottish basketball	9	47	21
Test and County cricket	984	782	713

1 Estimated.
2 Excluding speedway.
3 Car and kart racing only.
4 League matches only. Figures are for the seasons ending April of each year.
5 National league cup and championship matches only. Figures are for the seasons ending May 1972, May 1983, and May 1988.

Source: Organisations concerned

Holidays

The proportion of adult residents of Great Britain not taking any holiday was virtually the same in 1987 as in 1971, at just over 40 per cent (Chart 10.15). However, there has been a general trend for an increasing number of people to take more than one holiday each year. The proportion of adults taking two or more holidays a year increased from 15 per cent in 1971 to 21 per cent in 1987. Taking holidays varies considerably by age. In 1987, over half of adults aged over 65 did not have a holiday compared with around a third of those aged between 25 and 54. According to the English Tourist Board, Britons are increasingly choosing an activity holiday for their second break. These include hot-air ballooning, climbing, walking, potholing and hanggliding whilst the more off beat include everything from 'Dracula hunts' to 'murder weekends' and fighting mock battles.

The total number of holidays taken abroad by British residents trebled between 1976 and 1987 to 20 million (Table 10.16). The majority of adult residents of Great Britain who holiday abroad go to Europe. Spain has remained the most popular destination; its share of adult holiday makers fell between 1976 and 1981 but is now back to its 1976 level. The proportion of foreign holidays spent in Spain is about a third.

Between 1975 and 1987 short holidays in Britain increased by 37 per cent to 37 million (Chart 10.17). Since 1975, domestic holidays of 4 or more nights have gradually declined in popularity, and by 1987 the same number of long and short trips were taken. Holidays abroad have secured an increasingly significant share of all trips taken by British residents, representing 21 per cent of the total in 1987 compared to only 11 per

10.15 **Holidays[1]: number taken each year by adult residents of Great Britain**

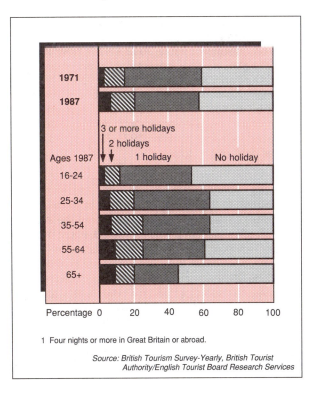

1 Four nights or more in Great Britain or abroad.

Source: British Tourism Survey-Yearly, British Tourist Authority/English Tourist Board Research Services

cent in 1975. (Figures are calculated on a different basis to those in Table 10.16 so are not directly comparable.)

10.17 **Holidays**

Great Britain

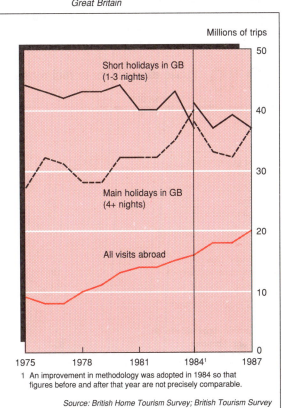

1 An improvement in methodology was adopted in 1984 so that figures before and after that year are not precisely comparable.

Source: British Home Tourism Survey; British Tourism Survey

10.16 **Destination of holidays abroad [1]**

Millions and Percentages

Destination	1976	1981	1986	1987
(percentages)				
Belgium or Luxembourg	3	2	3	1
France	20	27	21	20
Germany (Fed. Rep.)	2	3	2	3
Greece	5	7	8	9
Irish Republic	6	4	2	2
Italy	7	6	4	4
Netherlands	3	2	2	2
Spain [2]	30	22	31	31
Austria	2	3	3	3
Switzerland	2	2	2	2
All in Europe	91	87	91	90
United States	2	5	3	3
Other countries	7	8	6	7
Total (= 100%) (millions)	7	13	18	20

1 A holiday is defined as a visit of 1 or more nights made for holiday purposes. Business trips and visits to friends and relatives are excluded.
2 From 1981 includes Balearic and Canary Isles, but in earlier years only includes Balearic Isles.

Source: International Passenger Survey

Resources

The Arts Councils of Great Britain and Northern Ireland were established to develop and improve the knowledge, understanding and practice of the arts, to increase their accessibility to the public and to advise and co-operate with government departments, local authorities and other organisations. Table 10.18 shows how the Arts Councils allocate their government grant-in-aid. Total expenditure amounted to over £144 million in 1986-87, of which 22 per cent went to National Companies (theatre, ballet and opera). The proportion of expenditure on Regional Arts Associations has increased four-fold between 1971-72 and 1987-88 to 20 per cent of the total.

Business sponsorship is making an increasing contribution to the funding of the arts. In 1975-76 only a handful of major businesses sponsored the arts and the level of sponsorship was estimated at just over £½ million. However, following the establishment in 1976 of the Association for Business Sponsorship of the Arts, an independent organisation dedicated to raising more commercial sponsorship for the arts, and the introduction in 1984 by the government of its Business Sponsorship Incentive Scheme (BSIS) which offers matching grants for new sponsorship, the national arts sponsorship figure rose to over £25 million in 1986-87 and is estimated to be in the region of £30 million in 1987-88. Although the main source of sponsorship is still the banks, oil companies and insurance, medium and small sized businesses all over the country are now starting to sponsor artistic activities.

The Government is encouraging arts organizations to increase audiences and maximise their income through better marketing. In 1987, 22 awards were made to arts organizations for original or unusual marketing projects under a one-year experimental Arts Marketing Scheme. In 1988-89, the Government is supporting a distance

10.18 Arts Council expenditure

United Kingdom — Percentages and £ thousand

	1971 -72	1981 -82	1986 -87[1]	1987 -88
National companies [2]	29	27	23	22
Regional Arts Associations	5	11	21	20
Art	5	6	4	3
Drama	20	18	14	14
Music	20	19	17	17
Dance	4	4	5	5
Literature	2	2	1	1
Other [3]	15	12	15	18
Total (=100%) (£ thousand)	12,096	83,028	139,288	144,239

1 The total for 1986–87 includes £25m to cover the consequences of the abolition of the GLC and the Metropolitan Counties. £8.8m of this was paid to the South Bank Board and has been included in the 'Other' category. Most of the remainder was paid to Regional Arts Associations.
2 Includes the English National Opera in London and on tour, the National Theatre (in three auditoria), the Royal Opera and the Royal Ballet Companies in London and on tour, and the Royal Shakespeare company in Stratford-on-Avon and in London.
3 Includes arts centres and community projects, training in the arts, housing the arts, and general operating costs.

Source: Annual Reports, Arts Council of Great Britain; Arts Council of Northern Ireland.

learning package (instructional video and work book) and a programme of training courses for top management. They are also contributing to Business in the Arts, an organization set up by the private sector to encourage businessmen to put their talents and professional skills at the disposal of arts organizations, on a voluntary basis, to improve the quality of business management in the arts.

In real terms, that is adjusted for inflation, public expenditure on arts and libraries (Table 10.19) has

10.19 Public expenditure in real terms [1] on arts and libraries

United Kingdom — £ million (base year 1986-87)

	1982-83 outturn	1983-84 outturn	1984-85 outturn	1985-86 outturn	1986-87 outurn	1987-88 estimated outturn	1988-89 plans
Central government							
Museums and galleries	119	118	123	129	138	147	169
Other arts and heritage	134	124	132	129	158	155	162
Libraries	59	63	66	66	78	83	93
Administration	5	5	5	6	5	6	1
Total central government	317	310	327	329	379	390	425
Local authorities							
Museums and galleries	86	90	98	97	95	93	80
Libraries	448	462	466	467	480	506	470
Total local authorities[2]	534	552	564	564	575	600	550
Total public expenditure on arts and libraries	850	862	891	894	955	990	976

1 Real terms figures are the cash outturns or plans adjusted to 1986-87 price levels by excluding the effect of general inflation as measured by the GDP deflator.
2 Includes local authority expenditure on other arts and heritage which is too small to be shown separately in the table.

Source: The Government's Expenditure Plans (Cm 288), HM Treasury

increased by 12 per cent between 1982-83 and 1986-87. The estimated figures for 1987-88 show a continued rise in both central government and local authority expenditure.

In 1986, households spent an average of £5.93 each per week on alcohol drunk away from home (see also Table 10.3), the largest item of leisure expenditure included in Table 10.20. Not surprisingly households with higher income levels spent more on most categories. Holidays and television, radio and musical instruments formed the next largest areas of expenditure, with the highest income group spending more than twice as much as the next highest income group on holidays. Household expenditure on the leisure items covered in this table amounted to 16 per cent of total household expenditure in 1986, the percentage rising with income.

10.20 Household expenditure on selected leisure items: by household income, 1986

United Kingdom   £ and percentages

| | Gross normal weekly income of household | | | | | | |
	Up to £100	Over £100, up to £150	Over £150, up to £200	Over £200, up to £250	Over £250, up to £300	Over £300	All house-holds
Average weekly household expenditure on (£):							
Alcoholic drink consumed away from home	1.67	3.64	5.23	6.23	7.73	10.63	5.93
Meals consumed out [1]	1.03	2.00	3.00	3.66	4.65	9.43	4.38
Books, newspapers, magazines, etc	1.46	2.13	2.53	2.75	3.10	4.16	2.73
Television, radio and musical instruments	2.09	3.05	4.45	5.79	6.39	7.62	4.85
Purchase of materials for home repairs, etc	0.84	2.01	2.03	2.96	3.63	6.00	3.08
Holidays	0.65	1.75	3.24	4.30	5.26	12.95	5.39
Hobbies	0.03	0.03	0.06	0.07	0.06	0.11	0.06
Cinema admissions	0.03	0.04	0.08	0.09	0.11	0.20	0.10
Dance admissions	0.03	0.06	0.07	0.12	0.18	0.24	0.12
Theatre, concert, etc admissions	0.05	0.17	0.18	0.26	0.25	0.64	0.29
Subscriptions and admission charges to participant sports	0.08	0.36	0.38	0.68	0.86	1.59	0.71
Football match admissions	0.01	0.07	0.03	0.13	0.10	0.14	0.08
Admissions to other spectator sports	0.02	0.01	0.02	0.03	0.05	0.07	0.04
Sports goods (excluding clothes)	0.09	0.14	0.17	0.42	0.28	0.83	0.37
Other entertainment	0.10	0.19	0.31	0.33	0.49	0.86	0.41
Total weekly expenditure on above	8.18	15.64	21.76	27.83	33.15	55.46	28.54
Expenditure on above items as a percentage of total household expenditure	*11.3*	*12.6*	*13.7*	*15.7*	*16.2*	*18.3*	*16.0*

1 Eaten on the premises, excluding state school meals and workplace meals.   Source: Central Statistical Office, from Family Expenditure Survey

DEPARTMENT OF TRANSPORT

NATIONAL TRAVEL SURVEY REPORT

The only comprehensive, national source of travel information — linking different kinds of travel with the characteristics of travellers and their families. The NTS provides a picture of personal travel, particularly in terms of people and the distance they travel. It emphasises those characteristics of people and their households that have most effect on their extent of travel.

AN ANALYSIS OF PERSONAL TRAVEL

General Household Survey 1986

General Household Survey

The sixteenth edition of this annual publication from the Office of Population Censuses and Surveys contains statistics on population, family information, contraception, housing, burglary, employment, education, health, smoking, leisure and the elderly. Published by HMSO, it can be obtained from Government bookshops and through good booksellers.

£7.00

WOMEN AND MEN IN GREAT BRITAIN, 1987

A research profile

To inform the debate on equal opportunities the Equal Opportunities Commission has prepared a digest of statistics depicting the position of women and men in various facets of life in the mid-eighties.

HMSO

£7.00

Chapter 11: Participation

Charitable and voluntary organisations and religion
- Medicine and health-related charities received almost one-third of all charities' voluntary income in 1987-88. *(Chart 11.3)*

- There has been consistent and substantial growth in environmental organisations in recent years; between 1981 and 1987 the membership of the National Trust rose by 500 thousand. *(Table 11.6)*

- Membership of Trinitarian churches in the United Kingdom fell by over 1 million between 1975 and 1987, while membership of non-Trinitarian Christian churches and other religions rose by 85 thousand and 764 thousand respectively. *(Table 11.8)*

Trade unions
- Trade union membership in the United Kingdom grew from 12.4 million in 1976 to a peak of 13.3 million in 1979, but fell to 10.5 million by 1986, representing less than half of employees in employment. *(Page 179)*

Political participation
- Around 75 per cent of the electorate exercised their right to vote in the 1987 General Election, a greater proportion than in 1983 but much the same as in 1979. *(Table 11.11)*

Civic participation
- There has been a large increase in the number of people using advisory services in the United Kingdom; for example in 1987 over 5½ million more people used the Citizens Advice Bureau than used it in 1971. *(Table 11.14)*

- The use of counselling services in the United Kingdom has also increased dramatically; for example the number of clients visiting Alcoholics Anonymous rose six-fold between 1971 and 1987. *(Table 11.14)*

- Between 1971 and 1988, about 1,800 more women than men became magistrates; even so in 1988 there were still 4,000 more male magistrates than female. *(Table 11.15)*

11.1 Religious affiliation of the population

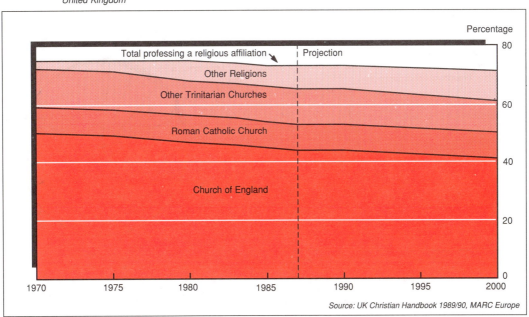

United Kingdom

Percentage

Total professing a religious affiliation | Projection

Other Religions

Other Trinitarian Churches

Roman Catholic Church

Church of England

1970 1975 1980 1985 1990 1995 2000

Source: UK Christian Handbook 1989/90, MARC Europe

This chapter measures some aspects of the ways in which people participate in the life of the community. Participation as defined here can take various forms such as: membership of trade unions; voting in elections; the exercise of the right to appeal against administrative decisions, or against discrimination on grounds of sex or race; and helping others in the community in their spare time.

Charitable and voluntary organisations and religion

Many people are involved in work carried out by charities. Around 4 thousand new charities were registered with the Charity Commission in England and Wales during 1987, and by the end of that year there were around 162 thousand charities on the register.

The total income and voluntary income of some of the larger charities are shown in Table 11.2 ranked by their total income for the latest year available, usually 1987. Although for some charities the majority of their income is derived from fees rather than voluntary donations, the charity with the highest voluntary income was the Royal National Lifeboat Institute with £35.9 million. Including rents, investments, statutory grants and fees, the National Trust had the largest total income, the next highest being The Salvation Army. The National Trust also had the largest expenditure in 1987 at yy74.8 million, 5 per cent of which was on administration, and it held the largest net assets with £171 million followed by the Salvation Army with £143 million.

In 1987-88 charities concerned with medicine and health accounted for nearly one third, £251 million, of the voluntary income of the top 200 grant seeking charities in the United Kingdom (Chart 11.3). More than one fifth, £163 million, of the voluntary income of these 200 charities was given in support of international aid. Nearly £53 million was given in support of animal protection charities such as the Royal Society for the Prevention of Cruelty to Animals (RSPCA). In 1987 the RSPCA had 3 hospitals, 45 clinics, 54 animal homes, and 31 animal welfare centres. It treated over 194 thousand animals, 6 per cent up on 1986, and found new homes for almost 114 thousand animals, 47 per cent of which were dogs. The society also obtained 1,805 convictions for animal cruelty.

11.2 Total income and voluntary income of selected [1] charities, 1987 [2]

United Kingdom   £ million cash

	Total income	Total voluntary income
National Trust	87.9	34.2
Salvation Army	55.8	24.0
Barnardo's	50.5	23.7
Oxfam	42.0	33.9
Imperial Cancer Research Fund	41.9	28.8
Spastics Society	40.2	12.6
Royal National Lifeboat Institution	39.4	35.9
Save the Children Fund	34.7	21.3
British Red Cross Society	32.7	11.0
Cancer Research Campaign	28.5	24.7
Royal National Institute for the Blind	28.5	14.6
Guide Dogs for the Blind Association	26.4	15.9
UNICEF	22.9	9.4
National Society for the Prevention of Cruelty to Children	20.7	15.9
Royal Society for the Prevention of Cruelty to Animals	18.3	13.8
Church of England Children's Society	17.8	9.4
Christian Aid	17.2	13.4
British Heart Foundation	16.0	13.3
Help the Aged	15.5	12.8
Royal British Legion	14.5	9.4
ActionAid	13.5	12.0
Marie Curie Memorial Foundation	13.2	9.2
Tear Fund	11.1	10.4
National Society for Cancer Relief	10.3	9.6
Jewish Philanthropic Association	9.7	9.7

1 Charities with a voluntary income of £9.0 million or over in the year, ranked by size of total income.
2 Accounting periods ending in 1987; although 12 month periods covered may differ.

Source: Charity Trends 11th Edition, Charities Aid Foundation

11.3 Voluntary income of the top 200 charities: by major sector, 1987/88

United Kingdom

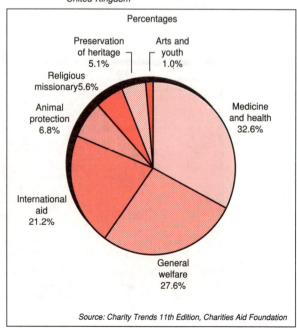

Percentages

- Preservation of heritage 5.1%
- Arts and youth 1.0%
- Religious missionary 5.6%
- Animal protection 6.8%
- Medicine and health 32.6%
- International aid 21.2%
- General welfare 27.6%

Source: Charity Trends 11th Edition, Charities Aid Foundation

11.4 Broadcast charitable appeals [1,2]: amount raised

United Kingdom				£ thousands
	1983	1984	1985	1986[3]
BBC 1 TV	373.8	113.7	522.7	325.6
ITV	94.5	142.9	160.4	42.1
BBC Radio 4	443.0	580.9	401.7	369.5

1 National appeals excluding extended appeals, British Wireless
  for the Blind and St Martin in the Fields.
2 Numbers of appeals per annum vary.
3 First 6 months only.

Source: Charity Trends 11th Edition,
Charities Aid Foundation

During 1987-88 the first year of the operation of the new tax free payroll deduction scheme, just over £1 million was passed to charity from employees and pensioners paid through the newly formed agency charities. The maximum amount it has been possible for employees or pensioners to authorise as a tax free deduction from pay was £120 per annum throughout the tax year 1987/88. Only those remunerated through a PAYE system are able to participate (ie not the self employed). The scheme, which is entirely voluntary both for employees and employers, was made possible by legislation introduced in the 1986 Finance Act. During the first year of the scheme approximately 1,500 employers offered payroll deduction to their employees/pensioners. In the year to April 1989 the scheme is hoping to raise £10 million.

Table 11.4 shows the amounts of money raised on regular broadcast appeals. In the first six months of 1986 there were 38 appeals, 12 on television and 26 on Radio 4. There was a significant difference in the average amount raised by appeals; BBC 1 averaged over £54 thousand per appeal in the first six months of 1986 while ITV averaged just over £7 thousand and BBC Radio 4 over £14 thousand. However, much larger sums are raised during large 'one-off' broadcast appeals. For example from 7.00pm on Sunday 29 May until 10.00pm on Monday 30 May 1988 all of the ITV companies combined to broadcast the ITV Telethon '88. The aim of Telethon '88 was to raise money for work in five main categories: disability, training and employment, children, special needs, self help and community groups. By 10.00 pm on Monday 30 May over £22 million had been pledged, considerably higher than the sums raised by the 1987 BBC Children in Need (about £14 million) and Comic Relief (about £15 million) appeals. Telethon '88 took 912 thousand telephone pledges; 72 per cent were cash pledges totalling £8.25 million. The remainder were credit card pledges totalling £4 million. Of the £22 million pledged, between £6 and £7 million came from commercial sources.

The Women's National Commission (WNC) was formed in 1969 as an advisory committee to the Government, with a small Secretariat from the Cabinet Office. Its terms of reference are 'to ensure by all possible means that the informed opinions of women are given their due weight in the deliberations of government'. The Commission consists of 50 women, elected or appointed by mainly national organisations with a large and active membership of women and which have been asked by Government to send are presentative. These include the women's voluntary organisations, the political parties, trade unions, churches, professional and business organisations and women participating in voluntary service and caring organisations. Although varying greatly in size and age the 50 constituent organisations of WNC represent a broad spectrum of women's experience and views in the UK today. The Commission works by responding to government papers and by setting up ad hoc working groups to study, report and make recommendations to government on issues of its own choosing. The Commission has two Co-Chairman, one a minister appointed by the Prime Minister and one elected from among the members by the members.

Table 11.5 gives the participation of women in some of the larger voluntary organisations. It shows that the Women's Institute was the organisation with the most members in 1987. While some organisations have a falling membership, others such as the Association of Inner Wheel Clubs and Soroptimist International are attracting more members. There are also many new women's organisations being formed often to meet a specific need or interest.

11.5 Membership of some womens' voluntary organisations

			Thousands
		Membership	
	1971	1981	1987
Mothers Union [1,2]	308	210	183
National Federation of Women's Institutes [1]	440	378	338
National Women's Register [3]	15	23	20
National Union of Townswomen's Guilds [1]	216	155	150[5]
Royal British Legion (Women's Section)	162	165	127
Church of Scotland Woman's Guild [1]	127	86	68
Scottish Women's Rural Institutes [1]	58	50	42
Association of Inner Wheel Clubs [1]	31	34	36
Soroptimist International of GB and Ireland [1]	13	14	16
National Council of Women [1,4]	. .	. .	2

1 Members of the Women's National Commission.
2 Includes Republic of Ireland.
3 Formerly the National Housewives Register.
4 An umbrella organisation with 87 affiliated national societies.
5 1986.

Source: Organisations concerned

There has been increasing awareness of the environment (see Chapter 9) in recent years and this is reflected in the remarkably consistent growth in membership of voluntary environmental organisations (Table 11.6). The World Wide Fund for Nature's membership grew 10 fold between 1971 and 1987.

Many rescue organisations are also manned by volunteers. It is estimated that the number of volunteer lifeboatmen in the Royal National Lifeboat Institute (RNLI) has remained fairly constant at around 5 thousand, of whom about half are crew members, since the beginning of the 1970s, but the number of calls on their services has increased very significantly. The Mountain Rescue Committees of England and Wales and of Scotland, with around 3 thousand volunteers, were called out on 586 rescue occasions in 1986 which was double the 1971 call out rate. In 1987, the Mountain Rescue Committee of Scotland were called to 237 incidents involving 149 casualties of which 27 were fatal. Around 60 per cent of calls were in summer. In addition, in 1986 the British Cave Rescue Council's one thousand volunteers in England and Wales were called out on 47 occasions to rescue 103 persons, 4 of which were fatalities and 11 injured.

11.6 Membership of selected voluntary environmental organisations

Thousands

	Membership		
	1971	1981	1987
Civic Trust [1]	214	. .	240
Conservation Trust [2]	6	5	4
Council for the Protection of Rural England	21	29	32
Friends of the Earth [3]	1	. .	55
National Trust	278	1,046	1,545
National Trust for Scotland	37	110	160
Ramblers Association [4]	22	37	57
Royal Society for Nature Conservation	64	143	184[5]
Royal Society for the Protection of Birds	98	441	561
Woodland Trust	. .	20	58
World Wide Fund for Nature	12	60	124

1 Members of local amenity societies registered with the Civic Trust.
2 In September 1987 the Conservation Society was absorbed by the Conservation Trust.
3 England and Wales only, Friends of the Earth (Scotland) is a separate organisation founded in 1978.
4 Includes Republic of Ireland.
5 Does not include 30,000 members in junior organisation WATCH.

Source: Organisations concerned

It can be seen from Table 11.7 that many thousands of adults put a great deal of time and effort into organisations for young people. For example around 173 thousand helpers were involved with the Girl Guide and Scout Associations in 1987. With a combined membership of 1.2 million in 1987 these organisations continue to attract large numbers of young people. Similarly, the Boys and Girls Brigades have retained around 200 thousand members between them, though numbers have fallen.

The Duke of Edinburgh Award Scheme, inaugurated in 1956, is not an organisation with members but a programme of activities for young people aged between 14 and 25, and is run by volunteers. In 1987 180 thousand young people were participating in the Scheme, 9 per cent more than 1986. Any organisation which is concerned with young people within the age range may apply to the National Award Office to be licensed as an Operating Authority. Since the Scheme began over 2 million young people from all parts of the world have taken part. The Award is a registered charity, which receives funding - largely for the provision of support services and publicity materials for users, from sponsorship and donations from industry and individuals, from an Entrace fee paid by young people taking part, and from national and local government.

11.7 Organisations for young people

United Kingdom   Thousands

	Members		Helpers	
	1971	1987	1971	1987
Membership				
Beaver Scouts		98 ⎫		
Cub Scouts	265	254 ⎪	75	97
Scouts	194	169 ⎬		
Venture Scouts	22	39 ⎭		
Brownie Guides	377	372 ⎫		
Girl Guides	295	241 ⎬	64	76
Rangers/Young Leaders	21	27 ⎭		
Sea Cadet Corps	18	17	..	4
Army Cadet Force	39	44	..	7
Air Training Corps	33	38	..	8
Combined Cadet Force	45	42	..	2
Boys' Brigade [1]	140	116	26	29
Girls' Brigade [1]	97	83[3]	8	9[3]
National Association of Boys' Clubs	164	166	..	30[3]
National Federation of Young Farmers' Clubs				
— Males [2]	24	23 ⎫	11	12
— Females [2]	16	19 ⎭		
British Red Cross				
Senior Members	62	10	6	2
Youth Members		13		
Methodist Association of Youth Clubs	..	100	..	10
Duke of Edinburgh's Award				
Participants	122	180	..	45[3]
Awards gained				
Bronze	18	20	.	.
Silver	7	8	.	.
Gold	3	4	.	.

1 Figures relate to British Isles.
2 Figures relate to England, Wales, and the Channel Islands and to young people aged between 10 and 25 in 1971, and between 10 and 26 in 1986.
3 1986.

Source: Organisations concerned

11.8 Membership[1] of churches and other religions

United Kingdom — Thousands and percentages

	1975	1983	1987
Trinitarian churches			
Anglican	2,270	2,083	1,928
Presbyterian	1,646	1,430	1,346
Methodist	615	529	517
Baptist	270	235	241
Other Protestant churches [2]	728	759	836
Total Protestant [2]	5,528	5,035	4,868
Roman Catholic	2,535	2,215	2,059
Total Trinitarian	8,063	7,251	6,927
Percentage of adult population [3]	*18.6*	*16.0*	*15.0*
Non-Trinitarian churches			
Mormons [4]	100	125	142
Jehovah's Witnesses	80	95	108
Spiritualists	57	52	52
Other Non-Trinitarian	97	107	116
Total	333	378	418
Other religions			
Muslims	400 [5]	750	900 [5]
Sikhs [5]	115	160	200
Hindus [5]	100	130	150
Jews	111	109 [5]	109
Others	88	176	220
Total	814	1,325	1,578

1 See Appendix, Part 11: Church membership.
2 Includes Orthodox churches.
3 Population aged 15 or over. The 1987 percentage has been calculated using 1981-based population projections.
4 Church of Jesus Christ of Latter-Day Saints.
5 Estimate.

Source: UK Christian Handbook 1989/90, MARC Europe

Membership of Trinitarian churches in the United Kingdom was 15 per cent of the adult population in 1987, Table 11.8. Between 1975 and 1987 the number of Trinitarian members fell by 14 per cent, while the smaller number of non-Trinitarians rose by 26 per cent and other religions almost doubled their membership. An important difference between the figures in Chart 11.1 and Table 11.8 is that Chart 11.1 includes nominal members who are not enrolled on church registers. While Chart 11.1 implies that in 1987 65 per cent of the population were affiliated to a Trinitarian church, Table 11.8 makes clear that only 15 per cent of the adult population were actually members of Trinitarian churches.

Between 1981 and 1987 the number of baptisms each year in Methodist Churches rose by around 4 per cent to just over 30 thousand. While during the same period infant baptisms in the Church of England fell by 14 per cent, to 188 thousand, other baptisms rose by 15 per cent to 45 thousand. In the Church of Wales, as in the Baptist Churches, the annual number of baptisms fell slightly between 1981 and 1987.

Between 1987 and 2000 the number of Trinitarian ministers is expected to fall slightly, while the number of churches is forecast to rise by over 600 taking it above its 1980 level but not as high as 1975. In non-trinitarian and other religions the number of both ministers/leaders and congregations/groups are predicted to rise between 1987 and 2000.

Table 11.9 shows that the number of marriages with a religious ceremony fell by 14 per cent between 1971 and 1987, in Great Britain; partly due to a drop in the total number of marriages (down by 13 per cent) but also somewhat compensated by the increased proportion of religious marriages which were second or subsequent marriages of one or both partners (going

11.9 Marriages: religious and civil ceremonies

Great Britain — Thousands and percentages

	1971	1987		
	All marriages	First marriages [1]	Second or subsequent [2]	All marriages
Manner of solemnisation				
Religious ceremony				
Church of England/Church in Wales	160	114	7	121
Church of Scotland	20	12	2	14
Roman Catholic	48	27	2	29
Other Christian	37	18	19	37
Jews and other non-Christian	2	2	—	2
Civil marriages	180	78	105	183
Total marriages	447	251	136	388
Civil marriages as a percentage of all marriages				
England and Wales	*41*	*31*	*78*	*48*
Scotland	*31*	*30*	*70*	*42*
Great Britain	*40*	*31*	*77*	*47*

1 First marriage for both partners.
2 Remarriage for one or both partners.

Source: Office of Population Censuses and Surveys; General Register Office (Scotland)

from 20 per cent in 1971 up to 35 per cent in 1987). Couples in Scotland are more likely to marry with a religious marriage ceremony than those in England and Wales; 58 per cent of marriages in Scotland in 1987 were soleminised with a religious ceremony whereas the corresponding proportion for England and Wales was 52 per cent. However, in Northern Ireland (not shown in the table) the proportion was 86 per cent in 1986. For more details on marriage and divorce see Tables 2.12, 2.15, 2.16, 2.17 and 2.20 and Chart 1.4.

Trade unions

In the United Kingdom between 1976 and 1986 the number of people belonging to a trade union fell by 15 per cent. Trade union membership grew from 12.4 million in 1976 to 13.3 million in 1979, but fell to 10.5 million by 1986, falling below 50 per cent of employees in employment. The decline in the number of trade unions since 1973 reflects a continuing process of mergers and transfers of membership as well as local and craft unions joining with national unions; between 1976 and 1986 the number of trade unions fell by 138, from 473 to 335. Table 11.10 shows the membership of selected trade unions since 1961. Between 1979, which was the year of peak membership for most unions, and 1987 the membership of the more traditional industrial unions, like the National Union of Mineworkers and the National Union of Railwaymen, fell quite considerably, as did that of the largest union

the Transport and General Workers Union. Over the same period the membership of the Royal College of Nursing rose by 96 thousand. In January 1988, the Association of Scientific, Technical and Managerial Staffs and the Technical Administration Supervisory Section (of the Amalgamated Union of Engineering Works) merged to form Manufacturing, Science and Finance (MSF) which, with 650 thousand members now forms the sixth biggest union in the United Kingdom and the largest white-collar union in Europe.

Many unions are relatively small; in 1986 over half the unions had fewer than 1 thousand members but these only accounted for 0.4 per cent of total union membership. In contrast, over 80 per cent of union membership was concentrated in just 24 unions with over 100 thousand members each.

11.10 Membership of selected trade unions

United Kingdom

Thousands and percentages

	1961	1971	1976	1979	1987	Percentage change 1979 - 1987
Transport and General Workers Union	1,358	1,580	1,930	2,086	1,349	− 35.3
Amalgamated Engineering Union [1]	.	.	.	.	815	. .
General Municipal Boilermakers and Allied Trades Union [2]	.	.	.	.	803	. .
National and Local Government Officers Association [1]	.	.	683	753	750 [5]	− 0.4
National Union of Public Employees	210	395	651	692	651	− 5.9
Association of Scientific, Technical and Managerial Staffs [1]	.	220	396	491	390 [5]	− 20.6
Union of Shop, Distributive and Allied Workers	351	319	413	470	387	− 17.7
Electrical Electronic Telecommunications and Plumbing Union	.	.	429	444	369	− 16.9
National Union of Mineworkers	675	417[4]	371	372	211 [5]	− 43.3
National Union of Teachers [1]	.	.	294	291	225	− 22.7
Confederation of Health Service Employees	58	87	201	213	208	− 2.3
Royal College of Nursing [3]	.	.	.	162	258	+ 59.3
Civil and Public Services Association	143	185[4]	231	224	149 [6]	− 33.5
National Union of Railwaymen	317	195	178	170	118	− 30.6
Iron and Steel Trades Confederation	125	133[4]	117	110	44	− 60.0

1 Owing to changes in the structure of the union comparable data for earlier years are not available.

2 The union was set up in 1982 following amalgamation. Comparable data for 1961 to 1979 are not available.

3 The union was set up in 1977. Comparable data for earlier years are not available.

4 Figure relates to 1970.

5 Figure relates to 1986.

6 Membership dropped by 43,000 in 1985 when there was a transfer of a block of members to the National Communications Union.

Source: Annual returns in the custody of the Certification Office for Trade Unions and Employers Associations

WOMEN AND MEN IN GREAT BRITAIN, 1987

A research profile

To inform the debate on equal opportunities the Equal Opportunities Commission has prepared a digest of statistics depicting the position of women and men in various facets of life in the mid-eighties.

HMSO

£7.00

Political participation

Table 11.11 shows that around 74.5 per cent of the electorate exercised their right to vote in the General Election held on 11 June 1987, more than in the 1983 election (71.8 per cent) but comparable with the 1979 election (75.1 per cent). In 1987 the outgoing Government was re-elected with 42.3 per cent of the votes cast and an overall majority of 101 seats, the second largest majority since the 1945 General Election. Labour won 229 seats with 30.9 per cent of the votes cast while the Liberal-Social Democratic Party (SDP) Alliance polled 22.5 per cent of the votes, but only won 22 seats, one less than in 1983.

11.11 Parliamentary General Elections [1]

United Kingdom

	26 May 1955	8 Oct 1959	15 Oct 1964	31 Mar 1966	18 Jun [2] 1970	28 Feb 1974	10 Oct 1974	3 May 1979	9 Jun 1983	11 Jun 1987
Number of votes recorded as a percentage of the electorate by party										
Communist	0.1	0.1	0.1	0.2	0.1	0.1	—	—	—	—
Conservative [3]	38.2	38.9	33.4	31.8	33.2	29.5	26.0	33.0	30.5	31.5
Labour	35.6	34.5	34.0	36.4	30.8	28.9	28.5	27.7	19.8	23.0
Liberal [4]	2.1	4.6	8.6	6.5	5.3	15.1	13.3	10.4	9.8	9.6
Social Democratic Party [4]	.	.	.	.	.	.	.	.	8.4	7.2
Plaid Cymru	0.1	0.2	0.2	0.2	0.4	0.4	0.4	0.3	0.3	0.3
Scottish National Party	—	0.1	0.2	0.4	0.8	1.6	2.1	1.2	0.8	1.0
Other [3]	0.7	0.3	0.5	0.5	0.9	2.3	2.3	2.6	2.2	1.9
Total voters	76.8	78.7	77.1	75.8	71.5	77.8	72.5	75.1	71.8	74.5
Non-voters	23.2	21.3	22.9	24.2	28.5	22.2	27.5	24.9	28.2	25.5
Members of Parliament elected (numbers)										
Conservative [3]	344	364	303	253	330	296	276	339	396	375
Labour	277	258	317	363	287	301	319	268	209	229
Liberal [4]	6	6	9	12	6	14	13	11	17	17
Social Democratic Party [4]	.	.	.	.	.	.	.	.	6	5
Plaid Cymru	0	0	0	0	0	2	3	2	2	3
Scottish National Party	0	0	0	0	1	7	11	2	2	3
Other [3]	3	2	1	2	6	15	13	13	18	18
Total	630	630	630	630	630	635	635	635	650	650
Government majority on election	59	99	5	97	31	0[5]	4	44	143	101

1 See Appendix, Part 11: Parliamentary elections.
2 The voting age was lowered from 21 to 18 on 16 February 1970.
3 Ulster Unionist MPs are included with Conservative members to 1970. There were 12 U.U. members in 1964, 11 in 1966, and 8 in 1970. After 1970 all Ulster Unionist MPs are included in 'Other'. The Speaker is also included in 'Other' but is not counted when calculating the government majority.
4 The Social Democratic Party was launched on 26 March 1981. In 1985 and 1987 the Liberal and Social Democratic Parties contested General Elections as the Liberal—SDP Alliance, with only one of the parties putting up a candidate in each seat contested.
5 This election resulted in a minority government.

Source: Home Office

In May 1988 elections took place for non-metropolitan district councils and county councils in England and Wales and in the London Boroughs and the Scottish regions, islands and districts. Fewer people exercise their right to vote in local and county council elections than in General Elections, and in many areas turnout is below 50 per cent. Table 11.12 shows the political composition of local councils. Under 'Party control', the column 'Other' includes councils where there was no clear control.

The United Kingdom sends 81 members to the European Parliament (EP): since the last elections held in 1985, 45 Conservatives sit in the European Democratic Group, the third largest (66 seats); 32 Labour members along with one member of the Social Democratic and Labour Party from Northern Ireland sit with the Socialist Group, the largest with 164 seats; one Scottish Nationalist sits with the European Renewal and Democratic Alliance (30 seats); one Ulster Unionist sits with the Group of the European Right (17 seats); and a Democratic Unionist, along with 11 others, sits as an Independent. None of the UK members sit with the second largest group, the European People's Party (115 seats). The next elections to the European Parliament will be held in 1989.

11.12 Local elections [1]

England and Wales and Scotland   Numbers

	Party control					Number of seats				
	Con-servative	Labour	Liberal — SDP[2,3]	Other[4]	Total	Con-servative	Labour	Liberal — SDP[2,3]	Other[4,5]	Total
England & Wales										
Counties										
Metropolitan [6]										
1981	0	7	0	0	7	162	476	51	4	693
Others										
1981	19	14	1	13	47	1,568	1,382	342	382	3,674
1985	10	9	1	27	47	1,374	1,262	644	284	3,564
1988	10	15	2	5	32	1,381	1,245	606	334	3,566
Districts										
Metropolitan										
1980	6	27	0	3	36	770	1,548	133	78	2,529
1982	8	23	0	5	36	751	1,457	222	51	2,481
1984	5	25	0	6	36	690	1,523	228	40	2,481
1986	1	27	0	8	36	545	1,649	237	50	2,481
1987	1	26	1	8	36	545	1,569	329	38	2,481
Others										
1980	150	70	3	110	333	6,614	4,022	809	3,564	15,009
1982	143	71	3	116	333	6,457	3,939	1,213	3,405	15,014
1984	145	69	2	117	333	6,651	3,927	1,482	2,875	14,935
1986	119	77	5	132	333	6,185	4,089	1,819	2,855	14,948
1987	128	69	8	128	333	6,283	3,864	2,344	2,346	14,927
1988	134	77	5	117	333	6,332	3,967	2,194	2,478	14,971
London Boroughs										
1982	16	11	0	5	32	979	783	124	28	1,914
1986	11	15	2	4	32	685	956	249	24	1,914
1988	11	16	1	4	32	693	944	248	33	1,918
Scotland										
Regions										
1988	0	4	0	5	9	62	221	34	134	451
Islands										
1988	0	0	0	3	3	0	0	0	79	79
Districts										
1988	2	24	—	27	53	164	554	64	384	1,166

1 Not all seats are at risk during local elections. The figures represent the total state of the councils after the elections. See Appendix, Part 11: Local elections, for details of how councillors become due for re-election.
2 On 26 March 1981 the Social Democratic Party (SDP) was formed. From then until 1988 the Liberals and SDP contested local elections as the Liberal-SDP Alliance. In 1988 the Social and Liberal Democrats formed. The Democrats contested the 1988 local elections separately from the SDP.
3 Pre-1951 Liberal; 1981-1987 Liberal-SDP Alliance; 1988 LSDP.
4 1988 includes SDP.
5 Includes a small number of vacant seats.
6 Includes the Greater London Council. Metropolitan counties were abolished on 1 April 1986.

Source: Various

Civic Participation

The means of appeal against the administrative decisions of central government departments is to complain to the Parliamentary Ombudsman - the Parliamentary Commissioner for Administration (PCA) - through Members of Parliament. In 1987 the PCA received slightly fewer complaints than in 1986. Of the total of 656 complaints dealt with in 1987 around three-quarters were rejected and 145 full investigations were completed and the results reported to MPs; around 43 per cent of these were found to involve maladministration leading to injustice. The Health Service Commissioners (HSC), who are statutory independent offices, deal with complaints about the administration of the National Health Service. The number of complaints received by the HSC also fell, by 10 per cent between 1986-87 and 1987-88. In the latter year 525 cases were reported upon, of which 321 were found to have involved failures in service, or maladministration, leading to injustice. Table 11.13 gives figures on the work of these Ombudsmen.

Table 11.13 also includes statistics about the work of the Commissions for Local Administration (Local Ombudsmen) who deal with complaints against local authorities and certain other authorities in Great Britain. There are separate Commissions for England, Scotland and Wales. The number of complaints received by the three Commissions increased by 5 per cent between 1986-87 and 1987-88. In 1986-87 431 cases were reported upon, of which 273 were found to have involved maladministration causing injustice to the complainant.

According to the Office of Fair Trading around 347 thousand consumer complaints were made to local enforcement authorities and advice agencies in the United Kingdom in the six months to 31 March 1988. About 92 thousand of the complaints received concerned motor vehicles and household appliances alone.

11.13 Complaints to Ombudsmen [1]

Great Britain   Numbers

	1971	1976	1983	1984	1985	1986	1987
Complaints to the Parliamentary Commissioner for Administration							
Received during the year	548	815	751	837	759	719	677
Dealt with during the year [2]							
Rejected	295	505	605	658	606	549	509
Discontinued after partial investigation	39	29	6	9	5	2	2
Reported upon							
Maladministration leading to injustice found	67	139	90	87	75	82	63
Other	115	190	108	96	102	86	82
Total dealt with during the year	516	863	809	850	788	719	656
Complaints to the Health Service Commissioner [3,4]							
Received during the year	.	582	895	815	926	883	794
Dealt with during the year [2]							
Rejected [5]	.	413	762	672	727	684	696
Discontinued after partial investigation	.	13	8	1	11	16	29
Reported upon							
Containing failures in service/maladministration leading to injustice found	.	61 [7]	167	209	302	290	321
Other	.	59	183	234	224	193	204
Total dealt with during the year	.	546	889	798	875	831	858
Complaints to the Commissioners for Local Administration [3,6]							
Received during the year	.	1,335	3,717	4,079	4,442	5,051	5,311
Dealt with during the year [2]							
Rejected/discontinued after partial investigation	.	772	3,223	3,542	3,577	4,451	4,768
Reported upon							
Maladministration leading to injustice found	.	143	242	227	256	266	273
Other	.	142	218	169	156	185	158
Total dealt with during the year	.	1,057	3,683	3,938	3,989	4,902	5,199

1 See Appendix, Part 11: Parliamentary Commissioner for Administration; Health Service Commissioner, Commissioners for Local Administration.
2 Some complaints will have been received during the previous year.
3 The Health Service Commissioner and the Commissioners for Local Administration report annually from April to the following March. The 1986-87 figures appear under 1986, etc.
4 The Health Service Commissioner started operating on 1 October 1973.

5 Includes cases referred back to complainant for more information and no response received.
6 The Commissioners for Local Administration for England started operating on 1 April 1974; for Wales in September 1974; and for Scotland on 1 January 1976.
7 From 1981 the figures refer to the number of individual grievances rather than reports issued.

Source: Annual Reports: The Parliamentary Commissioner for Administration ; The Health Service Commissioner ; The Commissioners for Local Administration in England, Scotland, and Wales

11.14 Selected advisory and counselling services

United Kingdom   Numbers and thousands

	Branches/centres (numbers)			Clients (thousands)		
	1971	1981	1987	1971	1981	1987
Al-Anon Family Groups[1]	135	612	952	1.2	7.3	11.4
Alcoholics Anonymous[2]	420	1,550	2,500	8.3	30.0	40.0
Catholic Marriage Advisory Council[3]	63	68	81	2.5	3.3	14.8
Citizens Advice Bureaux[4]	512	914	1,123	1,500.0	4,514.6	7,180.3
Cruse[5,6]	13	73	140	5.0	9.1	15.0
Disablement Information and Advice Services	.	44	82 [9]		40.0	250.0 [9]
Law Centres[6]	1	41	54[10]	1.0	155.0[10]	160.0 [9]
Leukaemia Care Society[6]	1	21	30	0.2	1.7	3.6
Relate[6,7,8]	141	178	166	21.6	38.3	48.4
Samaritans[8]	127	170	182	87.0	303.8	421.0
Young People's Counselling and Advisory Services	. .	55	88	. .	30.0	60.0

1 Support groups for alcholics' families. Includes Alateen which is part of Al-Anon. Data also include the Republic of Ireland.
2 Includes branches in the Channel Islands. The 1981 and 1987 figures exclude Northern Ireland.
3 Figures are for years ending March 1972, March 1982, and March 1987. They relate to Great Britain only.
4 Figures are for years ending December 1971, March 1982, and March 1987. The figures given for 'Clients' represent new enquiries in 1971, and new *plus* repeat enquiries in 1981 and 1987. Includes the Citizens Advice Scotland, which had 508 thousand new *plus* repeat

enquiries in its 62 outlets in 1987.
5 The National Organisation for the Widowed and their Children. Figures given for 'Clients' exclude many short-term contacts.
6 Figures given for 'Clients' represent numbers of families.
7 Includes National Marriage Guidance Council (now operating under the name Relate) in England, Wales, N. Ireland, Channel Isles and Isle of Man/and Scottish Marriage Guidance Council.
8 The figures given for 'Clients' represent new cases during the year.
9 1986.
10 1985.

Source: Organisations concerned

During the 1970s a substantial network of advisory and counselling services were developed providing general information and advice through largely volunteer-based advice centres (Table 11.14). All the advice networks shown record a continuing upward trend in enquiries. The number of clients who visited Relate, formerly the National Marriage Guidance Council for counselling on marriage or intimate personal relationships including Aids-related problems, more than doubled between 1971 and 1987. The fabled 'seven year itch' seems to have some justification, as according to the Scottish Marriage Guidance Council 'The years between 6 and 10 continue to represent the most vulnerable period in couple relationships' (see Table 2.17). Citizens Advice Bureau (CAB) dealt with over 7.7 million clients in 1987

an increase of 400 thousand over 1986. Almost 1.5 million enquiries in 1987 were about social security. Approximately 25,000 people work in the CAB service, 90 per cent of whom are volunteers.

The number of magistrates rose by 45 per cent between 1971 and 1988 (Table 11.15). Apart from a small number of stipendiary magistrates, magistrates are unpaid volunteers. These unpaid magistrates are also known as Justices of the Peace (JP) and have limited judicial and executive power to deal with minor cases and preliminary hearings. Over the period the number of female magistrates rose by 78 per cent, while males rose by only 27 per cent. Even so there are still 4,000 more male magistrates than female.

11.15 Magistrates [1] in service: by sex

England & Wales   Numbers

	1971	1976	1981	1982	1983	1984	1985	1986	1987	1988
Magistrates										
of which:										
Male	12,551	13,833	15,951	15,476	15,606	14,945	15,980	16,133	15,978	15,992
Female	6,699	8,096	9,484	10,189	10,328	10,833	11,264	11,554	11,672	11,934
Total	19,250	21,929	25,435	25,665	25,934	25,778	27,244	27,687	27,650	27,926

1 Excluding magistrates aged 70 or over who are no longer qualified to appear in court, and stipendiary magistrates (of which there are currently 63).

Source: The Magistrates Association: Lord Chancellor's Department

Home Office Statistical Bulletins

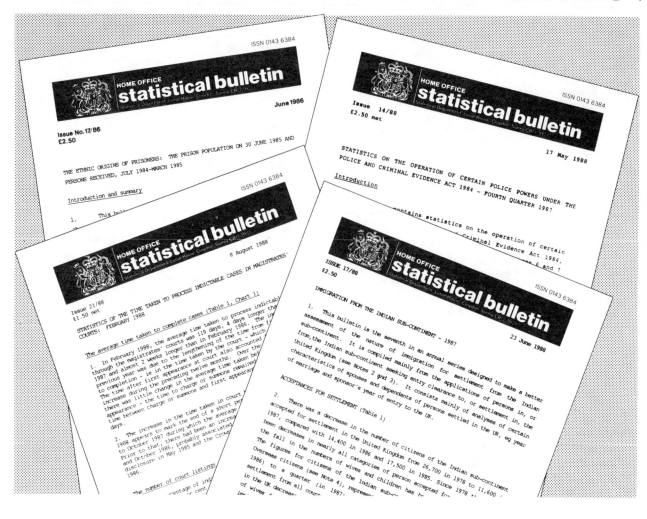

The Home Office publishes about 40 statistical bulletins each year, giving detailed information on special topics within the responsibility of the Home Secretary. Some of these bulletins are published regularly each quarter:

> Offences recorded by the police,
> Control of immigration statistics,
> The operation of the prevention of terrorism legislation.

Others are issued annually, for example:

> Statistics of breath tests,
> Offences relating to motor vehicles,
> Statistics of the misuse of drugs.

Other bulletins give summary figures, before more detailed statistics can be made available, for example:

> The prison population, 1987 (Issue 8/88), issued on 30 March 1988, some 9 months before publication of the detailed Command paper "Prison Statistics".

Yet other bulletins are issued on an ad hoc basis, for example:

> Criminal careers of those born in 1953, 1958 and 1963 (Issue 7/85). The results of a cohort analysis of the offenders index which makes it possible to link successive convictions of the same individual.

> The ethnic origin of prisoners published on 18 June 1986 (Issue 17/86) giving the first results of the collection of comprehensive information about the ethnic origin of prisoners.

A comprehensive list of bulletins issued in the last year is available from Home Office, Statistical Department, Room 1834, Lunar House, 40 Wellesley Road, Croydon, CR0 9YD, Telephone: 01-760 2850, or by personal application to the Home Office Library, Home Office, 50 Queen Anne's Gate, London, SW1 9AT. Bulletins may also be purchased from either of the above addresses and are currently priced at £1.50 or £2.50 according to their size.

Chapter 12: Law Enforcement

Offences

● There was an average increase of 5½ per cent per year in notifiable offences recorded by the police in England and Wales between 1981 and 1987. *(Chart 12.1 below)*

● Crimes against the person increased by 12 per cent between 1986 and 1987. *(Table 12.2)*

Police, court action and sentencing

● The number of 15 to 19 year olds found guilty or cautioned for indictable offences per thousand population in the age group trebled between 1961 and 1987. *(Chart 12.9)*

Prisons and probation service

● The average prison population in the United Kingdom in 1987 was 56.4 thousand, a rise of 3.9 per cent on the previous year. *(Table 12.12)*

● The prison population in England and Wales is projected to rise from 48 thousand in 1987 to between 63 and 69 thousand by 1996. *(Chart 12.11)*

● The remand population in prison in England and Wales more than doubled to 10,700 between 1971 and 1987, and the number of adult prisoners serving life sentences trebled to 2,230. *(Tables 12.13 and 12.14)*

Compensation and legal aid

● Over 700 thousand criminal legal aid applications were granted in the United Kingdom in 1986-87, over 3 times as many as in 1971-72. *(Chart 12.21)*

Resources

● Thirty thousand staff were in post in prison department establishments in Great Britain at the beginning of 1988, 2.7 per cent more than the beginning of 1987. *(Table 12.24)*

Public order in Northern Ireland

● There were 236 explosions in Northern Ireland in 1987, 64 more than in 1986, and 148 bombs were neutralised. *(Table 12.26)*

12.1 Notifiable offences[1] recorded by the police: rates

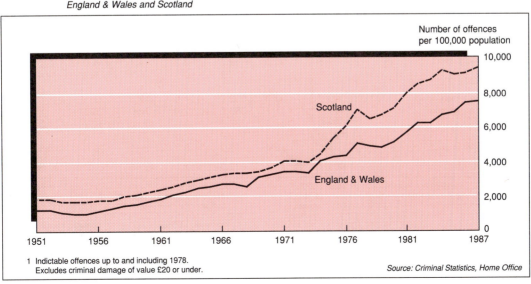

England & Wales and Scotland

1 Indictable offences up to and including 1978.
Excludes criminal damage of value £20 or under.

Source: Criminal Statistics, Home Office

Offences

Though the number of notifiable offences recorded by the police provides a measure of the amount of crime with which the police are faced, changes in the number recorded do not necessarily provide an accurate reflection of changes in the amount of crime committed as many offences are either not reported to the police or not recorded by them. This coupled with numerous small changes in coverage over the years makes it difficult to analyse long term trends of recorded crime. However, making such allowances as can readily be made, Chart 12.1, on the previous page, shows that the average annual increase in recorded crime per 100 thousand population in England and Wales was nearly 5 per cent per year in the 1950s, over 6 per cent in the 1960s, nearly 5 per cent in the 1970s, and in the 1980s to 1987 it was about 5½ per cent. The average annual increase for Scotland was only just over 1½ per cent in the 1950s, over 4½ per cent in the 1960s and rose to nearly 7 per cent in the 1970s. In the 1980s to 1987 it was 4 per cent.

In 1987 in England and Wales the police recorded nearly 3.9 million notifiable offences, an increase of 1 per cent over 1986, of which 94 per cent were crimes against property and 5 per cent crimes against the person (Table 12.2). Crimes against property are defined as the burglary, theft, fraud and forgery, and criminal damage groups, whilst offences against the person comprises violence against the person, robbery and sexual offences. Scotland showed an increase of 4 per cent between 1986 and 1987 but the figure for Northern Ireland dropped. Since the 1950s the number of notifiable offences have increased at an average of about 6 per cent each year, although individual year to year changes vary substantially. In the United Kingdom as a whole, theft and handling stolen goods accounted for over half of all notifiable offences recorded in 1987. Between 1986 and 1987 in England and Wales there was a rise of 81 thousand in thefts from vehicles but an appreciable fall in the numbers of thefts of motor vehicles and burglaries, with the recorded number of burglaries in 1987 showing a 3 per cent decrease. The number of recorded sexual offences rose by 11 per cent in 1987, after increases of 6 per cent in each of the two preceeding years. Home Office data suggest that there were further increases in 1987 in recorded numbers of offences against children though the numbers of such offences remain quite small. This may be a reflection of the growing awareness and concern about this type of offence leading to increased reporting and/or increased efforts by the police to deal with them. The incidence of crime against the person continues to rise. There was an increase of 12 per cent in England and Wales since 1986 compared with an average increase of 4 per cent a year between 1980 and 1986. Scotland showed a rise of 16 per cent between 1986 and 1987.

An offence is said to be cleared up if a person is either charged, summoned, or cautioned for the offence, or if the offence is admitted and is taken into consideration by the court, or if there is sufficient evidence to charge

12.2 Notifiable offences[1] recorded by the police: by type of offence

England & Wales, Scotland, and Northern Ireland Thousands

	England & Wales			Scotland			Northern Ireland		
	1971	1986	1987	1971	1986	1987	1971	1986	1987
Notifiable offences recorded									
Violence against the person	47.0 [2]	125.5	141.0	5.0	11.6	13.8	1.4	4.2	4.2
Sexual offences	23.6	22.7[5]	25.2[5]	2.6	2.7	2.9	0.2	0.8	0.8
of which, rape and attempted rape	..	2.3	2.5	0.2	0.4	0.4	..	..	..
Burglary	451.5	931.6	900.1	59.2	96.9	98.6	10.6	20.0	17.3
Robbery	7.5	30.0	32.6	2.3	4.1	4.6	0.6	2.2	2.5
Drugs offences	..	7.3	7.1	0.9	5.3	4.7	..	0.3	0.3
Theft and handling stolen goods	1,003.7	2,003.0[4]	2,052.0[4]	104.6	212.8	223.5	8.6	30.8	30.1
of which, theft of vehicles	167.6	411.1	389.6	17.1	28.0	26.2	..	..	..
Fraud and forgery	99.8	133.4	133.0	9.4	30.6	31.7	1.5	4.2	4.2
Criminal damage	27.0[3]	583.6	589.0	22.0	78.9	76.4	7.4[6]	4.1[6]	2.6
Other notifiable offences	5.6[4]	9.4	12.2	5.0	21.0	29.6	0.5	1.7	1.9
Total notifiable offences	1,665.7[3]	3,847.4	3,892.2	211.0	463.8	481.2	30.8[6]	68.3[6]	63.9

1 Offences which in 1978 and earlier years were 'indictable'. Scottish figures of 'crimes' have been recompiled to approximate to the classification of notifiable offences in England & Wales. However, because of differences in the legal system, recording and counting practices, and classification problems, Scottish figures are not strictly comparable with those for England & Wales.
2 Figures for 1986 and 1987 are not precisely comparable with those for 1971 because of changes made by new counting rules which were introduced at the beginning of 1980.
3 Excludes offences of criminal damage valued at £20 or less.

4 Offences of 'abstracting electricity', of which there were 5,572 cases in 1987 are included among 'Other offences' in 1971 and 'Theft and handling stolen goods' in 1986 and 1987.
5 Includes offences of 'gross indecency with a child.'
6 Figures for 1971 exclude criminal damage valued at £25 or less; 1986 and 1987 figures exclude criminal damage valued at £200 or less.

Source: Criminal Statistics, Home Office; Scottish Home and Health Department; Northern Ireland Office

12.3 Clear-up rates for notifiable offences[1] : by type of offence

England & Wales, Scotland, and Northern Ireland   Percentages

	England & Wales			Scotland			Northern Ireland		
	1971	1986	1987	1971	1986	1987	1971	1986	1987
Notifiable offences recorded									
Violence against the person	82[2]	71	75	87	82	79	28[7]	57	71
Sexual offences	76	71[5]	75[5]	77	76	78	87	79	91
of which, rape and attempted rape	..	62	71	81	77	77	..	..	..
Burglary	37	26	27	26	19	19	27	26	30
Robbery	42	20	21	21	29	29	7	19	18
Theft and handling stolen goods	43	31	32	37	29	29	46	38	43
of which, theft of vehicles	..	22	25	36	27	28	..	..	..
Fraud and forgery	83	67	67	80	75	74	84	70	79
Criminal damage	34[3]	21[3]	23[3]	32	22	23	10	31	43
Other notifiable offences	92[4]	93[6]	96[6]	85	95	96	89	43	42
Total notifiable offences	45[3]	32	33	38	34	35	32	37	43

1 See Table 12.2 footnote 1.
2 Figures for 1986 and 1987 are not precisely comparable with those for 1971 because of changes made by new counting rules which were introduced at the beginning of 1980.
3 Excludes criminal damage valued at £20 or less.
4 Includes offences of 'abstracting electricity'.
5 Includes offences of 'gross indecency with a child', recorded only from the beginning of 1983.

6 Includes offences of 'trafficking in controlled drugs', recorded only from the beginning of 1983.
7 Figures for 1986 and 1987 are not precisely comparable with those for 1971 because of a change in the definition of when a crime is recorded as cleared-up. The total notifiable offences for 1971 exclude criminal damage valued at £25 or less; 1986 and1987 figures exclude criminal damage valued at £200 or less.

Source: Criminal Statistics, Home Office; Scottish Home and Health Department; Northern Ireland Office

a person but the case is not proceeded with. Examples of the latter are where the offence is attributed to a child under the age of criminal responsibility, where the offender is already serving a long custodial sentence for another offence, or because the victim is unable to give evidence. As a percentage of offences recorded, the number cleared up in England and Wales in 1987 was 33 per cent compared to 32 per cent in 1986 and 45 per cent in 1971 (Table 12.3). Some offences tend to have much higher clear-up rates than others. For example, only 21 per cent of robberies, half the rate in 1971, and 23 per cent of criminal damage offences recorded by the police were cleared up in 1987 compared with 75 per cent of both offences of violence against the person and sexual offences. Thus the differences in the overall clear-up rates between years can be as a result of changes in the pattern of offences; for instance in 1987 there were larger than average

increases in recorded numbers of offences of violence against the person, which have high clear-up rates, and a drop in the recorded numbers of burglaries and theft of vehicles which have low clear-up rates.

Clear-up rates in both Scotland and Northern Ireland were both higher, 35 and 43 per cent respectively, than in England and Wales in 1987 (33 per cent).

Table 12.4 shows that the number of firearms certificates on issue in England and Wales remained constant at 160 thousand from 1983 to 1986, dropping slightly to 159 thousand in 1987. In 1987 the number of shotgun certificates on issue was about 860 thousand having steadily increased, by 10 per cent, since 1983.

In 1972, 1973, 1979 and 1980 and 1985 and 1986, the General Household Survey has included questions

12.4 Firearms and shotgun certificates: applications by outcome and number on issue

England & Wales, Scotland and Northern Ireland   Thousands and numbers

	Applications for					Applications for				
	Grant of firearms certificate		Renewal of firearms certificate			Grant of shotgun certificate		Renewal of shotgun certificate		
	Granted (thousands)	Refused (numbers)	Granted (thousands)	Refused (numbers)	Firearms certificates[1]	Granted (thousands)	Refused (numbers)	Granted (thousands)	Refused (numbers)	Shotgun certificates[1]
England & Wales										
1968	..	..	..	..	216					
1971	..	..	..	..	191	..	..	..	..	716
1983	11	234	43	205	160	47	495	234	170	783
1984	11	224	44	177	160	56	579	233	152	798
1985	12	215	44	145	160	61	691	233	167	819
1986	12	255	44	235	160	64	808	240	155	841
1987										
England & Wales	11	232	43	276	159	65	955	246	232	861
Scotland	3	22	..	..	38	5	83	..	..	89
Northern Ireland	4	298	29	42	88[2]	..	..	..	..	..

1 On issue at 31 December.
2 Includes shotgun certificates.

Source: Home Office; Scottish Home and Health Department; Northern Ireland Office

on household burglary, with the aim of identifying the extent and seriousness of burglaries in private households for which no routine statistics are available. The official statistics are based on crimes recorded by the police but some burglaries are not reported to the police and police do not always record an offence that is reported. Changes in the burglary rate as shown in the official statistics may therefore reflect changes in reporting rates by the police or public. A comparison of the rates for burglaries with loss reported in the GHS in England and Wales with those recorded by the police show that the survey rates increased less quickly than the police rates. Thus the increase in burglary rates in recent years shown by police figures is partly attributable to an increase in the number of burglaries recorded by the police rather than purely an increase in the number of crimes committed.

Police, court action and sentencing

This section looks at the action of the police and courts. As an alternative to court proceedings in England and Wales, the police may deal with an offender who admits his guilt by means of a caution. For motoring offences, the police have other options available: depending on the type and seriousness of the offence, they also have discretion on whether to give a fixed penalty or vehicle defect rectification scheme (VDRS) notice, or a written warning. On 1 October 1986, the extended fixed penalty system, the provisions for which were covered in Part III of the *Transport Act 1982*, was introduced. This allows the police to issue fixed penalty notices for a much wider range of minor traffic offences, such as speeding and neglect of traffic directions. The penalties are currently £12 for non-endorsable offences and £24 for endorsable offences. Drivers have 28 days (or longer in the case of parking and certain other offences where the owner, rather than the driver is liable) in which to pay or to request a court hearing, otherwise a fine, set at 50 per cent higher than the fixed penalty, is registered at the offender's local court. In 1987, the first full year of operation, the number of fixed penalty notices issued was 5.8 million, 1.3 million more than in 1985 and double the number 10 years earlier (Table 12.5). About half of the rise between 1985 and 1987 was due to the newly covered offences and half to a rise in offences already covered by fixed penalty legislation. Data from the Scottish Home and Health Department indicate that in the 13 months period from December 1986 to December 1987, over 515 thousand fixed penalty notices were issued in Scotland, and the Northern Ireland Office estimate that 77 thousand were issued in Northern Ireland in 1987.

12.5 Defendants proceeded against, cautioned, or given written warnings or fixed penalty notices

England & Wales   Thousands

	Indictable offences		Summary offences					
			Motoring offences			Other offences		
	Defendants proceeded against	Persons cautioned	Defendants proceeded against [1]	Written warnings	Fixed penalty notices [1,2]	Defendants proceeded against	Persons cautioned
1971	374	77	1,026	209	1,997	395	32
1977	474 [3]	115	1,222	198	2,831	466 [3]	34
1977	470	111	1,166	198	2,831	458	38
1981	523	104	1,299	253	4,317	472	50
1982	539	111	1,214	236	4,481	469	49
1983	530	115	1,252	235	4,619	521	51
1984	521	124	1,181	215	4,419	482	66
1985	520	145	1,158	205	4,522	469	73
1986	463	137	1,199	204	5,059	508	77
1987	488	150	850	165	5,814	505	87

1 For notices issued up to 1 October 1986 some persons were prosecuted following non-payment of a fixed penalty. The extended fixed penalty system was introduced on 1 October 1986. It allowed the police to issue fixed penalty notices for a much wider range of offences than hitherto, and to register fines automatically in the event of non-payment without the need for court proceedings.

2 Number of notices, not persons.

3 Series adjusted from 1977 following the implementation of the *Criminal Law Act 1977*, and a new procedure for counting court proceedings. See Appendix, Part 12: Criminal courts in England and Wales.

Source: Home Office

One of the aims of the extended fixed penalty system was to divert a large proportion of minor motoring cases from court proceedings, and Table 12.6 shows that in 1987, about 360,000 fewer court proceedings were recorded than in 1986. Most of this fall was in offence groups newly covered by fixed penalty arrangements such as speeding and neglect of traffic directions etc, as the falling proportion of total proceedings in Table 12.6 indicates. Conversely, the proportion of proceedings for licence, insurance and record keeping offences rose sharply in 1987, although the number of these offences rose only a little. Proceedings for drink-driving offences rose from 6 to 7 per cent of the total, reflecting in part a rise in the number of proceedings for these offences. The rise in drink driving offences may be related to increased levels of enforcement by the police. The effectiveness of drink-driving campaigns cannot be assessed from these figures, but Home Office figures on breath testing during these campaigns indicates a fall in the number of arrests in most recent years, despite very large increases in the rate of testing. Department of Transport figures also show a small fall in the whole of 1987 in the number of drivers and riders involved in injury accidents who failed the breath test, despite a substantial increase in the overall number of tests required.

Vehicle defect rectification schemes were introduced in most areas on 1 October 1986, although a few areas had been operating such schemes since 1983 and in Scotland since 1 May 1984; all areas had schemes by 1 April 1987. Under these schemes, drivers can avoid prosecution for vehicle defect offences if they repair or scrap their vehicles within the period allowed. In 1987, some 250,000 VDRS notices were issued in England and Wales, and about 80 per cent were complied with; 16,400 offences were dealt within this way in Scotland and in Northern Ireland 13,636 drivers had to produce their vehicles at a police station with the defects remedied.

12.6 Court proceedings for motoring and motor vehicle offences: by offence

United Kingdom   Percentages and thousands

Offence	1983	1984	1985	1986	1987
Driving etc after consuming alcohol or drugs	5	5	5	6	7
Careless, reckless driving etc	7	7	6	6	6
Licence, insurance and record keeping	35	36	36	36	43
Vehicle test and condition	15	14	14	13	14
Neglecting traffic signs, pedestrians rights etc	6	6	5	5	4
Obstructing, waiting and parking	4	4	4	4	3
Speeding	11	11	11	13	9
Total number of offences [1] (= 100%) (thousands)	2,656	2,518	2,493	2,524	2,163

1 Includes other offences which are not shown separately.

Source: Home Office; Scottish Home and Health Department; Northern Ireland Office

Table 12.7 shows the proportion of original sentences or orders which are breached. These are offenders who breach the original sentence or order and get caught: for example, failure to report for Community Service, or committing a further offence whilst under a suspended sentence. The different proportions vary according to the length of the original sentence and to whether the person is partly under some kind of supervision or not. In cases where offenders' sentences were fully suspended, one quarter of the orders were breached in 1987, the same proportion as 1986 but slightly lower than in 1985. This continues the slow downward movement from the percentage in 1971. There has been a steady, gradual increase in the percentage of community orders breached since 1984

12.7 Offenders breaching original sentence or order: by type of order

England & Wales   Percentages and thousands

Type of sentence or order	1971	1976	1981	1983	1984	1985	1986	1987
Partly suspended								
Orders made (thousands)	.	.	.	3.9	4.0	3.9	3.1	2.8
Orders breached (percentages)	.	.	.	5	8	11	11	11
Fully suspended								
Orders made (thousands)	31.7	34.7	38.4	32.9	29.2	30.9	27.7	29.2
Orders breached (percentages)	39	30	28	33	32	27	25	25
Community Service								
Orders made (thousands)	.	9.1	28.2	35.2	37.9	38.3	35.1	35.9
Orders breached (percentages)	.	4	18	16	16	17	18	18
Probation								
Orders made (thousands)	31.6	28.1	36.2	38.7	40.9	42.4	40.1	41.4
Orders breached (percentages)	30	20	14	15	15	17	18	19
Conditional discharge								
Orders made (thousands)	57.3	74.6	76.3	80.4	80.6	78.8	72.1	75.6
Orders breached (percentages)	9	9	10	11	11	11	11	11

Source: Home Office

12.8 Offenders sentenced [1] for indictable offences [2]: by sex, age, and type of sentence [3], 1987

England & Wales, Scotland and Northern Ireland

Thousands and percentages

	Males					Females				
	10—13	14—16	17—20	21 or over	All ages[4]	10—13	14—16	17—20	21 or over	All ages
England & Wales										
Type of sentence [3]										
1987										
Absolute or conditional discharge	1.8	8.4	10.3	19.5	40.1	0.2	1.3	3.4	8.2	13.0
Probation or supervision order	0.7	6.3	12.1	15.4	34.5	—	0.6	2.8	5.9	9.3
Fine	0.6	7.8	40.1	81.0	132.0	0.1	0.7	4.7	11.4	16.9
Community service order	—	1.6	13.4	14.4	29.4	—	0.1	0.6	1.0	1.7
Attendance centre order	0.9	5.3	2.2	—	8.4	—	0.2	—	—	0.2
Detention centre order	—	2.5	4.8	—	7.3	—	—	—	—	—
Youth custody	—	1.4	15.9	—	17.3	—	0.1	0.6	—	0.7
Imprisonment — fully suspended	—	—	—	23.2	23.2	—	—	—	2.6	2.6
— immediate[5]	—	—	—	42.0	42.0	—	—	—	2.5	2.5
Other	0.2	0.9	1.1	2.8	5.1	—	0.1	0.2	0.4	0.6
All sentences										
1981	15.1	62.0	114.4	206.9	399.2	1.8	7.4	14.6	41.6	65.4
of which, non-custodial (%)	*100*	*88*	*77*	*70*	*76*	*100*	*99*	*92*	*88*	*91*
1987	4.3	34.2	99.9	198.3	339.2	0.3	3.2	12.2	32.0	47.5
of which, non-custodial (%)	*100*	*89*	*79*	*67*	*74*	*100*	*98*	*95*	*84*	*88*
Rate per 1,000 population	3.5	30.7	62.0	11.5	16.0	0.3	3.0	7.9	1.7	2.1
Scotland [6]										
All sentences										
1981	.	0.6	22.1	27.6	50.3	.	0.1	2.4	6.1	8.5
of which, non-custodial (%)	.	*89*	*88*	*82*	*85*	.	*89*	*98*	*96*	*96*
1987	.	0.3	25.6	34.6	60.4	.	—	2.5	6.1	8.6
of which, non-custodial (%)	.	*87*	*85*	*82*	*83*	.	*100*	*94*	*92*	*93*
Rate per 1,000 population	.	0.5	118.8	20.1	24.4	.	0	11.9	3.2	3.2
Northern Ireland										
All sentences										
1987	0.1	0.8	3.0	5.5	9.5	—	0.1	0.3	0.8	1.1
of which, non-custodial (%)	*78*	*74*	*76*	*74*	*74*	*100*	*89*	*97*	*95*	*95*
Rate per 1,000 population	2.7	18.1	50.0	11.5	14.9	—	1.4	4.8	1.5	1.7

1 Sentences are shown on a principal offence/sentence basis.
2 See Appendix, Part 12: Criminal courts in England and Wales.
3 See Appendix, Part 12: Sentences and orders.
4 The figures include companies etc. and therefore the age breakdown does not add to the 'All ages' total.

5 Includes unsuspended and partly suspended imprisonment.
6 Scottish age ranges differ slightly and those shown are: under 16, 16—20, 21 or over.

Source: Criminal Statistics, Home Office
Scottish Home and Health Department;
Northern Ireland Office

after the sharp rise between 1976 and 1981 was followed by a slight drop. The percentage of probation orders breached has increased since the drop from 20 per cent in 1976 to 14 per cent in 1981; although it was still a third less than in 1971 it was only 1 per cent less in 1987 than in 1976.

Table 12.8 shows the number of people in each sex and age group given the different types of sentence available for indictable offences in England and Wales in 1987. Total figures for all sentences are given for Scotland and Northern Ireland. Following the *Criminal Justice Act 1982*, borstal training was abolished for young offenders as from 24 May 1983 in England and Wales and from 15 November 1983 in Scotland. Part 12 of the Appendix explains the new procedure of youth custody in England and Wales. In Scotland, young offenders now receive one sentence which, depending on its length and the circumstances of the offenders, is served either in a young offenders institution or a detention centre. Females are less likely than males to be given custodial sentences at all ages, and for both the males and

females the likelihood of receiving a custodial sentence increases with age.

Chart 12.9 gives the ages of offenders under 21 found guilty of, or cautioned for, indictable offences. This shows that the peak age for male offenders in 1961 was 14, after which the rate of offenders gradually fell. In 1971 the rate of offenders rose at all ages from 11 upwards, and particularly for those aged 13 upwards; there was no longer a distinct peak in the age distribution of offenders and the rate did not begin to fall until the age of 18. In 1987 the peak age range was 15 to 19 with an average increase of over a quarter in the rates of offenders in this age group over 1971; however, the overall shape of the age distribution was similar to 1971. For boys in the 15 to 19 age group the rate has tripled between 1961 and 1987.

The age distribution of female offenders show slightly less variation with the highest rates in both 1961 and 1971 amongst those aged 14, and in 1987 amongst those aged 14 and 15. However, there have been much greater proportionate increases between 1961 and 1987 in the rate of offenders in most age groups than amongst teenage boys.

The number of seizures of drugs controlled under the *Misuse of Drugs Act 1971* rose steadily over the period from 1974 to 1985, but since then appears to have stablised. In 1987 there were about 30,500 seizures, around the same number as in 1986. Overall, there was a substantial drop in the total number of seizures of class A drugs in 1987 - the number of seizures was about 3,500, some 800 (18 per cent) less than in 1986 and some 1,400 (about 29 per cent) less than in 1984 and 1985 (Chart 12.10). Nearly all of the fall between 1986 and 1987 was accounted for by the decrease in heroin seizures, although there were also falls in the number of seizures of class A drugs apart from cocaine. The number of seizures of class B drugs in 1987 was about 28,000, some 700 (3 per cent) more than in 1986. Most of this increase was accounted by the rise in seizures of herbal cannabis. Under the *Drug Trafficking Offences Act 1986*, a person convicted by a Crown Court in England and Wales of a drug trafficking offence (in addition to whatever other sentence is imposed) will also have a confiscation order imposed on him. This requires the offender to pay an amount equal to the full value of the proceeds from his drug trafficking activities, or that which is realisable. To the end of 1987 200 confiscation orders were made with a total value of £1.2 million. Confiscation orders were not introduced in Scotland until 1988 and do not yet apply in Northern Ireland.

12.9 Offenders aged under 21 found guilty of, or cautioned for, indictable offences: by sex and age

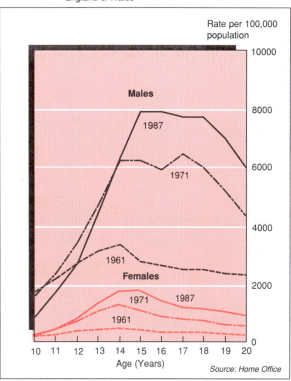

England & Wales

Source: Home Office

12.10 Seizures of controlled drugs: by drug type [1]

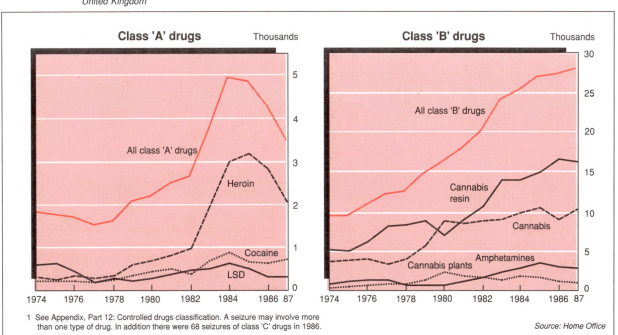

United Kingdom

1 See Appendix, Part 12: Controlled drugs classification. A seizure may involve more than one type of drug. In addition there were 68 seizures of class 'C' drugs in 1986.

Source: Home Office

Prisons and probation service

12.11 Average population of prison establishments[1]: actuals and projections[2]

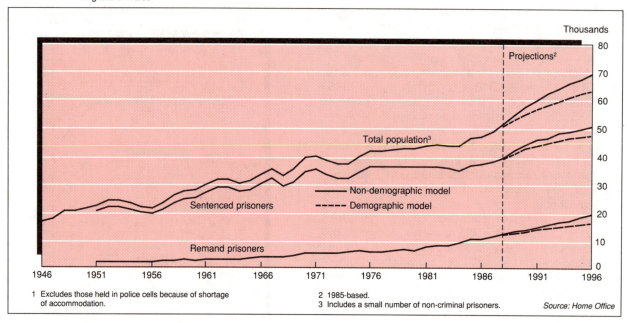

England & Wales

1 Excludes those held in police cells because of shortage of accommodation.

2 1985-based.

3 Includes a small number of non-criminal prisoners.

Source: Home Office

The total prison population in England and Wales is projected to continue to increase, reaching between 63 thousand and 69 thousand in 1996 (Chart 12.11). The mid point of the projected increase of between 14.6 and 20.6 thousand between 1987 and 1996 is more than 2½ times the increase of around 6.6 thousand over the nine years to 1987. The Chart shows that there was an increase almost every year since the second world war in the average prison population. There were small falls in numbers between 1983 and 1984 but between 1984 and 1987 the upward trend was resumed, there being an increase of 11.8 per cent in the average population to 48.4 thousand.

The average population of prison establishments in the United Kingdom in 1987 was 56.4 thousand, a rise of

12.12 Receptions [1] into prison establishments and population in custody

United Kingdom, and England & Wales   Thousands

	1961	1971	1976	1981	1982	1983	1984	1985	1986	1987
United Kingdom										
Receptions [1,2]										
Untried prisoners	39.1	67.2 [6]	59.9	60.1	63.2	61.9	67.4	72.0	73.0	76.0
Convicted prisoners										
awaiting sentence [3]	11.6	27.7	24.2	26.3	26.1	22.7	21.9	21.2	18.9	18.2
Sentenced prisoners	61.3	84.8	88.7	106.0	117.4	116.3	115.3	122.7	113.0	112.5
Non-criminal prisoners	9.8	6.7	6.0	4.8	4.8	4.1	3.8	3.5	3.7	3.4
Average population [2]										
Males	31.5	44.9	47.5	48.7	49.5	49.4	48.7	51.8	52.4	54.4
Females	1.1	1.2	1.5	1.6	1.5	1.6	1.6	1.7	1.8	2.0
Untried prisoners	1.9	3.5 [6]	4.5	5.8	6.4	7.2	8.3	9.4	9.6	10.6
Convicted prisoners awaiting										
sentence [3]	0.7	1.8	2.0	2.3	2.2	1.8	1.7	1.7	1.7	1.7
Sentenced prisoners [4]										
Adults	20.3	29.0	30.2 [7]	29.9	30.1	30.2	29.1	31.0	32.2	33.6
Young offenders [5]	7.1	10.8	11.7	12.0	11.9	11.4	11.0	11.1	10.4	10.0
Other sentences	2.1	0.3	—	—	—	—	0.1	—	—	—
Non-criminal prisoners	0.5	0.6	0.5	0.4	0.4	0.3	0.3	0.2	0.2	0.3
England & Wales										
Highest number of inmates sleeping										
Two in a cell	..	6.2	10.7	11.3	12.4	12.1	12.1	13.4	13.5	14.0
Three in a cell	..	8.2	5.7	5.6	4.4	5.0	4.4	5.1	4.9	5.3

1 Figures of receptions contain an element of double counting as
 individuals can be received in more than one category of prisoner.
2 Excludes internees in Northern Ireland.
3 Includes persons remanded in custody while social and medical
 inquiry reports are prepared prior to sentence. Prisoners in Northern
 Ireland are not committed for sentence but are sentenced at
 the court of conviction.
4 From 1983 onwards persons detained in Scotland under Section
 205(2) of the *Criminal Procedure (Scotland) Act 1975* are
 included as adults or young offenders according to the type of

establishment in which they were held. For earlier years they
are all included as young offenders.
5 See Appendix Part 12: Young offenders.
6 Scottish data for convicted prisoners awaiting sentence for 1961
 and 1971 are not separately available but are included in Untried
 prisoners.
7 Northern Ireland figures for young prisoners are not available
 separately before 1980; they are included with adults.

*Source: Prison Statistics, Home Office; Scottish Home and Health
Department; Northern Ireland Office*

4.1 per cent over 1986 continuing the increase which has followed a slight fall between 1983 and 1984 (Table 12.12). There were two main reasons for the fall: in England and Wales under the enabling powers of the *Criminal Justice Act 1982,* referred to earlier, the minimum qualifying period for parole was reduced from 1 July 1984 (see Table 12.17 and accompanying commentary); and in Scotland the *Criminal Justice (Scotland) Act 1980,* abolished borstal sentences from 15 November 1983.

About 22 per cent of the average prison population in the United Kingdom in 1987 were being held on remand, either untried or convicted awaiting sentence, compared to 8 per cent in 1961; over the period the number on remand increased nearly five-fold while the sentenced population increased by less than a half.

About half a per cent of the prison population were non-criminal prisoners, such as aliens and immigrants held under the *Immigration Act 1971;* persons in default of court orders, maintenance orders, alimony payments etc; and those in contempt of court. Just under a fifth of the average sentenced population in prison establishments were aged under 21, less than the proportion in 1961.

In England and Wales there were on average 540 prisoners, mostly on remand, accommodated daily in police station cells in 1987. During early 1988 the daily number rose rapidly to reach over 1,500 in early March. It then fell to under 700 in mid-July. But following industrial relations difficulties, there was a substantial increase again and at mid-October 1988 there were around 1,800 prisoners in police cells.

12.13 Prisoners [1]: by length of sentence and sex

England & Wales, Scotland and Northern Ireland Numbers and rates

	1971	1976	1981	1984	1985	1986	1987
England & Wales [2]							
Males							
Prisoners aged 21 or over serving:							
Up to 6 months	2,970	3,360	3,970	3,730	3,900	3,280	2,920
Over 6 months and up to 18 months	8,230	7,450	7,480	6,500	6,700	6,370	6,110
Over 18 months and up to 4 years	9,580	9,360	8,010	7,550	8,270	9,250	9,890
Over 4 years (excluding life)	3,320	3,740	3,700	4,220	4,750	5,490	6,590
Life sentences	770	1,110	1,530	1,760	1,880	2,020	2,170
All sentenced male prisoners	24,870	25,020	24,680	23,770	25,510	26,410	27,680
Rate per 100,000 population aged 21 or over	157	155	150	141	150	154	160
Females							
Prisoners aged 21 or over serving:							
Up to 6 months	130	170	230	270	260	250	180
Over 6 months and up to 18 months	210	280	300	300	300	290	310
Over 18 months and up to 4 years	170	170	170	200	220	290	390
Over 4 years (excluding life)	20	30	40	60	70	90	150
Life sentences	20	30	40	50	50	60	60
All sentenced female prisoners	540	690	790	880	900	980	1,090
Rate per 100,000 population aged 21 or over	3	4	4	5	5	5	6
Scotland							
Males							
Prisoners aged 21 or over serving:							
Less than 6 months	1,275	865	751	896	1,008	979	909
6 months and less than 18 months	503	541	411	448	459	488	472
18 months and less than 3 years	481	326	359	280	295	405	404
3 years and over (excluding life)	500	615	694	752	954	1,137	1,221
Life sentences	134	220	276	313	322	326	349
All sentenced male prisoners	2,893	2,567	2,491	2,690	3,039	3,335	3,356
Rate per 100,000 population aged 21 or over	183	160	155	161	179	195	195
Females							
Prisoners aged 21 or over serving:							
Less than 6 months	33	39	28	29	36	47	65
6 months and less than 18 months	12	12	14	13	19	18	10
18 months and less than 3 years	6	7	7	7	10	12	10
3 years and over (excluding life)	5	6	11	7	29	29	26
Life sentences	2	4	3	7	7	6	6
All sentenced female prisoners	58	68	63	64	101	113	118
Rate per 100,000 population aged 21 or over	3	4	3	3	5	6	6
Northern Ireland [3]							
Males							
Prisoners aged 21 or over serving:							
Up to 6 months	..	..	..	62	94	82	100
Over 6 months and up to 18 months	..	..	..	124	140	135	154
Over 18 months and up to 4 years	..	..	..	205	164	182	243
Over 4 years (excluding life)	..	..	..	587	495	397	369
Life sentences	..	..	..	292	304	334	335
All sentenced male prisoners	..	..	..	1,270	1,197	1,130	1,201
Rate per 100,000 population aged 21 or over	..	..	..	267	252	238	250
Females							
Prisoners aged 21 or over serving:							
Up to 6 months	..	..	..	2	3	2	4
Over 6 months and up to 18 months	..	..	..	3	7	1	4
Over 18 months and up to 4 years	..	..	..	1	2	2	2
Over 4 years (excluding life)	..	..	..	11	12	9	7
Life sentences	..	..	..	2	2	6	6
All sentenced female prisoners	..	..	..	19	26	20	23
Rate per 100,000 population aged 21 or over	..	..	..	4	5	4	4

1 Average population of sentenced prisoners aged 21 or over. Excludes untried prisoners, convicted prisoners awaiting sentence, and non-criminal prisoners.

2 Numbers of prisoners are rounded to the nearest ten.
3 Data taken at 30 June each year.

Source: Home Office; Scottish Home and Health Department; Northern Ireland Office

12.14 Untried and convicted unsentenced prisoners: by sex
England & Wales

Thousands and numbers

	1971	1976	1981	1983	1984	1985	1986	1987
Untried prisoners								
Males								
Average population (thousands)	2.8	3.2	4.6	5.8	6.9	7.8	8.2	8.7
Receptions (thousands)	45.5	42.7	44.7	45.3	49.4	52.0	52.8	56.8
Average number of days in custody [1]	21	27	38	47	51	55	57	56
Females								
Average population (thousands)	0.1	0.1	0.2	0.2	0.2	0.3	0.3	0.3
Receptions (thousands)	2.2	2.6	2.5	2.4	2.5	2.7	2.6	2.7
Average number of days in custody [1,2]	17	20	25	31	34	41	44	45
Convicted unsentenced prisoners								
Males								
Average population (thousands)	1.5	1.6	2.0	1.5	1.4	1.5	1.4	1.5
Receptions (thousands)	25.6	22.2	22.4	18.9	17.3	17.4	15.5	14.6
Average number of days in custody [3]	25	27	32	30	30	31	32	37
Females								
Average population (thousands)	0.1	0.1	0.1	0.1	0.1	0.1	0.1	0.1
Receptions (thousands)	2.1	2.0	1.7	1.3	1.2	1.2	1.1	1.0
Average number of days in custody [2,3]	21	26	31	30	33	26	24	27

1 Before conviction
2 Subject to wide variation because of the small sample size.

3 After conviction before sentence.

Source: Home Office

Apart from the rise in the number of remand prisoners, the increase in the average prison population since 1984 in England and Wales referred to earlier was mainly due to the rise in the numbers of adult males serving longer sentences of 18 months or more (Table 12.13). The population with sentences between 10½ and 18 months was, however, kept down by the lowering of the parole minimum qualifying period in July 1984, which extended parole to such inmates for the first time. There had also been a correspondingly sharp rise for similarly sentenced adult males in Scotland in 1986 now followed by a further, though much smaller, rise in 1987.

The proportion of sentenced adult male prisoners in England and Wales serving sentences of 6 months or less was 10½ per cent in 1987, a decrease in the proportion of 12 per cent in 1971. However the proportion serving sentences of four years or more or life doubled to 32 per cent. Both Northern Ireland and Scotland have higher number of sentenced male prisoners aged 21 or over per 100 thousand males in this age group than England and Wales.

Northern Ireland figures show that there has been a decrease between 1984 and 1987 in the number of prisoners serving over 4 years (excluding life) but increases in all other lengths of sentence. The largest increase since 1971 is in life sentences, which have trebled.

In England and Wales the average number of days spent in custody by male remand prisoners fell slightly for those awaiting trial, but not for those awaiting sentence, in 1987 compared with 1986 (Table 12.14). Untried male prisoners spent an average of 56 days in custody compared to 21 days in 1971 and 47 days in 1983. For female prisoners awaiting trial there was a slight rise; the average of 45 days in 1987 was almost three times as long as in 1971. Over the same period the average female remand population for untried prisoners trebled and receptions were up by over 20 per cent. The rise in the number of days convicted prisoners awaiting sentence spend in custody is not so pronounced, 37 days in 1987 against 25 in 1971 for male prisoners and the figure for females rising by 6 days to 27 days since 1971.

Of the 10.7 thousand prisoners on remand at the end of June 1987 21 per cent were known to be from ethnic minority groups, about half of which were of West Indian, Guyanese or African origin (Table 12.15). The proportion of young offenders among sentenced prisoners varied between the groups; a third of those of Chinese, Arab or mixed origin were young offenders compared to a sixth of prisoners of Indian sub-continent origin and about a quarter of those of White, West Indian, Guyanese or African origin. Adult prisoners from the ethnic minority groups tend to be serving longer sentences than white prisoners: under a quarter of ethnic minority prisoners were serving less than 18

12.15 Population in prison department establishments on 30 June 1987: by ethnic group and type of prisoner

England and Wales   Numbers

		Ethnic group				
	White	West Indian Guyanese African	Indian Pakistani Bangladeshi	Chinese Arab Mixed Origin	Other, not recorded (including refusals)	All
Prisoners on remand						
Untried criminal prisoners						
Aged 14 to 20	2,290	248	69	77	161	2,845
Aged 21 and over	4,865	774	160	136	359	6,294
Convicted unsentenced prisoners	1,265	142	18	28	77	1,530
All remand prisoners	8,420	1,164	247	241	597	10,669
Prisoners under sentence						
Young offenders						
Detention centre trainees	979	56	25	23	3	1,086
Youth custody trainees [1]						
Up to 18 months [2]	4,459	316	64	94	32	4,965
Over 18 months (inc. life)	2,872	417	74	105	37	3,505
All sentenced young offenders	8,310	789	163	222	72	9,556
Adults by sentence length						
Up to 18 months [2]	9,451	674	167	143	83	10,518
Over 18 months up to 4 years	8,689	1,087	206	183	120	10,285
Over 4 years (inc. life)	7,043	973	536	191	201	8,944
All sentenced adults	25,183	2,734	909	517	404	29,747
All sentenced prisoners	33,493	3,523	1,072	739	476	39,303
Non-criminal prisoners	128	66	36	16	47	293
Population of prison department establishments	42,041	4,753	1,355	996	1,120	50,265

1 Includes persons detained under Section 53 of the Children and Young Persons Act 1933 and custody for life cases.

2 Includes persons committed in default of payment of a fine, compensation order or costs.

Source: Home Office

months compared with over a third of White prisoners. This pattern will reflect different offence patterns for the various ethnic groups.

Before 1 July 1984 prisoners serving sentences of over 18 months might be considered for release on parole licence after serving a third of their prison sentence or

12.16 Cases considered and persons recommended for parole

England & Wales and Scotland   Numbers and percentages

	England & Wales			Scotland		
		Persons recommended for parole			Persons recommended for parole	
	Cases considered for parole	Numbers	Percentage of cases considered	Cases considered for parole	Numbers	Percentage of cases considered
1971	9,653	2,971	31	459	138	30
1976	10,077	4,995	50	676	227	34
1977	10,344	5,218	50	682	210	31
1978	10,183	4,815	47	708	228	32
1979	10,156	4,771	47	764	236	31
1980	10,070	5,088	51	729	219	30
1981	9,620	5,279	55	802	246	31
1982	9,193	5,200	57	678	261	38
1983	9,534 [1]	5,363	56	791	340	43
1984	19,071	11,909	62	719	245	34
1985	22,912	14,431	63	752	226	30
1986	24,380	14,805	61	972	274	28
1987	23,778	14,006	59	1,167	370	32

1 Figures from 1984 are not comparable with those for earlier years. See accompanying text for details.

Source: Report of the Parole Boards for England and Wales and Scotland

12.17 Percentage of time served under sentence by adults discharged [1] from determinate sentences on completion of sentence or on licence: by sex and length of sentence [2]

England & Wales   Percentages

	1976	1978	1979	1980	1981	1982	1983	1984	1985	1986	1987
Length of sentence											
Males											
Up to 3 months	66	65	64	65	60	60	61	60	60	58	52
Over 3 up to 6 months	63	63	62	62	59	60	60	60	60	59	52
Over 6 under 18 months	62	62	61	61	60	59	58	55	52	51	47
18 months	63	62	62	61	61	61	58	50	41	40	40
Over 18 months up to 4 years	53	53	53	52	51	49	49	45	43	44	44
Over 4 up to 5 years	54	53	53	52	49	47	47	48	50	51	50
Over 5 years, less than life	54	53	52	49	48	49	48	52	55	55	55
Females											
Up to 3 months	63	65	65	65	60	60	63	61	61	58	53
Over 3 up to 6 months	61	61	61	63	60	58	60	59	60	60	54
Over 6 under 18 months	62	61	61	62	62	60	59	56	54	54	49
18 months	64	62	62	63	64	60	61	48	36	37	37
Over 18 months up to 4 years	49	48	50	48	49	49	45	40	40	38	43
Over 4 years, less than life	46	58	51	41	37	44	50	40	58	52	39

1 Excludes discharges following recall after release on licence, non-criminals and persons committed to custody for non-payment of a fine.

2 On discharge; the sentence may change after reception if there are further charges or an appeal.

Source: Prison statistics, Home Office

12 months after sentence, whichever was longer. In 1975, the then Home Secretary made a statement encouraging the more widespread use of parole and its granting at an earlier stage. Additionally on 1 July 1984, under enabling provisions of the *Criminal Justice Act 1982*, the minimum qualifying period for parole was reduced from 12 to 6 months from sentence, although the overriding requirement to serve a third of the sentence if this was longer remained unchanged. As a result of these changes there was a large rise in England and Wales between 1975 and 1976 in the number of prisoners recommended for parole and between 1983 and 1984 the number of cases considered for parole doubled and the proportion of persons recommended for parole rose from 56 to 62 per cent of cases considered (Table 12.16). Compared to England and Wales, where in 1987 59 per cent of all cases considered were recommended for parole, the proportion in Scotland has always been far lower; for example, only 32 per cent in 1987.

In 1987 in England and Wales, males and females discharged from longer determinate sentences (over 5 years but less than life for males, over 4 years but less than life for females) had served on average 55 and 39 per cent respectively of their sentences in custody, not counting any time spent on remand (Table 12.17). Broadly speaking, the shorter the sentence the higher the proportion served, except for very short sentences. Both males and females discharged in 1987 from sentences of up to 3 months had served around half on average, the proportion having fallen from around two-thirds in the late 1970s. In Northern Ireland both males and females sentenced to 4 months and over up to but excluding life served an average of just over a half of their sentence. In short sentences of 3 months or less a larger proportion of the sentence was served

with males serving 68 per cent and females 89 per cent of their sentences.

Table 12.18 shows the proportion of offenders in England and Wales who were reconvicted within two years of their discharge in 1984. The greatest proportion of reconvictions was among young male offenders sentenced to youth custody. Over three-quarters of young male offenders aged 15-16 and sentenced to youth custody were reconvicted within two years. A much lower proportion of young female offenders were reconvicted. Less than a quarter of adult male prisoners with partly suspended sentences were reconvicted compared to half of those sentenced to imprisonment.

12.18 Offenders reconvicted within two years of discharge in 1984: by type of custody and sex [1]

England & Wales   Percentages

	Males	Females
Adult prisoners		
Partly suspended sentences	24	18
Unsuspended imprisonment	50	34
All	47	31
Young offenders		
Detention centres	62	..
Youth custody - aged 15-16 on sentence	80	43
- aged 17-20 on sentence	66	42
Young prisoners [2]	59	45
All	65	42
All offenders	55	34

1 Estimates based on samples of discharges.

2 Persons committed to prison who were under the age of 21 on the date of reception under sentence; including *Children and Young Persons Act 1933* and custody for life.

Source: Home Office

About 135 thousand people commenced supervision by the probation service in England and Wales during 1986, 8 per cent fewer than in 1985 (Table 12.19) after large increases in previous years. More than half of those under criminal supervision were either on probation or subject to a community service order. The number of those commencing parole increased slightly between 1985 and 1986 but is now nearly three times as many as in 1981, while there has been a decrease in the number commencing youth custody and detention centre supervision. The number of persons commencing supervision under the *Children and Young Persons Act* has halved since 1981, reflecting the much greater use by the police of cautioning of juvenile offenders and the large fall in the numbers dealt with in the courts.

12.19 Persons commencing supervision by the probation service: by type of supervision [1]

England & Wales   Thousands

	1981	1982	1985	1986
Criminal supervision				
Court orders	79	82	89	81
of which,				
Probation	36	37	42	39
Community service order	28	31	38	35
Supervision [2]	12	11	8	6
Statutory after-care	28	28	35	33
of which,				
Detention centre	10	10	8	7
Youth custody	.	.	17	16
Borstal/Young prisoner	14	14		
Parole	5	5	12	13
Voluntary after-care	22	23	30	28
Total criminal supervision	124	127	144	133
Domestic supervision	4	4	2	2
Total	128	131	146	135

1 Each person is counted once for each type of supervision commenced. Individual figures do not add to the total because each person is counted only once in the total irrespective of the number of types of supervision.

2 Under the *Children and Young Persons Act 1969.*

Source: Home Office

Compensation and legal aid

In 1987-88, 43,054 new applications for compensation under the Criminal Injuries Compensation Scheme were received, a slight increase on the year before, which brought the overall total to over 455 thousand since the scheme was introduced in Great Britain on 1 August 1964 (Chart 12.20). The 20,991 awards made in 1987-88 were slightly less than in 1986-87 with the number of applications rejected remaining the same. In Northern Ireland 9,249 applications were received in 1987-88 under the scheme with awards made in 4,170 cases.

The total number of certificates for civil legal aid issued in England and Wales in 1986-87 was 245 thousand (Table 12.21), up 6 per cent on the year before, continuing the general gradual increase in the total number issued since 1977-78. There was a substantial fall between 1976-77 and 1977-78 because of the withdrawal of legal aid for undefended divorce cases. There was also a fall between 1979-80 and 1980-81 because of the introduction in 1980 of the assistance by way of representation scheme which allows for representation of a parent or guardian in certain child care proceedings. Since 1981-82 the number of civil legal aid certificates issued in Scotland each year has been around 20 thousand and in Northern Ireland around 10 thousand with a slight increase in 1987 to 13 thousand. The number of criminal legal aid applications granted in the United Kingdom as a whole in 1986-87 was 715 thousand, over three times as high as the number granted in 1971-72. Excluding Legal Advice and Assistance and the Duty Solicitor Scheme,

12.20 Criminal injuries compensation

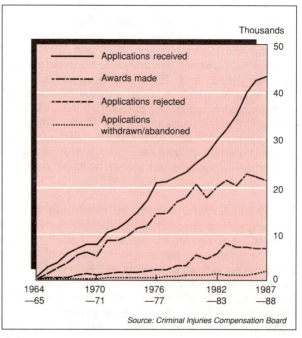

Great Britain

Thousands

Applications received
Awards made
Applications rejected
Applications withdrawn/abandoned

Source: Criminal Injuries Compensation Board

gross payments for criminal legal aid were £14 million higher than for civil legal aid. The 24 Hour Duty Solicitor Scheme (Advice and Assistance at Police Station) came into operation on January 1 1986 and expenditure under this scheme increased from nearly £12½ million in 1986 to over £21½ million in 1987.

12.21 Legal aid[1] and legal advice and assistance: by type of case

England & Wales, Scotland and Northern Ireland

Thousands and percentages

	1971 -72	1976 -77	1979 -80	1982 -83	1983 -84	1984 -85	1985 -86	1986 -87
England & Wales								
Civil legal aid: certificates issued (thousands)								
Matrimonial proceedings - issued to men	36[4]	32	25	33	35	36	37	36
- issued to women	118	123	94	85	85	86	87	90
Other cases	49	56	73	72	86	100	108	119
Total	202	211	192	190	206	222	232	245
Criminal legal aid: applications granted								
Total, all criminal proceedings and appeals[2] (thousands)	187	362	388	478	495	515	571	620
Legal advice and assistance[3]								
Type of case (percentages)								
Matrimonial and family	.	*56*	*59*	*47*	*46*	*43*	*41*	*41*
Criminal	.	*15*	*16*	*24*	*25*	*27*	*26*	*23*
Other	.	*29*	*25*	*29*	*29*	*30*	*33*	*36*
Solicitors' claims paid (thousands)	.	292	439	733	832	953	1,039	981
Scotland (thousands)								
Civil legal aid: certificates issued	11	13	17	19	18	19	20	20
Criminal legal aid: applications granted	13[5]	30	37	55	61	63	64	67
Northern Ireland (thousands)								
Civil legal aid: certificates issued	4	5	7	8	11	12	10	13
Criminal legal aid: applications granted	7	10	13	22	24	25	25	28

1 See Appendix, Part 12: Legal aid.
2 Calendar years. 1971 is shown under 1971-72, etc. Includes care proceedings.
3 Scheme began on 2 April 1973.

4 After 1975-76 data refer to offers of certificates accepted, some of which will have been issued in an earlier year.
5 Prior to 16 May 1975 legal aid was only available in criminal cases in High and Sheriff Courts.

Source: Legal Aid Annual Reports, Lord Chancellor's Department; Scottish Home and Health Department ; Northern Ireland Office

There has been a change in the distribution of type of case on which legal advice and assistance is sought; in 1973-74 (the first year that the Scheme was in operation), around 60 per cent of the cases involved marriage or family matters and only about 10 per cent related to criminal affairs, but by 1985-86 these proportions had changed to around 40 per cent and 25 per cent respectively. Almost all defendants appearing at the Crown Court for trial or sentence were legally aided in 1987 (Table 12.22) and nearly three-fifths of all defendents in criminal proceedings at juvenile courts received legal aid. Whereas only 28 per cent of adults tried for indictable offences in magistrates courts were legally aided in 1971, the proportion had risen to 91 per cent by 1987. In contrast only 3 per cent of adults tried for summary offences in magistrates courts in 1987 were legally aided (1 per cent in 1971).

12.22 Percentage of defendants on criminal charges who were legally aided[1]: by type of proceedings

England & Wales

Percentages

	Magistrates' court proceedings				Crown Court proceedings		
	Trials of adults for		Proceedings relating to committal for trial[2]	All criminal proceedings at juvenile courts	Trials at the Crown Court	Appearances for sentence following conviction at magistrates' court	Appeals against a decision of a magistrates' court
	Indictable offences	Summary offences					
1971	*28*	*1*	*71*	*5*[3]	*94*	*94*	*65*
1976	*53*	*2*	*70*	*21*	*96*	*98*	*64*
1978	*58*	*2*	*70*	*22*	*96*	*98*	*60*
1979	*60*	*2*	*68*	*27*	*96*	*98*	*64*
1930	*62*	*2*	*62*	*27*	*96*	*98*	*62*
1981	*65*	*2*	*57*	*31*	*97*	*97*	*67*
1982	*69*	*2*	*49*	*33*	*97*	*98*	*60*
1983	*71*	*2*	*55*	*38*	*98*	*98*	*60*
1984	*67*	*2*	*67*	*38*	*98*	*96*	*63*
1985	*75*	*2*	*72*	*45*	*98*	*95*	*64*
1986	*84*	*2*	*75*	*52*	*96*	*94*	*59*
1987	*91*	*3*	*76*	*58*	*99*	*94*	*62*

1 See Appendix, Part 12: Legal aid.
2 Figures should be treated with caution.

3 Figure includes some care proceedings.

Source : Lord Chancellor's Department

Resources

The strength of the police forces in the United Kingdom was 145.7 thousand in 1987 continuing the gradual increase in recent years (Table 12.23). The number of special constables in England and Wales and in Scotland has remained virtually constant at 16 thousand and 2 thousand over the last three years.

Table 12.24 presents data on manpower within prison department establishments in Great Britain, which include borstals, youth custody centres, detention centres, and young offenders institutions. The number of staff in post at the beginning of 1988 was 2.8 per cent higher than 12 months earlier, 12.5 per cent higher

than in January 1981, and 63.5 per cent higher than at the beginning of 1971. This growth has meant that despite the increase in the average population in prison establishments, the ratio of inmates to prison officers has fallen substantially in both male and female establishments from 3.5 and 2.3 respectively in 1971 to 2.4 and 1.4 in 1987. However, because the officers work in shifts, the numbers of inmates per prison officer on duty at any time are higher than the overall rates given in the table.

Data from the Northern Ireland Office shows that in Northern Ireland the number of staff in post in 1988 was 3,137 The ratios of inmates to prison officers was 1.7.

12.23 Police forces and police auxiliaries: manpower [1]

England & Wales, Scotland, and Northern Ireland

Thousands

	1961	1971	1976	1979	1981	1984	1985	1986	1987
Police forces — strength									
England & Wales[2]									
Men	73.5	93.5	102.4	103.8	108.8	109.5	109.4	109.8	111.5
Women	2.3	3.8	7.1	9.5	10.7	11.1	11.3	11.7	12.6
Scotland									
Men	8.8	10.4	11.6	12.4	12.4	12.4	12.5	12.6	12.5
Women	0.3	0.4	0.7	0.8	0.7	0.7	0.8	0.8	0.9
Northern Ireland									
Royal Ulster Constabulary									
Men	2.9	4.0	4.8	5.9	6.6	7.5	7.6	7.6	7.6
Women	0.1	0.1	0.4	0.7	0.7	0.6	0.6	0.7	0.6
United Kingdom total	87.9	112.2	127.0	133.1	140.0	141.8	142.2	143.2	145.7
Police auxiliaries									
England & Wales									
Special constables	47.6	30.0	21.4	16.0	14.6	16.1	16.2	16.1	16.2
Cadets	3.3	4.5	3.7	3.6	2.0	0.6	0.4	0.4	0.4
Traffic wardens	0.3	5.8	5.9	4.3	4.4	4.9	4.8	4.8	4.8
Civilians[3]	11.8	28.1	34.6	35.8	37.7	38.9	39.2	40.3	41.6
Scotland									
Special constables	7.3	4.3	3.4	3.1	2.8	2.5	2.0	2.0	2.0
Cadets	0.2	0.4	0.5	0.6	0.1	0.1	0.1	0.1	0.1
Traffic wardens	. .	0.6	0.8	0.7	0.6	0.5	0.5	0.5	0.5
Civilians[3]	0.9	1.9	2.7	2.8	2.8	2.9	3.0	3.1	3.1
Northern Ireland									
Special constables[4]	12.8	.	.	.	.	.	.	.	.
Cadets	.	.	0.2	0.2	0.1	—	—	—	—
RUC Reserve									
Full-time	. .	. .	. .	. .	. .	. .	. .	. .	3.0
Part-time	. .	. .	. .	. .	. .	. .	. .	. .	1.6
Total	.	1.3	4.7	4.5	4.9	4.4	4.5	4.4	4.6
Traffic wardens	.	0.1	0.1	0.1	0.1	0.1	0.1	0.1	0.2
Civilians	. .	0.9	1.5	1.8	1.9	2.6	2.6	2.7	2.9
Civilian Search Unit	.	.	0.5	0.3	0.3	0.1	0.1	0.1	0.1
United Kingdom total	. .	77.9	80.0	73.8	72.3	73.6	73.5	74.6	76.5

1 As at 31 December each year.
2 Includes additional constables and police on secondment until 1971, and police on secondment only from 1976 onwards.
3 Figures for 1971 onwards include part-time employees on a two for one basis. Figures for 1961 do not include part-timers.

4 Special constables were disbanded in Northern Ireland on 30 April 1970.

Source: Home Office; Scottish Home and Health Department; Northern Ireland Office

12.24 Prison service: manpower [1]

Great Britain   Numbers

	1971	1976	1981	1984	1985	1986	1987	1988
Prison officer class	13,087	16,865	19,441	20,305	20,902	21,223	21,849	22,512
Governor class	532	578	614	622	617	612	614	649
Other non-industrial staff	3,027	3,811	4,358	4,549	4,582	4,602	4,598	4,690
Industrial staff	1,825	2,219	2,426	2,291	2,201	2,279	2,309	2,350
Total staff in post	18,471	23,473	26,839	27,767	28,302	28,716	29,370	30,201
Number of inmates per prison officer [2]								
Male establishments	3.5	2.8	2.6	2.5	2.4	2.5	2.4	2.4
Female establishments	2.3	2.2	1.7	1.6	1.5	1.4	1.8	1.4

1 Manpower in male and female establishments as at
  1 January each year.

2 Prison officer class excluding prison officers under training or prison
  auxiliaries who are not directly involved in the supervision of inmates.

Source: Home Office; Scottish Home and Health Department

Table 12.25 shows trends in the size of the Judiciary and the numbers of legal representatives in England and Wales, Scotland and Northern Ireland, although figures are not directly comparable due to differences in the legal system and composition of the Judiciary.

In England and Wales High Court Judges try High Court civil work and the serious criminal cases in the Crown Court. Circuit Judges try the great majority of Crown Court cases and also sit in the county court to try civil actions. Recorders and Assistant Recorders are barristers or solicitors who undertake to sit in the Crown Court for a minimum of 20 days a year and who perform similar duties to Circuit Judges but usually deal with the less serious cases.

In Scotland, greater use is made of full-time legally qualified judges. The Court of Session, consisting of 22 judges, is the supreme civil court. The most serious criminal cases are dealt with in the High Court, where the judges are the same persons as in the Court of Session, or under solemn procedure in the Sheriff court. The Sheriff court is the principal local court of both civil and criminal jurisdiction. Sheriffs are qualified as advocates or solicitors. Sheriffs principal are full-time judges resident in their Sheriffdom.

In Northern Ireland High Court Judges try High Court civil work and the serious criminal cases in the Crown Court. County Court Judges try the great majority of Crown Court cases and also sit in the County Court to try civil actions. Deputy County Court Judges are drawn mainly from Senior and Junior Counsel, in addition, four Circuit Registrars, three Resident Magistrates and one practising Solicitor fulfil the same role which covers only the civil courts.

12.25 The Judiciary, and legal representatives

England & Wales, Scotland and Northern Ireland   Numbers

	1972	1981	1987
England and Wales			
The Judiciary			
Judges [1,2]			
Lord Justices	14	18	23
High Court Judges	70	74	79
Circuit Judges	233	334	393
Assistant			
Recorders	.	.	417
Recorders	325	446	609
Registrars [2]	134	150	212
Magistrates [3]	20,539	25,435	27,650
Legal representatives			
Barristers [4]	2,919	4,685	5,642
Solicitors [4]	26,327	39,795	48,937
Scotland [2]			
The Judiciary			
Judges	19	21	24
Sheriffs [5]	. .	78	88
Stipendiary Magistrates	3	3	4
Justices of the Peace [6]	. .	. .	961
Legal representatives [7]			
Advocates	48	134	221
Solicitors	3,374	5,065	6,496
Northern Ireland [8]			
The Judiciary			
Judges			
High Court Judges	. .	8	10
County Court Judges	5	10	12
Circuit Registrars	0	4	4
Resident Magistrates	17	15	17
Legal representatives			
Barristers	88	203	307
Solicitors	. .	888	1,151

1 Excludes deputy judges and, for 1972 and 1981, assistant recorders.
2 Figures relate to 31 December each year.
3 Figures relate to the 1st of January each year.
4 As at 31 October each year.
5 Numbers not available before local government reorganisation in 1975.
6 On rota for court duty, 31 March 1988.
7 Practising.
8 Figures are at 1971, 1981 and 1987.

Source: Lord Chancellor's Department; The Magistrates' Association;
The Senate of the Inns of the Court and the Bar; The Law Society;
Scottish Home and Health Department; Northern Ireland Office

Public order in Northern Ireland

12.26 Northern Ireland: terrorist activity and injuries connected with the civil disturbances

Numbers

	Type of activity			People injured				
	Shooting incidents	Explosions	Bombs neutralised	Royal Ulster Constabulary	Regular Services	Ulster Defence Regiment	Civilians	Total people injured
1970	213	153	17	191	620 [1]	. .	245	. .
1971	1,756	1,022	493	315	381	9	1,838	2,543
1972	10,628	1,382	471	485	542	36	3,813	4,876
1973	5,018	978	542	291	525	23	1,812	2,651
1974	3,206	685	428	235	453	30	1,680	2,398
1975	1,803	399	236	263	151	16	2,044	2,474
1976	1,908	766	426	303	242	22	2,162	2,729
1977	1,081	366	169	183	172	16	1,027	1,398
1978	755	455	178	302	127	8	548	985
1979	728	422	142	165	132	21	557	875
1980	642	280	120	194	53	24	530	801
1981	1,142	398	131	332	110	30	878	1,350
1982	547	219	113	99	80	18	328	525
1983	424	266	101	142	66	22	280	510
1984	334	193	55	267	64	22	513	866
1985	237	148	67	415	20	13	468	916
1986	392	172	82	622	45	10	773	1,450
1987	674	236	148	246	92	12	780	1,130

1 This figure includes substantially more minor injuries than those for later years.

Source: Northern Ireland Office

There were 236 terrorist explosions in Northern Ireland in 1987, 37 per cent more than in 1986 (Table 12.26). A further 148 bombs were neutralised in 1987, a rise of over 80 per cent over 1986 and bringing the total number of incidents avoided since 1970 to 3,919. There were 72 per cent more shooting incidents than in 1986, the highest number recorded since 1981 when there had been a sharp increase after a steady decline from 1972, the peak year for terrorist activity. Of the 1,130 people injured in 1987, 69 per cent were civilians, over twice the number of security forces injured. Nevertheless the number of civilians injured was still about a fifth of the number in 1972.

The number of deaths connected with the disturbances in 1987 was 50 per cent higher than in 1986. (Chart 12.27). The greatest number killed were in 1972, the year when terrorist activity was at its peak, when there were 467 deaths, and in 1976 with 297 deaths. In 1987 16 policemen were killed, over half of the total number of security service deaths. Sixty-six civilians died, nearly twice as many as those civilians that were killed in 1986 and the highest figure since 1977. This figure brings the number of civilians killed since 1969 to 1811 and is the highest number since 1977. Since 1969 there have been a total of 2617 deaths in Northern Ireland, connected with the civil disturbances.

12.27 Northern Ireland: deaths connected with the civil disturbances

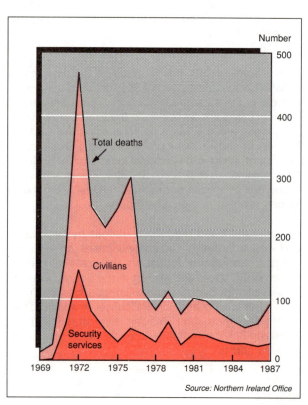

Source: Northern Ireland Office

APPENDIX: Definitions and Terms

Major surveys used in *Social Trends*

	Frequency	Sampling frame	Type of respondent	Location	Set sample size (most recent survey included in *Social Trends*)	Response rate (percentages)
Census of Population	Decennial	Detailed local	Household head	UK	Full count	100
British Social Attitudes Survey	Annual	Electoral Register	Adult in household	GB	4,240 addresses	67
British Tourism Survey — Yearly[1]	Annual	Electoral Register	Individual adult	GB	3,527 individuals [6]	58
Continuous Household Survey	Continuous	Rating valuation list	All adults in household	NI	4,500 addresses	69
Family Expenditure Survey	Continuous	Electoral Register	Household	UK	11,660 addresses	69
General Household Survey	Continuous	PAF [2]	All adults in household	GB	13,248 addresses	84
International Passenger Survey	Continuous	International passengers at ports and airports	Individual traveller	UK	175,000 individuals	82
Labour Force Survey	Continuous	PAF [2]	Adult in household [3]	UK	63,000 addresses	82
National Food Survey	Continuous	PAF [2]	Housewife	GB	13,344 addresses	54
National Readership Survey	Continuous	Electoral Register	Individual adult	GB	28,500 individuals	67
National Travel Survey	Intermittent	PAF [2]	Individual in household	GB	15,120 addresses	76
New Earnings Survey	Annual	Inland Revenue PAYE records	Employee [4]	GB	174,000 employees [4]	[4]
Survey of Personal Incomes	Annual	Inland Revenue	Tax unit [5]	UK	64,800 tax units	95

1 Previously known as the British National Travel Survey.
2 Postcode Address File.
3 Includes some proxy information.
4 In the New Earnings Survey employers supply data on a 1 per cent sample of employees who are members of PAYE schemes. 221 thousand were selected for the 1988 sample and there was

a 95 per cent response but some 35 thousand returned questionnaires did not contain data.
5 In the Survey of Personal Incomes local tax offices supply data on tax units to a central point in Inland Revenue.
6 Basic sample only; in 1987 a further 5,040 individuals were contacted in connection with holidays abroad.

The **Census of Population** was described in *Social Trends 17* (page 203.)

The first **British Social Attitudes Survey** was conducted in 1983 by Social and Community Planning Research. Technical details of the survey, which is conducted annually, are included in the Appendix to the article *'Recent Trends in Social Attitudes'* (page 22 of this edition).

A description of the **General Household Survey** was contained in the Appendix to *Social Trends 12* (page 253). In 1984 the sampling frame of the General Household Survey was changed from the Electoral Register to the Postcode Address file. The **Continuous Household Survey** in Northern Ireland is a similar survey to the General Household Survey in Great Britain.

A description of the **Labour Force Survey** was contained in the Appendix to *Social Trends 16* (page 204).

A description of the **National Food Survey** was contained in the Appendix to *Social Trends 12* (page 255). In 1984 the sampling frame of the National Food Survey changed from the Electoral Register to

the Postcode Address File, selecting the sample by means of a stratified random sampling scheme from 52 local authority districts.

Descriptions of these surveys were contained in the Appendix to *Social Trends 12* (pages 253, 255 and 256):
British Tourism Survey — Yearly, formerly the British National Travel Survey
Family Expenditure Survey
International Passenger Survey
New Earnings Survey
National Readership Survey

A description of the 1985-86 **National Travel Survey (NTS)** was contained in the Appendix to *Social Trends 18* (page 197).

Fieldwork for the latest NTS was begun in July 1988 and will run continuously with an annual sample of 5,040 addresses. The survey is being carried out by the Social Survey Division of the Office of Population Censuses and Surveys using the same methodology and covering the same topics as in the 1985-86 survey. Although the continuous survey will provide some results annually, the main results will only be available periodically as in the past.

APPENDIX

PART 1: POPULATION

Population and population projections

The estimated population of an area includes all those usually resident in the area, whatever their nationality. Members of HM and non-UK armed forces are taken to be resident at their stationed address. Students are taken to be resident at their term-time address. Population projections are on the same basis.

The current series of estimates are updated annually, starting with those derived from the 1981 Census of Population and then allowing for subsequent births, deaths and migration.

National population projections have recently been made every two years, but will from 1988 be made each year. The principal projections are supplemented by variants assuming higher or lower fertility or mortality rates to provide some measure of the uncertainties present in the principal projections. Sub-national projections continue to be made every two years. The projections given in this chapter are principal projections based on the estimated population at mid-1985.

Refugees

The basis for the granting of refugee status is the 1951 United Nations Convention relating to the Status of Refugees, extended in its application by the 1967 Protocol relating to the Status of Refugees. The United Kingdom is party to both. The Convention defines a refugee as a person who 'owing to a well-founded fear of being persecuted for reasons of race, religion, nationality, membership of a particular social group or political opinion, is outside the country of his nationality and unable or, owing to such fear, is unwilling to avail himself of the protection of that country '. Until July 1984 a significant number of applicants who failed fully to meet this criterion were granted asylum. This carried similar benefits to those accorded to a refugee. Since July 1984 anyone who previously would have been granted asylum has been granted full refugee status. In addition, the United Kingdom is prepared to grant, to applicants who do not fully meet the requirements of the Convention, exceptional leave to stay here for an appropriate period, both to individuals and to groups of nationals who could not reasonably be expected to return to their country of origin in the prevailing circumstances.

PART 2: HOUSEHOLDS AND FAMILIES

Households

A household: a single person or a group of people who have the address as their only or main residence and who either share one meal a day or share the living accommodation.

Size of household: is *de jure* household size and counts those people who are usually resident in the household irrespective of whether or not they are present on census night.

Families

A family: is a married couple, alone or with their never-married child or children (of any age), or a lone parent together with his or her never-married child or children. A lone parent (in the Census) is a married parent whose spouse does not reside in the same household, or any single, widowed, or divorced parent.

A one-parent family (in the General Household Survey): consists of one parent, irrespective of sex, living with his or her never-married dependent children, provided these children have no children of their own. Married lone mothers whose husbands are not defined as resident in the household are not classified as lone parents because it is known that the majority are separated from their husband either because he usually works away from home or for some other reason that does not imply the breakdown of the marriage (see OPCS's *GHS Monitor 82/1).* Parents describing themselves as married but who are in fact cohabiting are not counted as lone parents.

Children: children are never-married people of any age who live with one or both parent(s). This also includes step-children or adopted children (but not foster children) and also grandchildren (without parents) or great grandchildren (without parents or grandparents).

Dependent children: in the 1961 Census dependent children were defined as children under 15 years of age, and persons of any age in full-time education.
In the 1971 Census dependent children were defined as never-married children in families who were either under 15 years of age, or aged 15-24 and in full-time education. However, for direct comparison with the General Household Survey (GHS) data, the definition of dependent children used for 1971 in Table 2.9 has been changed to include only never-married children in families who were either under 15 years of age, or aged 15-18 and in full-time education.

In the 1981 Census and the GHS dependent children are never-married children in families who are aged under 16, or aged 16-18 and in full-time education. In the Labour Force Survey, dependent children are aged under 16.

Divorce

A decree of divorce or of nullity of marriage may be granted on certain grounds as set out in the *Matrimonial Causes Act 1973.* A divorce is a dissolution of marriage granted if the marriage has irretrievably broken down. Annulled marriages are either void (for example if it was bigamous) or voidable (for example if it has not been consummated). A decree nisi is granted by the Court at the time of the hearing, and normally becomes absolute after six weeks on the application of the party granted the decree nisi. The parties are then legally free to remarry. The law in Scotland did not change until the coming into effect of the *Divorce Reform Act (Scotland) 1976* on 1 January 1977.

Social class of father

The occupations of a sample of fathers at the birth of their first child after marriage were coded using the OPCS *Classification of Occupations 1980.* In addition, an employment status code for each father was allocated on the basis of the one most likely to be associated with his given occupation, from which his social class was derived (see *Classification of Occupations 1980).* The 1980 social classes are:

I	Professional occupations
II	Intermediate occupations (including most managerial and senior administrative occupations)
IIIN	Skilled occupations (non-manual)
IIIM	Skilled occupations (manual)
IV	Partly skilled occupations
V	Unskilled occupations
Other	Residual groups including, for example, armed forces, students, and those whose occupation was inadequately described.

PART 3: EDUCATION

Main categories of educational establishments
Educational establishments in the United Kingdom may be administered and financed in one of three different ways:

Public sector: by local education authorities, which form part of the structure of local government;

Assisted: by governing bodies which have a substantial degree of autonomy from public authorities but which receive grants direct from central government sources; or

Independent: by the private sector, including individuals, companies, and charitable institutions.

Direct grant schools
Prior to 1976 there were about 170 direct grant schools in England and Wales, that is schools which catered for pupils on behalf of whom a direct grant was paid to the schools by central government under the *Direct Grant Schools Regulations 1959.* In 1975 the then Government began to phase out this scheme.

Schools were required to elect either to enter the maintained sector or else to become independent. About a quarter of them chose to enter the maintained sector, a process which was carried out over the next five years or so. A few chose neither option and closed.

Stages of education
There are three stages of education: primary (including nursery), secondary, and further (including higher) education. The first two stages are compulsory for all children between the ages of five and sixteen years (fifteen before 1972/73); and the transition from primary to secondary education is usually made between ten and a half and twelve years but is sometimes made via middle schools (see below) after age twelve. The third stage of education is voluntary and includes all education provided after full-time schooling ends.

Primary education
Primary education includes three age ranges: nursery, under five years of age; infant, five to seven or eight years; and junior, seven or eight to eleven or twelve years. The great majority of public sector primary schools take both boys and girls in mixed classes. In Scotland the distinction between infant and primary schools is generally not made.

Middle schools
In England and Wales middle schools take children from first schools and generally lead on, in turn, to comprehensive upper schools. They cover varying age ranges between eight and fourteen. Depending on their individual age range they are deemed either primary or secondary.

Secondary education
Provision of maintained secondary schools in an area may include any combination of types of school. The pattern is a reflection of historical circumstance and of the policy adopted by the local education authority. Comprehensive (including middle deemed secondary) schools account for about 90 per cent of pupils in a variety of patterns as to forms of organisation and the age range of the pupils attending. Comprehensive schools normally admit pupils without reference to ability and aptitude, and cater for all the children in a neighbourhood; but in some areas they co-exist with modern, grammar, and technical schools. Scotland has a few schools which are part comprehensive/part selective; these are comprehensive in intake but selective as regards level of courses offered (typically not beyond 'O' grade).

In Northern Ireland secondary education normally begins when pupils reach the age of 11. Under current transfer procedure arrangements pupils transferring from primary education take two tests which are compiled and marked by the Department of Education for Northern Ireland. Parents who do not wish their children to take the tests are free to say so and those children transfer to secondary (intermediate) schools. Most of the pupils who are successful in the tests transfer to secondary (grammar) schools and the remainder transfer to secondary (intermediate) schools. Secondary schools of all types operate under common regulations and are staffed under a common formula based on the numbers and ages of the pupils enrolled.

Special schools
Special schools, either day or boarding, provide education exclusively for children who are so seriously handicapped, physically or mentally, that they cannot profit fully from education in normal schools.

Further education
The term 'further education' may be used in a general sense to cover all non-advanced education after the period of compulsory education. More commonly it excludes those staying on at secondary school, and those studying at universities, polytechnics and colleges. The figures in Table 3.15 cover all courses taken in public sector and assisted establishments of further education.

Higher education
The term 'higher education' as used in this chapter (Tables 3.16, 3.17 and 3.18) covers all courses (including teacher training courses) in universities, polytechnics and colleges (including Scottish Central Institutions), that is those leading to qualifications above General Certificate of Education 'A' level, Scottish Certificate of Education 'H' grade, and Ordinary National Diploma, or their equivalents.

The Youth Cohort Study
The sample size for cohort 2 (first eligible to leave school in 1985), taken in Spring 1986 was 20,000. The net response rate (after allowing for non-contact) was 75 per cent giving 14,430 usable responses. The data are weighted, based on sex, region, school type and, for school leavers, examination attainment.

School-leaving qualifications
In England, Wales and Northern Ireland, the two main examinations for school pupils at the minimum school leaving age are the Certificate of Secondary Education (CSE) and General Certificate of Education (GCE) 'O' level. Both CSE and 'O' level examinations are taken in a wide range of subjects. The CSE is awarded at grades 1 to 5 and 'O' level at grades A to E. Grade 1 CSE results are deemed equivalent to higher graded results (grades A-C) at 'O' level and both are considered to be at the standard required for the GCE 'O'-level pass grade, which operated up to 1974. The GCE is also offered at 'A' level and usually taken after a further two years of study in a sixth-form, or equivalent. These examinations are also awarded at grades A-E.

In Scotland there is no general counterpart to the CSE in England, Wales and Northern Ireland; although the examination is taken in some schools, data on the results are not available. The counterpart to the GCE examination is the Scottish Certificate of Education (SCE). The SCE Ordinary ('O') grade course leads to an examination (of approximately equivalent standard to the GCE 'O' level) at the end of the fourth year of secondary schooling, which in Scotland starts at age 12. In 1986 the first phase of the new Standard Grade examinations was introduced. These examinations, which are aimed at a wider ability range, will replace 'O' grades by the early 1990s. From 1973 to 1985 'O' grades were awarded in a 5-band, A to E, structure; awards in bands A to C correspond to what were previously rated passes. From 1986 Standard grades are being awarded on 1-7 scale, with 'O' grades being awarded on a comparable 1-5 scale; grades 1-3, in total, are equivalent to the previous A-C. The examination of the Higher (H) grade requires, basically, one further year of study and may be taken at the end of the fifth or sixth year. For the better 'H' grade candidates the range of subjects covered may be almost as wide as for the 'O' grades - it is not unusual for candidates to study five or six subjects spanning both arts and science. The breadth of study inevitably means that an individual subject in the 'H' grade course is not taken to the same depth as the more specialised GCE 'A' level course.

Pupil/teacher ratios
The pupil/teacher ratio within schools is the ratio of all pupils on the school register to all teachers employed in schools on the day of the annual count. Part-time teachers are included on a full-time equivalent basis, with part-time service calculated as a proportion of a full-time school week. Part-time pupils are counted as 0.5.

APPENDIX

PART 4: EMPLOYMENT

Labour force
The civilian labour force includes employees, employers, and self-employed (but excludes those in HM Forces), together with those identified by censuses and surveys as seeking work. Also included in the civilian labour force as unemployed are those waiting to start a job they have already obtained and those who are unemployed but prevented from seeking work by temporary sickness or holiday. Persons employed under special employment measures (other than those measures providing full-time training) are included in the civilian labour force. The civilian labour force differs from the total labour force only by the exclusion of those in the Armed Forces. The civilian labour force includes students in full-time education if they did any work in the reference week, or if they sought work and were not prevented from starting work by the need to complete their education.

Workforce
Workforce in employment plus the unemployed.

Workforce in employment
Employees in employment, self-employed, HM Forces and participants on work-related government training programmes.

GHS definition of unemployed
The unemployed consist of those who, in the week before interview, were looking for work, would have looked for work if they had not been temporarily sick, or were waiting to take up a job they had already obtained. In this context temporary sickness refers to illness lasting 28 days or less. These definitions apply whether or not the person was registered as unemployed or claiming unemployment benefit.

In 1985 full-time students were classified according to their own reports of what they were doing in the reference week; in previous years they were classified as 'inactive'. Also, in 1985 people on the Youth Training Scheme were classified as 'working' if they were with an employer providing work experience in the reference week and as 'inactive' if they were at college.

Sector classification
The Post Office has been included in public corporations from 1961 onwards although employees were still civil servants until 1969. In 1974 water services (previously undertaken by local authorities) passed to Regional Water Authorities classified to public corporations; trust ports were reclassified from local authorities to public corporations; and most local authority health services were transferred to the Regional and Area Health Authorities which form part of the central government sector. From 1970 employees of some local authority transport under-takings were taken over by passenger transport authorities classified to public corporations. Most of the steel industry was nationalised in 1967, and the aircraft and shipbuilding industries in 1977. The Royal Ordnance Factories, Royal Mint, Property Services Agency (Supplies Division) (now the Crown Suppliers), and Her Majesty's Stationery Office were established as trading funds and reclassified to public corporations from 1974, 1975, 1976, and 1980 respectively. British Aerospace and part of Cable and Wireless Ltd (operating mainly overseas) were reclassified to the private sector in 1981. The National Freight Company Ltd, formerly the National Freight Corporation, and Britoil were reclassified to the private sector in 1982, and Associated British Ports were transferred to the private sector in 1983. Enterprise Oil was reclassified to the private sector in June 1984. British Telecom plc was reclassified to the private sector in November 1984, and Trust Ports (Great Britain) in April 1985. Between 1984 and 1986 British Shipbuilders were transferred to the private sector. In April 1986 both United Kingdom Atomic Energy Authority and English Industrial Estates Corporation were reclassified from central government to public corporations. In December 1986 the British Gas Corporation was reclassified to the private sector as was British Airways plc in February 1987 and Royal Ordnance plc in April 1987.

Industrial disputes
Statistics of stoppages of work owing to industrial disputes in the United Kingdom relate only to disputes connected with terms and conditions of employment. Small stoppages involving fewer than 10 workers or lasting less than one day are excluded from the statistics except where the aggregate number of working days lost in the dispute exceeds 100.

Workers involved and working days lost relate to persons both directly and indirectly involved (unable to work although not parties to the dispute) at the establishments where the disputes occurred. People laid off and working days lost at establishments not in dispute, due for example to resulting shortages of supplies, are excluded.

There are difficulties in ensuring complete recording of stoppages, in particular near the margins of the definition; for example short disputes lasting only a day or two. Any under-recording would particularly bear on those industries most affected by such stoppages, and would affect the total number of stoppages much more than the number of working days lost.

The unemployed
People claiming benefit (that is unemployment benefit, supplementary benefits, or national insurance credits) at Unemployment Benefit Offices on the day of the monthly count, who on that day are unemployed and able and willing to do any suitable work. (Students claiming benefit during a vacation and who intend to return to full-time education are excluded.)

Unemployment rate
In 1986 the unemployment rate was made available on a new basis. National and Regional unemployment rates are now calculated by expressing the number of unemployed as a percentage of the latest available mid-year estimates of the workforce *including* the self-employed and the armed forces.

Previously all rates were expressed as a percentage of employees *plus* the unemployed only. The narrower based rates continue to be available for comparison with the rates for local areas (travel-to-work areas and counties) which cannot be calculated on the new basis because the information on the self-employed needed for the calculation of the new rates is not available below regional level.

Unemployment — Discontinuity
In Chart 4.23, figures up to October 1982 relate to the registered unemployed. From October 1982 the figures are on the claimant basis. From April 1983 some men aged 60 or over did not have to sign on at an Unemployment Benefit Office to receive the higher rate of supplementary benefit or national insurance credits. Between March and August 1983 the number affected was 162 thousand of whom about 125 thousand were in the over 52 weeks category. Other changes in coverage have also affected the figures, but to a much lesser extent; eg the change in compilation in March 1986 to remove over-recording reduced the number in the over 52 week category by some 15,000.

Definition of unemployment — OECD concepts
The unemployment figures used in these standardised rates are estimated by the OECD to conform, as far as possible, with the definition of unemployment in the guidelines of the International Labour Organisation (ILO), and the rates are calculated as percentages of the total labour force, again as defined in the ILO guidelines. According to these guidelines the unemployed covers all persons of working age who, in a specified period, are without work, who are available for work, and who are seeking employment for pay or profit. The total labour force consists of civilian employees, the self-employed, unpaid family workers, professional and conscripted members of the armed forces, and the unemployed. The standardised

rates will therefore differ from the unemployment rates published in national sources whenever the national definition of unemployment differs from that indicated above, or the denominator used to calculate the national rates is other than the total labour force.

The ILO/OECD measure of unemployment used in Tables 4.25 and 4.26 comprises people without a job who were available for work and had either looked for work at some time in the last four weeks or were waiting to start a job they had already obtained. Table 4.6 defines the Great Britain labour force unemployed as those who were without a job who were seeking work in the referee week, or prevented from seeking work by temporary sickness or holiday, or were waiting for the results of a job application or were waiting to start a new job they had already obtained.

Employment and training measures
In Chart 4.27 Department of Employment schemes include:

Current schemes:
Job-Share Scheme
Enterprise Allowance Scheme
Job Start

Past schemes:
Temporary Short-Time Working Compensation Scheme, which placed the Short-Time Working Compensation Scheme in the textiles, clothing, and footwear industry
Temporary Employment Subsidy
Small Firms Employment Subsidy
Adult Employment Subsidy

Job Realease Scheme (full-time and part-time schemes)
Young Workers Scheme (applications approved)
New Workers Scheme
Youth Employment Subsidy

Training Agency schemes include:

Current schemes:
Youth Training Scheme
Employment Training

Past schemes:
Youth Opportunities Programme
Job Creation Programme
Community Enterprise Programme
Special Temporary Employment Programme
Job Introduction Scheme
Work Experience Programme
Training in Industry
Community Programme
Voluntary Projects Programme
Community Industry

Work related government training programmes
Participants in the YTS who receive work experience except those who have contracts of employment (who are included in employees in employment), plus participants on new YTS and, in Northern Ireland, those on Youth Training Programme, Job Training Programme, and Attachment Training participants and other management training scheme participants training with an employer.

PART 5: INCOME AND WEALTH

The household sector
The household sector includes private trusts and individuals living in institutions as well as those living in households. It differs from the personal sector, as defined in the national accounts, in that it excludes unincorporated private businesses, private non-profit-making bodies serving persons, and the funds of life assurance and pension schemes. More information is given in an article in *Economic Trends*, September 1981.

Household disposable income is equal to the total current income of the household sector *less* payments of United Kingdom taxes on income, employees' national insurance contributions, and contributions of employees to occupational pension schemes. It is revalued at constant prices by a deflator implied by estimates of total household expenditure at current and constant prices. This deflator is a modified form of the consumers' expenditure deflator.

Social security benefits
The National Insurance Fund provides insurance against loss of income in the event of unemployment, sickness and invalidity, widowhood or retirement. These, with the various industrial injury benefits, are generally known as contributory benefits. Non-contributory benefits include means-tested support to people or families with low income (income support and family credit). Payments, often in the form of loans, may also be made from the social fund to assist people with exceptional expenses which they would find difficult to pay out of their regular income. Non-income-related support is available through child benefit and, for the long-term sick or disabled, through severe disablement allowance, attendance allowance and mobility allowance. A separate war pensions scheme pays benefit to people widowed or disabled as a result of wars since 1914.

For the purpose of the *Social Security Act 1975* there are four classes of contribution to the National Insurance Fund. Class 1 is payable by employed earners and their employers, Class 2 and Class 4 are payable by the self-employed, and Class 3 is payable on a voluntary basis by the non-employed. Class 1 contributions are wholly earnings-related and Class 4 contributions are related to the level of profits or gains. Class 2 and Class 3 contributions are flat-rate. In general, unemployment benefit and industrial injuries benefits are only payable to Class 1 contributors.

The weekly standard rates of benefits introduced in April 1988, and personal allowances for income support are:

Rates of benefits, April 1988   £

	Stand-ard rate	Adult depend-ant	Each child
Retirement pension (single person)	41.15	24.75	8.40
Widow's pension	41.15		8.40
Unemployment benefit	32.75	20.20	
Invalidity pension	41.15	24.75	8.40
Industrial disablement benefit (100%)	67.20		
Invalidity allowance[1]			
Age 40	8.65		
Age 50	5.50		
Age 60 (men) (55 women)	2.75		
Sickness benefit	31.30	19.40	
Child benefit			7.25
One-parent benefit (first or only child of certain lone (persons)	4.90		

1 Payable with Invalidity pension when incapacity began before each age shown.

Income support personal allowances, April 1988 £

Couple	One aged 18 or over	51.45
	Both under 18	38.80
Single claimant	Aged 25 or over	33.40
	18 – 24	26.05
	under 18	19.40
Lone parent	Aged 18 or over	33.40
	under 18	19.40
Dependent	Child under 11	10.75
	11 – 15	16.10
	16 – 17	19.40
	18	26.05

Income support is income-related and non-contributory. From September 1988 it will not normally be available to people aged below 18. People in full-time education or working more than 24 hours are also excluded. Couples (whether married or not) and any dependent children are assessed as a unit. Claimants with one or more dependent children also receive a family premium of £6.15. Certain 'client groups' are entitled to additional payments:

Additional payments, April 1988 £

	Single	Couple
Disability premium	13.05	18.60
Pensioner premium	10.65	16.25
Higher pensioner premuim (80 or over)	13.05	18.60
Lone parent premium	3.70	

It is not possible to receive more than one of these. There is also a severe disability premium of £24.75 and a child disability premium of £6.15.

Unemployed claimants

The data for 1983 onwards presented in Table 5.9 are taken from the count of unemployed claimants taken for the Department of Social Security (DSS). This count is different from that taken for the Department of Employment (DE), which is used in Chapter 4. The DE count is designed to produce quick simple figures for all unemployed claimants. In order that the statistics are as accurate a record as possible of the status of claimants on the count date, they are compiled retrospectively 3 weeks later rather than on the count date itself, to take account of later notifications of both new and terminating claims.

The DSS count is more detailed and includes information on the claimant's benefit position on the date of the count. Unlike the DE count, no retrospective adjustment is made to the figures and the DSS count includes only those claimants who declare unemployment for that day or are expected to, given their firm evidence of unemployment during the previous fortnight. Students on vacation and temporarily stopped workers are included in the DSS count if they are claiming benefit. The differences between the DE and DSS counts reflect the different objectives which the two counts serve.

Redistribution of income

Estimates of the incidence of taxes and benefits on households of different types and in different income groups, based on the Family Expenditure Survey, are published by the Central Statistical Office in *Economic Trends*. The article covering 1986 appeared in the issue for December 1988, and contains details of the definitions and methods used.

Households below average income

The tables are derived from the Family Expenditure Survey which covers private households only. The income used is the net household income before housing costs. Income tax, employees' national insurance contributions and superannuation are deducted, but housing costs are not. The income is adjusted for household size and composition using 'equivalence scales' which reflect the extent to which households of different sizes require different incomes to achieve the same living standard; full details are given in an article in *Social Trends 8*, page 28. The unit of analysis is the individual so that all individuals receive equal weight whether they live in large or small households. All members of any one household will occur at exactly the same point in the income distribution since they are all taken to have an income level determined by the income (after adjustment) of the household as a whole.

In the analysis by economic status, individuals are classified by the economic status of the head of their social security benefit unit. In the economic status breakdown the 'other' category includes men aged 60 – 64 not in full-time work, people looking after sick relatives, widows, students, persons temporarily away from work (for reasons other than sickness) on reduced or no pay and any others not working and not apparently seeking work.

More details may be found in *Households Below Average Income: A Statistical Analysis 1981–85* published by the Department of Health and Social Security.

Personal wealth

The estimates of the distribution of the marketable wealth of individuals relate to all adults in the United Kingdom. They are produced by combining estimates of the distribution of wealth identified by the estate multiplier method with independent estimates of total personal wealth derived from the Central Statistical Office personal sector balance sheets. The methods used for combining the two sets of information were described in an article in *Economic Trends* (November 1978) entitled 'The distribution of personal wealth'.

Estimates of the distribution of wealth allowing for pension rights cover both rights in occupational pension schemes and rights to state retirement pensions and widows' benefits. Certain assumptions are necessarily involved in the valuation of the rights taken in aggregate, and a description of the main assumptions used in the calculations was given in the Royal Commission on the Distribution of Income and Wealth's (RCDIW) *Report No 5* (paragraph 189). Further assumptions are involved in allocating pension rights to various size holdings of marketable wealth. Below the upper percentiles the distribution estimates vary significantly depending on the allocation assumptions used, and ranges are therefore shown for the 25th and 50th percentiles in Table 5.23. A fuller account of the scope of the estimates is given in *Inland Revenue Statistics, 1986*.

Balance sheet estimates of the net wealth of the personal sector, analysed by type of asset and liability, are published annually in the February issue of *Financial Statistics*.

In 1987, revised estimates were published, along with new estimates of the physical assets of other sectors, in an article, 'National and sector balance sheets 1957–85', in *Economic Trends* (May 1987). Figures for each year from 1976 to 1987 were subsequently published in *United Kingdom National Accounts, 1988* edition.

PART 6: RESOURCES AND EXPENDITURE

Retail prices
The General Index of Retail Prices measures the changes month by month in the level of prices of the commodities and services purchased by all types of household in the United Kingdom, with the exception of certain higher income households and households of retired people mainly dependent on state benefits. These households are:

(a) the 4 per cent (approximately) where the total household recorded gross income exceeds a certain amount (£600 a week in 1987).

(b) those in which at least three-quarters of the total income is derived from state pensions and benefits and which include at least one person over the national insurance retirement age.

The weights which are used to calculate the index are based on the pattern of household expenditure derived from the continuing Family Expenditure Survey. Since 1962 the weights have been revised in February of each year.

Expenditure patterns of one-person and two-person pensioner households differ from those of the households upon which the General Index is based. Separate indices have been compiled for such pensioner households since 1968, and quarterly averages are published in the Department of Employment 's *Employment Gazette*. They are chain indices constructed in the same way as the General Index of Retail Prices. It should however be noted that the pensioner indices exclude housing costs.

An explanation of the methods used in calculating the retail prices index is contained in *'A short guide to the RPI'*, published in the August 1987 issue of the *Department of Employment Gazette* and also available as a booklet from HMSO.

Household expenditure
Household expenditure consists of: personal expenditure on goods (durable and non-durable) and services, including the value of income in kind; imputed rent for owner-occupied dwellings; and the purchase of secondhand goods *less* the proceeds of sales of used goods. Excluded are: interest and other transfer payments; all business expenditure; and the purchase of land and buildings (and associated costs). In principle, expenditure is measured at the time of acquisition rather than actual disbursement of cash. The categories of expenditure include that of non-resident as well as resident households and individuals in the United Kingdom.

For further details see the article entitled *'Consumers' expenditure'* in *Economic Trends,* September 1983.

Household saving
Household saving is the balance of income and expenditure on the current account of households, and is derived from the personal sector account, mainly by subtracting the income and expenditure (and hence saving) of the other parts of the personal sector. The household savings ratio is household saving expressed as a percentage of household disposable income.

Household income comprises:
Wages and salaries, and forces' pay
Self-employment income
Rent, dividends, and interest
Income in kind
Pensions and benefits paid by life assurance and pension schemes
Social security benefits
Other current transfers
Household expenditure comprises:
Interest payments
Expenditure on goods and services
United Kingdom taxes on income and social security contributions (excluding employers' contributions)
Contributions to life assurance and superannuation schemes
Other current transfers

PART 7: HEALTH AND PERSONAL SOCIAL SERVICES

Expectation of life
The expectation of life at a given age, shown in Chart 7.1 and Table 7.2 as applying to a particular year, is the average number of years which a person of that age could be expected to live, if the rates of mortality at each age experienced by the population in that year (or in a period including that year) were assumed to be experienced thereafter in all future years. The mortality rates which underlie the expectations of life figures in Table 7.2 are based on total deaths occurring in the three-year period of which the year shown is the middle year (except in the case of 1906 for which a longer period was used).

Drinking habits
Chart 7.15 compares the result of a survey of adults' alcohol consumption in England and Wales in 1987 with that of a survey carried out in 1978.

Informants' descriptions of the amount they had drunk (glasses of wine, pints of beer, etc) were converted into units containing broadly similar amounts of alcohol. A standard unit is equivalent to a half pint of beer, 1/6 gill of spirits (an English single measure), a glass of wine (4 fl oz) or a small glass of fortified wine (2 fl oz). (One unit is roughly equivalent to 8½ grammes of absolute alcohol.)

Accidental deaths
The data in Table 7.18 exclude deaths where it was not known whether the cause was accidentally or purposely inflicted, misadventure during medical care, abnormal reactions, late complications and late effects of accidental injury. It does however include a small amount of double counting; these are cases where the accident occurred while the deceased was working at home or in residential accommodation. Figures for Scotland comprise accidents occurring on farms and in forests, in mines and quarries, and in industrial places and premises.

Road accident deaths
The data in Chart 7.20 relating to road transport accidents are not comparable with those issued by the Department of Transport, whose figures are restricted to deaths occurring within 30 days of an accident on the public highway and relate to the date of the accident rather than the date of registration of death. All road accident deaths have to be referred to the coroner and therefore there is inevitably a time-lag between death and registration. An assessment of this time-lag shows that at least 50 per cent of all road accident deaths are registered within three months and over 90 per cent within six months.

Unrestricted principals

An unrestricted principal is a medical practitioner who provides the full range of general medical services and whose list is not limited to any particular group of persons. In a few cases (about 20), he may be relieved of the liability to have patients assigned to him or be exempted from liability to emergency calls out-of-hours from patients other than his own. Doctors may also practise in the general medical services as restricted principals, assistants or trainees.

Manpower

The total of Health Authorities' staff and family practitioners would contain an element of duplication, since some practitioners have been counted under more than one of the categories shown. Figures for England, Scotland and Wales relate as closely as possible to 30 September, except those for ophthalmic family practitioner staff which refer to 31 December. Figures for Northern Ireland relate to 31 December, except those for family practitioner staff which relate to 31 July.

Staff of the Post Graduate Specialist Health Authorities and those Family Practitioner Committee staff on health authority payrolls are included in Regional and District Health Authorities' staff, as are Common Services Agency staff in Scotland. In 1982, due to the restructuring of the NHS in England and Wales, Area Health Authorities were removed and their functions devolved to District Health Authorities.

The figures for medical and dental staff in Regional and District Health Authorities include permanent paid and honorary staff in hospital and community health services, hospital practitioners and part-time medical/dental officers, but exclude locum staff in Great Britain. Northern Ireland figures include all community sessional staff.

Figures for family practitioner staff include General Medical Practitioners (principals, assistants and trainees), General Dental Practitioners (principals and assistants) and staff of the General Ophthalmic Service.

Health and Personal Social Services Statistics for England 1988

The fourteenth in a series of annual publications in which information is presented on a wide variety of developments in NHS manpower and hospitals, family practitioner committee services, community health services and personal social services. There is a section covering the financial implications of providing these services and a supporting section on population trends.

HMSO   Price £8.95

PART 8: HOUSING

Dwellings

Estimates of the stock of dwellings are based on data from the Censuses of Population, with adjustments for enumeration errors and for definitional changes. The figures include vacant dwellings and temporary dwellings occupied as a normal place of residence. Privately rented dwellings include those rented from housing associations, private owners and other tenures; including dwellings rented with farm or business premises and those occupied by virtue of employment.

Low cost home ownership initiatives

Under low cost home ownership initiatives, local authorities receive capital payments from sales, a part of which they may use for further housing programmes.

Land sales for starter homes

A local authority can encourage the provision of low cost homes by selling land to private builders for starter homes or self-build schemes. Starter homes are usually small houses or flats built at high densities for small households expected to move on fairly quickly to other homes.

Building under licence

Builders are licensed to build low cost homes on land owned by local authorities, new towns, or housing associations. On completion the freehold of the land usually passes to the purchasers of the individual dwellings.

Built for sale

Local authorities contract a builder to develop a site according to their requirements. This may occur, for example, where the site is difficult and development costs are high.

Voluntary sales of vacant dwellings

In addition to 'right to buy' and other sales to sitting tenants, local authorities may voluntarily sell vacant dwellings (for example, 'difficult to let' dwellings) to provide low cost homes. Discounts of up to 30 per cent of the market value may be allowed.

Homesteading

Homesteading is the sale of substandard dwellings on condition that they are improved by the purchaser, usually within a certain time. Local authorities may also offer discounts, mortgages, and improvement grants and loans.

Improvement for sale

Local authorities and housing associations which improve or repair substandard property and then sell it can claim central government funds towards the cost.

Shared ownership

As an alternative to outright sale, local authorities and new towns can offer shared ownership as a means of lowering the cost of entry to home ownership. In shared ownership the equity of the dwelling is shared between the tenant and the authority. The tenant continues to pay rent for the portion of the equity retained by the authority, in addition to any mortgage repayments on the portion he has purchased.

Renovations

House renovation grants are available from local authorities for improving the standard and preserving the fabric of sound, older housing, or for the conversion of houses or other buildings into flats to increase the stock of dwellings. The notes below refer to the grants available in England and Wales under the legislation current at the time of the latest figures shown. In Northern Ireland a broadly similar scheme is in operation. Separate legislation in Scotland provides for a broadly similar scheme of house improvement and repairs grant.

Private owners, landlords, and tenants with security of tenure are eligible for any of three grants: improvement grants (discretionary) for substantial improvements and conversion (conversion grant not available to tenants), intermediate grants (mandatory) for the provision of standard amenities (eg bath, hot and cold water, and WC), and repairs grants (discretionary) for substantial and structural repairs to pre 1919 dwellings. The amount of grant varies, but intermediate and repair grants, together with improvement grants in priority cases (ie premises in housing action areas, and dwellings elsewhere in particularly bad condition), are payable at 75 per cent of eligible costs, or up to 90 per cent in cases of hardship. In non-priority cases the maximum grant is 50 per cent or 65 per cent in general improvement areas. A fourth kind of grant, a special grant, may be made for the provision of standard amenities and/or means of escape from fire in houses in multiple occupation. Temporary measures made grants available at an enhanced maximum rate of 90 per cent for repairs and intermediate grants for applications that were approved by local authorities after 12 April 1982 or submitted to them before 1 April 1984.

Assistance is potentially available to local authorities towards the costs of renovating their housing revenue account dwellings, subject to the detailed subsidy rules.

Housing benefit

From April 1983, housing benefit replaced the provision of assistance with rent and domestic rates through supplementary benefit and the former rent and rate rebate and rent allowance schemes. The responsibility for paying housing benefit to all eligible persons whether or not in receipt of supplementary benefit was given to local authorities. A new housing benefit scheme was introduced from 1 April 1988 but no information on the new scheme is available yet. A brief description of how the benefit was calculated up to March 1988 is given below. Further details including the rates used for assessment are given in *Social Security Statistics 1988*.

Calculation of housing benefit up to March 1988
Under the housing benefit scheme assistance is given with rent and rates but not with mortgage interest or water rates. A person may be eligible for housing benefit for any rent or rates paid, but the actual rent and/or rates on which benefit is assessed may be reduced in some circumstances.

Certificated housing benefit
The Department of Health and Social Security issues a certificate of entitlement to housing benefit for all householders who qualify for supplementary benefit or whose partners qualify. This certificate is submitted to the appropriate authority responsible for paying the benefit. Housing costs are normally met in full for householders on certificated benefit unless the household includes non-dependants such as lodgers or grown up children.

Standard housing benefit
Other householders apply for standard housing benefit. Entitlement to benefit is assessed on the basis of a claimant's income in relation to their housing benefit 'needs allowance '. Although all sources of income are taken into account, specified amounts of income of certain types are disregarded for the purpose of calculating total income — for example, for the year beginning November 1984 the first £17 of a claimant's weekly earnings and the first £5 of their partner's earnings were disregarded. The claimant's needs allowance is primarily based on marital status and the number of dependent children present. However, additional amounts are given where either the claimant or their partner is over pensionable age or one of them is handicapped.

Although housing benefit for rent and for rates is calculated separately, the method of calculation is similar for each case: 60 per cent of eligible rent or rates is taken as the starting point for benefit, awarded when the claimant's income is exactly equal to their needs allowance. If a claimant's income exceeds their needs allowance, benefit is reduced by a proportion of the amount by which the needs allowance is exceeded. If a claimant's income is less than their needs allowance, benefit is increased by a proportion of the deficiency. These proportions, known as 'tapers', differ for rent and rates, and in some circumstances for pensioners and others. If the calculated amounts are below certain minimum levels for rent and rate rebates, then no benefit may actually be paid. Maximum benefit cannot exceed the claimant's actual rent and rates.

PART 9: TRANSPORT AND THE ENVIRONMENT

Passenger transport prices
Implied consumer price indices for individual items of consumers' expenditure on passenger transport are calculated by dividing the consumers' expenditure at current prices for each item by the corresponding estimate at constant prices. More detailed information can be found in Chapter VI of *National Accounts Statistics: Sources and Methods* (HMSO, 1985), and the notes section in *United Kingdom National Accounts, 1988 Edition* (HMSO, 1988).

Journey purpose
The purpose of a journey is taken to be the activity at the destination, unless that destination is 'home' in which case the purpose is defined by the origin of the journey. A journey is defined as a one-way course of travel having a single main purpose.

To and from work: journeys to a usual place of work, or from work to home.

In course of work: personal journeys in course of work. This includes all work journeys by people with no usual place of work (eg site workers) and those who work at or from home.

Education: journeys to school or college etc. by full-time students, students on day-release and part-time students following vocational courses.

Escort for work/education: used when the traveller has no purpose of his or her own, other than to escort or accompany another person; for example, taking a child to school. 'Escort-work' is escorting or accompanying someone to, from, or in course of, work. 'Escort-education' is escorting or accompanying someone whose journey purpose is education. All other escort purposes are included with the purpose of the person being escorted.

Shopping: all journeys to shop or from shops to home, even if there was no intention to buy.

Personal business: visits to services, eg hairdressers, launderettes, drycleaners, betting shops, solicitors, banks, estate agents, libraries, churches; or for medical consultations or treatment; or for eating and drinking, unless the main purpose was entertainment or social.

Social and entertainment: visits to meet friends, relatives, or acquaintances, to all types of entertainment or sport, clubs and voluntary work, non-vocational evening classes, political meetings, etc.

Holidays and day trips: journeys (within GB) to or from any holiday (including stays of 4 or more nights with friends or relatives), or journeys for pleasure (not otherwise classified as social or entertainment) within a single day.

Quality of popular coastal bathing waters
Directive (76/160/EEC) concerning the quality of bathing water sets the mandatory values for bacteriological parameters:

— for total coliforms   10,000 per 100 ml; and

— for faecel coliforms   2,000 per 100 ml.

In determining compliance with the coliform standards the following method has been used:

a. where 20 or more samples are analysed, 95 per cent of coliform results must not exceed the mandatory value;

b. where less than 20 but more than 11 samples are analysed, no more than 1 coliform result may exceed the mandatory value;

c. where 11 or fewer samples are analysed, no coliform result may exceed the mandatory value.

This method is applied separately to results for faecal coliforms and for total coliforms. If one of the bacteriological parameters fails to comply with its standard then the water is said to fail to comply with the coliform standards.

The table includes some bathing waters for which only a limited number of samples were analysed. In 1986 this occured at 83 bathing waters. In 1987 this occurred at just 1 bathing water.

Transport Statistics Great Britain 1977-87

The fourteenth edition of this annual publication consists of 242 pages with over 180 statistical tables, charts and maps with associated commentary on all matters relating to Transport. Separate sections include articles on selected transport subjects.

HMSO   **Price £18.95**

PART 10: LEISURE

General Household Survey

Questions on leisure were included in 1973, 1977, 1980, 1983, and 1986. In 1986 they took the form: *We are interested in the things people do in their leisure time, when they are not working or at school, or looking after the house and family. Can you tell me if you have done any of the following things in your leisure time in the four weeks ending last Sunday?*

> *Watched television?/Listened to the radio?*
> *Listened to records or tapes?*
> *Read books?*
> *Visited friends or relations, or had them come to see you?*
> *Gone out for a meal to a restaurant, pub, or club (not in working hours)?*
> *Gone out for a drink (not in working hours)?*
> *Done any gardening?*
> > *dressmaking, needlework or knitting?*
> > *house repairs, or do-it-yourself jobs?*

What other things have you done in your leisure time (or on holidays) in the four weeks ending last Sunday?

This was followed by showing a prompt card and asking:
Apart from those you have already mentioned, have you done any of the types of activity listed on this card in the four weeks ending last Sunday?

The GHS sample is taken continuously throughout the year, but results for a full quarter are a balanced sample, so that although the question refers to the four weeks preceding the week of the interview, the rates and frequencies of participation over any four weeks within a quarter are assumed to be representative of the quarter as a whole. These were aggregated over the year to produce annual figures. More details of this process and of limitations of the data are given in the *General Household Survey, 1973, 1977, 1983, and 1986* (forthcoming) reports along with details of the questionnaires and the coding of leisure activities.

Social class: Institute of Practitioners in Advertising (IPA) definition

Social class categories are based on head of household's occupation as follows:

Class A   Higher managerial, administrative, or professional

Class B   Intermediate managerial, administrative, or professional

Class C1   Supervisory or clerical, and junior managerial, administrative, or professional

Class C2   Skilled manual workers

Class D   Semi and unskilled manual workers

Class E   State pensioners or widows (no other earners), casual or lowest grade workers, or long-term unemployed

---

PART 11: PARTICIPATION

Church membership

Definitions of membership vary according to the church denomination or religious group in question. For the purpose of Table 11.8 adult church membership is defined as appropriate to each particular group, so that for example the Electoral Roll (not to be confused with the Local Authority Electoral Roll) has been used for the Church of England, the Easter communicant figure has been used for the Church in Wales, whilst estimates comparable to the Protestant definitions of membership, have been made for the Roman Catholic churches.

Churches

Figures for the Church of England relate to the Provinces of Canterbury and York, and include the Isle of Man and the Channel Islands but exclude the Diocese of Europe. Church of Scotland data include all baptisms in the United Kingdom; data for the Methodist church relate to England, Wales, Scotland, the Isle of Man, and the Channel Islands; and those for Roman Catholic churches to England and Wales only.

Parliamentary elections

A general election must be held at least every 5 years, or sooner if the Prime Minister of the day so decides. The United Kingdom is divided into 650 constituencies, each of which returns one member to the House of Commons. To ensure equitable representation, four permanent Boundary Commissions (for England, Wales, Scotland, and Northern Ireland) make periodic reviews of constituencies and recommend any redistribution of seats that may seem necessary in the light of population movements or for some other reason.

Local elections

Under the *Local Government Act 1972*, England and Wales (outside Greater London and the Isles of Scilly) were arranged into 47 non-metropolitan counties. The term of office of a councillor elected to any local authority is usually four years.

From 1973, county council elections take place every four years with the next due in 1989. The London borough councils elections are also held at four-yearly intervals.

Metropolitan district councils have elections by thirds — a third of the councillors resigning in each year except for years when county council elections are held.

Non-metropolitan district councils have the choice between whole council elections, which take place in years midway between county elections, or elections by thirds as in Metropolitan district councils — see above.

Parliamentary Commissioner for Administration

The Parliamentary Commissioner is a statutory independent officer appointed by the Crown. His function is to investigate complaints of maladministration brought to his notice by Members of Parliament on behalf of members of the public. His powers of investigation extend to actions taken by central government departments and certain non-departmental public bodies in the exercise of their administrative functions, but not to policy (which is the concern of Government) or legislation (which is the concern of Parliament).

Certain administrative actions are, however, outside his jurisdiction; these include matters affecting relations with other countries, contractual matters, hospitals (but see the note on the Health Service Commissioners) and personnel questions of the armed forces and the civil service. The Commissioner cannot investigate any matter where the complainant has exercised a right of appeal to a tribunal or court of law. However, he may, at his discretion, conduct an investigation if such a right of appeal exists and it is held that the complainant has, with good reason, not resorted to that right.

In the performance of his duties, the Parliamentary Commissioner has the power to require the production of evidence, including official papers, and the attendance of witnesses. He reports his findings to the Member of Parliament who presented the case. The Commissioner reports annually to Parliament and may submit such other reports at he thinks fit. An all-party Select Committee considers his reports.

Health Service Commissioners

The function of the Health Service Commissioners, who are statutory independent offices appointed by the Crown, is to investigate complaints of failure in provision or in execution of a service provided by a health authority, or maladministration by or on behalf of these authorities. The authorities concerned include Regional Health Authorities, District Health Authorities and Family Practitioner Committees. A complaint may be made directly to the appropriate commissioner, but only after it has been brought to the attention of the relevant health authority and an adequate opportunity given to that authority to investigate it and reply. Matters outside jurisdiction include action taken solely in the exercise of clinical or medical judgment and any action taken by doctors, dentists, pharmacists and opticians who provide services under contract to a health authority.

There are three Health Service Commissioners: one each for England, Scotland and Wales. All three posts are at present held by the Parliamentary Commissioner.

The Commissioners report annually from April to the following March and as they see fit.

Commissioners for Local Administration

The Commissioners investigate complaints from members of the public about injustice caused by maladministration in local government in England, Scotland and Wales.

Examples of faults or failures which the Local Commissioners have treated as maladministration are: neglect and unjustified delay; malice or bias or unfair discrimination; failure to observe relevant rules or procedures; failure to take relevant considerations into account; and failure to tell people of their rights. Commissioners have no power to question the merits of a decision taken without maladministration.

A complaint should be made in writing and may be sent direct to the Local Commissioner or to a member of the authority complained against with a request that it should be sent to the Local Commissioner.

Certain administrative actions are outside the jurisdiction of the Commissioners; these include matters where the complainant has a right of appeal to a tribunal or court of law, personnel matters, contractual and commercial transactions, complaints about public passenger transport, docks, harbours, entertainment, industrial establishments and markets, and the internal affairs of schools and colleges.

If a report by a Local Commissioner finds that injustice has been caused by maladministration, the Council must consider the report and tell the Local Commissioner what action they propose to take. A Local Commissioner cannot force a Council to act if they decide not to.

Since 1 January 1985 the statistical records of the Local Commissioner for Wales relate to all complaints, not only to formally referred complaints as hitherto.

PART 12: LAW ENFORCEMENT

Criminal courts in England and Wales

The courts of ordinary criminal jurisdiction in England and Wales are the magistrates' courts, which try the less serious offences and the Crown Court which deals with the serious cases. The Crown Court was established by the *Courts Act 1971,* which came into effect on 1 January 1972. From that date the former courts of assize and quarter sessions were abolished.

Part III of the *Criminal Law Act 1977,* which came into effect on 17 July 1978, redefined offences according to three new modes of trial, namely:

    i.   offences triable only on indictment

    ii.   offences triable either on indictment or summarily, but which are triable summarily only with the consent of the accused

    iii.   offences triable only summarily

For statistical purposes the figures for court proceedings and for police cautioning for 1979 to 1986 are shown in two groups; the first group is a combination of i. and ii. above which has been called 'indictable' and covers those offences which must or may be tried by jury in the Crown Court and the second group, 'summary' offences, covers iii. above and can only be tried at magistrates' courts.

Where possible comparable figures have been given for 1977 and 1978 to take account of both these changes in legislation and changes in counting practice (to remove an element of double counting).

Controlled drugs classification

The Misuse of Drugs Act 1971 divides drugs into three categories according to their harmfulness and drugs are shown according to two of these categories in Chart 12.6. In addition to the drugs shown in the chart, class 'A' drugs include dextromoramide, dipipanone, methadone, morphine, opium and pethidine; class 'B' drugs include cannabis liquid and methylamphetamine. Class 'C' drugs include methaqualone. A full list of drugs in each category is given in Schedule 2 to the *Misuse of Drugs Act 1971,* as amended by Orders in Council. The list of controlled drugs was extended to include barbiturates from 1 January 1985.

Sentences and orders

The following are the main sentences and orders which could have been imposed upon those persons found guilty in 1984, 1985 and 1986 (during 1983, the *Criminal Justice Act 1982* was implemented and this changed the sentences available). Some types of sentence or order can only be given to offenders in certain age groups.

Absolute and conditional discharge

A court may make an order discharging a person absolutely or (except in Scotland) conditionally where it is inexpedient to inflict punishment and a probation order is not appropriate. An order for conditional discharge runs for such period of not more than three years as the court specifies, the condition being that the offender does not commit another offence within the period so specified.

Attendance centres

This sentence, available in England, Wales, and Northern Ireland, involves deprivation of free time. The centres are mainly for boys between the ages of 10 and 16 found guilty of offences for which an adult could be sentenced to imprisonment. At the end of 1984, however, in addition to the 102 centres for boys aged 10 to 16, 13 of which also took girls in the same age group, there were 18 centres for males aged 17 to 20, and 7 centres solely for girls usually in the age range 14 to 16. Attendance is on saturday mornings or afternoons for up to three hours on any one occasion and for a total of not more than 24 hours and (normally) not less than 12. The activities include physical training and instruction in handicrafts or other practical subjects.

Probation orders

Probation is designed to secure the rehabilitation of an offender while he remains at liberty and under the supervision of a probation officer (social worker in Scotland), whose duty it is to advise, assist, and befriend him. A cardinal feature of the service is that it relies on the co-operation of the offender. Probation orders may only be made on people aged 17 or over; juveniles aged under 17 may receive supervision orders and care orders (see below). Probation orders may be given for any period between 6 months and 3 years inclusive (until 15 May 1978 the minimum period was 1 year).

Community service

An offender aged 17 or over (16 or over in Scotland) who is convicted of an offence punishable with imprisonment may be required to perform unpaid work for not more than 240 hours, and not less than 40 hours. From 24 May 1983 an offender aged 16 in England and Wales may be required to perform unpaid work for not more than 120 hours, and not less than 40 hours.

Detention centres

Detention centres are intended to provide a method of custodial treatment for young offenders who have committed an offence for which an adult could be sentenced to imprisonment and for whom a long period of residential training does not seem necessary. They are available for offenders who have reached the age of 14 (16 in Scotland) but are not yet 21. A person released from a detention centre in England and Wales comes under the care of a probation officer or social worker for a period of 3 months. Those released before 24 May 1983 were subject to 12 months supervision, but their supervision ended on 24 May 1983, or as soon thereafter as 3 months supervision had been completed.

Borstal training

The borstal training system, which, until 24 May 1983 (15 November 1983 in Scotland), was available for offenders who had reached the age of 15 (16 in Scotland) but were not yet 21, and who had been convicted of an offence punishable in the case of an adult with imprisonment, comprised borstals specialising in treatment of different types of young offenders, classified according to such criteria as age, intelligence, and type of offence. Release from a borstal sentence was followed by a period of supervision by a probation officer or social worker as for youth custody (see below). Those released from borstal in England and Wales before 24 May 1983 were subject to 12 months supervision, but their supervision ended on 24 May 1983, or as soon thereafter as 12 months from the start of the sentence had elapsed.

Youth custody/custody for life

Part 1 of the *Criminal Justice Act 1982,* which came into force on 24 May 1983, made major changes in the custodial sentences available to the courts in England and Wales to deal with offenders aged under 21. The sentence of borstal training was abolished, the sentence of imprisonment was prohibited, and detention in a detention centre was substantially modified to become the new 'detention centre order '. A determinate 'youth custody ' sentence, normally of over 4 months, was introduced for offenders of both sexes aged 15 to 20, but with a maximum sentence of 12 months for those aged under 17. Imprisonment for life was replaced by the sentence of custody for life for offenders aged 17 to 20. Release from youth custody is followed by a period of supervision by a probation officer or social worker. Most people are granted remission and released before the expiration of their sentence. The period of supervision lasts until the time the sentence would otherwise have expired, subject to a minumum of 3 months and a maximum of 12 months, and termination on the person's 22nd birthday.

Imprisonment

The custodial sentence for adult offenders is imprisonment or, in the case of mentally abnormal offenders, hospital orders with or without restrictions on when the offender may be discharged. A third of a prisoner's sentence (half in Northern Ireland) is remitted subject to good conduct and industry, and those serving sentences of over 9 months (18 months in Scotland and prior to 1 July 1984 in England and Wales) may be released under the parole scheme after serving 6 months (12 months in Scotland and prior to 1 July 1984 in England

and Wales) or a third of that sentence whichever is the longer. A life sentence prisoner may be released on licence subject to supervision and is always liable to recall.

Fully suspended sentences of imprisonment and
suspended sentences with supervision order
In England, Wales and Northern Ireland, sentences of imprisonment of two years or less may be fully suspended. The period for which a sentence may be suspended is between one and two years at the discretion of the court. The result of suspending a sentence is that it will not take effect unless during the period specified the offender is convicted of another offence punishable with imprisonment. The *Criminal Justice Act 1972*, which came into force on 1 January 1973, gave the courts power, on passing a suspended sentence of over 6 months, to impose a 'suspended sentence with supervision order ' placing the offender under the supervision of a probation officer for a specified period not longer than the period of suspension.

Partly suspended sentences of imprisonment
Section 47 of the *Criminal Law Act 1977* was implemented on 29 March 1982. As amended by Section 30 of the *Criminal Justice Act 1982*, this gives the courts the power to suspend not less than a quarter of a sentence of imprisonment of between 3 months and 2 years.

Young Offenders Institutions: Scotland
The *Criminal Justice (Scotland) Act 1963* laid down that Young Offenders Institutions should be provided to avoid sending to prison young people aged 16 to 20 inclusive for whom neither borstal nor detention training was appropriate, but who still required custodial treatment. The sentencing arrangements for young offenders in Scotland were also changed by the *Criminal Justice (Scotland) Act 1980*, on 15 November 1983.

Young Offenders Centres: Northern Ireland
On 1 June 1979 provisions in the *Treatment of Offenders (Northern Ireland) Act 1968* were brought into operation so that those under 21 years of age would no longer be sent to prison unless the court wished to impose a sentence of 3 years or more, but would be detained in a Young Offenders Centre.

Fines
Fines may be imposed with or without time to pay the fine. If the fine is not paid in the time allowed imprisonment or detention may result.

Supervision orders and care orders: England and Wales
Under the *Children and Young Persons Act 1969*, which came into force on 1 January 1971, supervision and care orders may be made on people aged under 17 in both criminal and care proceedings.

Legal aid
Advice and assistance provided by a solicitor, short of actual representation in court and tribunal proceedings, may be obtained either free or on payment of a contribution by those whose capital and income are within certain financial limits.

Assistance by way of representation covers the cost of a solicitor preparing a case and representing a client in court. It is available (either free or on payment of a contribution to those who are financially eligible) for most civil cases in the magistrates' court, for proceedings before Mental Health Review Tribunals', and for certain proceedings relating to the care of children and young people.
Legal aid in civil cases, such as county court and higher court proceedings, covers all work up to and including court proceedings and representation by a solicitor and a barrister, if necessary. Legal aid in these cases is available free or on a contributory basis to those whose capital and income are within certain financial limits. Applicants must show that they have reasonable grounds for asserting or

disputing a claim. Certain types of action, including libel and slander, are excluded from the scheme.

In the criminal courts in England and Wales a legal aid order may be made if this appears desirable in the interest of justice and the defendant's means are such that he requires financial help in meeting the costs of the proceedings in which he is involved. No limit of income or capital above which a person is ineligible for legal aid is specified, but the court must order a legally-aided person to contribute towards the costs of his case where his resources are such that he can afford to do so.

Advice and assistance and civil legal aid in Scotland operate on the same basis. In the case of advice by way of representation (ABWOR), however, this is granted mainly for summary criminal cases rather than civil cases and applies where a plea of guilty is made. Mental health appeals are also covered by ABWOR. Criminal legal aid, which is granted by the Scottish Legal Aid Board, for summary cases and for all appeals, and by the courts for solemn cases, is not subject to a contribution.

Civil courts in England and Wales
The main civil courts in England and Wales are the county courts, which are the courts for the lesser cases, and the High Court, where the more important cases are heard. Magistrates' courts have limited civil jurisdiction covering such matters as matrimonial proceedings for separation and maintenance orders, adoption and affiliation and guardianship orders, and care proceedings. Most appeals in civil cases go to the Court of Appeal (Civil Division) and from there may go to the House of Lords.

County courts are presided over by a judge, who almost always sits alone, although he may in a very limited number of cases sit with a jury consisting of eight persons if either party wishes it and the court makes an order to that effect. The jurisdiction of the county courts covers: actions founded upon contract and tort (except libel and slander) where the amount claimed is not more than £5,000 (increased from £2,000 in 1981); equity matters, such as trusts and mortgages, where the amount does not exceed £30,000; and actions concerning land where the net annual value for rating does not exceed £1,000 (£1,500 in London). Cases outside these limits may be tried in the county court by consent of the parties, or may be transferred to the High Court.

Other matters dealt with by the county courts include adoption cases, bankruptcies (which are dealt with in certain courts outside London), and undefended divorce cases (which are heard and determined by county courts designated as divorce county courts).

Civil courts in Scotland
The Court of Session is the supreme civil court in Scotland. As a general rule it has the original jurisdiction in all civil cases and appellate jurisdiction (that is the power to hear and give decisions on appeals) over all civil courts, unless such jurisdiction, original or appellate, is expressly excluded by statute. The Court is divided into two parts, the Inner House and the Outer House. The Inner House exercises appellate jurisdiction on reclaiming motions from the Outer House and on appeals from the inferior courts. Appeals from the Court of Session may go to the House of Lords.

The Sheriff court is the principal local court of civil, as well as criminal, jurisdiction in Scotland. Its civil jurisdiction is comparable with that of the county courts in England and Wales but is more extensive in certain directions. There is no limit to the sum which may be sued for in the Sheriff court. The Sheriff's jurisdiction now includes actions of divorce, but does not extend to actions of declarator of marriage, or to actions of declarator involving the personal status of individuals or to certain other actions; but, with these exceptions, the civil jurisdiction of the court is general similar in scope to that of the Court of Session. In addition, the Sheriff deals with a mass of quasi-judicial and administrative business, some of which is similar to that deal with in county courts in England and Wales, but of which a large part is particular to the Scottish system.

Index

The references in this index refer to table and chart numbers, or entries in the Appendix.

Expenditure
  see 'Government expenditure
  'Household expenditure '
  'Public expenditure'

Families, App. Pt 2
  household type 2.9
  expenditure 6.3
  with lower incomes 5.17, 5.19, 5.18
  poverty trap 5.19
Family Expenditure Survey, App. Major Surveys
Family practitioner services 7.27, App. Pt 7
Fertility rates 1.9
  by country of birth of mother 1.13
Firearms and shotgun certificates 12.4
Food
  consumption 7.11
  diet 7.12, 7.13
  household expenditure 6.1, 6.2, 6.3
  purchases from supermarkets 6.4
  retail prices index 6.8
Free time use 10.1
Fuel
  household expenditure 6.2, 6.3
  retail prices index 6.8
Further education
  see 'Education, further '

General Household Survey
  App. Major Surveys, App Pt. 2
General medical practitioners
  see 'Doctors '
Government
  expenditure 6.17, 6.18
    as a percentage of GDP 6.17
    on education 3.26
  income 6.19
Graduates
  by subject group of study 3.18
  destination of 3.19
Gross domestic product 6.21
  international comparison 6.22

Handicapped
    see 'Disabled '
Health
  manpower 7.36, App. Pt 7
  prescriptions 7.26
  private services 7.24, 7.28
  public expenditure 7.37
  see also 'Hospitals ', 'Prevention ', 'Private
    medical insurance '
Health Service Commissioner, complaints to 11.13,
    App. Pt 11
Holidays 10.15, 10.16, 10.17
  entitlement 10.2
Hospitals
  beds 7.26
  in-patients 7.24
    maternity 7.22

operations 7.26
private 7.24, 7.28
waiting lists 7.25
out-patients 7.24
private 7.28
Hours of work 4.16, 10.2
  EC comparison 4.19
  necessary to pay for goods and services 6.10
  number working
    overtime 4.17, 5.7
    short-time 4.17
Household sector, App. Pt 5
Households, App. Pt 2
  availability of durable goods
    by usual gross household income 6.5
  below average income 5.20, 5.21, App. Pt 5
  cars with 9.7
  European Communities comparison 6.6
  expenditure 6.1, 6.2, App. Pt 6
    by household type and income, 6.3
  housing 8.14
  family type 2.9
  homeless 8.4, 8.5, 8.6
  income 5.1, 5.2
    distribution 5.18
    redistribution 5.17, App. Pt 5
  in local authority and new town rented
    accommodations 8.10
  one-person 2.1
    projections 2.5
  receiving housing benefit 8.15
  savings 6.16, App. Pt 6
  size 2.2, App. Pt 2
  EC comparison 2.8
  taxes and benefits 5.17
  tenure
    by age of head 8.20
    by socio-economic group 8.21
  type 2.3, 2.4, App. Pt 2
  video-casette recorders, with 10.6
Household Survey (Continuous) App. Major Surveys
Housing
  accommodation type, 8.21
  benefit supplement, App. Pt 8
  benefit recipients of 5.8, 8.15, App. Pt 8
  building society possession and arrears 8.19
  dwelling price to earnings ratio 8.16
  dwellings 5.22, 8.1, 8.3, 8.19, App. Pt 8
  energy conservation, 8.13
  homeless households 8.4, 8.5, 8.6
  household expenditure 6.2, 6.3, 8.14
  local authority
    allocation of 8.8
    households reasons for not buying 8.10
    sales of 8.9
  low cost home ownership initiatives 8.11, App. Pt 8
  mortgage or loan, source of 8.18
  mortgages, building societies, balances, arrears
    and possessions 8.19
  mortgages by institutional source, 8.17
  public expenditure 8.7
  renovations 8.12, App. Pt 8
  retail prices index 6.8
  shared ownership, App. Pt 8
  stock
    by tenure 8.1
    changes in 8.3
    completions 8.2
Immigration
    see 'Migration'

Annual Abstract of Statistics

1989 Edition

For about 140 years the Annual Abstract of Statistics has probably been the most quoted source of statistics about the United Kingdom.

348 tables in 18 separate chapters cover just about every aspect of economic, social and industrial life

Area and climate	Education	Transport
Population	Employment	Communications
Vital Statistics	Defence	Retailing
Social Services	Energy	External Trade
National Insurance and Health	Iron and Steel	National Income and Expenditure
Public Health	Building	Home Finance
Housing	Manufacturing	Banking
Elections	Agriculture and Food	Insurance
Law Enforcement	Fisheries	Prices

Most of the data in the Abstract are annual and cover periods of about 10 years

HMSO £18.50 net

ISBN 011 620346 3

Printed in the UK for HMSO   Dd. 289332   C65   1/89   4073